See p 291

Looking for Ground

Relational Perspectives Book Series

Volume 21

Relational Perspectives Book Series

Stephen A. Mitchell and Lewis Aron
Series Editors

Volume 1
Rita Wiley McCleary
Conversing with Uncertainty: Practicing Psychotherapy in a Hospital Setting

Volume 2
Charles Spezzano
Affect in Psychoanalysis: A Clinical Synthesis

Volume 3
Neil Altman
The Analyst in the Inner City: Race, Class, and Culture Through a Psychoanalytic Lens

Volume 4
Lewis Aron
A Meeting of Minds: Mutuality in Psychoanalysis

Volume 5
Joyce A. Slochower
Holding and Psychoanalysis: A Relational Perspective

Volume 6
Barbara Gerson, editor
The Therapist as a Person: Life Crises, Life Choices, Life Experiences, and Their Effects on Treatment

Volume 7
Charles Spezzano and Gerald J. Gargiulo, editors
Soul on the Couch: Spirituality, Religion, and Morality in Contemporary Psychoanalysis

Volume 8
Donnel B. Stern
Unformulated Experience: From Dissociation to Imagination in Psychoanalysis

Volume 9
Stephen A. Mitchell
Influence and Autonomy in Psychoanalysis

Volume 10
Neil J. Skolnick and David E. Scharff, editors
Fairbairn, Then and Now

Volume 11
Stuart A. Pizer
Building Bridges: Negotiation of Paradox in Psychoanalysis

Volume 12
Lewis Aron and Frances Sommer Anderson, editors
Relational Perspectives on the Body

Volume 13
Karen Maroda
Seduction, Surrender, and Transformation: Emotional Engagement in the Analytic Process

Volume 14
Stephen A. Mitchell and Lewis Aron, editors
Relational Psychoanalysis: The Emergence of a Tradition

Volume 15
Rochelle G. K. Kainer
The Collapse of the Self and Its Therapeutic Restoration

Volume 16
Kenneth A. Frank
Psychoanalytic Participation: Action, Interaction, and Integration

Volume 17
Sue Grand
The Reproduction of Evil: A Clinical and Cultural Perspective

Volume 18
Steven H. Cooper
Objects of Hope: Exploring Possibility and Limit in Psychoanalysis

Volume 19
James S. Grotstein
Who Is the Dreamer Who Dreams the Dream? A Study of Psychic Presences

Volume 20
Stephen A. Mitchell
Relationality: From Attachment to Intersubjectivity

Volume 21
Peter G. M. Carnochan
Looking for Ground: Countertransference and the Problem of Value in Psychoanalysis

Looking for Ground

Countertransference and the Problem of Value in Psychoanalysis

Peter G. M. Carnochan

THE ANALYTIC PRESS
2001 Hillsdale, NJ London

Published by The Analytic Press, Inc.
101 West Street, Hillsdale, NJ 07642

Set in Garamond Antiqua 11/13 by EVS Communications, Point Pleasant, NJ
Index by Leonard Rosenbaum, Washington, DC

Library of Congress Cataloging-in-Publication Data

Carnochan, Peter, 1960–
Looking for ground : countertransference and the problem of value in psychoanalysis / Peter Carnochan
p. cm.
Includes bibliographical references.
ISBN 0-88163-324-0
1. Countertransference (Psychology). 2. Epistemology. 3. Values—Psychological aspects. 4. Psychotherapist and patient.

RC489.C68 C37 2000
616.89′17—dc21

00-026372

Printed in the United States of America
10 9 8 7 6 5 4 3 2 1

Table of Contents

Acknowledgments

The idea of writing this book came to me while I was reading Freud's *Papers on Technique* (1911–1915). The depth of his insight and the clarity of his style left me giddy and determined to pursue this work. This book owes its beginnings to Freud and the analytic tradition that he nurtured. Freud and the philosophic dialogue he engaged have helped shape what we imagine it means to be human.

This book emerged out of my doctoral work at the University of Denver. The faculty at Denver showed real faith in me when they allowed me to write a theoretical dissertation. I am quite grateful to them for allowing me this freedom. Charles Spezzano, Karen Rosica, and Helen Hand all played an important role in my early analytic education. I want to thank both Wyndol Furman and Steven Shirk for their support of my work. I also want to especially thank Paul Ornstein for agreeing to serve as my advisor. I could not have completed this project without his help. Paul and his wife Anna were both extremely generous toward me.

The process of turning a dissertation into a book is harder than I would have known. In the case of this work, it would not have happened without the support of the people at the Analytic Press. I want to thank Stephen Mitchell and Lewis Aron for their sympathetic reading of my manuscript and their editorial suggestions. John Kerr, my editor, provided substantial and incisive help in shaping this work into its final form. He helped me make changes at a point when it was difficult for me to see the work clearly. Lesley Bonnet provided tireless help with the final proofreading. I also want to thank Lenni Kobrin, Meri Freedman, and Shari Buchwald, who helped oversee the production of the book.

Finally, I want to dedicate this book to my father and mother for helping me first make sense of thinking and feeling, and to Diane for keeping me company while I wrote.

Preface

This work is an attempt to bring sense to the meaning and use of the countertransference. While it has been well celebrated in the last half-century of analytic practice, the countertransference, persistent intimation of our subjectivity, remains a source of controversy. At the edges of the debate there are both those who would call for its elimination and others who would suggest it is the most fertile ground of analytic activity. In the wide middle the voices are quieter, yet still not unanimous. This clangor of opinion leaves us to ask how the countertransference should best be understood? In what ways does it impede or facilitate the analyst's activity? Does it serve diagnostic understanding or is it merely the reflection of inappropriate analytic zeal? When we risk speaking about the countertransference do we necessarily subvert the analytic frame, or are there ways to utilize disclosure that further the rigor of the analytic process?

To address these questions entails revisiting the foundations of analysis. We must consider the historical, epistemological, and moral questions that form the backdrop for analytic discussions of objectivity, neutrality, gratification, and abstinence. I argue that the countertransference, understood as the whole range of the analyst's feelings toward the patient, is inevitable. For an analysis to make a difference in how we live, the countertransference must be engaged as a source both of knowing and of action. Consequential change, change that makes a difference to our suffering, occurs only within the context of an engaged human relationship. To be of real help to our patients we must not be shy of our loving, nor of the moments of hate. Yet the utilization of the analyst's affectivity requires careful structure and discipline if we are to avoid the degeneration of our craft or the risk of naive sentimentality or inauthenticity.

By regrounding our consideration of the countertransference in the historical progression of psychoanalysis and in the wider issues of epistemology and morality, we gain a perspective on the psychoanalytic debate that allows us to integrate more fully the contending voices that have spoken on this issue. This book seeks to provide a deeper view of the countertransference that will allow us to rethink the problem of knowing and gratification in analysis.

To suggest that the countertransference can function as a source of therapeutic action as well as information is controversial, and may conjure up images of "wild analysis." If analysts' emotions are brought into the treatment, what prevents the therapy from becoming a context for analysts to play out their own needs and issues? If affect is part of knowing, what marks the line between objectivity and bias? If we move beyond the prescription of abstinence, what determines the boundaries of the therapeutic frame? I argue that to make use of the countertransference does not entail the necessity of capricious technique. To make this claim, though, is to put in dispute important parts of the psychoanalytic legacy. This should not be done lightly. To reach an adequate understanding of where we stand with the countertransference, we must be aware of history. In this history, the empirical record of our field, lies evidence that the countertransference must not be avoided. But the turn toward history is not just a statement of the known. The historical is never merely found; it is always reconstructed and reformed through the process of interrogation. By tracing the history of psychoanalysis as the evolution of ideas concerning countertransference, we gain an opportunity to re-understand the significance of analytic activity.

In approaching psychoanalysis through the historical view, we begin with Freud. In reading his work it becomes clear that the initial proscription of the countertransference rests on his understanding of epistemology and morality. These two themes are pivotal in the attempt to reach a coherent account of the countertransference. Freud cautions against the countertransference in part because he feels that the intrusion of feeling must act to subvert the analyst's objectivity. To make sense of the countertransference we must take up this epistemological theme and rethink the role of affect in the process of knowing. Traditional notions of analytic objectivity and abstinence are grounded in positivism.

When we transcend the bias of the personal, the press of passion—positivism holds—reality can be known without distortion. This attempt to make all knowing scientific, however, has been undercut by more recent accounts of the inevitability of perspectivism. The constructivist school suggests that knowing is fundamentally based in the perceiver's relationship to the perceived. To understand this shift is to see that objectivity cannot be understood as the opposite of subjectivity. The dichotomy between these two must be overcome. The analyst must necessarily be grounded in subjectivity, but this subjectivity does not imply doing away with the concept of objectivity.

Freud's proscription of the countertransference, however, also stems from his economic theory of motivation and his ideas about the teleological significance of human existence. For Freud, the goal of analysis is to help the individual forsake hallucinatory or compromise pleasures, and make the difficult but ultimately more satisfying step, toward real objects and complete genital release. This goal, however, is placed at risk by the operation of the pleasure principle. In Freud's mind, the individual is governed by the desire to reduce the buildup of psychic tension. Gratification in the transference, then, provided through complementary countertransferential behavior, can only act to siphon away therapeutic initiative, and must be avoided in order not to derail the analytic process. Psychoanalysis, however, has not remained static in its understanding of therapeutic action and metapsychology. Just as psychoanalysis has evolved in its epistemological understanding, so too has it undergone profound changes in this second area of thought. We have moved away from mechanistic accounts of drive toward relational accounts of development. According to these models, developmental progress requires experiences of satisfaction. As we have moved in our understanding from drive to relational models of human functioning, our understanding of motivation and human health have changed, and these changes must be tested for their implications for psychoanalytic technique.

Yet in approaching this part of the psychoanalytic evolution we quickly run into difficulty. If we call the first part of our work epistemology, and describe the changing view as the move from objectivism to constructivism, what corresponding label might mark the changes in the second area of our work, the area that concerns metapsychology and therapeutic action? As of yet the field is lacking an organizing term, and the discussion remains segmented and provincial. This asymmetry between analytic discussions of epistemology and discussions of therapeutic action seems peculiar, leaving the analytic dialogue lopsided as it struggles forward. To correct our posture we would do well to gather this second line of analytic evolution under the organizing rubric of a larger theme. When we take up the question of what the patient needs, I suggest that we have entered the domain of moral theory. Questions about human nature and correct action bring us squarely into the realm of value and morality. While discussing these changes in theories of metapsychology and therapeutic action as part of moral theory may seem unfamiliar, this categorizing suggestion should not be unexpected. When we consider philosophic discourse, questions about knowing and valuing have acted as twin siblings. To the extent that psychoanalysis matters, it cannot avoid addressing these seminal issues of our culture and thought.

To reach a comprehensive view of the countertransference and its role in analytic therapy, we must revisit the teleological assumptions of analysis and try to make explicit the moral frame from which we operate. Analysis, to the extent it is therapeutic, must work toward goals, and to imagine that it could operate outside the realm of value and morality is a fictitious hope. Therefore, we must make clear the moral ground on which analysis has been founded and try to discern how that ground has changed over the last century of analytic practice. By bringing this emergent mode of valuing into focus, the significance and correct use of the countertransference becomes more clear. I find myself sympathetic to perspectives that advocate a more active utilization of countertransference phenomena. Common to these perspectives is the idea that the countertransference, rather than being a necessary obstacle to analytic work, can become an ally. Countertransference is valuable in part because it is a way of knowing our patients. What we feel about someone can be as informative as what we think. But countertransference is more than just a source of information–it is also the ground of the human relationship in analytic work. There are times in analytic work, I will argue, when we need to do more than merely observe our affect; we need to act from it.

CHAPTER ONE

ATLAS'S PERCH

Analysts, in the attempt to help patients, shoulder substantial burdens. They must provide a platform from which the patient can begin to sort through the false turns and recesses of personality. We can risk further metaphor and say the analyst is a kind of modern Atlas. Analysts are asked to bear the analysand's transference and possess a firmness of vision that will allow them to distinguish distortion from reality. But when I think about Atlas with the world on his shoulders, I cannot help but wonder about his perch. On what does Atlas stand? In the analytic encounter we are faced with the same question as we strive to get our footing. Analysts, too, are bound to subjectivity, and any knowing gained is dependent on perspective, any action must rest on an implicit theory of value. If this is the case, then what keeps our feet from dangling in analytic work? To face this question is to grapple with the significance of the countertransference. The emergence of the countertransference serves as the clearest reminder to the analyst of the subjectivity of vision. These feelings push us back toward our self–they underline the limits of objectivity. But this is not to say that the presence of the countertransference is cause for grief. The merely human is also the basis of our humanity and in the countertransference lies the possibility of a living analysis. I see this as a critical question of analytic technique: How should analysts make use of their emotional response to the patient? To pursue an answer is to try to find an adequate foundation as we do this work.

The temptation is to look toward neutrality for this foundation. In the world of psychoanalysis, neutrality has been equated with abstinence (Freud, 1915a). By keeping the analyst's self out of the treatment, Freud felt the patient's transference could be analyzed objectively. There are advantages to this approach. In the analytic attitude (Schafer, 1983), we reflect emotions and ask patients how they imagine us. We subordinate our personality and avoid judgments. We may use the analytic attitude as a means to keep us separated from our gravity-bound emotions. This stance toward ourselves, perhaps, allows us to become more like mirrors, and permits the development of an analyzable transference. By avoiding gratification we disabuse ourselves of the illusion that through the unlimited provision of love we can circumvent suffering. At the beginning, then, we may rely on neutrality. Yet neutrality, in truth, is not separate from us and our inventions, and if we stay too tightly bound to neutrality, understood only as abstinence, then as an analysis develops we will end up obscuring the atmosphere of honesty.

Levenson (1972) suggests that the analyst, despite his best efforts, is inevitably drawn into a reenactment of the transference drama.[1] The attempt to remain neutral becomes precisely the set of actions that cause the patient's suffering. The meaning of our interpretations and silence are not determined within themselves. We may remain silent with the intention of not disturbing the patient's associations. Yet, to the patient, our silence may be experienced as abandonment or criticism. We may interpret with the hope of illuminating the patient's psychology. But to the patient this may seem like only another attempt to avoid blame or exposure. The truth of our action lies not solely in our intentions, or in the patient's feelings, but in the interaction between these two fields of experience. These kinds of moments in therapy lead to an experience of paralysis for the analyst. The meaning of neutrality has been coopted, but to abandon neutrality is to fly in the face of the transference and the re-creation of the past. The patient's tenacity in transforming the meaning of our efforts to help is difficult to accept. Over the course of an analysis, the analyst is bound to have feelings toward the analysand that are stirred up by the effort to help and by the demands of the relationship.

[1] Writers, in using the English language, face a difficult challenge. To use "he" or "she" in designating the third person is to retain sexism in our language. When possible I avoid this difficulty by using the plurals "they" and "them" and "we" and "us." There are times, however, when the singular third person cannot be avoided. In these instances, I will use "he" to refer to the analyst, and "she" to refer to the analysand. In alternate chapters I reverse this reference: the analyst will be referred to as "she" and the analysand as "he." However, in instances when I am writing about actual analysts and analysands I, naturally, preserve their gender in pronoun usage.

At this point neutrality can become a curtain behind which shadows move. Now, if the analyst asks, "How do you imagine me?" he implies that the analysand's perceptions are based in fantasy. To continue shielding one's subjectivity behind the attitude of neutrality creates ghosts that prevent patients from distinguishing between themselves and the therapist. In this gap between the analyst's private and therapeutic self the patient is left alone with an unvalidated sense of reality. If this account is correct, then somehow the curtain must be drawn back. Merely using the countertransference as a source of information about the client is inadequate. The problem is: how can we act from the countertransference without acting it out?

Authenticity as Accident: The Quandary of Skillful Affectivity

The difficulty of the countertransference becomes clearer the closer we get to the analytic situation. Lucia Tower (1956) describes a case where the difficulty of acting from the countertransference, rather than acting it out, is central. In this case, Tower has seen a female patient for several months. The patient, who was referred to Tower after a near-psychotic reaction in an unsuccessful analysis, is enraged by the earlier failure and brings this anger to bear on Tower:

> Week after week, and month after month, she raged at me in a vituperative manner, despite my having the greatest of patience with her. I endured a quantity of abuse from her, such as I have never taken from any other patient. At times, I would get irritated with the abuse, but mostly I rather liked the patient, was genuinely interested in helping her and was somewhat surprised at my ability to control my irritation with her [p. 141].

When Tower says that she was surprised at her ability to control her irritation, we can readily empathize with her position. Vituperative rage is trying, and to remain unaffected in the face of such an onslaught seems unexpected. Given the intensity of this patient's initial transference, how should the analyst behave?

If we take neutrality as our starting point, then the aim will be to endure and interpret the abuse. We are to understand that the abuse is a statement about the patient's intrapsychic landscape, not about us. For the Kleinians, the task will be to interpret the patient's primitive anxiety and destructive rage. For the Kohutians, on the other hand, the aim is to understand the patient's rage as arising from genuinely painful responses in her world and, therefore, to see it as not merely unjust. To the extent that we are able to remain patient and compassionate with the patient, we avoid the cycles of revenge and mutual misunderstanding. The hope is that, through this sustained compassion, we can begin to form an alliance with the patient. From this alliance we can strive to help the patient begin to be able to observe her rage, and to know more clearly the pain and fear that fuels it. In essence, what we ask the patient to do is to risk moving closer, in our presence, to her more vulnerable feelings, and so explore the boundaries of trust.

But our good intentions and compassion are not always enough. Tower's patient does not seem to notice the analyst's patience, let alone her compassion. In fact, we may wonder if the analyst's patience is not precisely the fuel that stokes the patient's rage. What the analyst experiences as patience may to the analysand feel like pity. By staying impervious to the analysand's rage, the analyst makes her ineffective. The fly that bites an elephant may wonder about the elephant's failure to swat it. Is the elephant large of spirit, or just large? If the analyst is experienced as simply large, then the analysand's continued rage may be an attempt to inflict a bite that is deep enough to gain a response. Only through this response can the patient feel herself to be substantial and her concerns registered.

At this point in the work the neutrality of the analyst has been coopted by the analysand's transferential system. Patience has been translated into indifference. The question then is how this continual translation affects the analyst. Tower writes that at this juncture she forgot an appointment she had with her client:

> One beautiful spring day I walked out of my office, twenty minutes before this patient's hour, with my appointment book lying open on my desk. I had a delicious luncheon, alone, which I enjoyed more than usual, and strolled back to the office, in time for my next appointment, only to be informed that my patient had been there and had left extremely angry. It was obvious that I had forgotten her appointment, unconsciously and purposely, and it suddenly came over me that I was absolutely fed up with her abuse to the point of nonendurance [p. 142].

In this passage Tower suggests that her acting out sprang from her countertransferential anger. By her acting out—by missing an appointment—her unconscious feelings became manifest. This analysis seems correct in part. But we may also wonder if it was only after acting out her frustration that her anger grew into full form. Before Tower misses the appointment, she can hold on to her conception of herself as genuinely patient and trying to help. Her acting out, however, undermines that self-image, and makes true her patient's rageful perception of her. Now Tower is vindictive and vengeful. This exposed truth about the analyst is a blow to her self-esteem and produces a defensive anger. Despite all intentions to the contrary, she has hit out at her patient.

Clearly the analyst has acted out the transference–countertransference drama. She has sailed into the face of the hurricane she was seeking to avoid. If the maintenance of neutrality and countertransference-free functioning were essential, we would expect this breach in technique to lead to disaster for the analysis. The patient's transferential view has been confirmed in the actual world of the moment. Forward progress should be forfeited. But this is not the result Tower describes. When the patient arrives for her next session, she begins to attack Tower anew for this lapse. Tower apologizes and then remains silent. After ten minutes of abuse, though, the patient reigns herself in, and says, "Well, you know, Dr. Tower, really I can't say that I blame you" (p. 142). Tower writes that, following this incident, the tone of the therapy changed. The analysand was able to form an alliance with her and move into more productive levels of work.

Tower concludes that her acting out resulted in a critical resolution of her own countertransference problem. The obstacle in the therapy had concerned Tower's own overly great reticence to act aggressively in the face of her client's abusive behavior. Why the emergence of the analyst's aggression was a positive force in the treatment is a question open for speculation. Tower talks about the breakthrough as a facilitation of the patient's "passive homoerotic" transference. I would be more inclined to speak about it as the analyst's engaging her countertransference in the service of a necessary confrontation of the patient's destructiveness. But the ultimate explanation of the breakthrough can wait.

What is more troubling for the reader of this account is its implications for the management of the countertransference. Tower does not suggest that acting out unconscious countertransference aggression is a recommended procedure. Missing appointments with abusive clients is problematic, and there are clearly many forms of countertransferential action that are destructive. Where does this leave us? Tower writes that she needed to be "freer to be more aggressive" (p. 142). But how does this differ from acting out the aggressiveness by missing an appointment? In the current literature (Chused, 1992a) on the analyst's subjective participation in analytic treatment, there is a tendency to suggest implicitly that enactments, while unavoidable and sometimes helpful, must be left in the unconscious realm. To deliberately behave with emotion, these voices suggest, is to enter into the domain of the "corrective emotional experience" and fall prey to manipulative action. While I agree that analysis depends on truthful response, I feel it is critical that we unlink authenticity from the unconscious. We need ways to consciously shape our analytic technique and our affective responses in the countertransference that do not entail debasing our reality or the authenticity of response.

Countertransference and the History of Psychoanalytic Technique

I began with an assertion that countertransference and subjectivity are inevitable. One must ask about the foundation for this claim. This turns us toward the history of psychoanalysis. I argue that this history is a chronicle of the necessity and value of the countertransference.

This is a controversial claim that Freud (1912d) did not share. He wrote: "I cannot advise my colleagues too urgently to model themselves during psychoanalytic treatment on the surgeon, who puts aside all his feelings, even his human sympathy, and concentrates his mental forces on the single aim of performing the operation as skillfully as possible" (p. 115). In this passage, Freud suggested that all manifestations of the countertransference, regardless of whether we subscribe to the wider or the narrower definition, are obstacles to correct analytic technique. But we must wonder how literally Freud intended this principle to be understood. In Freud's description of his own work, evidence of his nonsurgical manner is widespread. Freud brought patients with him on vacation, lent them money, and considered some of them his friends (Gay, 1988). Perhaps the safest reading of Freud's intention here is to caution analysts against an inadequate distance from their feelings. As new converts came to the analytic cause, enthusiasm for the cure often led to excesses in the relationship (Freud, 1910d).[2] Yet whatever Freud's intention, the result of this kind of instruction was that the field as a whole came to advocate minimal participation on the part of the analyst. Analytic behavior that failed to meet these standards of self-restraint was seen as evidence of an insufficient training analysis.

For psychoanalysis to have proscribed the countertransference betrays a peculiar logic. Freud's central discovery was the unconscious and the sexually determined basis of behavior. In Freud's story, the ground of human life is primitive and driven by libidinal strivings represented as affect. The ego and the civilized restraint of a surgeon, therefore, would have to depend not on the overcoming of the id, but on a series of compromises that would act as reigns on the impulses. Any behavior or attitude, traced through its origins, draws its energy from the soil of sexuality. For Freud to state that all feelings should be set aside, the countertransference overcome, is tantamount to a biologist insisting that life should overcome its dependence on carbon. It would seem more consistent if Freud, rather than asking for the eradication of feeling in the analyst, had offered suggestions on how the countertransference should be managed.

To understand the factors that determined this apparent contradiction in Freud's technical position, we need to turn to his epistemological and moral context. At one level this context is well-traveled ground, and it has become almost a truism to state that for Freud the epistemological ground was positivism. By embracing positivism, one turns away from metaphysical explanations of forces behind phenomena, and toward the power of observation and reasoning. Science begins with the observation of facts. In this view of knowledge, facts are apparent and can be gathered without bias. With the facts in hand, reason intervenes to uncover the laws that govern phenomena, and understanding can progress.

---

[2] Freud (1910d) described the case of a woman who had received problematic "psychoanalytic" treatment from her physician. This woman had begun suffering anxiety states after she divorced her husband. Her physician, who had evidently read some of Freud's writings, told this woman that her anxiety stemmed from her lack of sexual satisfaction. He stated that she could recover only if she returned to her husband, took a lover, or engaged in masturbation. The woman was unwilling to take any of these courses of action and remained mired in her anxiety. Freud, in recounting this case, suggested that the physician in question had taken a too simple view of sexuality and had ignored the difficulties of repression and defense in the enthusiasm with which he gave advice.

While this characterization of Freud's epistemological position is not untrue, it fails to capture the wider complexity of his thought. At times, Freud's discoveries about the unconscious push him to the brink of a constructivist sensibility, and his views about the relationship between truth and affect are more subtle than are often portrayed. I present some of this complexity in chapter three. Yet it remains true that Freud's platonic sensibility, his desire to be scientific, his faith in pure thought, lead him away from the countertransference. By eliminating the countertransference, Freud hoped both to secure the analytic method on a foundation of reason rather than emotion and to assist the analysand in the difficult path away from fantasy toward a clarity of perception that would allow a marriage with the real.

But the importance of putting aside human feelings stems as much from Freud's metapsychology—his moral or teleological view of humankind—as it does from his epistemology. Freud's metapsychology places sexuality at the root of all behavior and motivation. In the drive model, the analyst's activity is inevitably defined by the sexual fantasies of the patient (and perhaps by the sexual longings of the analyst). To embrace the countertransference, then, would imply that analysis was an enactment of a sexual affair, in symbol if not in fact. And if only in symbol, then it is the worst kind of sexual relationship for Freud, a kind of coitus interruptus. To play out a symbolic coitus could lead to nothing but further damage to the patient. Abstinence on the part of the analyst, then, is essential to prevent an entrenchment of the difficulty.

Freud's disdain for symbolic enactments is based on his understanding of the role of unconscious conflict. In his view, the neurosis acts as a compromise solution for the patient. The patient's symptoms lie at the point of equilibrium between the demands of the id and the prohibitions of society. In analysis, the patient strives to sneak satisfactions for the id from the analyst. The danger of analytic activity, under this conception, is that if the analyst gives in to these pulls from the patient, it will lead to sexual gratification. The sexual gratification, then, will lead to a reduction in psychic tension, and the pressure that might drive the complex from the somatic to the psychic and conscious level is lost. This loss also decreases motivation; if the patient is gratified by the analyst then all impetus to change is lost. Again, this is familiar territory, and it has been well explicated in modern critiques. Yet here, too, Freud's view of gratification is complex and is not done justice by this overly simple characterization. Freud's model led analysts to become deeply cautious about giving in to drive needs. The assumption was that if a need was gratified it could never be analyzed. By staying at the observing and interpreting level, however, the analyst acted as a mirror for the analysand. The frustration this abstinent stance engendered pulled the sexual strivings to the surface and helped the analysand understand the shape of the transference distortions. In essence, the analyst became an attendant to patients in helping them move toward a positivist relationship to themselves. Here the epistemological and the moral meet to define the necessary direction of analytic action.

Psychoanalysis, then, began with a hypothesis about the possibility and necessity of rising above subjectivity. This is the starting point for our discussion. The chapters on Freud are intended both to take seriously his arguments against the countertransference and to reawaken our curiosity. To embrace subjectivity is unsettling and can make us long for the seemingly clearer ground of objectivity and neutrality. To see the roots of Freud's technical recommendations vaccinates us against the temptation to close prematurely our speculation about technique. Freud (and the culture that gave birth to analysis) led his followers to believe that analysts needed to work through and so do away with their tendency to react to the patient with feeling. Out of loyalty to Freud (and perhaps for fear of the alternative), the field continued to test this notion long after it first showed signs of weakness. In chapter 5 I discuss how the early analysts sought to implement Freud's technique and trace the difficulties they encountered. These analysts attempted to carry out Freud's recommendations in a literal manner. They saw the analytic cure as resting in the proper telling of the transference myth. But in practice not all analytic patients were sufficiently cooperative. They failed to free associate; they grew angry at their analysts rather than falling in love with them. These difficult patients were initially labeled unanalyzable or were maligned for their faulty characters, and in these moral judgments we can see unconscious manifestations of countertransference.

Ultimately, the attempt to expand the reach and utility of analysis led the analytic community to reassess its practice with such patients. In the works of Ferenczi (1919a), Reich (1933), and Alexander (1925) we find the recognition that the mere voicing of the unconscious narrative, if it remains an intellectual exercise, lacks the power to produce change. With this realization came an increasing focus on the analysis of resistance and the importance of emotional processes in the analytic hour. The transference came to be seen more as a living transaction than as the static re-creation of a past reality. In Ferenczi's desire to help he experimented with more active techniques. At times he forbade patients to practice their symptoms; he tried setting ending dates to push the work forward; and, finally, he tried more supportive techniques. Ferenczi felt the limitations of analysis most acutely and struggled with this issue in his relationship with Freud. It is in Ferenczi's passion and pain that the dilemma of early analytic practice can most clearly be seen. Despite the experiments in analytic technique that Ferenczi and others carried out, the field as a whole remained loyal to the Freudian vision of the analyst. Objectivity and analytic reserve remained at the center of analytic practice, and manifestations of the countertransference were seen as evidence of an incomplete training analysis.

The patients who came to analysis, though, were not swayed from making new demands of the field. As psychoanalysis turned to the treatment of children and more disturbed patients, the boundaries of theory and technique were stretched (Tansey & Burke, 1989). These patients were not willing to tolerate the analytic reserve of traditional analysts. Children tend not to free associate; analysts have to be willing to play with them. With patients suffering from narcissistic and borderline disorders, rigid analytic restraint can be so wounding that it leads to unanalyzable affective storms. These patients required a less impersonal analytic technique and a more comprehensive account of development that extended further back than the oedipal phase. These encounters led to the development of the object relational, self psychology, and interpersonal schools. Central to these schools of thought is an emphasis on relationships as the driving force in motivation. In chapter 6 I discuss how these schools emerged out of the analytic encounter with the patient and how, in turn, these schools influenced analytic practice. In these models, the emphasis on relationships in the formation and maintenance of personality led to a reconsideration of analytic technique.

The move from drive theory to relational models was not easily embraced. Yet despite the attempts to hold fast to objectivity and the sanctity of Freud, the field has changed its structure. Increasingly, psychoanalysis has come to see relationships, rather than drives, as the principal motivating force in human behavior. In this view people are no longer seen as solipsistic, egocentric beings who seek out other people only as objects for drive gratification. Rather than the individual beginning as a self who seeks out others for pleasure, the individual is a self only by virtue of a history of relationships to others. The being and character of the individual, then, come to be seen as inevitably conditioned by the web of interpersonal relationships in which she is immersed. While psychoanalysis has undergone paradigmatic change in its theoretical underpinnings, these changes have yet to be fully integrated into the technical practice of analysis. If we accept a relational view of human development and motivation, what are the implications for our understanding of the countertransference? For practicing therapists this situation can be confusing. Often we are left with a vague sense that we should follow the prohibitions and proscriptions of traditional technique, but without knowing why. The irony here is that Freud's technical recommendations stemmed from his effort to secure analysis on science rather than on dogma. This book's journey through history is an attempt to free us from our troubled conscience as we move into new technical realms.

Accounts of Inquiry: Epistemology and the Countertransference

In the current psychoanalytic dialogue, the issue of epistemology has come to the forefront; it forms the first arm of psychoanalytic thought. To make sense of the countertransference, we must address the problem of how affect intersects with the process of knowing. In what ways does our affectivity, the countertransference, interfere with or inform our judgments? Does objectivity depend on the suspension of our emotional involvement, or is participation an essential part of understanding? These are epistemological questions and they require that we articulate a coherent position about the problem of knowing.

The by now familiar dichotomy between objectivism and constructivism is overly simple. Human inquiry is too variegated to be neatly divided into opposing camps. We think magically and construct egocentric worlds of causality; we think artistically and draw unexpected links. When we turn to mature modes of inquiry, however, it may be useful to specify, without lapsing into reification, three stages of historical and personal development: the Platonic, the objective, and the constructive. Each of these forms of inquiry has its own idea about the nature of truth and the necessary method for contacting it. These modes of inquiry, while sequential, are not mutually extinguishing. As in human development, the establishment of more mature forms of experience does not permanently do away with the more primitive. In the attempt to know, the individual and the culture may vary in the methods used to conduct inquiries.

The first mode of inquiry, the Platonic, is born from the breakdown of omnipotent/magical perception, and arises out of the recognition that truth is not immediately available. Experiences of the senses may mislead us and impulse is an unreliable guide to action. For Plato and the theological tradition that followed him, the mutability of the world cannot be indicative of the realm of being. Being, in contrast to the world that presents itself to our senses, must be pure and eternal. To locate truth, then, inquiry must be modified; methodology is required. In Platonic inquiry, knowing rests on the shoulders of revelation and disembodied reason. Truth is a quality of being that exists above the mortal plane, and our access to its fruits depends on our capacity to rise above the limits of ordinary sense perception. In the theological aspect, effective inquiry requires that the individual turn away from the unreliable input of the senses and move toward oracular experience. Through the process of revelation, truth is transmitted from the authority of the divine to the mortal receiver. Within the Platonic aspect, effective inquiry is still based on turning away from the senses. In this aspect, however, epistemological authority flows from the revelation of reason rather than the divine. By turning toward reason the mind is able to sort through the false impressions of experience and becoming, and reach a transcendent knowing of being. Here, reason is set above the fallibly human and is appealed to as the final arbiter of the real. What we must realize about both theological and Platonic inquiry, however, is that they rely on an elusive epistemological method. Only the select are chosen for revelatory experience; only the deeply philosophical capture metaphysical systems. For those who are denied revelatory experience, truth must be determined through second-hand reports. Within the theological aspect, the Bible and the ecclesiastic hierarchy must serve as the authoritarian arbiter of reality. When we turn to philosophy, the access to truth is similarly limited. For those less skilled at philosophic thought, truth is based on the conclusions brought forward by the more adept, and texts become the authoritative purveyors of truth.

While Freud conceived psychoanalysis in an objectivist epistemological climate, the primacy of objectivism in the birth of psychoanalysis does not mean that the Platonic/theological mode of inquiry has no part in the history of our field. Within psychoanalysis there is a long history of depending on Freud's texts as sources of truth. We have wanted to find validation for our thinking in Freud's seemingly more authoritative words. The struggles within psychoanalysis over which branch of thought is the true heir to the Freudian legacy, and the assertion that the analyst is the arbiter of the real, as well as the tendency to dismiss the countertransference out of hand as an obstruction to effective analysis, all betray a reversion to Platonic/theological modes of knowing. In these acts we seek to rely on authority as a source of knowing.

This mode of knowing, in both its theological and Platonic aspects, however, while full of self-confidence, lacks adequate means of adjudication. Whose revelatory experience should be accepted as authentic? Whose interpretation of the Bible should be recognized as authoritative? The problems of adjudication are no less daunting in the realm of Platonic reasoning. As metaphysical systems proliferate, each claiming to be self-evident through the appeal to reason, who is to decide which system is most reasonable? This quandary touches psychoanalysis as well. Psychoanalysis has had to ask which analytic school, which member of the analytic dyad, is the most reliable oracle of the unconscious? We realize that there are reasonable disagreements about Freud's intent, and that there are moments when the analysand seems to make more sense than the analyst. The Platonic/theological mode of inquiry has no procedure for securing agreement among discussants, and so the process of inquiry degenerates into declamation. Religion and metaphysics are founded on unstable ground, and this form of knowing culminates in a crisis of faith. The failure to reach a secure mode of adjudication in this form of inquiry leads to the overturning of religious authority and pure reason as modes of determining truth. It is this resentment of the authoritarian aspects of Freud's legacy that leads detractors to reject his conclusions as unsubstantiated and to attack his integrity as if he were a contemporary rather than a historical figure.

As the flaws in the Platonic/theological mode of inquiry become more visibile, the objective or scientific mode of inquiry emerges to fill the epistemological vacancy. In objective inquiry, reality becomes available through the suppression of subjectivity and the suspension of empirically ungrounded speculation. By avoiding the distorting pull of desire and affect, egoism is overcome. Rather than turning away from the data of the senses, objective inquiry seeks to draw on this information to systematically uncover its regularity. In a reversal of the Platonic hierarchy, the material world, as known through the senses, must govern the conclusions of the mind. Through empirical observation, the scientist locates reality, a reality that is material and makes itself felt through its technological achievements. Truth, under this paradigm, is opposed to the tyrannical claims of authority. It transcends the cultural organization of opinion and, as long as objective method is obeyed, becomes available in democratic form to the individual. This is the climate of thought in which Freud reached his maturity. For his generation, maintaining an objective attitude toward experience was the critical aim. To position oneself to perceive truth required that the affective side of the self be contained and kept out of the laboratory or consulting room. It is this concept of objective method and attitude that shaped the debate surrounding the countertransference for most of the twentieth century. It is the dictates of the objectivist paradigm that have demanded that abstinence govern the terms of analytic inquiry.

While objectivism provided resolution of the problems plaguing theological knowing, it has since revealed its own weaknesses. Objectivism displaced theological knowing both because it offered a more secure process for arbitrating between competing claims of truth and because its attention to the material world allowed it to score significant advances in the technological realm. Yet over the course of this century both of these achievements have begun to show flaws in their structure. Critics of the philosophy of science have suggested that the seemingly secure principles offered by science for adjudication of truth claims are less immutable than predicated. Bernstein (1983) writes, "It is an illusion to think that there is or must be a permanent, neutral matrix to which we can appeal that will tell us once and for all what is to count as better and worse substantive arguments or even what is properly a scientific argument" (p. 72). Scientific method and the objective attitude are as much a human creation as any other activity in which we might engage. Their capacity to secure truth must still be verified through investigation; it does not exist independently of the process of human knowing.

The difficulties with objectivism are not simply external to the analytic situation. If they were we would feel no obligation to import these conundrums of philosophy into the already complicated realm of analytic technique. But objectivism's difficulties are robust and they make themselves felt within the therapeutic context as well. When the analyst operates from an objectivist stance, I believe, damage is done to the therapeutic relationship, and the possibilities of change are curtailed. In the attempt to be neutral, we may turn to silence and a position behind the couch. In this way the analyst strives to be a pure observer. However, in the post-Newtonian world there is no static matrix to which we can affix our stillness, and staying silent and out of sight are actions in their own right, subject to interpretation. In the attempt to reach objectivity through minimal participation, the analyst still participates in and colors the analytic setting. We can agree with Sullivan (1953) when we say that we are inevitably participant observers. The analyst, no matter how quiet or still, necessarily participates in the analytic interaction. Whether we sit behind the patient, or behind glass, we must still sit somewhere, and this position will help determine what there is for us to see. Observation plays a critical role in shaping the observed.

Once the force of perspectivism makes itself felt, clinging to an objectivist sensibility is harmful to the analytic relationship. When the perspectival quality of knowing is denied, the atmosphere of honesty is injured. Silence does not render the analyst immune from the stirrings of the countertransference, and the analysand is sensitive to these movements. The analysand who gains some sense of perspectivism (a shift that is facilitated by the nature of analytic work) can no longer be expected to sit back and accept the analyst's behavior as simply neutral. Its meaning is determined not only by scientific intent. The analyst's insistence on the privileged quality of his knowing can act as a traumatic event that derails the analytic treatment. To avoid this kind of iatrogenic damage, psychoanalysis must acknowledge the subjectivity of the analyst as well as that of the analysand. Objectivism is an unworkable epistemology for psychoanalytic practice.

In the face of the difficulties that objectivism presents, analytic thinking has increasingly acknowledged the necessity of perspectivism. The significance of this recognition, however, has not yet come into clear focus. The undermining of positivism makes the technical field more complex. When neutrality is understood as the therapist acting as a blank slate, questions about technique are simplified. The therapist's role, then, is to reduce his activity to a minimum. Yet when we come to see this kind of abstinence as problematic, we are thrown into greater uncertainty. Even the best training analysis cannot purify the analyst in a way that robs him of his subjectivity. This is good news. But it leaves us with the question of how the therapist's self should be brought into the analytic context. We have to start asking, what kinds of activity are helpful and at what phases in the treatment? We must ask, what are the implications of constructivism for psychoanalytic theory and technique? At first glance it may be tempting to suggest that the analyst should behave like a constructivist. The analyst, under this impulse, should be willing to entertain the analysand's ideas as a version of truth, and ask the analysand to offer the same consideration toward the analyst's interpretations. Since neutrality can no longer be equated with abstinence or silence, perhaps the analytic situation should mirror the more free ranging methodology of constructivist knowing. Writers like Tansey (1992) and Hoffman (1992) seem to make this precise suggestion. I would argue, however, that it is a mistake to assume that this conclusion is a necessary implication of constructivist epistemology. To move from seeing the sense in constructivism to arguing that its method must govern our analytic behavior is to lose track of constructivism's first insight. Truth, including the truth of constructivism, is created through the process of human interpretation, and to suggest that constructivism should become superordinate to our activity is to revert to the claims of necessity embedded in the Platonic/theological and objectivist modes of knowing. To stay closer to constructivist insights we should realize that the analyst's behavior should also be governed by pragmatic considerations. We have to ask not merely what is true, but what is useful. What epistemological attitude is most therapeutic, and on what basis do we derive our confidence? While I too believe that a candid and explorative attitude is a necessary component of the analytic attitude, this view remains a practical matter rather than an a priori necessity.

When we begin to comprehend the relational nature of being and knowing, our connection to the countertransference changes. Rather than seeing affect as necessarily clouding judgment, constructivism suggests that affect serves as an inescapably human form of judgment. Our affective reactions act as perspectival promontories through which we come to know aspects of the world. Our anger, our interest, our sadness, our fear—all of these are reactions to real aspects of other people and things. To turn away from the countertransference, then, would be to discard critical information about the interpersonal exchange of the analytic environment. This recognition of the countertransference as a source of knowing has increasingly penetrated the analytic debate. To make full use of this source of insight, however, we must clarify our understanding of emotion. We need to go past intuitive accounts, and answer more precisely what constitutes an emotional reaction. What does it mean when we become bored or angry? What information does this convey? In trying to answer these questions, I examine psychoanalytic theories of emotion and how these relate to theories of emotion from the empirical branch of psychology.

Constructivism's acceptance of perspectivism and affect as a source of knowing, however, should not be read as an abandonment of discerning judgment or standards of truth. While we cannot imperially claim that one version of truth invalidates all others, this does not entail that all versions of reality are of equal value, or that affect provides a categorical access to truth. We must be able to first contain our affective reactions within a field of reverie and consideration before they can reliably provide useful insights. Some constructions of reality are more useful than others; they help us make changes in the world and in ourselves that allow us to feel better. In a perspectival world, versions of truth are arbitrated through pragmatic considerations (Rorty, 1982). This is not to say that truth is whatever the individual finds convenient at the moment. The pragmatic standard is saved from pure anarchic relativism through the limiting conditions of the human body and mind. How we feel over time is governed to some extent by the unchanging terms of human affectivity. These terms cut across individuals, and provide a reference point for interpersonal agreement.

In a constructivist view, reality moves closer to the human, but this increase in proximity is won through a decrease in the sense of certainty. To think relationally is to give up claims to know absolutely. When we see that truth is multifaceted, we must recognize that while we do know something about the world, this knowing does not exhaust the available perspectives. As we move forward in inquiry, we should expect surprise and new insight. The result of the progressive and constructivist nature of truth is that the analyst can no longer be the exclusive keeper of reality. Instead, the truth of interpretation must lie somewhere between the analyst and the analysand. Schafer (1983) refers to this emphasis on the conditioned nature of interpretation to reassess our relationship to metapsychology in psychoanalysis. Metapsychology, rather than designating absolutely the truth of what occurs in development, is seen as a narrative structure that we can use to retell our lives. This act of retelling is not a movement from falsehood to truth, but is instead a movement from partial truth to less-bounded truth. The value of interpretation lies in its ability to unfreeze our perception of reality. In this unfreezing, alternatives and choice reemerge.

The Evolution of Morality

When we turn to the second arm of psychoanalytic thought—metapsychology and the problem of gratification and need—we must take up the issue of morality. How we understand the problem of value, how we map out the route to virtue, plays a critical role in shaping our view of the countertransference. The countertransference has been proscribed out of fundamental beliefs about motivation, health, and the therapeutic process. The traditional line of thought holds that to provide gratification in the transference is to strengthen the grip of fantasy and to lead the analysand away from the assumption of self-responsibility. The countertransference, a source of affective entanglement, must be contained in order to avoid this kind of false palliative. When we turn from the drive model to relational theories of developmental arrest (Mitchell, 1988), and from the problem of gratification to the question of need, the hesitation surrounding the countertransference as a source of action has remained. To allow the countertransference to intrude on the psychoanalytic environment, this thinking holds, is to burden the analysand with responsibilities for the analyst that will serve to abort the therapeutic process of regression. When we prematurely demand that the analysand recognize the subjectivity of the analyst, the analysand is prevented from contacting the submerged core of the self. These ideas about the curative process of psychoanalysis derive from beliefs about the constitution of correct living, and I suggest that they belong to the realm of moral theory. The drive and developmental-arrest models are based on different moral foundations—on different views of health and the therapeutic process—but each requires analysts to keep important aspects of their countertransferential subjectivity to themselves. As we move toward a third paradigm in psychoanalysis, what Mitchell calls the relational-conflict model, we must revisit the questions of gratification and need in the therapeutic environment, and specify its portrait of virtue. By defining and clarifying this moral position we rework our relationship to psychoanalytic technique and the problem of subjectivity; it is a reworking that points us toward a more active use of the countertransference in the therapeutic relationship.

In making this argument about the role of morality in psychoanalytic technique and the utilization of the countertransference, it is useful to turn again toward the evolutionary view. By tracing the development of moral understanding—as we did with epistemology—we extricate ourselves from anachronous assumptions that interfere with the formulation of a congruent understanding of the countertransference. Within psychoanalysis, as well as in cultural history, we can make out three stages of moral evolution that roughly parallel the stages we outlined with epistemological evolution: transcendent virtue, natural virtue, and constructed virtue. In each of these stages the conception of human nature and the route to virtue varies. Transcendent virtue is based on the attempt to overcome animal physicality. It calls for abstinence as a way of disembedding ourselves from problematic impulse. Natural virtue moves in the opposite direction. It suggests that human nature is essentially good, but becomes corrupted by the press of civilization. To reach virtue, repression must be undone, and the natural core of the self allowed to grow without traumatic constraint. Constructed virtue, the third stage, is only slowly emerging into our awareness. It suggests that our biological or animal nature is neither something that must be overcome nor inherently pure. Rather, virtue requires a developmental environment that allows us to construct ways to skillfully shape the expression of our endogenous impulses. This third stage in the trajectory of moral development, I suggest, requires fuller articulation for us to make intelligent use of the countertransference.

As humanity moves into its long period of self-consciousness, morality emerges as a question. In tandem with the emergence of self-consciousness comes an immediate experience of choice. To possess self-consciousness is to sense that affectively determined impulse does not necessarily entail immediate action. This nascent sense of free will, however, also makes action more difficult. It requires that we justify our choices through some theory of value. Now on the surface, it seems, the awakening of self-consciousness does not necessitate the movement away from impulse. We might feel that humanity could self-consciously observe itself choosing to consistently be guided by impulse. Yet the seeming compatibility of self-consciousness and impulse-determined action is fictitious. Self-consciousness itself, I would argue, only arises through the emergent awareness that impulse is unreliable as a guide to action. To suggest otherwise is to fall into the trap of homuncular experience; it is to imagine a silent being residing behind the movement of the impulsive self. As Wittgenstein argues that a private language is impossible, otherwise imagining one were following a rule would be the same as following a rule, I would suggest that an unconflicted self-consciousness is impossible, otherwise the chosen could not be distinguished from the impul-

transcendent virtue – impulses transcended

sive. Self-consciousness makes itself known through the gap between impulse and action.

As self-consciousness emerges out of the awareness of impulse, the necessity for moral structure becomes clear with the realization that to be guided immediately by the tempestuous hand of emotion—to bite, to punch, to flee, to grope, without caution—is to invite catastrophe. When the body reveals the unreliability of its impulse, the first impetus is to work to transcend its limitations. The result is what I will call "transcendent virtue," the first stage in the evolution of morality. In this mode of valuing, the hope is that by forsaking the body as a source of guidance, the suffering it engenders through its unreliability can be overcome. It is this hope that leads toward abstinence as a mode of living. By avoiding sensual gratification, by the move away from the body and toward the mind, the expectation is that the dangers of acting on base impulse will be averted. When the body is disqualified as a source of guidance, a higher standard of moral authority must be located. Within the paradigm of transcendent virtue that standard is located beyond the self. It becomes equated with God, reason, and the purity of the real. In this form of virtue the aim is to align action and choice with the moral dictates of the transcendent standard. The Platonic version would ask us to accept the primacy of reason in the formulation of moral doctrine. The theological version posits the primacy of divine canon. In both versions, however, the debased realm of passion and appearance is split off from the purity of the transcendent principle. This version of virtue emphasizes the role of self-discipline and moral choice. When the impulse is curtailed, and perception and choice are brought into alignment with the transcendent standard, virtue is established.

While the paradigm of transcendent virtue begins with the hope for salvation, this optimism hides within itself darker shadings. When the pure is split off from the base, part of the self becomes discredited. If this part of the self gains precedence we become vulnerable to judgement. Within the theological tradition this takes shape in the concept of sin. In other versions of transcendent virtue, terms like "childish," "depraved," or "perverse" fill the same function of reproof. Transcendent virtue, then, carries within it a reprobative attitude. It condems as beyond salvation parts of the self. In this way it creates a backdrop of humiliation and shame. The virtue of abstinence, while initially based on an accurate perception of the unreliability of impulse, hides within itself a hatred of the body. This derogative attitude toward the body and its desires is problematic. The insistence on transcendence slowly diminishes the energy of the body, and leaves us in a devitalized state.

In response to this devitalizing effect of transcendent morality, a second trend in morality emerges. This second form of morality expresses the hope that the damage to human valuing can be righted through a partial resurrection of the natural state of mankind. In the morality of naturalism, perhaps most clearly represented in Rousseau's work (1750), lies the recognition that the demands of society and intellectual culture, rather than alleviating the distress of living, have in some cases compounded its difficulty. The morality of natural virtue, rather than calling for abstinence as a route to salvation, stresses the innate goodness of mankind, and prescribes the need to reach below the level of civilizing trauma to recover the inherent virtue of humanity. The aim is not to reveal the sinful nature of mankind, but to recognize the effect of traumatic living conditions and how they distort our essential benevolence. By recognizing how we are the object of trauma–how events determine us–naturalism seeks to release us from the damaging effects of blame.

Psychoanalysis, paradoxically, begins its life spanning these two moral positions. On one hand, Freud (1898), in his earliest theory, suggests that hysteria stems from the toxic effect of suppressed sexuality. The restrictive demands of society lead to certain sexual practices–coitus interruptus, masturbation–that interfere with the proper flow of the reflex arc. Even in his more mature theories, Freud (1923) retained a view of health that centered on the ability to establish genital object relations. In this emphasis on overcoming the damaging effects of repression, Freud clearly has aligned himself with the morality of natural virtue. Health is reached through undoing the repressive effects of civilization. Yet even while Freud keeps one foot in this circle, he quickly places the other in the realm of transcendent virtue. For the analysand to reach health, Freud argues, she must be willing to forsake hallucinatory pleasures and bear the difficult abstinence of the therapeutic context. Real health is available only through adult relationships and the nonsensual realm of sublimated satisfaction. In this aspect of his work, Freud demanded that we rise above the press of the unconscious drives and accept responsibility for how we shape our experience.

In the period after Freud's death, his followers seemed to embrace more fully the transcendent aspects of his account of virtue. Early analytic writers (Abraham, 1919; Nunberg, 1928) increasingly spoke of the necessity for therapeutic abstinence in gaining the leverage to make recalcitrant analysands forsake "childish" erotic longings. The ego psychologists stressed the need to make adaptations to reality and modulate the difficult powers of the id. Embedded in this reprobative tilt lies an implicit directive for the analyst to avoid responding affectively to the analysand. For the analyst to allow himself to be moved by the countertransference, either positively or negatively, would be to fall back toward the body and its problematic urges, and so drag the analysand down after him. The analysand was only too willing to make this journey, but it was a journey that moved in opposition to virtue. For these analysts, discipline in the realm of affect required the suspension of countertransferential feeling.

In response to this increasing conservatism, the middle school theorists countered by emphasizing more fully the natural virtue aspects of psychoanalysis. We can see this in Winnicott's (1962) writing about the true self and how it must be protected from impingement. In these writings the stress is placed more on providing for the analysand's developmental needs than on withholding damaging gratification. While not often discussed as a form of countertransference, the emphasis on the supportive holding environment implicitly suggests that the analyst must be willing to supply a positive emotional presence. In a sense, then, the positive countertransference becomes part of the curative process in the paradigm of natural virtue. It is what allows the lifting of the false self, the narcissistic defenses, and the resumption of the true self's authentic development. It is this emphasis on the reworking of developmental failures that leads Mitchell (1988) to label this paradigm in psychoanalysis the "developmental-arrest" model. By stressing how the analysand is the object of the analyst's ministrations, these theorists, on the whole, ask the analyst to assume responsibility for the undoing of the traumatic past. The analyst must contain the negative countertransference, or the desirous positive countertransference, in order to allow the analysand to experience an optimal therapeutic-developmental environment.

The tilt toward the morality of natural virtue, however, has come under increasing criticism (Mitchell, 1988). While it corrects some of the excesses of the transcendent approach, it has its own limiting factors. On epistemological grounds we should be suspicious when the dialogue moves to a discussion of a *true self* that exists prerelationally. If we accept the critique of constructivism, how can we know this self from a stance transcendent to perspective? How would we divine the invariant sequence of its needs? To imagine that humans have a pure core that lies below the shaping press of experience is to retreat to the fiction of the thing-in-itself. These epistemological difficulties are not ephemeral; rather, they make themselves felt in tangible ways in the therapeutic context. When we split sullied from pure experience, we solidify both pathology and health. This split leads us to believe that we could somehow escape from the difficulty of choice and find a reliably authentic relationship to impulse that is unmarred by ambivalence and ambiguity. But this hope for natural purity, a hope that echoes Plato's belief in the realm of forms, is a fabrication whose surface benevolence conceals damaging hopes. By holding out the prospect of perfectibility, it prevents us from moving forward with the real difficulty of choice. The emphasis on inadequate holding environments, on missing developmental experiences, can lead the analysand to reify the feeling of emptiness. The fluid affective state becomes tangible, and the analysand comes to believe that the move toward affective fullness depends on perfect reparative ministrations. In the face of this belief, analytic empathy takes on a magical quality in the analysand's mind, a quality that is never quite met in actuality. The hope for compensation, a compensation that is bound to fall short, then sets off a second round of affective distress and hopelessness. The analysand, sensing her history as an object, is left helpless in the face of the current situation. The psychoanalytic version of naturalism runs aground through its inability to reveal the optimism inherent in the acceptance of imperfection and the empowerment implicit in taking agentive responsibility for suffering.

The psychoanalytic morality of natural virtue runs into further difficulty around the problem of entitlement and victimization. By stressing the authority of impulse and how this initiative is damaged through trauma, naturalism underlines how we are the object rather than the agent of our experience. We suffer because of what has been done to us rather than from what we do; we have been victimized, and in our passivity we are entitled to compensation. Shabad (1993) suggests that the attempt to recover the preexperiential self leads to a distortion of wish: "Unlike the wish experience, which may implicitly communicate a request to receive from the other, the experience of need, with its implication of demand, may do violence to the free social discourse of giving and receiving" (p. 487). When desire becomes demand, the analyst may struggle with feelings of withholding, and the analysand, even if the demand is met, may be unable to internalize this experience as a tangible sign of the analyst's concern. If need rules the day, then the analysand may see the analyst as having no choice, as being bound by professionalism, and the act of giving becomes devalued. The analyst gives out of obligation rather than concern. The atmosphere of necessity curtails the process of interpersonal negotiation. Yet negotiation, I suggest, is critical to adult relationships, and if it is not practiced within the consulting room, the analysand is left underprepared for relationships where both parties come with an agenda of wish.

As these difficulties with naturalism as a moral foundation have become increasingly evident, a new moral position has struggled to emerge. In the morality of constructed virtue lies a recognition of both the body's essentiality and its unreliability. The goal of value is not to return us to a primordial mode of authentic being or to allow us to transcend the material constraints of mortality, but to invent a marriage between the two, between inheritance and conscious creation, that generates a new view of what it might mean to be a human. In this emergent stage of morality the aim of value is not to overcome the body, but to work skillfully with the information provided in its affects and impulses to reach a mode of living that we can fully endorse. The morality of constructed virtue holds an essentially more active view of virtue. It suggests that health—rather than being dependent on overcoming the body or the damaging effects of civilization—requires the active construction of new skills. Virtue must be constructed, not simply uncovered. Psychoanalysis is in the midst of a transition to this third, still uncertainly defined, moral position.

In turning toward a discussion of virtue, however, we may expect the rejoinder that psychoanalysis is not bound by the conclusions of philosophy. The practice of psychoanalysis is governed by its own empiricism, by the weight of clinical experience. This rejoinder is well founded, but empiricism and theory are not simply connected in hierarchical sequence; instead they are partners in a game of leapfrog, each hopping over the back of the other. The empiricism of practice has brought us to the front end of the new moral paradigm; now theory must take its turn and leap. To reach a coherent approach to the countertransference we must try to clarify the shape of constructed virtue and specify its ramifications for technique.

This new paradigm of virtue has been most clearly articulated by Mitchell (1993), who frames the shift as a revolution in the understanding of what the patient needs. To Mitchell's mind, the field of psychoanalysis has moved away from the rationalism of drive theory, to an emphasis on creativity and subjectivity. Psychoanalysis can no longer rest on Freud's call—based in the ethic of transcendent virtue—for renunciation of fantasy in return for increased technological control. This kind of material rationalism can no longer generate meaning and value. Instead, if we are to construct meaning that retains vitality, psychoanalysis must enrich our imaginative capacity: "What the patient needs is not a rational reworking of unconscious infantile fantasies; what the patient needs is a revitalization and expansion of his own capacity to generate experience that feels real, meaningful, and valuable" (p. 24). In this revised view, the fundamental conflict in human experience stems not from warring drives, but from the tension between preserving relationship—meeting the fundamental need to be connected with others—and retaining a sense of affective authenticity and vitality. The morality of constructed virtue suggests that our suffering stems from the experience and belief that maintaining connection requires the subjugation of our affective response. In this subjugation, in the degradation of affect, we lose track of aliveness and meaning.

In the morality of constructed virtue, affect moves to the center stage of analytic attention—it serves as the agent of our motivational concerns (Frijda, 1986). Our anger, our fear, our sadness, our joy are all biologically based action tendencies that are in the service of core motivations. Whether we see these concerns as primarily libidinal, or if we take a more modern view and see them in Greenberg's (1992) terms as divisible into the need for safety and effectance, emotions are evolutionary strategies to help us reach these goals. We react with emotion out of the need to protect, relinquish, or celebrate a concern. It is through affect, then, that our most essential concerns announce themselves; affect serves as the energetic wellspring of our motivational life. Spezzano (1993) suggests that

> psychoanalysis is psychoanalytic—because it emphasizes the ways in which "wired-in," preexperiential *affective* meaning categories are immanent in all immediate human experience. One might say that what distinguishes psychoanalysis from hermeneutics is that where hermeneutics tends, in general, to point first to culture and language as the major preexperiential mediums for the basic constitution of human experience, psychoanalysis points first to affects [1993, p. 211].

Affect is the primary preexperiental organizer of experience, and the root of meaning, because it is the structured impetus of our concerns. To preserve our vitality, our sense of meaning, then, we must not turn away from emotion.

There are two primary ways we run aground in relation to emotion. The first, and perhaps more conventionally understood, is through the failure to modulate emotions adequately. When we are overwhelmed by emotion, our actions are unskillful, and this is the side that transcendent morality sees. Yet, a second difficulty can arise in the tension between concerns. Our emotions can work against each other and constrict the energetic pathways. When we find ourselves angry at an intimate partner, we may feel an impulse to speak forcefully, even to yell, about the perceived transgression. The thought of expressing this anger, however, may elicit fear of further negative consequences—anger enacted may lead to abandonment. At this moment we have been drawn into an emotion loop (Fischer, Shaver, and Carnochan, 1989); we have an emotion about an emotion. In this case we are afraid of our anger and its consequences. This fear then leads us to freeze or run away from the anger. If the fear becomes too strong, rather than leading to a useful reworking of the basic impulse of anger, it leads to its truncation, and the initial concern that was at the root of the anger becomes misplaced. This kind of compromise between fear and anger is a poor one, where neither the sense of safety nor effectance is well served—to avoid overwhelming danger we settle for an attenuated sense of security and vitality. In this emotional reflexiveness, the relationship to the motivational wellspring becomes distorted. Our fluidity and spontaneity become tangled. This is the emotional danger that spurs naturalism. To reach a position of health, to construct a workable virtue, we must find ways of skillfully acting from affect that do not elicit untenable secondary dangers. Here the task would be to rework the appraisal that led to anger or to find a mode of anger that does not entail isolation. Health, in the paradigm of constructed virtue, requires that we construct emotion skills that allow us to reach greater levels of experienced safety and effectance.

If we find the move toward an affective-relational model convincing, we must reevaluate the nature of therapeutic action. When we see suffering as stemming from misplaced libidinal strivings—strivings directed at a misimagined version of the therapist—then the idea that interpretation and insight are curative is coherent. The task is to oblige the analysand to recognize the illusionary nature of the transferential perception and renounce trying to induce the analyst to occupy the role of libidinal object. Analysis must reveal the impossibility of the transference rather than demonstrate alternate modes of relating. If, however, we see suffering as arising out of affective-relational conflict, the idea that interpretation and insight alone can overcome the difficulty loses coherence. The problem is not that the analysand wants the impossible—desires the fulfillment of oedipal longings—but that the analysand believes that the necessary is impossible. The analysand is convinced that life demands a choice between connection and vitality, when both are in fact necessary. Assurances that this is not the case are inadequate to dispel the analysand's dread. Interpretation, as a strictly informational communication of meaning, must remain only an assertion since it lacks the substance of proof. To alleviate the flow of suffering, the analysand must reach a tangible experience of relationship where affective vitality, the authentic striving for concerns, does not disrupt the bonds of interpersonal connection. The emphasis on actual experience in the therapeutic relationship is central to the work of Weiss and Sampson (1986). They suggest that the therapeutic action of psychoanalysis depends on the disconfirmation of pathogenic beliefs through contact with the analyst's actual behavior. It is with the analyst that the analysand can untangle the fear-based emotion loops and construct new emotion skills. What must occur is not merely the discarding of past illusion, but the creation and discovery of formerly unimagined patterns of relationship. Under the morality of constructed virtue, the therapeutic relationship becomes the crucible where dread can be converted to hope, and more satisfying ways of being with another can be discovered.

The Nature of Therapeutic Action

If we accept this much of the metapsychological or moral revision, then we must examine more carefully what it is about the therapist's presence, rather than absence, that allows the analytic relationship to be transformative. The answer to this question has many facets, but for each of these the management and utilization of the countertransference is central. I argue that the skillful working with the countertransference, the capacity to be emotionally present in particular ways, is an essential feature of psychoanalytic practice. This fact requires that we move beyond seeing the countertransference merely as a source of information and begin to draw on it as a source of action. To make sense of this still controversial aspect of constructed virtue we must examine both the necessity of the countertransference, and the necessity of transforming the countertransference through self-analysis.

The first part of our consideration is an accounting of why the countertransference is a necessary source of action. From a relational perspective the therapeutic action of psychoanalysis is dependent on the tangible connection between the analysand and the analyst. I suggest that it is through the interplay between transference and countertransference that this tangibility is established. For the relationship to become tangible the analysand must sense the analyst's affective participation. The advent of emotion offers more substantial proof to the analysand because it is something that happens to us; unlike words, it is not readily manipulated. This quality of arising unbidden, of lying beyond the realm of the technically produced, allows affect to convert the professional relationship into the actual. It is in the affective response that the analytic relationship becomes real. When we come to feel emotion about another, it is a signal that she has entered the realm of our concern; the countertransference offers a kind of proof to the analysand that the relationship matters to the analyst. For the analytic relationship to become a transformative experience, a place where the unimagined becomes actual, the analyst must be willing to bring emotion forward. Only in this way can the analysand's limiting beliefs about relationship be challenged.

While an affective presence is required for the analytic relationship to gain the substance to be transformative, we should be clear that this is not a call for affective impulsiveness. Although affect provides reality, this does not mean that emotion is real only when left in its raw form. For the analyst to act immediately on the impulse of countertransferential feeling would be to re-create the disruptive events that initiated the analysand's suffering. Unmodulated acts or statements of fear, anger, boredom, or lust can only be hurtful in the analytic context. For the countertransference to be a therapeutic source of action it must be managed and transformed.[3] The nature of that transformation, an uncertain and difficult process, is a central concern of our work. But if, in the face of this rightful caution, we turn away from the expression of emotion, then we sabotage the analytic process. We sabotage its honesty and reality. To concede to the anxiety of expression is to betray a distrust of the

[3] The reader may argue that to transform the countertransference is to abandon honesty. Under a constructivist frame, however, our immediate impulse is only one facet of us; it is not necessarily more authentic or "true" to speak impulsively rather than judiciously. See chapters 7 and 8 for a more extensive discussion of this issue.

therapeutic compact. In the morality of constructed virtue the attempt to bring affect constructively into relationships is the linchpin of health. Within this position we suggest that affective authenticity and vitality do not have to lead to the dissolution of relationship. We assume that emotions make sense and can be the basis for generative action. The danger lies in those instances when we behave merely impulsively or turn our emotions back on themselves and distort them. To resort to silence, to leave the countertransference unspoken, is to undercut our credibility. As therapists we ask patients to make the shift from suppressing to experiencing emotion. How can we ask our patients to take this unsettling step if we are unwilling to model ourselves on that kind of capacity and courage?

To become credible proponents of our analytic vision, we must find a way to bring the countertransference into the therapeutic transaction. The steps and sequence involved in transforming the countertransference into an analytic attitude and basis for action require tracing. While this process is deeply complex, a complexity I return to in chapter 10, I suggest that when it is simplified in a schematic form we can identify a few key components. At the center of constructed virtue is a belief in both the body's essentiality and its unreliability. In the face of the countertransference, then, nodding to its unreliability, we must begin with an attitude of patience or containing. When the analyst is sitting with an analysand and the countertransference begins to assert itself, the analyst must turn his attention to it without a sense of urgency–try to decipher its significance, locate its underlying concern–before he sets about formulating a response. In this moment of delay (and it may be a long moment), the first step is to separate the emotion's underlying concern from its prefabricated strategy for action. When he notices that he is angry with the analysand, the analyst must work to sort out the concern–perhaps a sense of worry that the therapeutic process is derailed–from the impulse to accuse or confront. The approach of constructed virtue is to accept our biological nature and the validity of its goals, without granting it executive authority.

When we locate the concern behind the countertransference, a hope to establish a particular kind of investigative and constructive relationship with the analysand, we are naturally led to expand our emotional view to include the analysand. Our anger, if it is to achieve its goal, must move beyond attacking. Stern (1994), tracing this process, writes, "The transformation begins *within* the analyst as he or she begins to get space from the complementary countertransference affects and 'remembers' the traumatized child within the patient whose developmental-relational needs have been thwarted and whose current response to the analyst makes sense as an adaptation to that trauma" (p. 337). While I feel hesitant to endorse the language of "the child within," Stern's injunction to remember the pressure of the patient's developmental history is important. What begins as simple anger becomes transformed through this act of compassionate remembrance. In this paradigm, the analyst's neutrality is not based on a belief that the analysand's transference is unreal. Unlike the drive model, where neutrality depends on seeing that the analysand, in her difficulty, is not really speaking about us, the morality of constructed virtue is more willing to grant reality to the present transference. Instead, constructivism asks us to look at the analysand with a more penetrating sight, to look past the trying behavior, the vitriol, to see the reasonable concerns that lie below. Neutrality, then, rather than stemming from abstinence, becomes an extension of compassion. It is based on the analyst's capacity to maintain, despite numerous assaults, both his own and the analysand's genuine desire to reach a certain quality of connection.

When transformed in this way, the countertransference loses some of its thorns. In the compassionate attitude, we approach our emotions and the actions of others as statements about the breach in the relationship. We assume that beyond the difficult feelings lies a potential desire to be connected in a way that neither of the participants must sacrifice his or her integrity. If we bring this understanding of neutrality to Tower's case, then we may move beyond seeing the frustration she felt toward her patient as a narcissistic reaction to her patient's abuse. Tower was able to tolerate the abuse for months. The abuse, per se, is not the difficulty; it is the abuse that leads nowhere, and so becomes abusive to the patient herself, that is the problem. When the analyst holds in awareness the centrality of the therapeutic concern, the initial anger, the desire to leave the analysand to her own ranting, was transformed. The desire for revenge, for a lunch without the analysand, became a compassionate anger directed more at the impasse than at the analysand. When the analyst acknowledges the reality of the countertransference, the door may be opened for the patient to begin to see both how she affects the world and how other responses to anger may be possible.

In chapters 9 and 10 I return to these questions and specify more fully the terrain of constructed virtue. When this emergent form of valuing is brought into focus, the problems surrounding gratification and abstinence, neutrality and affective engagement, are dislodged from their intractable positions. In those chapters I speak of how we might view human nature and the problem of psychological health. This is necessary groundwork for formulating a coherent approach to the countertransference. Finally, having established this ground, I treat the problem of countertransference disclosure in greater detail.

CHAPTER TWO

Freud and the Advent of Psychoanalysis

In a field so inherently disturbing and uncertain as psychoanalysis, the desire for authority is significant. Freud's writing has filled that role. He mapped the territory of analytic therapy, establishing critical questions and themes. Those who have followed Freud in trying to understand human functioning and the process of change have been both inspired and constrained by his insights. The scope of Freud's genius has kept the field from making changes capriciously. This intellectual tradition is part of what gives psychoanalysis its substance and rigor, and it speaks to the advantage of having a seminal figure like Freud. But Freud's role as an authority has also served to limit vision in the field. As the source of psychoanalysis, Freud tugs at our thinking, coloring how we understand human functioning and the problems of therapy. At times this infusion is so complete that we fail even to see it. In a country where iron infuses the soil, people will believe that the ground everywhere is red. Freud's writings on psychoanalytic technique have functioned similarly: they have filtered through the soil of therapy, permeating it. In this section I argue that we have lost track of the fact that the call for analytic neutrality has a beginning, and that if we examine that beginning it becomes clear that it is deeply tied to the arguments that fueled Freud's work.

Prohibition of the Countertransference

Freud was specific in stating that all his psychological insights stem from the discoveries made through the practice of analysis. Yet, while Freud writes extensively about the findings that emerged from analytic practice, his descriptions about how to practice analysis are more scarce. Apart from his early writings in hypnosis and the cathartic technique, Freud's recommendations concerning analytic technique are confined to his case histories, a few chapters in his longer works, and, most important, a series that has been called the *Papers on Technique.* These papers, written by Freud (1911–1915) to provide some basic guidelines to the analytic practitioner, are quite short and, in them he makes recommendations about technique without making explicit how he reached his conclusions. The contrast between Freud's willingness to argue exhaustively for his psychological and metapsychological positions and his terse prose in the technical papers is striking. Freud's reluctance to make explicit the argument behind his suggestions strikes me as having a paradoxical effect. Rather than weakening the claim these papers have had on analytic practice, the brevity of his argument has served as a kind of consecration and placed these suggestions in the realm of received wisdom. To make these texts penetrable to reconsideration, we must first recreate the argument and reasoning that drove Freud's position.

Freud (1912d) draws an outline of the analytic attitude that stresses the importance of remaining emotionally removed from the analysand. He writes, "I cannot advise my colleagues too urgently to model themselves during psycho-analytic treatment on the surgeon who puts aside all his feelings, even his human sympathy, and concentrates his mental forces on the single aim of performing the operation as skillfully as possible" (p. 115). The severity of this analogy is striking, though not accidental. Throughout his mature writing, Freud consistently advocates that the analyst stay distant from the emotional pulls of the treatment setting. For Freud (1919), analytic austerity is required both to provide an environment that motivates the analysand to struggle against the resistance toward real improvement and to ensure the objectivity of the analyst in the interpretative process. Putting aside "human sympathy" is necessary to prevent the analysis from becoming a theater of substitutive satisfaction:

> *Analytic treatment should be carried through, as far as is possible, under privation–in a state of abstinence.* . . . Any analyst who out of the fullness of his heart, perhaps, and his readiness to help, extends to the patient all that one human being may hope to receive from another, commits the same economic error as that of which our nonanalytic institutions for nervous patients are guilty. Their one aim is to make everything as

> pleasant as possible for the patient, so that he may feel well there and be glad to take refuge there again from the trials of life. In so doing they make no attempt to give him more strength for facing life and more capacity for carrying out his actual task in it. In analytic treatment all such spoiling must be avoided [pp. 162, 164].

In this model, human activity is determined by the pleasure principle. Motivation to act, either in the external world or intraphysically, arises only from the buildup of tension and the feeling of displeasure it evokes. If the analyst, motivated by feelings of empathy, discloses too much positive affect toward the analysand, the analysand will become spoiled and feel no pressure to do the hard work that will allow him to change his life beyond the sphere of the consulting room. The first layer, then, in excavating Freud's technical position concerns his view of motivation and the curative factor in psychoanalysis. Yet Freud's insistence on an analytic attitude unsullied by emotion has roots that extend beyond his ideas on gratification. Countertransference, in Freud's (1910b) thinking, is grounded in the unconscious of the analyst and is therefore not susceptible to the taming influence of reason. The countertransference has to be overcome so that the analyst's interpretative activity can be free from egocentric pressures that would interfere with objectivity. He writes, "We have become aware of the 'counter-transference,' which arises in him as a result of the patient's influence on his unconscious feelings, and we are almost inclined to insist that he shall recognize this counter-transference in himself and overcome it" (pp. 144–145). Freud's theory of epistemology, of the possibility of knowing in an intersubjective field, then, is the second key layer in understanding his work.

This exposition of the reasoning behind Freud's prohibition of the countertransference is enough only to locate the surface of his thought. The aim of this section is to penetrate more deeply his view of gratification and objectivity in treatment. But from the outset I want to draw attention to an apparent contradiction between Freud's technical recommendations and his theory of human motivation and mind. Throughout his work, Freud is concerned with the instinctual basis of human life. For Freud (1910c), the id is the basis of human energy and is the driving force of all activity. While the pleasure principle can be modulated by the reality principle, it is never supplanted. Even science cannot escape the economic necessity of serving pleasure. Freud writes, "Science is, after all, the most complete renunciation of the pleasure principle of which our mental activity is capable" (p. 165). Science may distance itself appreciably from the hallucinatory pressures of the pleasure principle, but not free itself. Freud (1895) remains consistent with this reasoning when he writes that even the working of logic is governed by pleasure: *"The existence of biological rules of this kind can in fact be proved from the feeling of unpleasure at logical faults"* (p. 386). This brings us to the leading aspect of the paradox: if science and reason are still at least partially tied to the operation of the pleasure principle, it would seem that the countertransference cannot be done away with. To some extent, the action of the analyst must be governed by the search for pleasure.

Freud's account of the analytic attitude seems, at first reading, to be guilty of several internal tensions. In examining his patient's symptoms and associations, Freud (1910a) adamantly maintains that all the phenomena presented are meaningful and can be decoded. He writes, "As you see, psycho-analysts are marked by a particularly strict belief in the determination of mental life. For them there is nothing trivial, nothing arbitrary or haphazard" (p. 38). Once the determination of mental life is seen, then even the errors in our behavior become a source of information. When it comes to the countertransference, however, Freud (1905b) does not seem to hold to his faith. Instead he writes that the countertransference must be "overcome," rather than understood or unraveled. As we continue to pursue this paradox in Freud's position, we are led to his ideas about normality and illness. For Freud, the division between sickness and health shows no sharp boundaries. He writes, "In the sphere of sexual life we are brought up against peculiar and, indeed, insoluble difficulties as soon as we try to draw a sharp line to distinguish mere variations within the range of what is psychological from pathological symptoms" (p. 161).

The contiguity between normality and pathology is further demonstrated by Freud's work on the psychopathology of everyday life. He underlines the regular presence of meaningfully distorted actions in his own and others' daily lives. The possibility of "overcoming" countertransference, then, seems increasingly hard to imagine. In the same vein, Freud specifies that analysis must be carried out in a state of abstinence, yet in his case histories he repeatedly describes analytic behavior that seems to break this prohibition. Freud (1913b) writes, "During the treatment it happened now and again that her husband's remittances to her were delayed, so that she was left without resources in a foreign city. After she had told me this once, I made her promise that if it happened again she would borrow the small sum necessary from me" (p. 306). During the course of his analytic practice, Freud had dinner with his patients, took them with him on vacation, and brought them into his circle of friends. These actions are not easily reconciled with his prescription of therapeutic abstinence. Finally, Freud (1912d) specifies that the analyst should allow his attention to be evenly suspended. In describing the analytic posture he writes:

> It consists simply in not directing one's notice to anything in particular and in maintaining the same "evenly-suspended attention" (as I have called it) in the face of all that one hears. In this way we spare ourselves a strain on our attention which could not in any case be kept up for several hours, daily, and we avoid a danger which is inseparable from the exercise of deliberate attention. For as soon as anyone deliberately concentrates his attention to a certain degree, he begins to select from the material before him; one point will be fixed in his mind with particular clearness and some other will be correspondingly disregarded and in making this selection he will be following his expectations or inclinations. This, however, is precisely what must not be done. In making the selection, if he follows his expectations he is in danger of never finding anything but what he already knows; and if he follows his inclinations he will certainly falsify what he may perceive [pp. 111–112].

To prohibit the countertransference entails the risk that rather than its being resolved it will be repressed, and in this repression information will be missed that is critical for the analysis at hand. We must ask again how the call for the analyst to allow her attention to float freely can coexist with the insistence that the countertransference be "overcome."

These tensions surrounding Freud's technical recommendations regarding the countertransference underscore the necessity of tracing the development of his technical position. Freud is too rigorous a thinker to let easily detected contradictions remain in his work. When read closely, these surface contradictions shift, and a more congruent consistency emerges. To make full sense of Freud's technical recommendations, however, we must examine the larger body of his work. This is work that has to be pursued on several fronts. The first front, the focus of this chapter, concerns the development of his thought. Freud developed his technical position on the basis of clinical experience. The analytic technique of 1911 (when Freud wrote the first technique paper) had been shaped by years of working with patients and confronting the obstacles to therapeutic progress. To understand Freud's recommendations about countertransference, we must place them in a developmental context. Freud's personal history and clinical experience, though, are embedded in the wider history of Europe at the turn of the century. Freud's cultural environment gave shape to how suffering took form and put pressure on the psychoanalytic movement to defend itself against misinterpretation and misuse.

Mental illness at the turn of the century manifested itself primarily in the form of hysteria and obsessional disorders. These disorders, I argue, mask the interpersonal roots of suffering, and so underwrite Freud's idea that the analyst can remove himself from the emotional interchange. Freud also had to contend first with the culture's negative response to his work, and then to that work's growing popularity and the risk that it would be appropriated naively and so discredited. To make full sense of Freud's technical recommendations we must see how they are written in response to the culture that surrounded him.

While the recognition of Freud's historical context is not new (see Gay, 1988; Bettelheim, 1956; among others), its reexamination from the perspective of its effect on analytic technique may still enhance our understanding. Psychoanalytic technique, as Freud prescribes it, is definitely the product of Vienna at the turn of the century. His work in psychoanalysis was shaped by the historical press of both the cultural attitude toward suffering and mental illness and the understanding of science and epistemology after Darwin.

Epistemological Foundation

Freud approached the therapeutic field with a perspective shaped by his experience as a biologist (Sulloway, 1979). Freud's medical and scientific roots inform not only his view of pathology but also his ideas about the nature of investigation and the accumulation of knowledge. Even after the abandonment of the *Project for a Scientific Psychology* (1895), Freud retained his faith in the power of science to know the world objectively, apart from the prejudices of the observer. While Freud became increasingly aware that objectivity was not simple, this awareness did not allow him to shift his fundamental view of epistemology.

Freud was not unique in his faith in the power of science; it was ubiquitous in his time. Born almost simultaneously with the publication of *The Origin of Species*, Freud grew up in the midst of the Darwinian revolution. Freud (1925) writes, "At the same time, the theories of Darwin, which were then of topical interest, strongly attracted me, for they held out hopes of an extraordinary advance in our understanding of the world" (p. 8). Critical here is the hope that Darwin's work would stir up in the scientific community. Darwin's dethroning of mankind, according to Freud (1916b), pulled humankind from the realm of religion back into the ranks of animals (p. 285). At first glance this fall would seem to be cause for pessimism—we lose any claim to divine origin. But the exposure of false faith gave rise to new optimism. When naive belief was discarded, the possibility of a firmer means of knowing the world emerged.

In Freud's Vienna the route to knowledge was specified by the school of positivism (Gay, 1988). His teacher and mentor, Brücke, was a leading proponent of positivism, and Freud embraced its teachings. Positivism was grounded in the idea that only common physical-chemical forces are in operation in the organism, and the only basis for knowing is observation. Freud (1895) reveals his positivist assumptions: "Out there, according to the view of our natural science, to which psychology too must be subjected here, there are only masses in motion and nothing else" (p. 308). This is a movement in opposition to vitalism as a trend of thought, and it stresses the necessity of reducing the forces that constitute life to their material components. In the emphasis laid on observation, the positivist movement sought to distance itself from the blind faith of religion and the unanchored speculation of metaphysics. These modes of knowing had proven their unreliability. In a discussion of the progress of medicine, Freud (1906) writes:

> After a somewhat unfruitful period during which it was dependent on what was known as "Natural Philosophy," it came under the happy influence of the natural sciences and has achieved the greatest advances alike as a science and as an art: it has shown that the organism is built up from microscopically small elements (the cells), it has learnt to understand the physics and chemistry of various vital processes (functions). . . . All of these advances and discoveries were related to the *physical* side of man, and it followed, as a result of an incorrect though easily understandable trend of thought, that physicians came to restrict their interest to the physical side of things and were glad to leave the mental field to be dealt with by the philosophers whom they despised [pp. 283–284].

The disdain for philosophy unanchored in the ground of empiricism is a sentiment to which Freud is constantly sensitive, and the charge of being merely philosophical is one he guards against. With the overthrow of metaphysical speculation, the positivist revolution advances science. By renouncing the search for absolute knowledge and the hope of discovering a final cause, positivism sought to regain a basis for certainty through the process of observation and the scientific method. For Freud and his contemporaries, science offered the hope of knowledge that was definitive and unblemished by personal bias.

While positivism stressed its discontinuity with religion and metaphysics, it nonetheless still bears their characteristics and in some sense represents their continuation. Platonic metaphysics ventures two critical premises: a separation between the world of appearance and being, and an identification of the good with the real. Positivism maintains the separation between the world of appearances and that of being by stressing the importance of method in gathering knowledge and by its insistence that only physical-chemical forces are in operation. For positivism, the realm of appearances is populated by false assumptions about the existence of animate forces. Objective reality, a realm that is secure from the flux of belief, can be secured by not venturing beyond facts and observation. The second principle strand of Platonism, the identification of the good with the real, is preserved in the positivist faith that science will provide a foundation for the moral life of humanity. Both elements play a critical role in Freud's work, as he wrestles with the question of what is the truth that lies beyond the false front of the symptom. The split between appearance and reality can be seen in the distinction he makes between the manifest and latent content of the dream. Freud also embraces the second principle of Platonism. For Freud, too, the good—or in the psychoanalytic case, the healthy—is identical with a perception of the real. This is merely another way of stating Freud's view that the curative factor in psychoanalysis lies in making the unconscious conscious. As we trace the development of Freud's thought and the emergence of his technical position, these Platonic influences will become increasingly clear.

While positivism sought to do away with ungrounded speculation, it contained within itself an unexamined assumption. It presumed that observation could occur separately from the process of construction and interpretation, and that the observed would remain unaffected by the observer. Freud and his academic contemporaries displayed an untested optimism that phenomena could be apprehended without distortion through observation allied with reason. The strength of this optimistic view concerning scientific epistemology reveals itself in Freud's (1887–1904) correspondence with Fliess. In the early letters, Freud suggests that he is on the cusp of solving the problem of nervous illnesses. While Freud's partial insecurity and desire to maintain some modesty keep him in check when he writes about his own discoveries, he does not feel this restraint in speaking about Fliess's work, and describes him as a scientific "messiah." Critical discoveries are within reach for Freud, too. In his early work, Freud believes that both he and Fliess are on the trail of the key to human suffering. He feels that his work on sexual trauma and Fliess's work on the theory of periodicity will intersect to form a complete solution to human neurosis. Within this assumption lies the idea that phenomena as complex as neurosis might be traced to a single cause. In this early work there is no sign that Freud is aware that his or Fliess's work might be tainted by personal bias in the process of observation and gathering information.

This depiction of Freud's intellectual context is far from new. But I risk being repetitive not because this piece of the history of science is so vital in its own right, but because it forms the launching pad for Freud's own struggles with epistemology. Freud was too strong a thinker not to confront the obstacles to knowing as he struggled to form his theory and technique of psychoanalysis. But in his struggles he worked always to retain the ground of perceived knowability that he had inherited from positivism. As we move to a consideration of the development of Freud's work, the question of how he fought to preserve the possibility of objectivity must be revisited.

Culture and Mental Illness

The second aspect of the historical context concerns the culture's attitude toward mental illness. Freud's work and recommendations about technique were shaped both by how suffering was expressed in the bourgeois culture of that time, and by how that culture responded to Freud's ideas and practices. Just as positivism led to a retreat from emotion as an obstacle to knowing, so too did the culture retreat from emotion as a form for expressing suffering. One of Freud's (1893–1895) earliest patients remembered being chastised for her emotional outbursts as a child: "First when I was five years old and my brothers and sisters often threw dead animals at me. That was when I had my first fainting fit and spasms. But my aunt said it was disgraceful and that I ought not to have attacks like that, and so they stopped" (p. 52). But this stopping came at a cost; repression failed to account for suffering or give it an avenue for expression. Here lies the paradox: the act of repression increases suffering, but the forces that generate the repression are precisely those which prohibit an expression of the pain it engenders. To be too angry, too sad, too lascivious in reaction to the repression would only constitute a further breaking of the rule of stoicism. In Freud's energetic model of human functioning, this is the root of the damming up of instinctual forces. The forces of repression are quite willing for the damming up to be interminable, but the energy for repression in some is inadequate to contain the energy of suffering, and the suffering begins to leak out around the edges. Where it emerges—at least in those patients who constituted Freud's initial practice, the hysterics—is the body.

Hysteria can be seen as half social protest, and half dutiful compliance. Freud (1893–1895) clearly states that hysteria often befalls those women who are the most talented and least able to accept the constraints on their creativity: "Adolescents who are later to become hysterical are for the most part lively, gifted and full of intellectual interests before they fall ill. Their energy of will is often remarkable. They include girls who get out of bed at night so as secretly to carry on some study that their parents have forbidden from fear of their overworking" (p. 240). The act of falling ill and the opportunity to form such creative symptoms is one way to refuse the role society has prescribed for them; it is a statement of how intolerable the prohibition is. By transferring the suffering from the mental to the physical, the hysteric finds an avenue of expression for her suffering that the culture can comprehend. Freud (1893–1895) writes: "The need to be ill arises from the patient's desire to convince herself and other people of the reality of her illness" (p. 243). Hysteria as a form of mental illness demands that the culture attend to the suffering it engenders; but, at the same time, hysteria adapts to and accepts the terms of the culture. It depends on the dissociation from the emotional and instinctive elements of human experience. The hysteric who suffers from paralysis in her arm has twice distanced herself from her emotional experience. First, in the moment of trauma, she represses her feelings of rage or desire, which she finds offensive. But this emotional energy is durable, and it joins other associative strands and begins to search for an action in which to express itself. At this point the second level of dissociation occurs: the hysteric severs her associative link to her arm as the agent of the forbidden action, and the arm becomes paralyzed. Now the pain that was emotional and linked to the interpersonal has been transmuted into physical disability, and the suffering can take shape around a more permissible, physical, malady.

This cultural shaping of mental suffering through dissociation, a dissociation that parallels the attempt of the scientist to dissociate the process of reason from the press of emotion, has the result of supporting the belief that hysteria can be studied in an entirely objective, scientific manner. This belief can be seen in the practice of demonstrating the symptomatology of hysteria in academic auditoriums. Before the Vienna Society of Medicine, Freud (1886b) presents the case of a male hysteric:

> And now to consider the patient—a rather pale man of mediumly powerful development. The examination of his internal organs reveals nothing pathological apart from the dull cardiac sounds. If I press on the point of exit of the supra-orbital, intra-orbital or mental nerves on the left side, the patient turns his head with an expression of severe pain. There is therefore, we might suppose, a neuralgic change in the left trigeminal. The cranial vault too is very susceptible to percussion in its left half. The skin of the left half of the head behaves, however, quite differently to our expectation: it is completely insensitive to stimuli of any kind. I can prick it, pinch it, twist the lobe of the ear between my fingers, without the patient even noticing the touch [p. 27].

In reading this passage we should keep in mind that Freud is actually carrying out all of these acts on the docile patient. The self-anesthesia of the hysteric, coupled with the somatization of suffering, allows Freud and the medical community to assume that the phenomenon of the disorder will not be affected by the interpersonal press of being observed. If the hysteric could be poked with a pin and not be affected, it must have seemed unextraordinary to assume that subtler actions on the part of the analyst would also pass without effect. Freud's faith in the objectivity of the analyst is supported by the nature of the pathological conditions he confronts. This passage, however, demonstrates more than the assumptions about objectivity in the medical field. It also points to the position of the patient relative to the doctor. In this demonstration the patient is passive and allows Freud to have full authority in the treatment relationship. In the asymmetry between the patient's passivity and Freud's activity, the patient surrenders his autonomy in the treatment process. Part of

Freud's development as a clinician was his increasing recognition of the importance of bringing the patient into the treatment process as a full participant; it was a shift that allowed him to overcome the infantalizing inherent in cures based on relationships of authority.

Freud began his clinical work, then, embedded in a specific cultural and intellectual milieu. This environment had an impact on the epistemological assumptions he made and shaped the disease processes he observed, and these, in turn, left their mark on his technical recommendations. As we read Freud and consider our current therapeutic practice, we must be willing to question how the contextual press has changed and to what extent this change requires corresponding changes in our technique.

Freud's Early Practice

Freud came to the practice of therapy reluctantly, giving up his more prestigious practice as a research neurologist only out of financial necessity. Freud's hesitancy to move into private practice as a specialist in nervous diseases is readily understandable given the state of the medical arsenal at the time. When Freud began his private practice the nature of hysteria was still quite controversial. The lack of organic changes behind the somatic symptoms gave rise to a view that hysterics were malingerers, and their suffering was sometimes treated with derision. In a report on his work with Charcot, Freud (1886a) writes:

> Up to now, hysteria can scarcely be regarded as a name with any well-defined meaning. The state of illness to which it is applied is only characterized scientifically by *negative* signs; it has been studied little and unwillingly; and it labours under the odium of some very wide-spread prejudices. . . . During the last few decades a hysterical woman would have been almost as certain to be treated as a malingerer, as in earlier centuries she would have been certain to be judged and condemned as a witch or as possessed by the devil [p. 11].

When hysteria was seen as a legitimate disorder, it was perceived to be due to "nervous exhaustion." One standard therapeutic program for hysterics was directed at remedying this exhaustion. Very early in his career Freud (1887) wrote a favorable review of Weir Mitchell's paper on the treatment of neurasthenia and hysteria: "This procedure, by a combination of rest in bed, isolation, feeding-up, massage and electricity in a strictly regulated manner, overcomes severe and long-established states of nervous exhaustion" (p. 36). In some respects we can see that Freud's therapeutic endorsement of the Weir Mitchell rest cure rests on an attempt to cure the patient by supplementation. The physician strives actively to provide nourishment to the patient's depleted nervous system. While the Weir Mitchell rest cure forms only a minor footnote to Freud's work, it is helpful to see that, although Freud eventually prescribes the necessity of abstinence to cure, he began by trying to supplement. This initial optimism about the rest cure, however, quickly faded as he realized that the relief that came from the sanitarium or electricity was neither predictable nor durable. In his autobiography Freud (1925) writes:

> Anyone who wants to make a living from the treatment of nervous patients must clearly be able to do something to help them. My therapeutic arsenal contained only two weapons, electrotherapy and hypnotism, for prescribing a visit to a hydropathic establishment after a single consultation was an inadequate source of income. My knowledge of electrotherapy was derived from W. Erb's text-book [1882], which provided detailed instructions for the treatment of all the symptoms of nervous disease. Unluckily I was soon driven to see that following these instructions was of no help whatever and that what I had taken for an epitome of exact observations was merely the construction of phantasy [p. 16].

This passage reveals how Freud early in his career met the collapse of false optimism—optimism grounded on observation that appeared objective but was, in fact, biased. It is an encounter that marks the beginning of his struggle with epistemology, objectivity, and therapeutic technique. The failure of both the rest cure and electrotherapy left Freud with hypnotism as his only recourse, and it was his struggles to perfect this art that led to the development of psychoanalysis.

While Freud (1893–1895), in a number of the cases he reports in *Studies On Hysteria*, continued to use massage and electricity at least as late as 1892, these became unimportant factors in his work, and he increasingly turned to hypnotism. In a letter to Fliess, he writes, "During the past weeks I have thrown myself into hypnosis and have achieved all sorts of small but noteworthy successes" (1887–1904, p. 17). In his earliest therapeutic technique, Freud would begin with a hypnotic induction to place the patient in a trance state and then suggest that the troubling symptom was no longer in effect. Freud (1891) writes, "These suggestions consist in an energetic denial of the ailments of which the patient has complained, or in an assurance that he can do something, or in a command to perform it" (p. 110). This approach to treatment stands in marked contrast to his later recommendations about the necessity for abstinence in psychoanalytic technique. With the hypnotic procedure Freud attempts to directly change the patient's behavior through the force of his suggestive power. The use of suggestion is a fully active technique, and it pits the force of the analyst's personality and will against the patient's unconscious desire to remain ill.

Freud's initial optimism about hypnosis, however, collided with the cultural bias against it and the inherent uncertainty of the technique. Vienna's desire for rationality was not easily reconciled with the seeming mysticism of hypnosis. When Freud began his clinical practice, hypnotism was only beginning to gain some reluctant credence in the scientific community. In part this may be due to its links to Mesmer's theories of magnetism. Freud (1889b) writes that Mesmer suggested that "in the act of hypnotizing, an imponderable material–a fluid–passes over from the hypnotist into the hypnotized organism. Mesmer called this agent 'magnetism'" (p. 97). For Freud and his contemporaries the idea that an "imponderable" fluid could exist, much less be transmitted, lacked the grounding in materialism that would be required for admission into the positivist pantheon, and Freud sought to distance himself from Mesmer's legacy: "His theory has become so alien to our contemporary mode of scientific thought that it may be considered as eliminated" (p. 97). To imagine the imponderable was to flirt with a regression to magical thinking. To practice hypnotic therapy, according to Freud (1889a), was to risk being enveloped by the "halo of absurdity" that surrounded hypnosis (p. 75). The prejudice against hypnosis, however, went beyond the assertion that it was nonsense. As hypnosis gained recognition as an actual treatment, it began to elicit fears that it was dangerous. Part of this fear seems to have stemmed from the belief that hypnosis would debilitate the patient's nervous system. Hypnotism was accused of being a form of artificial insanity or hysteria. But the fear of hypnotism also stemmed from concern about the physician taking advantage of patients while they were under his suggestive influence. In describing the context of hypnotic work, Freud (1891) writes:

> When we have made our patient's acquaintance and established the diagnosis, the question arises of whether we are to undertake the

> hypnosis in a *tête-à-tête* or to introduce a trustworthy third person. This measure would be desirable to protect the patient from an abuse of hypnosis as well as to protect the physician from being accused of it. And both of these things are on record. But it cannot be applied universally. The presence of a woman friend, of the patient's husband, and so on, often disturbs the patient very considerably and decidedly diminishes the physician's influence [p. 107].

What is notable about the skepticism and concern surrounding hypnotism is that it is a reaction Freud repeatedly encounters early in his career. In trying to understand the forces that drive his later writing on the countertransference, it is useful to see how the need to allay public concern was etched into his thinking from an early point. To protect his reputation and income, he is forced to defend the validity of his therapeutic technique and stress the need for personal integrity to avoid the possibility that therapy would become an avenue for countertransferential acting out. In his treatment of Emmy Von N., Freud, responding to her concern that she might fall under the sway of an unscrupulous physician, even tried to counter this risk by making a suggestion that she would be unable to be hypnotized by anyone besides himself. In prohibiting the countertransference, Freud is particularly concerned with avoiding charges of impropriety.

The public antipathy toward hypnosis, coupled with the elusiveness of the trance state, made hypnosis an unruly therapeutic mount. As Freud (1891) begins to work with a wider range of patients, he encounters the difficulty of consistently inducing a trance state: "It would be a mistake to think that it is very easy to practice hypnosis for therapeutic purposes. On the contrary, the *technique* of hypnotizing is just as difficult a medical procedure as any other" (p. 105). Freud's cautionary tone here stems from his own difficulty in adequately hypnotizing some patients. The public concern about hypnosis made many of his patients reluctant to undergo the procedure. This deepened the difficulty of induction; hypnotism is not a therapy that can be easily imposed on a reluctant subject. As Freud suggests, hypnotism cannot be "dosed." When patients fail to enter trance states there is no way to increase the dosage of hypnotism rendered as there is with drugs. Initially Freud tried to overcome this difficulty by working to strengthen his technique, and in 1889 he traveled to Nancy to study hypnosis under Bernheim. In his paper "Hypnosis," Freud (1894a) outlines the results of this effort. He suggests that the patient must first be willing to be hypnotized. Freud's patients were often skeptical or afraid of the hypnotic procedure, and he describes this reaction in a case history:

> I found her lying in bed with flushed cheeks and furious at her inability to feed the baby—an inability which increased at every attempt but against which she struggled with all her strength . . . Far from being welcomed as a saviour in the hour of need, I was obviously being received with a bad grace and I could not count on the patient's having much confidence in me . . . Before I left the house I was also under the necessity of contradicting a worried remark by the patient's husband to the effect that a woman's nerves might be totally ruined by hypnosis [p. 119].

Freud learns that when the patient shows too much skepticism about the process, the resistance must first be worked with and mitigated before proceeding. The physician's first task is to lower the conscious resistance through education and reassurance about hypnosis so that the patient will at least collaborate sufficiently to pay attention to the induction process. Freud (1891) writes: "In such a case we say to him: 'I do not require your credence, but only your attention and some compliance at the start.' And as a rule we find excellent support in this indifferent mood of the patient" (p. 106).

The physician must also remain confident in his tone. If the physician feels and expresses doubt, it becomes contagious, and the force of the inductive suggestions are undermined. The expression of confidence, for Freud, is essential in overcoming the resistance. He writes: "Each separate suggestion must be made with the greatest decisiveness, for any hint of a doubt is noticed by the patient and unfavorably exploited; no contradiction whatever must be permitted and, if we are able, we should insist upon our power to produce catalepsy, contractures, anesthesia, and so on" (p. 112). In contrast to the assumed indifference the physician must bring to the patient's belief in hypnosis, the physician must be ready to proceed energetically in overcoming objections that emerge during the induction process. Freud recommends that during the induction, suggestions must be given vigorously and rapidly to prevent the patient from coming to his senses, and to prevent him from having "time to test whether what is said to him is correct" (p. 109). Furthermore, in the course of a hypnotic treatment, the induction process and the nature of the suggestions given must be varied to prevent the procedure from becoming monotonous for both the physician and patient. This paper shows Freud's increasing skill and subtlety as a hypnotist, but it also underscores the fragility of the therapeutic procedure. Resistance, in the form of disbelief and frustration, readily obstructs the physician's therapeutic efforts.

Freud's early struggles with hypnosis force him to confront the problem of faith and skepticism in the therapeutic process. In the aftermath of Darwin and the decline of religion, faith, as an avenue for healing, is discredited. To place faith over proof is to engage in an ascientific attitude. As a result the doctor replaces the priest as the agent of healing. Yet in Freud's early work with hypnosis, this changing of the guard is really more substitution than revolution. For hypnotism to work, patients must still let go of skepticism and place their faith in the doctor. While Freud tries to sidestep this challenge to his positivist sensibility by telling patients that he doesn't require their "credence," only their attention, it is an evasion that fails to solve the problem.

If we ascribe the roots of the scientific method to Descartes and to his insistence on doubting anything prior to proof, then radical skepticism is critical to the scientific attitude. To move from religion to science, skepticism must be indulged. But in his early technique, Freud fails to give this permission to his patients. Rather than allowing patients their skepticism, Freud is specific in stating that the patient must be denied the opportunity to "test whether what is said to him is correct" (p. 109).

In essence, then, hypnosis as a therapeutic technique depends not on the physician's ability to overcome prescientific modes of thought, but on the capacity to deliberately marshal the power of faith. Freud (1889b) states: "A physician—even a non-hypnotist—is never better satisfied than when he has repressed a symptom from a patient's attention by the power of his personality and the influence of his words—and his authority. Why is it then, that the physician must not endeavor to achieve systematically the influence which always seems to him so desirable when for once he stumbles on it unawares?" (p. 94). Here Freud suggests that the essence of hypnotism lies in the physician's capacity to discover scientifically the ability to marshal the curative power of faith in the patient. But this discovery is not one that the patient is allowed to grasp. While the physician abandons unexamined faith in favor of deliberate method, the patient is kept in the dark. In his treatment of Emmy Von

N., Freud, rather than seeking to expand the extent of her conscious awareness, seeks to diminish it. In the face of his patient's troubling memories, Freud uses suggestion to increase her dissociative capacity. He (1893–1895) writes: "My therapy consists in wiping away these pictures, so that she is no longer able to see them before her" (p. 53).

This expunging of memory is a kind of theft of the patient's identity and past, and it relies on the same process of repression and splitting that underlies the initial formation of the pathology. Rather than increasing the patient's connection with the real, it diminishes it. Frau Emmy Von N. points to this when she describes the nature of the relief she receives under Freud's early care: "The improvement of her general condition was shown by her remark that she had not done any reading today, she was living in such a happy dream—she, who always had to be doing something because of her inner unrest" (p. 59). She feels better because she has turned away from the waking torment, inward to a happy dream. But dreams are insubstantial in the realm of positivism, and their lack of durability and trustworthiness as a mode of cure is shown by our obstinate tendency to wake up. Freud is driven to the discovery of the analytic method by the pressure to find a curative process that is coincident with the state of wakening.

The inherent instability of a therapeutic technique that depends on the suppression of skepticism and memory becomes increasingly evident to Freud even as his well-practiced hypnotic technique proves inadequate with some patients. Freud describes the somewhat comical nature of a failed hypnotic induction in his "Studies on Hysteria":

> I soon began to tire of issuing assurances and commands such as: 'You are going to sleep! . . . sleep!' and of hearing the patient, as so often happened when the degree of hypnosis was light, remonstrate with me: 'But, doctor, I'm *not* asleep', and of then having to make highly ticklish distinctions: 'I don't mean ordinary sleep; I mean hypnosis. As you see, you are hypnotized, you can't open your eyes', etc., 'and in any case, there's no need for you to go to sleep', and so on [p. 108].

Early in his therapeutic career, Freud faced the difficulty of employing a technique that actively demands change from the patient. To issue this demand makes the physician dependent on the compliance of the patient. And in the case of hypnosis the failure to comply is easily masked under phenomena, the state of trance or being asleep, that appears involuntary. Because sleep, like breathing, is only partially under the control of volitional processes, the physician cannot conclusively argue that the failure to enter a trance is a problem of resistance rather than physiological inability. Furthermore, even when patients are susceptible to a hypnotic trance, there is no guarantee that the therapeutic suggestion will be effective. While hysterical patients readily submitted to innocuous suggestions that were unrelated to the illness, they were much less readily influenced by suggestions that took away the manifestations of the illness. Freud (1893-1895) writes: "I have been deeply impressed in another of my patients by this interesting contrast during somnambulism between a most far-reaching obedience in everything unconnected with the symptoms and the obstinacy with which those symptoms persist because they are deeply rooted and inaccessible to analysis" (p. 100). In this passage Freud begins to struggle with the implications underlying the resistance. The problems with hypnosis as a therapeutic technique, and with the resistance it engenders, give rise to the first transference-countertransference reactions.

In both his published papers and his letters to Fliess, Freud (1887–1904) describes the frustration he and his patients feel with one another as a result of the failures of hypnotic suggestion to cure. When one symptom is removed under hypnotic suggestion, the patient, resourceful in his need to be ill, quickly creates a substitute difficulty; this capacity for substitution means that "the physician will not be spared the depressing feeling of being faced by a Sisyphean task" (p. 263). In his footnotes to Charcot's work Freud (1894b) writes: "In the long run neither the doctor nor the patient can tolerate the contradiction between the decided denial of the ailment in the suggestion and the necessary recognition of it outside the suggestion" (p. 141). Part of Freud's ultimate success as a theoretician and therapist stems from his incessant desire to be effective; he genuinely wants to help his patients get better. But the presence of this motive also becomes the source of desire in the therapeutic setting, and when this desire is thwarted, frustration grows and countertransference is engendered. As Freud struggles to be of use he first tries to increase the force of his hypnotic suggestion. In his early case histories in "Studies on Hysteria" (1893–1895) this led to somewhat pitched exchanges. With Frau Emmy Von N., Freud uses hypnotic suggestion to prohibit her from throwing away her dry pudding and to insist she drink some alkaline water. While she initially complies with his request, she makes it clear that she follows his suggestion reluctantly, and only because of their positive alliance. But this compliance is short-lived, and the next day she resists being put under hypnotic trance:

> For when, soon afterwards, I tried to put her to sleep, for the first time I failed to bring about hypnosis; and the furious look she cast at me convinced me that she was in open rebellion and that the situation was very grave. I gave up trying to hypnotize her, and announced that I would give her twenty-four hours to think things over and accept the view that her gastric pains came only from her fear. At the end of this time I would ask her whether she was still of the opinion that her digestion could be ruined for a week by drinking a glass of mineral water and eating a modest meal; if she said yes, I would ask her to leave. This little scene was in very sharp contrast to our normal relations, which were most friendly.
>
> I found her twenty-four hours later, docile and submissive [pp. 81–82].

When the patient takes a deliberate stand for her autonomy in the face of the objectionable hypnotic injunctions, Freud clearly becomes angry and resorts to withholding his presence to make her comply. This threat can be seen as a manipulation of the transference relationship to serve Freud's countertransferential need to be of help. This outbreak was not an isolated event in Freud's early practice. In another case he (1893–1895) describes how his frustration with his patient's continuing hysterical limping pushed his patience past breaking: "One day, after she once more came tottering into the room, one arm supported on her father's, the other on an umbrella whose tip was already much worn down, I lost patience and shouted at her in her hypnosis: "This has gone on too long. Tomorrow morning that umbrella of yours will break in your hands and you'll have to walk without it" (p. 100). In considering Freud's later proscription of the countertransference, we must see it in the context of his own early struggles with countertransference. Part of Freud's injunction stems from his own hard-earned awareness that the therapeutic process posed many frustrations to the ambitions of the analyst, and that succumbing to these frustrations with an increase of affect and applied force was ultimately problematic.

Freud's Early Theory

When Freud came to the study of mental disorders, the theories available to explain these syndromes were uncertain and vague. In the case of hysteria, there was a lingering sense that, in keeping with its etymological connection to "womb," it was related to the genitals or sexuality. But Charcot, by demonstrating the existence of male hysterics, challenged this notion. In its place, Charcot forwarded the idea that hysteria was due to a "dynamic" lesion of the nervous system, a lesion that affected the function but not the structure of the organism. For Freud, given his personal and professional background, there was some intuitive appeal in both these approaches. Freud's frustration because of sexual abstinence during his long courtship gave him tangible experience with the power of sexuality to upset calm mental functioning (Gay, 1988). Furthermore, his own work on the nervous system of the eel made him intimately familiar with the functioning of neurons and the concept of the reflex arc. In his early work, Freud developed both of these ideas in formulating his theory of the etiology of neurosis.

Above all, Freud prided himself on being a rational man, wed to the world of science. This loyalty drove him to formulate a theory of mental functioning that was ostensibly based on biological principles. Implicit references to this effort are scattered throughout his writing, but are most compactly stated in his (1895) unpublished draft, *Project For A Scientific Psychology*. In this work, a precursor to modern connectionist theory, Freud tries to found the principles of mental functioning in the elementary working of the neuron. The scientific community had already discovered that the neuron was the basic element in the nervous system, and that it functioned by transmitting electrical energy to other neurons in an all-or-nothing fashion. Central to this early theory of the nervous system was the idea of the reflex arc—that when neurons are stimulated they undergo an increase in electrical charge, and that when this charge becomes high enough they distribute this energy forward in the nervous system, eventually leading to a disbursement of the energy in action. The process of the loading and unloading of neurons and their associative connection with other neurons becomes the basis of Freud's early theory. In the *Project,* he establishes several key premises, the most important being the principle of constancy. He suggests that the basis of motivation is the organism's attempt to return to a state of rest after any impinging stimulus:

> *The nervous system endeavors to keep constant something in its functional relations that we may describe as the 'sum of excitation.' It puts this precondition of health into effect by disposing associatively of every sensible accretion of excitation or by discharging it by an appropriate motor reaction* [pp. 153–154].

In this model pain is formed by the buildup of excitement in the nervous system, and pleasure comes about when the increased stimulation gains the opportunity to be released through associative or active linkages. The principle states that the organism is motivated not by the opportunity to gain or develop, but by the desire to remain constant and reduce irritating stimulation. It is a negative theory of motivation–the organism is not motivated by desires *for*, but instead only by desires *against*. When seemingly positive motivations occur, such as the desire for food or sex, they are in fact only intermediate agents that will allow the eventual reduction in built-up stimulation. Once the charge is released, the organism will remain at rest until further tension builds.

Freud's view of human functioning shapes his idea about the nature of mental disturbance. At the simplest level–a level of explanation we will let stand for the moment–pathology develops when the individual is unable to release the built-up tension or excitation in the nervous system. When discharge is blocked, affect becomes "strangulated," and a kind of fermentation process is begun that leads to symptom development. In Victorian Europe, the buildup of tension that was most restricted from release was sexual arousal, and Freud increasingly sees disturbances in the sexual field as the causal element in hysteria and neurosis. In his early work, Freud formulates a theory about the etiology of mental disorder that centers on sexual noxae and repression. He identifies a number of sexual noxae, including abstinence, coitus interuptus, the use of condoms, masturbation and, perhaps most importantly, childhood seduction. An understanding of Freud's conception of how all these practices act as noxae is critical in understanding the changes in his early therapeutic technique.

As Freud confronts the difficulties and limitations of hypnotic suggestion, he increasingly makes use of Breuer's cathartic technique, the "talking cure." Hypnotic suggestion that directly prohibited the symptom or prescribed an alternate course of action was too fragile, too readily defeated by the patient's resistance to hypnosis or by the process of symptom substitution. With his economic model of motivation in hand, Freud can now explain these failures. Direct suggestion only strengthens the repressive power available to conceal the symptom; it fails to provide an avenue for the release of accumulated tensions. This difficulty is avoided, though, when hypnosis is used to provide an avenue of expression, rather than as an additional restrictive force. As with Breuer, Freud begins to use hypnotism to evoke the memory of the events which led up to the symptom's formation. This shift in technique, a shift away from suggestion and toward uncovering, marks the beginning of psychoanalytic technique, but Freud continues to rely on force and authority in his practice. At first he uses full hypnotic induction to begin the memory-retrieval process. Induction, however, requires that the patient submit to the physician's suggestion to enter a trance, and this evokes the difficulties of resistance we have already outlined. Furthermore, while the patients are in a trance, Freud pursues an active questioning technique that places further demands on them, and these demands were not always well tolerated. Frau Emmy Von N. responded quarrelsomely to the procedure: "She then said in a definitely grumbling tone that I was not to keep on asking her where this and that came from, but to let her tell me what she had to say" (1893–1895, p. 63). As Freud encounters more patients whom he is unable to hypnotize, he begins to abandon hypnotism in favor of the pressure technique. Rather than demanding a state of trance, Freud asks only for concentration, and then asks the patient to remember the pertinent traumatic events. This change in technique depends on a critical assumption:

> I decided to start from the assumption that my patients knew everything that was of any pathogenic significance and that it was only a question of obliging them to communicate it. Thus when I reached a point at which, after asking a patient some question such as: 'How long have you had this symptom?' or: 'What was its origin?' I was met with the answer: 'I really don't know,' I proceeded as follows. I placed my hand on the patient's forehead or took her head between my hand and said: 'You will think of it under the pressure of my hand. At the moment at which I relax my pressure you will see something in front of you or something will come into your head. Catch hold of it. It will be what we are looking for' [p. 110].

When Freud presses on the patient's head he insists that some thought will come to mind, and whatever that thought is, no matter how little it seems to apply to the matter at hand, it will provide the clue that will lead to the necessary traumatic event. The pressure technique no longer depends on compliance with hypnotic induction, and in this sense it leads to a reduction in the necessary authority of the physician. Now Freud is much closer to a technique that is immune from the stymieing effect of the resistance. While patients can claim that they are unable to fall into hypnotic sleep, and that they are unable to remember a specific memory or event, it is untenable for them to claim that they have no thought whatsoever at a given moment. Furthermore, by assuming that the patient "knew everything" that was of significance, Freud subtly moves away from the prohibition of memory that keeps the patient in an infantilized role. But the pressure technique still contains within it the demand for obedience when Freud states that the task is to "oblige" the patient to communicate the necessary memory. It is within this period of therapeutic development, a period that still relies heavily on the activity and authority of the analyst, that Freud formulates the seduction theory.

As Freud makes use of the cathartic procedure with both hypnosis and the pressure technique, he begins to see a pattern to the formative events in the etiology of neurosis. In each case, his patients report that they experienced a traumatic event, an event which elicited a strong affective reaction. The context of the traumatic event, however, led to a suppression of that reaction, and the energy that should have been released in emotional expression or action was bottled up in the nervous system. Freud (1893–1895) writes: "We must presume rather that the psychical trauma—or more precisely the memory of the trauma—acts like a foreign body which long after its entry must continue to be regarded as an agent that is still at work" (p. 6). As Freud pursues the cathartic technique, he finds that the traumatic force which causes the disorder is not singular. The most immediate trauma is invariably connected to earlier trauma and when this chain is traced to its source, he discovers (or initially believes he discovers) that the root of the difficulty concerns trauma from childhood seduction. His patients begin to describe events from their childhood in which they were sexually seduced by an adult. By 1896 Freud (1896b) has gained enough confidence in these reports to ascribe childhood seduction as a necessary cause of hysteria: "*These sexual traumas must have occurred in early childhood (before puberty), and their content must consist of an actual irritation of the genitals (of processes resembling copulation)*" (p. 163). Freud initially is quite confident in this view.

Freud's belief in the seduction theory stemmed from both his clinical practice and his emerging model of the nervous system. As his patients, under the influence of hypnosis, begin to recollect the traumatic events leading to symptom formation, he is struck by the incongruity between the intensity of the trauma and the nature of the pathology. His patients describe events that, while distressing, were not extraordinary, and would not seem to justify an emotional reaction strong enough to fuel the symptom's creation. The need to locate a source of sufficient affect brings him to the area of sexual seduction—sexuality clearly is capable of producing the strongest affect. But the need for a source of intense affect to explain the etiology of hysteria still does not account for Freud's insistence that the seduction must be prepubertal. His justification for this claim seems to rest on two assumptions, one more biological, the other more ethical. Freud's (1896c) first line of reasoning concerns the biological and hinges on the relatively late development of the sexual instinct in human beings. He suggests that in a child the sexual instinct is not yet mature or in place, and so the stimulation of the genitals does not arouse a full charge of sexual excitation. This lack of sexual maturity at the time of the trauma is one source of pathology: "Injuries sustained by an organ which is as yet immature, or by a function which is in process of developing, often cause more severe and lasting effects than they could do in maturer years" (p. 202). Freud then extends this idea to explain the delay between the traumatic event of seduction and the onset of hysteria. He suggests that the advent of sexual maturity that comes with puberty leads to a strengthening of the instinctual forces, and this strengthening reawakens the traumatic memory with an additional charge of affect. In essence, Freud proposes that it is only with the advent of puberty that the full emotional significance of the seduction can be felt. This affect is blocked from expression, however, and the memory of the seduction begins to function as a suggestion that causes mental disorder.

This is primarily a biological argument based on the theories of embryology and on his model of excitation and satisfaction. In the same paper, however, he also recasts this argument in more humanistic terms. He writes:

> All the singular conditions under which the ill-matched pair conduct their love-relations—on the one hand the adult, who cannot escape his share in the mutual dependence necessarily entailed by a sexual relationship, and who is yet armed with complete authority and the

> right to punish, and can exchange the one role for the other to the uninhibited satisfaction of his moods, and on the other hand the child, who in his helplessness is at the mercy of this arbitrary will, who is prematurely aroused to every kind of sensibility and exposed to every sort of disappointment, and whose performance of the sexual activities assigned to him is often interrupted by his imperfect control of his natural needs—all these grotesque and yet tragic incongruities reveal themselves as stamped upon the later development of the individual and of his neurosis, in countless permanent effects which deserve to be traced in the greatest detail [p. 215].

In this passage, one that passionately recognizes the rights and sensitivities of the child, Freud shows an awareness of the problem of authority and imbalanced relationships. While Freud ultimately abandons the seduction theory as an explanation of the cause of hysteria, he preserves a sense of the danger of seduction. This passage on the adult's abuse of his power when translated into the terms of psychoanalytic therapy and technique can be seen as a foreshadowing of Freud's later prohibition of the countertransference. Freud's early attention to childhood seduction is one source of his continuing concern with protecting the patient from intrusions from the physician's need-based countertransference.

During this early stage of his work, when the seduction theory still holds ascendancy in his thought, Freud seems to see pathology as a fairly discrete entity. He suggests that the source of the difficulty and the driving force in symptom formation is the presence of strangulated affect acting like a "foreign body" in the individual. The problem, then, is a kind of "electrical charge" in the system that interferes with proper functioning. The structure of the system itself, however, does not seem to be altered by the traumatic events. As a result, Freud is able to maintain the optimistic position that psychoanalysis will lead to the complete cure of hysteria when it is able to provide an associative outlet for the excess excitation connected to the memory of the traumatic event. Freud does not yet perceive pathology as an elaborate structure, nor does he have a sense of the activity involved in health. While modern analytic practice is concerned with the developmental capacity to integrate negative and positive affect, to soothe oneself, to modulate self-esteem, Freud does not yet recognize this. His failure to fully grasp that health involves the development of skill supports his framing of the technical practice of psychoanalysis in terms of undoing repression, rather than facilitating development that depends on interpersonal involvement.

As Freud begins to gain notoriety for his therapeutic technique, he comes under increasing scrutiny from the professional community. Spending hours a week alone in a room with young women, pressing them to talk about their most intimate sexual history, was provocative to say the least. Aware of this controversy, Freud (1888) writes: "A doctor, I hear it being said, has no right to intrude upon his patients' sexual secrets and grossly injure their modesty (especially with women patients) by an interrogation of this sort" (p. 264). Furthermore, as Freud begins to venture an explanation of mental disorder that is based in the psyche, rather than soma, his contemporaries begin to question his competency as a scientist, despite Freud's own continued faith that his theory is congruent with the positivist insistence on explanation based on the chemical-physical makeup of the world. In a letter to Fliess, Freud (1887–1904) tries to remain indifferent to this development: "Today I learned that a colleague at the university declined to have me as a consultant, with the explanation that I could not be taken seriously; but I have been so fortified by my vacation that I felt nothing at all" (p. 198).

But Freud's calm front, given his continued financial difficulties and the uncertainties of his client base, is perhaps more bravado to protect his self-esteem than genuine indifference. These are trying years for Freud, and his anxiety gives rise to multiple somatic symptoms. He begins to believe that he has heart trouble and is dying, and his letters to Fliess are full of personal worry about his health and practice. When seniors with the status of Kraft-Ebing call his work "a scientific fairy tale" Freud must take notice and feel doubt, regardless of his protestation, "They can go to hell" (p. 184). But Freud, in part, relished the role of heretic and might have withstood these protests if his practice had flourished. But not only was he still having difficulty persuading patients to undergo psychoanalytic therapy, a fact he blames on the culture's blanket repression of sexuality and its unwillingness to face difficult truths, he was also having difficulty inducing even his best patients to complete the analytic process. He writes:

> A proud ship was wrecked for me a few days after my return. My banker, who was furthest along in his analysis, took off at a critical point, just before he was to bring me the last scenes. This certainly also damaged me materially, and convinced me that I do not yet know everything after all about the mainspring of the matter [p. 243].

Freud's etiological theory of neurosis requires that the chain of traumatic scenes lead to a particular form of childhood seduction. As he approaches what he believes he must find in the etiological chain, however, his patients respond with greater hesitancy and resistance. Freud reacts to this hesitancy by increasing the force of his insistence that they produce the necessary memories. But, rather than this working to reduce what he considers resistance, the pressure only serves to drive the patients out of therapy, leaving Freud frustrated and worse off financially.

Freud's initial response to this explicit criticism from the academic community and implicit criticism from his patients was to redouble his defense of his method and its results. Before he abandons hypnosis, Freud heralds it as a means to manipulate human phenomena scientifically. He (1889b) writes: "Anyone who has assembled a few personal experiences with hypnotism will recall the impression it made on him for the first time he exercised what had hitherto been an undreamt-of influence on another person's psychical life and was able to experiment on a human mind in a way that is normally possible only on an animal's body" (pp. 98–99). What is striking here, is that Freud forwards hypnosis and the use of suggestion as a means to further the objectivity of the observer. In emphasizing this point, Freud concentrates on how the existence of suggestibility allows the scientist to manipulate the independent variable, and so bring the contents of the mind into line with the requirements of scientific method. But if we take this same phenomena and give it a half turn, the fact of suggestibility can be seen to imply a breakdown in the separation between the observer and the observed, and so to undermine scientific method. From this perspective the problem with suggestion is that it may also be at work outside the intention of the scientist and so work to vary not only the intended independent variable, but also the unintended dependent variable. As hypnosis and suggestibility gain increasing credence in the scientific community, this is the very charge that is brought to bear against Freud and his work.

He first confronts this critique when he is still immersed in the use of hypnotic suggestion. In a preface to Bernheim's book on suggestion, Freud (1889a) writes: "If the supporters of the suggestion theory are right, all the observations made at the Salpêtrière [Charcot's lab] are worthless; indeed, they become errors in observation. The hypnosis of hysterical patients would have no characteristics of its own; but every physician would be free to produce any symptomatology that he liked in the patients he hypnotized" (p. 78). In regard to Charcot's work, Freud brushes off this critique by reference to the historical record claiming that hysterical symptomatology was well described before Charcot began his work. But the charge that his findings are merely the result of suggestion comes back to haunt him again as he develops the seduction theory:

> But other people, too, although they may be less averse to psychological theories of hysteria, will be tempted, when considering our analytic finds, to ask what degree of certainty the application of psycho-analysis offers. Is it not very possible either that the physician forces such scenes upon his docile patients, alleging that they are memories, or else that the patients tell the physician things which they have deliberately invented or have imagined and that he accepts those things as true? [p. 204].

These are serious charges brought against Freud's epistemological foundation. To the extent that they are true, and the separation between observer and observed dissolves, objectivity is debased, and Freud would be forced to rework his positivist assumptions. He is ready with a defense against this charge, but its shape is surprising and counterintuitive. Rather than defending himself on the grounds that he has not forced anything on the patient, that he has carefully maintained his neutrality, he seems to argue that it is his very forcefulness in the observation process that guarantees the validity of his findings. He (1896a) writes: "One only succeeds in awakening the psychical trace of a precocious sexual event under the most energetic pressure of the analytic procedure, and against an enormous resistance" (p. 153). The reasoning here is that the high level of resistance and the psychic pain produced are signs that the memory eventually extracted must be genuine; they demonstrate that the patient is not willfully misleading the physician nor quickly trying to oblige him in showing compliance with suggestion. Here Freud (1896c) seems to respond to the prejudice that hysterics are malingerers, and relies on this charge coupled with the resistance to defend the objectivity of his observation:

> While they are recalling these infantile experiences to consciousness, they suffer under the most violent sensations, of which they are ashamed and which they try to conceal; and, even after they have gone through them once more in such a convincing manner, they still attempt to withhold belief from them, by emphasizing the fact that, unlike what happens in the case of other forgotten material, they have no feeling of remembering the scenes [p. 204].

Freud reasons that if the hysteric were concocting a story out of a desire to manipulate, or out of complicity with the suggestive power of the therapist, we would expect a show of enthusiasm rather than reluctance in remembering these scenes. The other aspect of his reasoning seems to be based on the quality of affect that his patients demonstrate during the cathartic moment. Freud gives greater credence to the apparent genuineness and force of the accompanying affect than he does to the felt sense of disremembering that occurs in the cognitive sphere.

Freud's attempt to preserve the seduction theory against mounting criticism is further reflected in his analytic technique. While he has moved away from the use of hypnosis and suggestion, he brings forward from that training a belief in the importance of confidence and assertion on the part of the therapist. Freud (1893–1895) writes: "The task of the therapist, therefore, lies in overcoming by his psychical work this resistance to association. He does this in the first place by 'insisting,' by making use of psychical compulsion to direct the patient's attention to the ideational traces of which he is in search" (p. 270). While Freud has begun to make use of association as a starting point in his analytic technique, this passage makes it clear that it is a compelled rather than a free process of association. This reliance on compulsion suggests that Freud is still bound to a curative process that is wedded to authority. At this point he does not allow the patients autonomy to challenge his position or doubt his interpretations. When patients fail to produce associations or produce irrelevant ones, the physician must insist on the effectiveness of the pressure technique, and "represent himself as infallible" (p. 279). By stating that the key involves an act of representation, Freud deliberately aligns himself with the processes of faith that constitute the curative power of religion. Freud is striving to increase the patient's belief in the power of the physician in order to maximize therapeutic effectiveness. But the dependence on this belief prevents the patient from engaging in a search for truth that includes the full exercise of skepticism.

Again Freud writes: "It is of course of great importance for the progress of the analysis that one should always turn out to be in the right *vis-à-vis* the patient, otherwise one would always be dependent on what he chose to tell one" (p. 281). In this direct attack on the patient's resistance, Freud does not yet see the value in the analysis of resistance, but views its function only as an obstacle. When Freud demands that the patient surrender his resistance without exploring it, the problems of hypnosis are maintained. After fifteen years, Freud (1909a) is able to see this more clearly when he writes: "Hypnosis conceals the resistance and renders a certain area of the mind accessible; but, as against this, it builds up the resistance at the frontiers of this area into a wall that makes everything beyond it inaccessible" (p. 26). Freud ultimately comes to see that the use of force in therapeutic technique, while it provides some short-term gain, ultimately conceals more under the scar tissue of superficial compliance.

Freud's struggles with the resistance–in his patients, the academic community, and finally himself–ultimately lead to a dissruption in his confidence in the seduction theory. It is characteristic of his evolution that he begins by redoubling his arguments, but under continued pressure and difficulty he demonstrates a willingness to question himself and his most dearly held beliefs. The questioning process is set into motion by the claims that his findings are only the result of suggestion, and by his continued failure to bring an analysis to the expected completion. But it would seem that the final straw in the collapse of the seduction theory comes from Freud's own self-analysis. During this period of his work, Freud is beset by increasing neurotic difficulties of his own. Discussion of these symptoms take up a good portion of his correspondence with Fliess. His bouts with depression and hypochondriacal brooding lead Freud (1887–1904) to describe himself as hysterical: "The chief patient I am preoccupied with is myself. My little hysteria, though greatly accentuated by my work, has resolved itself a bit further" (p. 261). In the attempt to cure himself of his difficulties, Freud applies to himself the same procedures and obedience to theory that he has used with his patients. This willingness to be consistent, even when it is personally unpleasant, illustrates Freud's unceasing intellectual integrity. Freud seems to argue, with the force of logic, that if he is hysterical, and hysteria stems from childhood seduction, then it follows he too must have been sexually abused as a child. This conclusion forces Freud to search his memories of his father to extract incidents when his father abused him. Now as Freud personally experiences the sense of disremembering any of these incidents, the sense of memory being fabricated, he encounters a dilemma. With his patients, Freud has taken this sense of disremembering as proof of the theory's validity, but he expects of himself greater ability to make the unconscious conscious, and yet he is unable to break through the barrier of disbelief to gain a sense of conviction that his father actually did abuse him. This inability to gain a sense of personal conviction about the memory is the final blow to the theory:

> I no longer believe in my *neurotica* [theory of the neuroses]. This is probably not intelligible without an explanation after all, you yourself found credible what I was able to tell you. So I will begin historically [and tell you] where the reasons for disbelief came from. The continual disappointment in my efforts to bring a single analysis to a real conclusion; the running away of people who for a period of time had been most gripped [by analysis]; the absence of the complete successes on which I had counted; the possibility of explaining to myself the partial successes in other ways, in the usual fashion—this was the first group. Then the surprise that in all cases, the *father*, not excluding my own, had to be accused of being perverse [engaging in seduction of children]—the realization of the unexpected frequency of hysteria, surely such widespread perversions against children are not very probable. The [incidence] of perversion would have to be immeasurably more frequent than the [resulting] hysteria because the illness, after all, occurs only where there has been an accumulation of events and there is a contributory factor that weakens the defense. Then, third, the certain insight that there are no indications of reality in the unconscious, so that one cannot distinguish between truth and fiction that has been cathected with affect [p. 264].

This passage suggests that Freud went through a period where he began to believe his father was perverse, perhaps creating memories to support this idea, but then realigned himself with his sense of disbelief and abandoned the seduction theory. In the exploration of his own psyche, he recognizes that his own ability to distinguish between truth and fantasy is limited. This limitation to reality testing is a serious blow to his epistemological foundation. If the presence of affect can invest constructed memory with the felt sense of reality, the process of observation, the cornerstone of the positivist method, is undermined. Freud is forced to confront the fact that the expectations of the observer can shape the nature of what is observed through the process of suggestion.

Freud's recognition of the role of fantasy leads him to abandon the seduction theory. It is a painful abandonment and it leaves him feeling lost for a number of years. When he abandons the seduction theory of the neuroses, he moves away from the etiological role of trauma, and reemphasizes the importance of sexual constitution. From a technical standpoint, then, we might expect that this should free the physician from unnecessary fears that his activity might constitute another event in the traumatic series. If trauma doesn't cause hysteria, activity on the part of the therapist should not arouse the risk of furthering the damage. But Freud doesn't pursue this implication of his changing theory, and instead focuses on the importance of not reinforcing the fantasy elements in his patients' associations. Part of his mature insistence on abstinence in psychoanalytic technique is the remnant of his painful recognition of early errors. By withholding activity Freud strives to create greater distance between the transference fantasies and his own behavior. This distance is useful, as we will see in greater detail, in helping the patient see the elements of fantasy and distortion in the transference. If this defect in reality testing can be demonstrated to the patient, then Freud has reason to believe that the patient will also be more readily convinced that the falsely remembered scenes of childhood seduction are also based in fantasy. In part, Freud adopts abstinence in his technique, I argue, to help his patients make the same discovery about the error of the seduction theory that he had to make in his early practice.

As Freud abandons his seduction theory, he undergoes another round of technical innovation. He was led down the false path of the seduction theory by placing too little value on the role of fantasy and underestimating the capacity of suggestion to activate this process. While he never makes explicit statements concerning why he came to abandon the pressure technique, it is clear that the change came about during the upheaval concerning his theoretical base, and it seems reasonable to suppose that these two changes are related. In his practice, Freud takes another step away from actively trying to force change on the patient or asking for obedience. Instead, he relies more fully on free association and its ability to access the unconscious. Now Freud (1910a) merely asks the patient to follow the fundamental rule of psychoanalysis, to say everything that comes to mind:

> He must, we tell him, entirely renounce any critical selection of this kind and say whatever comes into his head, even if he considers it incorrect or irrelevant or nonsensical, and above all if he finds it disagreeable to let himself think about what has occurred to him. So long as this ordinance is carried out we are certain of obtaining the material which will put us on the track of the repressed complexes [p. 32].

Through the use of free association, Freud (1925) feels he aligns himself more closely with the attitude of objectivity that is necessary for a scientist.

When the amount of compulsion is reduced to a minimum, the influence of the observer is reduced and "guarantees to a great extent that no factor in the structure of the neurosis will be overlooked and that nothing will be introduced into it by the expectations of the analyst" (p. 41). In this statement made at the end of Freud's career, it is apparent that a key factor in the shaping of his mature technical positions is his epistemological concern about objectivity. Freud advocates analytic abstinence out of an experientially based awareness of how expectations can influence what is observed. He is able to leave behind the use of more directive techniques for accessing material because he has gained confidence that the interlocking associations of the unconscious, as long as the analyst is sufficiently fluent in that language, will reveal the material necessary to analyze the ground of the pathology. The move away from activity and force on the part of the analyst is critical in disengaging from futile battles with the patient's resistance. While the patient can claim he is unable to enter a trance, or resurrect a specific memory, he cannot claim to be devoid of all association. Freud (1901) writes: "If he should then assert that his attention is unable to grasp anything at all, we dismiss this with an energetic assurance that a complete absence of any ideational subject matter is quite impossible" (p. 635). This insistence on the necessity of thought realigns Freud with Descartes. Now, rather than prohibiting the patient from exercising his skepticism, Freud employs a reversal of Descartes' inference *cogito ergo sum.* While Descartes reasons, "I think, therefore I am," Freud seems to move in the reverse, and suggests to the patient, "You are, therefore you think." In insisting on the relevance of any association, Freud now gives full reign to any skeptical thoughts to which the patient may be prone. This move away from compulsion becomes a critical component of the analytic approach to virtue. Rather than relying on authority or suggestion to overcome the patient's resistance and skepticism, Freud relies on the force of logic. As the patient produces associations, there will be gaps or inconsistencies that render the account incoherent. By pointing out these holes in the structure of meaning, the analyst can expect to activate in the analysand displeasure from the breakdown of logic, and so to create energy in the associative chain to break through resistance and uncover the missing material. By relying on the power of logic and the appetite for truth in the analysand, Freud now completes a move from cures based on faith to a cure that fully includes the patient in the scientific process.

CHAPTER THREE

FREUD: GRATIFICATION, VIRTUE, AND THE THERAPEUTIC PROCESS

To understand Freud's proscription of the countertransference we must trace his view of virtue, motivation, and therapeutic change. Freud bases his theory of cognition on his biological model of motivation and gratification. The proscription of the countertransference is a direct corollary of Freud's view of the psychic economy. The individual, he argues, is motivated only by the desire to reduce the level of psychic tension. In analytic treatment then, to gratify, is to siphon off motivation and reduce the analysand's impetus to change. To redirect the analysand's desire toward real objects, the analyst must maintain an environment of frustration.

On the surface, this is a theory of biology and instinct. Within this apparently biological formulation, however, there is embedded a complex and sometimes paradoxical view of virtue. On one hand, Freud emphasizes the traumatic effect of frustration. He suggests that only when sexuality can free itself from the restrictions of guilt and repression can health or virtue be reached. This is a view that is in direct accordance with the theory of natural virtue. Health depends on reclaiming the instinctual base. At the same time, however, Freud is firmly wed to a transcendent account of virtue. He suggests that elemental motive is indolent; the analysand, left to her own devices, will subvert the therapeutic context, and convert the attempt to reach virtue into a regressive enactment of fantasy. To achieve virtue, discipline is required. Only when immediate temptation is resisted can mature object relations take shape. Only when the baser instincts are contained and redirected can they serve the higher goals of civilization. This transcendent bent is critical in shaping Freud's technical recommendations and in underwriting the proscription of the countertransference. By tracing this paradox in Freud's work—the tension between natural and transcendent accounts of virtue—we begin to reveal the moral terrain of psychoanalysis and how it has informed our theory of technique.

Gratification, Motivation, and Making the Patient Work

The abandonment of the seduction theory, a shift based on inverting the relationship between fantasy and reality in the analytic reproduction of the past, required a willingness on Freud's part to stand his conceptual perspective on its head. But in the disequilibrium that accompanies this kind of revision, we can lose track of what is preserved. Until virtually the end of his career, Freud continued to view the human economy of energy as governed solely by the need to reduce impinging stimuli. It is a belief that was pivotal in determining his view of human motivation and shaping his thinking on analytic technique. Shortly after he completed the *Papers on Technique* (1911–1915), Freud (1915b) reiterated his belief in the constancy principle: "The nervous system is an apparatus which has the function of getting rid of the stimuli that reach it, or of reducing them to the lowest possible level; or which, if it were feasible, would maintain itself in an altogether unstimulated condition" (p. 120). This last phrase is an unequivocal statement of Freud's teleological orientation. The organism, he suggests, not only seeks less rather than more stimulation, it also strives after a condition of complete isolation from stimuli; it would prefer a state of autism if this could be maintained while still addressing the basic needs of life.

Under this model, the accumulation of tension makes itself felt in the psyche through the sensation of pain. Pain is the indicator of the need to free the self of harmful stimulation. When tension finds an outlet and is released, the psychic experience is one of pleasure. Ultimately, the individual will turn away from all situations that lead to a buildup of tension or pain, and toward opportunities for release or pleasure. This economic model forms the basis for Freud's theory of pathology. When the organism is prevented from discharging tension, its integrity is compromised; for Freud, pathology is the product of frustration. "The most obvious, the most easily discoverable and the most intelligible precipitating cause of an onset of neurosis," he writes (1912b), "is to be seen in the external factor which may be described in general terms as *frustra-*

tion" (p. 231). Energy, in this view, is toxic and leads to neurosis. When obstacles block the associative outlets for energy, tension accumulates and the individual, unable to tolerate this situation for long, attempts to find other, compromise outlets for the toxic energy. The adhesiveness of these compromise modes of satisfaction, and their imperfect ability to meet the individual's needs, constitutes the core of neurotic suffering.

Freud's continued loyalty to the negative concept of motivation contained in the constancy principle is striking in view of the difficulties he had in trying to make it account for the actions of his patients. Freud goes to great lengths to argue that apparent exceptions to the constancy principle in human behavior—foreplay in sexuality, masochism, amongst others—are only momentary detours, and that at bottom these behaviors, also, aim for the reduction of stimuli. His obstinate faith seems to stem from a desire to make analytic findings remain in accordance with the principles of physics. Freud suggests that the law of the conservation of energy or mass in physics provides the ground for this premise concerning human motivation. Again, we can see the positivist influences at work shaping Freud's theory. This is apparent not only in the language of energy and mass, but also in the desire to unify the separate fields of science. The obstinate hold Freud keeps on the principle of constancy reflects his optimism that science will readily reveal the secrets of nature and human functioning and demonstrate their adherence to essential laws.

Having ventured into the field of motivation, we must return to the question of its relevance to the countertransference and analytic neutrality. The first corollary of the pleasure principle is that all activity, including activity oriented toward change or growth, is motivated only by the experience of frustration. Freud has formulated a negative theory of human motivation. Individuals will remain static unless they are impinged upon by irritating excitation. In taking this position, he aligns himself with a transcendent account of virtue. We begin life with unrighteous motive and to reach virtue we must transcend this biological limitation. Freud's belief in the inertial trend in human motivation shapes his concept of how learning takes place. If people are motivated only by the desire to reduce the painful buildup of excitation, then it naturally follows for Freud (1885) that "unpleasure remains the only means of education" (p. 370). The impetus for our moral work must come from the press of suffering. In this view, there is no inherent drive toward learning or growth in the individual.

This statement about learning is critical for Freud because it governs his view of how development takes place in the human life span as well as how change occurs in the therapeutic context. For Freud, the energy to move away from instinctual or habitual action can be generated only by conditions of deprivation. As a result, the analyst must remain vigilant to insure that the pleasure available in therapy does not lead to a premature decrease of the impinging tension, and so result in a state of inertia in the therapeutic work. He writes (1919): *"Analytic treatment should be carried through, as far as is possible, under privation–in a state of abstinence"* (p. 162). Privation is necessary to ensure the continued internal impetus toward change. To admit the countertransference into the analytic relationship, to abandon neutrality, would be to move away from abstinence and allow purloined gratification to undermine the therapeutic enterprise.

The idea that gratification will lead to therapeutic indolence in the patient brings us back to the reprobative strand in Freud's thought that springs from his allegiance to transcendent virtue. Therapy, he cautions, must be wary of spoiling the patient. This moral outlook is deeply embedded in Freud's vision and it colors his view of pathology. At times he seems to see hysteria as due to a kind of greediness of impulse. When Freud (1900) writes, "This had stirred up her old sensitiveness, which is a principal trait in the character of children inclined to hysteria: they are insatiable for love" (p. 200), he suggests that hysteria is a kind of self-indulgent behavior. If hysterics suffer from their greediness rather than from deprivation, as he suggests elsewhere, then this in turn provides further justification for his prohibition of gratification in the therapeutic setting. At this level of Freud's work, the reprobative stance is clear. But there is a basic tension here between the idea of spoiling and gratification on one hand and the pathological press of frustration on the other. Freud is clear that it is the experience of frustration that begins the development of neurosis (suggesting an alliance with natural virtue), but he is equally insistent that frustration is necessary to motivate the process of unraveling neurosis in the analytic setting. Given the uneven terrain in his theory of frustration and motivation, it is puzzling why Freud maintains, at least on the surface, such consistency in stressing the dangers of gratification in analytic therapy.

Yet when read more closely, this surface consistency contains submerged ambiguity, and Freud's view of gratification and his moral stance are more complex than we have yet indicated. From the beginning, Freud had to reconcile the economic theory of motivation with the apparent fact of self-driven activity in human beings. People do not uniformly retreat into autistic positions, shunning experience and stimulation. They seek social contact and sexual experience; they search out excitement. In his early theory, to account for apparent exceptions to the pleasure principle, Freud amends the principle of constancy. While the organism is always motivated by the desire to reduce stimulation, there are sources of stimulation within the organism, such as the drives, that cannot be reduced without the execution of a number of activities that do not permit the immediate release of energy. The individual—to preserve herself—must feed herself, protect herself from the elements, and engage in coitus to ensure the continuation of her species, and only by the serving of these needs can instinctual pressures be lessened. Behaviors that seem to violate the pleasure principle can now be seen as being in the service of the ego instincts, and so indirectly addressing the needs of self-preservation. This is the origin of what Freud calls the "reality principle." Immediate gratification is forestalled because of the recognition that more complex action is required to address the instinctual needs in a way that prevents them from continually reasserting their irritating stimulation.

The tension between the immediate urge to reduce stimulation and the drive toward preservation that arises out of the ego pushes Freud to adopt (although this may lie outside of his awareness) a two-faceted theory of energy. On one hand the buildup of tension is unpleasurable and, if unremitting, pathological in the individual. Energy, understood as tension or stimulation, then, is clearly a toxic force. But Freud also speaks of another form of energy when he recognizes the individual's motivation to survive. In these contexts, he often suggests that questions of efficiency and preservation are critical. When Freud (1900) writes in *The Interpretation of Dreams*, "But on the other hand it would be an unnecessary expenditure of energy if it [the mind] sent out large quantities of cathexis along the various paths of thought and thus caused them to drain away to no useful purpose and diminish the quantity available for altering the external world" (p. 599), he suggests that there is another form of energy besides the irritating energy that accrues from stimulation. He writes repeatedly about the value of efficiency in action, and how efficiency is undercut by neurotic behavior. In *The Interpretation of Dreams* Freud speaks somewhat counterintuitively of the need to preserve energy to remain asleep. And in his later work, he writes about how anticathexes disturb the efficiency of the self. In speaking about the benefit of analytic therapy, he writes (1940): "In either case [whether the repressed instinctual demand is accepted or consciously dismissed] a permanent danger has been disposed of, the compass of the ego has been extended and a wasteful expenditure of energy has been made unnecessary" (p. 179). If the pleasure principle were complete in specifying the nature of energy or stimulation, then we could not imagine an expenditure of energy that *was* wasteful. Expending energy is the sole goal and purpose of the individual. In part, Freud seems to admit this apparent inconsistency in to his writing out of his allegiance to Darwinian perspective–preservation is the driving force of evolution. He seems to be caught between physics and evolutionary biology; but the source of this tension in Freud's (1898) work also stems from his moral sensibility. Energy is valuable, he suggests, because it serves the higher aims of mankind: "It seems that in man the sexual instinctual forces are meant to be stored up so that, on their release at puberty, they may serve great cultural ends" (p. 281). The idea that there is something valuable to be accomplished in life that extends beyond the random activity of chemical and physical forces, leads Freud to discuss the utility of energy that is not immediately apparent in his statements on the constancy principle, and this suggests that in gratification there may be value that is not evident in his technical recommendations.

The paradox of gratification continues to assert itself in Freud's (1905b) writings on development. In these writings, he suggests that the mother must navigate a middle approach between too free and too stingy loving. On the side of frustration, he points out that "an excess of parental affection does harm by causing precocious sexual maturity and also because, by spoiling the child, it makes him incapable in later life of temporarily doing without love or of being content with a smaller amount of it" (p. 223). Here, Freud again puts forth the moral imperative of disciplining the child by being careful not to permit gratification too readily. The capacity to tolerate and store energy, a capacity that is necessary for both the preservative and the cultural activity of the individual, is developed gradually in the child by controlled experiences of frustration. Frustration is the first impetus to the reality principle and is the basis of character formation.

But Freud is equally clear that it is gratification that fuels the development of adequate object relations. In defining the core of neurotic difficulty, Freud (1904) writes: "The other, no less essential, factor, which is all too readily forgotten, is the neurotic's aversion from sexuality, his incapacity for loving" (p. 267). If the inability to love is central to neurosis, we are led to inquire about the conditions that support the development of that capacity. For Freud, this depends on early experiences of affection and gratification. Freud (1909a) writes about Little Hans, "The boy had found his way to object-love in the usual manner from the care he had received when he was an infant" (p. 111). The gratifying care provided by the mother becomes a template that guides the search for later loving experiences. It is her affectionate attention that teaches "the child to love" (1905b, p. 223). If gratification in childhood teaches the child the necessary skills for loving, we must again question whether Freud's proscription of gratification in therapy is consistent. The neurotic, we are told, suffers from an inability to love, and the capacity to love is learned through the experience of being loved as a child. These principles would seem to indicate that what is required in therapy is gratifying experience. Freud (1909a), perhaps, has provided us with ammunition against his own position when he writes: "In bringing up children we aim only at being left in peace and having no difficulties, in short, at training up a model child, and we pay very little attention to whether such a course of development is for the child's good as well" (p 143). In advocating the necessity of avoiding gratification in the treatment setting, perhaps Freud has fallen into the same predicament of convenience over benefit. Freud clearly feels otherwise, but an understanding of why he advocates the importance of gratifying experience in infancy but warns about its harmful effects in therapy, calls for an exposition of the problem of fixation in instinctual object choice.

Freud's central realization in his *Three Essays on the Theory of Sexuality* concerns the displaceability of sexuality. Rather than being firmly attached to the sexual object, the sexual drive only seeks pleasurable release, and the object is found secondarily as an outlet for that release. In simpler language, the child feels desire for food, later for orgasm, and happens upon other people as a conduit to pleasure, not as a desired end. Freud (1905b) writes:

> It has been brought to our notice that we have been in the habit of regarding the connection between the sexual instinct and the sexual object as more intimate than it in fact is. Experience of the cases that are considered abnormal has shown us that in them the sexual instinct and the sexual object are merely soldered together—a fact which we have been in danger of overlooking in consequence of the uniformity of the normal picture, where the object appears to form part and

> parcel of the instinct. We are thus warned to loosen the bond that exists in our thoughts between instinct and object [pp. 147–148].

This view concerning the structure of instinct is a further elucidation of Freud's understanding of motivation. The first aspect of motivation, discussed above, is that the individual seeks to reduce stimulation and is oriented to pleasure. The primacy of pleasure already acts to separate the individual from the relational world; motivation concerns events in the organism, not in the environment. The solipsistic tone of Freud's theoretical view, then, is only furthered by the severing of instinct from object. The individual becomes interpersonal only secondarily, driven by the need to find adequate sources of satisfaction and release. The secondary connection between instinct and object makes it fragile, and Freud suggests that the individual initially readily transfers the instinctual cathexis from one object to the next as it provides opportunity for pleasure. The tendency to displacement in sexuality, however, has limits, and as objects are found that provide pleasure, they become preferred out of force of habit: "A child who is indulging in sensual sucking searches about his body and chooses some part of it to suck—a part which is afterwards preferred by him from force of habit" (p. 183). While Freud does not specify the mechanism that allows the force of habit to supplant mutability of object choice, we may allow ourselves license to look again at the principle of constancy. His inertial view of motivation suggests that once a source of a satisfaction is located, there will be no energy left over to drive the individual toward an expanded portfolio of object choices.

In infancy, then, the sexual instinct is still fully mobile, and will naturally direct itself to sources of gratification. But this early plasticity is limited. Gratification in infancy forms the prototype for object relations in adulthood, and once formed they are not easily realigned. If early experience has led to pathological object relations, these will tend to become fixated and lead to pathology. "His task is to exchange one kind of satisfaction for another," Freud (1912b) writes, "and he breaks down from his inflexibility" (p. 233). The analyst, then, is confronted by the inflexibility of an adult who is fixated on sources of gratification that are problematic. The gratifications available from these sources are familiar to the analysand, and she sets about trying to procure these same forms of gratification in the analytic relationship. This search for the familiar gratifications becomes the basis of the transference. To the extent that the analysand successfully re-creates these outlets in the analytic relationship, the willingness to change is undercut. Freud's prohibition of gratification in the therapeutic relationship, despite the value of gratification in development and health, stems from the desire to loosen the bonds of fixated object choice through the accumulation of energy that arises through frustration. But again we have not escaped the paradox. Freud (1908a) writes that sources of pleasure can never be surrendered without replacement: "Actually, we can never give anything up; we only exchange one thing for another. What appears to be a renunciation is really the formation of a substitute or surrogate" (p. 145). If Freud, then, is to ask the patient to surrender pathological fixations, he must be prepared to aid the analysand in finding substitutive satisfaction. Gratification must be forthcoming, but the question is, from where?

Gratification and Sexual Noxae

For Freud, the question of gratification is essentially the question of sexual gratification. Pathology, in his model, stems from disturbances in the capacity for genital sexual enjoyment, and the process of analysis sets about rectifying these difficulties. In his earliest work, he takes a literal view of the pathological significance of "sexual noxae." He (1887–1904) writes: "The core and mainstay of the whole story remain, of course, the fact that as a result of particular sexual noxae even healthy people can acquire the various forms of neurosis" (p. 75). In his work, Freud identifies abstinence, coitus interruptus, the use of condoms, and masturbation as problematic sexual behaviors, and he views them as playing an etiological role in the genesis of mental disorder. When we encounter this view in Freud's work, it is easy to dismiss it as the obsolete and inessential relic of nineteenth-century medical prejudice. But to bypass these ideas is a mistake, for they are critical in shaping Freud's view of health and his technical recommendations. As Freud develops his theory of the unconscious and the role of the drives, the role of sexual noxae as the critical pathogen in neurosis recedes. But this shift in emphasis should not be taken as an indication that Freud changed his views on the danger of these practices. As late as 1912, when he was writing his technical papers, Freud participates in a conference on masturbation where he continues to insist, despite growing opposition from followers within the analytic movement, that masturbation is harmful and a cause of neurasthenia. Reading Freud's writings on sexual noxae helps clarify his understanding of the relationship between gratification, reality, and virtue.

The first strand of this theory, the danger of sexual abstinence and coitus interruptus, is relatively straightforward and immediately congruent with the stress placed on satisfaction. Sexual arousal, when unable to locate an outlet for gratification, becomes toxic. This is in direct accordance with the constancy principle. But his view of how other sexual noxae lead to pathology, as we will see, shows more clearly the paradox of energy. Although Freud states that the goal of the organism is to reduce stimulation through acquiring opportunities for satisfaction and pleasurable release, a closer reading shows that the manner of release is critical to the organism's health. In his early work, in addition to emphazing the harmful quality of abstinence involved with coitus interruptus and celibacy, he writes repeatedly about the harmful effects of masturbation and the use of condoms. These sexual practices, he believes, although offering some form of gratification, are nonetheless harmful.

Freud's stress on the importance of the reality principle and the aims of civilization lead him to suggest that energy and postponed release of sexual tension has value for the health of the individual. It becomes clear that he sees danger not only from the toxic effects of backed-up sexual tension, but from the exhaustive effect of overly frequent emissions. In speculating about the mechanism of the damage from masturbation, Freud (1912e) writes: "*Organic* injury may occur by some unknown mechanism. Here we must take into account the considerations of excess and of inadequate satisfaction" (p. 251). He believes that masturbation, because it provides a vehicle for overly frequent, pre-pubertal ejaculation, causes neurasthenia, a kind of depressive exhaustion. Masturbation leads to a depletion of the energy necessary to carry out the aims of the instincts.

Freud's (1912c) criteria for sexual release, then, is more complex than the constancy principle suggests. Rather than advocating the immediate release of sexual tension, he suggests that a full sexual charge must be first built up, and only then, when fully loaded, released.

> But at the same time, if sexual freedom is unrestricted from the outset the result is no better. It can easily be shown that the psychical value of erotic needs is reduced as soon as their satisfaction becomes easy. An obstacle is required in order to heighten libido; and where natural resistances to satisfaction have not been sufficient men have at all times erected conventional ones so as to be able to enjoy love [p. 187].

Masturbation, a practice that circumvents any obstacles to satisfaction, must lead to a reduction of the value of erotic pleasure. If the sexual charge is released too frequently, as is the case with masturbatory practices, then the individual never develops the capacity to tolerate larger quotients of sexual energy. Like when a runner trains for a marathon, longer distances can be tolerated only through practice.

As we try to make sense of Freud's view of sexual noxae, it seems that he believes that there is something necessary and unique about the quality of pleasure that is available in genital orgasm that can not be replicated through other sexual practices. He (1895) writes: "Neurasthenia develops whenever the adequate unloading (the adequate action) is replaced by a less adequate one" (p. 109). For Freud, the intensity of achieved pleasure in sexual contact seems to be the tonic element that assures healthy functioning. Masturbation (even if practiced infrequently) or the use of condoms, because they do not offer full pleasurable contact between penis and vagina, that exquisite moment of skin-to-skin touch, can not offer adequate unloading of sexual tension and so are damaging.

Here we come to the border between Freud's biological speculations and his moral, humanistic leanings. While he creates his theory based on biological perspectives, he simultaneously holds on closely to cultural values in his vision. This is in keeping with his positivistic sensibility and the desire to found the moral sphere on scientific observation. Freud is worried about these irregular sexual habits both because they threaten to divert the individual from genital attachment to another and because they drain away energy that is intended to fuel the goals of civilization. Part of Freud's definition of mature health is the capacity to handle the full loading of the neuronal system, and then to be able to release this loading fully in an orgasmic, genital climax, or channel this energy to cultural uses through sublimation. His polemics against masturbatory practices and various modes of birth control stem from his conviction about the necessary good of a bonded marriage relationship and the capacity to form a stable, genital attachment. Freud is concerned that if the individual chooses the easy path of sexual gratification through masturbation or through non-marital intercourse that is made possible by the protection of a condom, he will not feel the pressure of the instinct to drive him forward in development to achieve a mature relationship with a partner, where the sexual drives are united with affectionate emotions. In describing the roots of a patient's neurotic difficulties, Freud

(1887–1904) writes: "But above all, it cannot be disputed that the fear of infection and the decision to use a condom laid the foundation for what I have described as the factor of *alienation* between the somatic and the psychic. . . . One may add that his readiness to take precautions, instead of finding adequate satisfaction in a secure relationship, points to sexuality which was from the first of no great *strength*" (p. 93). Here Freud seems to equate the man's inability to tolerate sexual frustration until an adequate marriage could be made (in his mind a biological weakness) with moral weakness. This same transcendent moralizing is evident in Freud's concern about masturbation. He (1908b) writes:

> [Masturbation] vitiates the character through *indulgence,* and this in more than one way. In the first place, it teaches people to achieve important aims without taking trouble and by easy paths instead of through an energetic exertion of force—that is, it follows the principle that *sexuality lays down the pattern* of behavior; secondly, in the phantasies that accompany satisfaction the sexual object is raised to a degree of excellence which is not easily found again in reality [p. 199].

The first objection Freud levels against masturbation is familiar. With his mixed model of energy he believes that resources must be stored up to accomplish the aims of survival and of civilization. But, here, Freud suggests a second reason for the practice's harmful effects. It leads to a separation between the world of fantasy and reality, and in this separation the individual loses the capacity to tolerate the imperfect excellence of the real. This is critical in Freud's thinking, and it is a theme that we will return to when we move to a discussion of epistemology.

When we turn back to the consideration of Freud's technical recommendations, it seems, on the surface, peculiar that while he stresses the danger of masturbatory activity—that is, sexual practice that does not involve the full presence of the other—he insists that the analyst should present himself as a blank screen to the analysand. If the analyst fails to interact with the analysand, is not the analysand forced into a kind of masturbatory practice of free association? In the emotional realm, if not the sexual (a division that Freud might not accept as valid), the analysand is left to gratify herself, and to fantasize about the analyst; these seem to bear a strong resemblance to the dangers of masturbation Freud outlined. If the analyst is prohibited from gratifying the analysand, thereby insuring "inadequate satisfaction," why does Freud insist on the stoic demeanor of the analyst? The solution to this paradox lies in an appreciation of Freud's views of the analytic context as necessarily unreal, and so potentially masturbatory.

Gratification and the Development of Freud's Technique

Freud's technical practice of analysis was affected by his ideas on the nature and utility of gratification. In retrospect, we can detect an early tension between Freud's belief in the inertial tendency in human motivation and his own technical practice of therapy. At the simplest level this tension can be seen in Freud's use of restorative practices. When he uses massage to alleviate "nervous exhaustion" we can imagine that it arouses pleasure in the patient, and this pleasure, according to Freud's view, should undercut the patient's urge to carry out the hard work of abreactive therapy. In his early papers, Freud's use of expressed compassion, an expression that stands in contrast to his later work, can also be seen as an outlet for the patient's tension, and so pose problems to the motivation for continued work. In his *Studies On Hysteria* Freud (1893–1895) writes:

> One works to the best of one's power, as an elucidator (where ignorance has given rise to fear), as a teacher, as the representative of a freer or superior view of the world, as a father confessor who gives absolution, as it were, by a continuance of his sympathy and respect after the confession has been made. One tries to give the patient human assistance, so far as this is allowed by the capacity of one's own personality and by the amount of sympathy that one can feel for the particular case [pp. 282–283].

In this passage Freud explicitly directs the analyst to provide absolution, and so reduce the patient's guilt-induced torment . To provide this kind of gratification, the analyst must take on the role of "father confessor." This is the other side of Freud's early technique. Not only did Freud seek to marshal the authority that was previously granted to religious figures, he also sought to enlist their capacity for granting forgiveness and sympathy. We have already seen how this alignment with authority runs into epistemological difficulty, but the problems with this technique extend even further. If the attempt to oblige patients to change fails because of the resistance it arouses, the attempt to give succor, according to Freud's economic view, must run into difficulty through the weakening of motivation that follows from the reduction of tension.

The change in Freud's use of compulsion or authority to elicit analytic material is mirrored by a change in his attitude toward gratification in the treatment situation. He becomes increasingly cautious of providing gratification in the analytic setting out of a concern that gratification will undercut the motivation to change. His growing caution is a logical corollary of the constancy principle, but it is a caution that is further supported and made feasible by changes in his clinical practice. During the middle phase of his career, the period when he writes the *Papers on Technique* (1911–1915), Freud gains increasing fame and recognition. In contrast to the early years when he struggled to keep patients in therapy, Freud now must contend with the opposite difficulty: he is besieged by requests for therapy, and his patients, once in therapy, are reluctant to leave. He (1913c) writes: "In the early years of my psychoanalytic practice I used to have the greatest difficulty in prevailing on my patients to continue their analysis. This difficulty has long since been shifted, and I now have to take the greatest pains to induce them to give it up" (p. 130). Freed from his precarious financial position, Freud no longer needs to rely on overtly compassionate or gratifying behavior to keep patients in treatment and solidify the working alliance. He has the stature and reputation to risk behaving abstinently as an analyst.

Coupled with this shift in his popularity is a change in the makeup of his practice. With the abandonment of the seduction theory and the pressure technique, Freud is no longer consistently thwarted by resistance in the form of open rebellion. Overt rebellion requires a foil, and Freud, who has turned to the technique of free association, has abandoned making specific demands on memory. Yet the patient's attachment to their illness is strong, and the resistance now takes on more subtle forms. Freud begins to see that patients seem to use therapy as a retreat from the rigors of life and as a means of remaining ill. They follow the analyst's instructions, attend their therapeutic sessions, and speak about their symptoms, but their illness remains unchanged. These impasses lead Freud to feel that he is only providing comfort, not cures, to these patients.

This form of resistance is particularly evident in phobic and obsessional patients, a class of patient that increasingly takes up Freud's attention. While Freud's (1919) early case histories are about hysterics, he now begins to see a growing number of obsessional or phobic personality types. These patients, while hopelessly burdened by the need to practice elaborate pathological rituals, are still nominally able to function in the world, and can find ways to conceal their difficulties from the general public. They can show significant insight into their difficulties, yet remain unchanged in their behavior. Freud writes: "Their analysis is always in danger of bringing to light a great deal and changing nothing" (p. 166). Nothing is changed because the analytic production is kept separate from the affective core that maintains their character structure. Outside of awareness, the analyst and analysand play out scenes of gratification that prevent the essential aspects of the complex from reaching consciousness. The balance between neurotically induced suffering, a suffering that is reduced by the gratification available in the therapeutic setting, and the discomfort of genuine analytic work, is not in favor of the analyst. To shift this balance, and perhaps to vent his frustration, Freud begins to advocate more strongly the importance of analytic abstinence. Thwarting gratification is necessary to retain the pressure on the patient to change.

The evolution in Freud's (1915a) position concerning abstinence is evident in his proscriptions in his technical papers. He has moved beyond the desire to provide "absolution," and now evidences a sterner aspect. Yet in these writings, while he has gained a clear sense of the danger of gratification in the treatment, he does not yet endorse draconian measures to guard against it:

> I have already let it be understood that analytic technique requires of the physician that he should deny to the patient who is craving for love the satisfaction she demands. The treatment must be carried out in abstinence. By this I do not mean physical abstinence alone, nor yet the deprivation of everything that the patient desires, for perhaps no sick person could tolerate this. Instead, I shall state it as a fundamental principle that the patient's need and longing should be allowed to persist in her, in order that they may serve as forces impelling her to do work and to make changes, and that we must beware of appeasing those forces by means of surrogates [pp. 164–165].

Freud states clearly that providing satisfaction to the patient threatens therapeutic progress, but he stops short of prohibiting all forms of gratification. At this point he believes that would be intolerable for the patient, and would undermine the alliance, driving the patient from analysis. Freud's (1909b) willingness to provide some gratification to the patient during this period is evident in his case history of the Rat Man. When the Rat Man shows concerns about the possibility of changing himself and overcoming his obsessional ideas, Freud responds with assurances: "In this connection I said a word or two upon the good opinion I had formed of him, and this gave him visible pleasure" (p. 178). Aware of the Rat Man's suffering, Freud seems to retain his sympathetic spirit of inquiry. But the presence of "visible pleasure," given Freud's economic view of motivation, suggests trouble for analytic progress, and as Freud increasingly confronts the resiliency of mental illness he further modifies his position in this area.

The difficulties with patients using therapy as a means to remain ill are most clearly outlined in Freud's case history of the Wolf Man, and it is in response to this case that Freud further modifies his technical position concerning gratification in treatment. The Wolf Man, a member of the Russian aristocracy, suffers from numerous obsessional difficulties, but these difficulties do not easily succumb to analytic pressure. Freud (1918) writes:

> The patient with whom I am here concerned remained for a long time unassailably entrenched behind an attitude of obliging apathy. He listened, understood, and remained unapproachable. His unimpeachable intelligence was, as it were, cut off from the instinctual forces which governed his behavior in the few relations of life that remained to him. It required a long education to induce him to take an independent share in the work; and when as a result of this exertion he began for the first time to feel relief, he immediately gave up working in order to avoid any further changes, and in order to remain comfortably in the situation which had been thus established. His shrinking from a self-sufficient existence was so great as to outweigh all the vexations of his illness [p. 11].

In this passage we can see how Freud's belief in the constancy principle shapes his perception of the clinical material, and how the difficulties he begins to encounter in his practice work to reinforce his economic view of the indolence of motivation. The problem, as Freud sees it, is that while the force of suffering drives the patient into therapy, the conditions of the therapeutic environment are gratifying enough—which we can translate as providing enough subconscious outlets for the tension that causes suffering—that the energy to work on the psychic underpinnings of the suffering is depleted. The Wolf Man, to Freud's mind, when offered the substitutive satisfaction of therapy, feels greater pain when he approaches the critical "instinctual forces," than he does when living his life compromised by his illness. This is a view, grounded in the reprobative stance of transcendent virtue, that focuses more on the role of laziness in precipitating impasse, than it does on the role of fear.

Freud's previous difficulties with hypnosis and the pressure technique have made him acutely aware of the difficulties in trying to oblige a patient to do dynamic work; these efforts lead only to an increase in overt resistance. Freud, then, feels he cannot do more to force the patient to produce the relevant associations and affects without regressing to the difficulties of suggestive therapy. This puts him in an untenable position: to continue the analysis as it is would be to make the same mistake as sanitariums, but to use direct force would only lead the resistance to mutate into an equally unworkable form. Freud's solution is to place limits on the satisfaction that is available in the therapeutic setting—rather than increase the use of force, he decreases what he gives. To overcome the Wolf Man's resistance via apathy, Freud (1918) resorts to limiting the duration of the treatment:

> I was obliged to wait until his attachment to myself had become strong enough to counterbalance this shrinking, and then played off this one factor against the other. I determined—but not until trustworthy signs had led me to judge that the right moment had come—that the treatment must be brought to an end at a particular fixed date, no matter how far it had advanced. I was resolved to keep to the date; and eventually the patient came to see that I was in earnest. Under the inexorable pressure of this fixed limit his resistance and his fixation to the illness gave way, and now in a disproportionately short time the analysis produced all the material which made it possible to clear up his inhibitions and remove his symptoms [p. 11].

By setting a limit to the duration of the treatment, Freud believes he can reconstruct the energetic dam that initially led to the pressing need for action in the Wolf Man that induced him to undertake therapy, and turn this need toward the work of analysis. At the time of this writing, Freud seems optimistic that this parameter he has placed on analytic technique has made it possible to reach a resolution of the Wolf Man's difficulties. By thwarting gratification, Freud believes he has found the source of "inexorable pressure" (a source he first sought to find in hypnosis) that is necessary to produce change.

The publication of this innovation in technique, however, has influence beyond Freud's own thinking. By the time Freud writes the Wolf

Man's case history, he is no longer isolated in his clinical practice. He has secured a significant following, and these analysts have begun to employ the analytic method to make their own discoveries. In the field of technique, Sandor Ferenczi is the most prolific in seeking to expand the effectiveness of analysis. In response to Freud's case history of the Wolf Man, Ferenczi begins to experiment with setting limits on the substitutive satisfactions available in the therapeutic setting. In a case he (1919b) reports in the seminal article "Technical Difficulties in the Analysis of a Case of Hysteria," Ferenczi initially mimics Freud's use of a mandatory termination date to spur analytic progress. But this measure is only partially effective, and the patient returns to Ferenczi after a few months with renewed difficulties and symptoms. Ferenczi accepts the patient back into treatment and seeks other routes to create energy for analytic work.

In this process, he begins to notice that the patient rubs her legs together during the session and in doing this procures masturbatory pleasure for herself. Given the assumptions of the constancy principle, the energy released through this masturbation is energy taken away from the work of analysis, and Ferenczi comes to see this behavior as the source of the analytic stalemate. In response, he prohibits all of these movements in the analytic session, and eventually asks the patient to give them up all together. Ferenczi (1919a) formulates this experiment into a rule of analytic technique and suggests that the analyst must take an active role in closing off these furtive channels for satisfaction: "Just as in experiments on animals the blood pressure in distant parts can be raised by the ligature of large arterial vessels, so in suitable cases we can and must shut off psychic excitement from unconscious paths of discharge, in order by this 'rise of pressure' of energy to overcome the resistance of the censorship and of the 'resting excitation' by higher psychic systems" (p. 116). The idea of "shutting off" of discharge is equivalent in this model of energy to the prohibition of symptoms that give pleasure to the patient. The difficulty in this approach to treatment is that Ferenczi, in seeking to shut off unconscious paths of discharge, reenlists the analyst in trying to actively control the behavior of the analysand. While limiting the duration of the treatment is a prescription that is entirely under the control of the analyst, forbidding masturbatory practice requires the participation and cooperation of the analysand with the analyst's authority. In pursuing the prohibition of gratification, Ferenczi has made abstinence dependent on the analyst's activity.

Ferenczi's paper, initially influenced by Freud, now influences Freud. Freud is receptive to the ideas about active technique, and incorporates them into his own recommendations about the practice of analysis. At this point in his career, he takes his strongest position in stressing the importance of abstinence. He (1919) writes:

> You will remember that it was a *frustration* that made the patient ill and that his symptoms serve him as substitutive satisfactions. It is possible to observe during the treatment that every improvement in his condition reduces the rate at which he recovers and diminishes the instinctual force impelling him towards recovery. But this instinctual force is indispensable; reduction of it endangers our aim—the patient's restoration to health. What, then, is the conclusion that forces itself inevitably upon us? Cruel though it may sound, we must see to it that the patient's suffering, to a degree that is in some way or other effective, does not come to an end prematurely. If, owing to the symptoms having been taken apart and having lost their value, his suffering becomes mitigated, we must reinstate it elsewhere in the form of some appreciable privation; otherwise we run the danger of never achieving any improvements except quite insignificant and transitory ones [p. 163].

Freud almost seems to suggest here that the analyst must have a sadistic streak in order to be effective in bringing about structural change. Like penitents scourging themselves with whips, analysands reach virtue through the sharp prod of privation. While the idea of reinstating suffering in order to further the possibility of conducting analytic work may seem contrary to the spirit of the therapeutic endeavor, it is a position that is entirely consistent with Freud's view of motivation and growth. Suffering, placed in opposition to gratification, is the only force that drives the analysis forward. Freud's demand that the analysis preserve the conditions of frustration is relevant to the question of countertransference. On one hand, unexamined positive countertransference, if manifest in the analytic situation, would only further the pleasure available to the analysand and diminish the analysand's willingness to undertake the work of analysis. But the need to avoid gratification from the positive transference is perhaps secondary to the importance of not resorting to sadism based on the negative countertransference when barring substitute satisfactions in the analytic relationship.

Freud's more extreme proscriptions against gratification during this period of his work bring his technical position into one of exact consistency with the dictates of the constancy principle. But the surface consistency of that principle, as we have seen repeatedly, conceals submerged complexity. Freud's technical position then shifts again toward a somewhat more lenient one that implicitly recognizes the paradox of energy and gratification contained within his theoretical model. This final shift in Freud's thinking is precipitated by his experience with another category of patients, namely melancholic or depressive patients. These patients, in contrast to hysterical or obsessional patients, do not seem to be governed by the search for substitute or compromise sources of satisfaction through symptom formation. Instead, puzzlingly, they seem to have directed their aggressive instincts toward themselves. These patients punish themselves repeatedly and are tortured by a sense of guilt. Freud (1916a) writes:

> So much the more surprising, and indeed bewildering, must it appear when as a doctor one makes the discovery that people occasionally fall ill precisely when a deeply-rooted and long-cherished wish has come to fulfillment. It seems then as though they were not able to tolerate their happiness; for there can be no question that there is a causal connection between their success and their falling ill [p. 316].

These patients, when confronted with success in their analysis, and a corresponding reduction in their suffering, react by reintensifying their illness. Initially, Freud tries to cope with these patients by analyzing their negative therapeutic reaction as a form of oedipal defiance against the analyst or as a manifestation of their fixation on the gains they procure from the illness. But these interpretations, all shaped by the conceptual frame that self-punishment must ultimately serve the dictates of the pleasure principle, ricochet off the patient without effecting change, and return to haunt the analyst.

The difficulty of helping this class of analysands overcome their self-destructive need for punishment leads Freud to a final major revision of his theory. The first part of this revision concerns the adaptation of the structural model of mental functioning. Moving beyond the simple dichotomy of conscious and unconscious processes, Freud postulates the existence of three mental faculties: the id, the ego, and the superego. The recognition of the superego is a dramatic shift in his priorities. While early in his career, Freud is concerned with the id–driven search for pleasure and the ego-mediated compromises between instinct and the demands of the external world, now he increasingly senses the importance of the internal struggle between the ego and the punitive tendencies of the superego. The growing awareness of guilt and the superego leads Freud to make a parallel revision to his theory of the pleasure principle. In his paper "The Economic Problem of Masochism" (1924), Freud surrenders his adherence to the strong model of the constancy principle. In this paper, he admits that some experiences of pleasure are characterized by increases in tension. In a passage that is remarkably nonchalant given the magnitude of the reversal, Freud writes:

> It seems that in the series of feelings of tension we have direct sense of the increase and decrease of amounts of stimulus, and it cannot be doubted that there are pleasurable tensions and unpleasurable relaxations of tension. The state of sexual excitation is the most striking example of a pleasurable increase of stimulus of this sort, but it is certainly not the only one [p. 160].

The implications of this reversal, given the centrality of the constancy principle in Freud's theory of motivation and in shaping his technical principles, would seem to be pervasive. But this change in his theoretical position comes later in his career, and he no longer has the ambition to rework his technical recommendations.

If the individual is motivated by pleasure and deterred by pain, and pleasure can accompany the rise in tension and pain its reduction, it would seem that analysands, if gratified, would not naturally move to a state of stasis. Analytic work, perhaps, could proceed even under conditions of gratification. These questions, however, are never addressed by Freud, and the closest he comes to revealing his view on the subject is in a paper published in 1940. In contrast to his earlier statements about the need to reinstate suffering, Freud now writes that steps must be taken to mitigate the pain felt in relationship to analytic investigation. In discussing the resistance that the ego puts up in the face of analytic exploration, he (1940) writes: "The ego draws back in alarm from such undertakings, which seem dangerous and threaten unpleasure; it must be constantly encouraged and soothed if it is not to fail us" (p. 178). But we should be cautious in ascribing too much weight to this passage as evidence that Freud has realigned his technical position. This statement about "soothing the ego" seems to be a retreat from the extreme position he took toward gratification after Ferenczi's paper on the active technique. It is more a return to his early statements about not asking the analysand to do without any pleasure in the treatment setting, than a reversal of his basic prescription of abstinence in the treatment relationship.

CHAPTER FOUR

Freud: Reality Testing and the Pleasure Principle

While we would wish otherwise, reality is elusive, shot out of reach by our hand as we try to grab hold of it. Freud was no stranger to this elusive quality, and in trying to grasp his technical recommendations concerning the countertransference and his prescriptions for analytic abstinence we must consider his view of epistemology and the status of reality. The question of epistemology is critical to how we understand both the interpretive activity of the analyst and the nature of neurotic suffering in the analysand. While Freud is adamant that the capacity to procure gratification is the first pillar of health, he is equally clear that the attainment of this first goal is dependent on another: a strengthened connection to the real.

Freud and the Search for the Real

For Freud, the second pillar of health is the individual's epistemological capacity to separate fact from fantasy, and to find objects in reality to satisfy genuine instinctual need. For both the analyst and the analysand, the success of analysis depends on, and is measured by, the capacity to overcome the egoism of the pleasure principle and secure an undistorted capacity to embrace the hard but sustaining contours of reality. To begin with, this emphasis on reality informs the interpretive activity of the analyst; it concerns the problem of objectivity. This is not surprising–it touches ground we have already considered in the evolution of Freud's technical practice and the problems inherent in therapeutic suggestion.

Freud proscribes the countertransference out of a fear that it will cloud the analyst's objectivity. His model of perception demands that the analyst avoid strong countertransferential emotional reactions because he sees them as necessarily interfering with the clarity of thought. Without this connection to reality, the analyst loses her objectivity and risks spinning tales out of her personal need.

The second aspect of the problem of epistemology, however, may be less familiar. By the time of his technical papers, Freud (1905a) has extended his concern about the connection to reality beyond the analyst. While in his early therapeutic work, as has been described, Freud tried to enlist the naive powers of faith and complicity in the patient, this is a direction that he abandons in his mature writing. Instead, he comes to believe that the health of the individual is ultimately bound up with that person's ability to renounce fantasy for the world of real objects and effort. Treatment by suggestion is problematic because it results in a "blind dependence and a permanent bond between a patient and the physician" (p. 117). It must be avoided because it fails to ground the analysand's health in a direct connection to reality; the patient is cured by belief, rather than knowing. Analytic treatment, on the other hand, seeks to help the patient overcome dependency and reach a more solid autonomy.

This hypothesis, though, immediately runs into difficulty. The therapeutic context and the transference relationship, for Freud, are only a transitional realm halfway between fantasy and reality. The analyst must guard against the tendency toward dependence in the analysand that would subvert the desire for reality. He prescribes analytic abstinence and neutrality in order to ensure that the analysand moves forward to real relationships, and does not remain in the transitional realm of the treatment. Abstinence, according to Freud, is necessary to jar the analysand out of the hallucinatory comforts of neurotic symptoms and suffering. Freud strives to push the analysand toward the real. The distance to be traveled is one that begins in the unreality of neurosis, passes through the transitional realm of the treatment setting and the transference, and ends in the attainment of relationship to real objects in the world beyond the consulting room. The real, in Freud's model of health and epistemology, becomes equivalent to the good and is placed above the injurious realm of appearance; in this moral valuing, this dualism, he has positioned himself as a Platonic descendent.

Freud's dualism, however, is not straightforward, and his epistemological theory, as was the case with his views on gratification, conceals competing trends. The location of the real, the avenues to knowing, the role of affect, the possibility of objectivity—when examined closely—all reveal paradox and exception. While Plato draws the contrast between the real and the apparent in our knowledge of things and concepts, Freud extends this dualism inward. He separates the unconscious from the conscious, and so creates a second split between appearance and reality in the internal realm. In the mind it is the unconscious, however irrational and conditioned by fantasy, that is the real, and consciousness, seemingly rational but superficial, that is appearance. By extending Platonic dualism to the interior of the self, Freud threatens to overturn it. If consciousness is no longer the ruler of its own domain, then the whole field of observation, introspection, and the possibility of objective knowing are called into question. These are all activities that belong to the realm of consciousness, and that realm has become shaky, threatened by rebellious forces.

While Freud begins his therapeutic endeavors from a positivist perspective, these hopes must contend with the unruly epistemological pressures of the treatment setting. In his work with patients, Freud constantly encounters reality's slipperiness, and this impels him toward a more hermeneutic understanding of the world. Freud briefly seems to sense that reality is constructed from the interplay between perspectival positions. Yet this pressure on Freud's sensibility threatens to completely undermine the possibility of objectivity, and so demote his work to personal prejudice. This is a fate he finds unacceptable, and he fights against it. The paradoxes we find in his work are the remnants of the struggle between the hermeneutic pressures of the analytic setting and his competing desire to fight for the possibility of objectivity.

Reality Testing and Perception

For Freud, epistemology is not a derivative question. As a positivist, he begins with the assumption that when one adheres to facts over theory, knowledge can be approached, and this will provide a guide for correct action. Positivism, as a governing ethic, demands the possibility of objectivity; it is this distinction between objectivity and metaphysics on which positivism bases its claim to value. Yet in this refusal of metaphysics, positivism prohibits an epistemological foundation based on abstraction. Without an explanation of knowing, there can be no criteria of objectivity. It would seem positivism has amputated its own legs. To avoid this conundrum (an avoidance whose success we will come to argue), Freud turns toward the organic. As a biologist, he frames the epistemological in neurological terms. The nature and possibility of knowing is determined, in his mind, by the structure of the perceptual system. Therefore, in developing a model of perception, if he is to remain a positivist, Freud must preserve the individual's capacity to perceive without distortion.

In his clinical practice, however, he is confronted by patients whose reality testing has faltered. From the beginning, in his work with hypnosis, Freud sees patients who—under the influence of trance states—hallucinate objects and physical states that are not grounded in a material reality that can be perceived by others. In discussing hypnotic suggestions' capacity to create symptoms, Freud (1889a) writes: "They arise, that is from a suggestion, a conscious idea, which has been introduced into the brain of the hypnotized person by an external influence and has been accepted by him as though it had arisen spontaneously" (p. 77). Under hypnosis, the brain makes an error in assessing the origin of the thought. Inside and outside become confused, and there is a lapse in the mind's capacity to perceive the separation between self and other. The production of hallucination is a quality that is also present in hysteria. Anna O, in a sense the first analytic patient, has vivid hallucinations that black snakes are crawling up her arm. She perceives objects that cannot be confirmed in the consensual field, yet for her have the strongest affective reality. The hysteric's breakdown in reality testing extends to the formation of somatic symptoms. The hysterical paralysis of an arm can be seen as an internal failure of perception, the mind creating an incapacity that does not actually exist in the body or the physical world. The same breakdown in reality testing is evident in dreaming, another key phenomenon in Freud's clinical purview. The objects of imagination in dreams gain such vividness that the individual lacks an awareness that the dream products are not real. These clinical phenomena all underscore the potential fragility of reality-based perception and they place a second demand on his model of perception. In addition to securing the possibility of objectivity, Freud's theory of mind and perception must simultaneously explain the route by which this capacity breaks down.

The nature of Freud's (1895) perceptual and epistemological model takes shape in the *Project for a Scientific Psychology*. While he ultimately abandons this effort to place psychology on a neurological footing, its themes—perceptual regression, hallucination, the energetic pressure of the wish—continue to inform his work. The more purely neurological references are dropped, but he seems to preserve the *Project's* overall framework as his epistemological foundation. In approaching epistemology, the first question Freud must address is, what motivates this line of questioning, what drives us toward reality? In keeping with the constancy principle, he suggests that the impulse to conjoin with reality begins with the search for pleasure. This coupling of epistemology and hedonism is a startling reversal of traditional dualism, and it seems to offer objectivity a shaky foundation. To see the difficulties this coupling presents for epistemology, we must trace the nature of pleasure in Freud's model.

Pleasure, in his scheme, is really only "the sensation of discharge" (p. 312). Initially, then, the individual is motivated only to discharge the excitation that has built up within him, and reality gains importance secondarily as it facilitates or interferes with this effort. When the source of stimulation is external, excessive heat for instance, the route to eliminating the impingement and allowing discharge is simple—remove the self from the source of heat. We learn about the world, about fire, because it causes pain.

However, in the case of endogenous stimuli—the appetites or instincts—the situation is more complex. These internal stimuli will lead to an urgency to discharge, and typically the first route of discharge is emotional expression. Freud (1895) writes:

> Experience shows that here the first path to be taken is that leading to *internal change* (expression of the emotions, screaming, vascular innervation). But, as was explained at the beginning, no such discharge can produce an unburdening result, since the endogenous stimulus continues to be received . . . [p. 317].

The buildup of tension that stems from the instincts is initially released through the action of emotional expression. The baby, when hungry, feels this as tension, and that energy is discharged through the act of screaming. But screaming does nothing to remove the source of the tension—the need for food—and soon the tension reasserts itself. The baby fails to perceive the tension of appetite as a need for food; he misperceives his own insides. Freud continues:

> The removal of the stimulus is only made possible here by an intervention which for the time being gets rid of the release of Q'η in the interior of the body; and this intervention calls for an alteration in the external world (supply of nourishment, proximity of the sexual object) which, as a *specific action*, can only be brought about in definite ways [pp. 317–318].

Crying will not take care of the infant's tension; he needs food. With the endogenous stimuli or instinctual needs of the organism, the experience of satisfaction is dependent on specific changes in the external world. Now, rather than fleeing from pain, objects must be brought close.[1] In the course of human development, these satisfactions initially come about as the result of parental intervention. The baby is hungry and cries—an emotional expression—and this elicits feeding behavior by the parent and the breast is brought close. The act of being fed leads to a discharge of tension and to an experience of pleasure for the infant. The relationship between the presence of the parent and the experience of satisfaction begins to form an associative link in the child's memory. Now when the infant experiences the pain that is associated with hunger it leads to a wish for the parent. This is where the possibility of trouble begins. When the hunger reappears, the charge of this tension flows back into the image of the parent and food, bringing them into consciousness as a memory: "I do not doubt that in the first instance this wishful activation will produce the same thing as a perception—namely a *hallucination.* If reflex action is thereupon introduced, disappointment cannot fail to occur" (pp. 317–318).

When these images of the parent are brought into consciousness, the force of the wishful activation can endow them with the sense of reality. The memory of the object is mistaken for a current perception. Here Freud has ventured a radical proposal that touches at the core of mental disorder. He suggests that the human perceptual system is such that it does not readily distinguish between perception and memory. As a result the infant, in the process of wishing for the mother and the

---

[1] Freud argues that it is this unshakeability of the instincts, the fact that they remain with us even when we flee, that provides the basis for the infant beginning to distinguish between his internal world, that which is him, and the external world, that which is other.

satisfying food she brings, may hallucinate her presence and begin the sucking process, but fail to accrue any nourishment from this effort. In sucking at a non-existent breast, energy is further expended diminishing the resources available for later feeding attempts, and the infant risks starving itself to death like a trout chasing after artificial flies. In establishing the possibility of hallucination, however, Freud seems to have undercut the possibility of objectivity. How is the analyst, if driven by pleasure, able to avoid hallucinatory experience in the analytic situation?

This is a critical point: when Freud writes that reality is known as real by an "indication," he suggests that the epistemological connection to reality depends on more than information—it requires a feeling state as well. We see a chair—perceive its flat and curved surfaces; the smoothness of wood, the cool of metal, the possibility of sitting—but none of this separates memory from actual perception of the real object. Instead, each of these points of awareness must have a certain qualitative element to indicate its actuality. In this way "feeling," or the subjective tone of experience, takes on a vital role in thought. The question of how we gain a conviction of reality is critical to the therapeutic effort. It is an issue that Freud struggles with, as we will see, in trying to help his patients come to terms with the reality behind his interpretive statements.

This issue, however, must wait while we continue to elucidate Freud's perceptual model. Freud recognizes that this indication of reality has to be fallible to account for errors the mind makes under hypnosis or hysteria. In these cases the mind mistakes memory and imagination for reality; the indicator of reality has broken down. Freud suggests that what occurs in these cases is a "regression" along the neuronal pathways. Now, excitation, rather than flowing from the sense organs to consciousness, flows from memory back to the senses, and so activates a hallucinatory perception. This perceptual regression is the original meaning of "regression," a concept that will later be used developmentally. To satisfy the requirement that the perceptual system is capable of both accurate perception and hallucination, Freud (1895) introduces the concept of the inhibiting ego:

> For the difference is the *indication of quality* follows, if it comes from outside, whatever the intensity of the cathexis, whereas, if it comes from ψ, it does so only when there are large intensities. It is accordingly

> *inhibition by the ego which makes possible a criterion for distinguishing between perception and memory* [pp. 325–326].

The language of the *Project* is not easy to follow, but in this passage, Freud suggests a way to handle the problem of hallucination. The capacity to perceive external reality objectively is present at birth and works automatically. This avenue of knowing provides the foundation for Freud's positivist sentiments; it makes objectivity possible. The phenomenon of wishful memory, however, is different. Here, the wishful cathexis will also activate indications of quality and the suggestion of reality. But this source of excitation is subject to inhibition by the ego, and so will only give indications of quality and reality, and lead to hallucination, when the absolute level of excitation is high enough to breach the defensive inhibition. This second form of perception, the perception of mnemic images, does not function adequately at birth. As infants, we fail to perceive that these images and need states are internal. This realization depends on the development of an ego with sufficient structure and strength to inhibit the excitatory charge of the image.

This solution to the problem of objectivity and hallucination sheds further light on Freud's view of the epistemological indications of reality. The indication, since it stems from excitation, must be predicated on levels of intensity. Freud seems to suggest that we know reality as real, rather than imagined, because it offers a kind of intensity of perception. This is tricky ground. While positivism suggests that objectivity depends on cool rationality, Freud's perceptual model demands that our awareness of reality can be felt as such only with the heat of excitation. This is the first point of entry to the paradox surrounding his epistemological work. To suggest that an affective charge is critical to our perception of reality puts him on the precipice of abandoning Western metaphysical ideals as to what constitutes knowing. Yet Freud draws back from this edge to rescue the idea of the detached observer. While intensity indicates reality and creates belief, it is inhibition from the cathected ego that allows us to be accurate. By emphasizing the importance of restraint in knowing he reclaims his intellectual roots. With this two-fold route for the belief in reality Freud has managed to carve out a realm where perception remains objective and reliable, while simultaneously accounting for the possibility of hallucination and wishfully determined bias.

Affect and Reality Testing

While the perceptual system, in Freud's model, provides a direct window to the world,[2] these perceptions must compete with images provided from memory that have been cathected by wishful impulse. In the id, there is no easy way of distinguishing fantasy from reality. Freud (1887–1904), in a letter to Fliess, describes his own struggle to sort out fantasy from reality in his self-analysis and speaks of "the certain insight that there are no indications of reality in the unconscious, so that one cannot distinguish between truth and fiction that has been cathected with affect" (p. 264). Here Freud identifies affect as a culprit in the undermining of reality testing. It provides the energetic force to lend internally generated images the indication of reality and so become hallucination. This characterization brings us to the question of affect and how Freud understands its functioning in the mental economy. On one hand, Freud is suspicious of affect and its negative effect on thought. He wants to view affect as a kind of fluid–in contrast to the electrical energy of thought–that floods the mental system and diminishes its functioning. This suspicion contributes to his proscription of the countertransference. When examined more closely, however, Freud's writings reveal a more complicated position. Freud also sees affect as a kind of information; it functions as a signpost to the unconscious. While affect may act to create neurosis, it is also a force the must be actively engaged to activate health. The tension between Freud's negative and positive views of affect permeates his work, and to see this is to clarify his views on the countertransference.

When we first consider Freud's view of emotion, he appears to hold conventionally negative ideas about its role in human functioning. In keeping with the constancy principle, Freud, through most of his writ-

---

[2] Later in his career, Freud (1915a) retracts his strong faith in perception's capacity to provide an exact duplicate of the world for the mind to study. He writes: "Just as Kant warned us not to overlook the fact that our perceptions are subjectively conditioned and must not be regarded as identical with what is perceived though unknowable, so psychoanalysis warns us not to equate perceptions by means of consciousness with the unconscious mental processes which are their object" (p. 171). This change in his views, though, does not appear to have impact on his technical recommendations and his understanding of the countertransference.

ing, defines emotion as the subjective experience of dammed-up libido, a kind of accumulated toxic waste. While affect may once have played a useful role in guiding behavior, it now merely interferes with the operation of the reality principle. In this light, Freud's Darwinian frame leads him to see affect as an atavistic remnant, outdated in function like the neonatal tail or the intestinal appendix. He (1893–1895) writes: "All these sensations and innervations belong to the field of 'The Expression of the Emotions,' which, as Darwin has taught us, consists of actions which originally had meaning and served a purpose" (p. 181). Whatever meaning and purpose they once had has now dissipated, and, like the ruins of abandoned buildings, they stand in the way of new, more flexible constructions.

The threat from affect stems from two difficulties it poses. Emotion's energetic value readily facilitates hallucinatory perception, overcoming the ego's necessary inhibition. In the case of phobias, the high degree of fear becomes linked with the memory of the feared object, and may give it the force necessary to override the ego's inhibition, creating the indication of reality. Freud (1895) writes in *The Project:* "It is quite an everyday experience that the generation of affect inhibits the normal passage of thought" (p. 357). Under the influence of affect, old pathways are too readily followed, and action is initiated prematurely. The second pitfall of affect is that it obstructs thought by filling up the associative outlets that might have led to a discharge of accumulated tension. In his earliest work, Freud saw affect as the key ingredient leading to dissociation in hysterical paralysis. He (1892) writes: "If the conception of the arm is involved in an association with a large quota of affect, it will be inaccessible to the free play of other associations. *The arm will be paralyzed in proportion to the persistence of this quota of affect or to its diminution by appropriate psychical means"* (p. 171). Freud suggests that affect is a kind of energetic fluid that clogs all the portals through which a volitional thought could grasp the neurological input of the arm, and move it to action. While thought is electrical, in Freud's model, and so quick to cathect and decathect, affect is more viscous, and cannot be so readily displaced. In all of this, Freud succumbs to the view that affect interferes with reason and judgment, undercutting the possibility of an objective viewpoint.

To align oneself with objectivity, then, requires that the pull of affect be resisted. Only when the ego is able to inhibit the wishful impulses that would cathect memory and falsely lend these images the felt sense of reality, can the world be accurately perceived and reality separated from fantasy. The analyst, then, must control the countertransference because it generates affect, and this will interfere with the capacity to accurately perceive the analysand. The countertransference, understood in this vein as backed up libidinal energy, will exert hallucinatory pressure on the analyst, leading her to perceive the analysand as a source of satisfaction to be seduced or as a threatening object that must be punished, rather than as a patient in need of assistance. Clearly Freud had good reason to fear this outcome, given the strength of the erotic and hostile transference and the temptations to mistake this clinical phenomena for genuine relationship. He has chronicled his own struggles in his earliest work with hypnotic treatment and in his aborted work with Dora. Although Freud never speaks about his own countertransference, he does talk about his technical errors and implies that they stem from emotional reactions. His followers in the analytic movement also fall prey to this breakdown in analytic judgment and indulge their libidinal countertransference. Freud's (1915a) technical proscription of the countertransference is intended to act as a warning against this error in the analyst's reality testing:

> For the doctor the phenomenon [transference] signifies a valuable piece of enlightenment and a useful warning against any tendency to a countertransference which may be present in his own mind. He must recognize that the patient's falling in love is induced by the analytic situation and is not to be attributed to the charms of his own person; so that he has no grounds whatever for being proud of such a 'conquest,' as it would be called outside of analysis [p. 161].

Freud proscribes the countertransference to ensure that analysts do not indulge their own libidinal or aggressive needs at the expense of the patient's treatment. The acting out of the transference drama through the consummation of the erotic affair, because it leads to gratification, removes the pressure on the transference to become conscious and stymies the analytic enterprise. The opportunity for understanding and genuine change has been surrendered to reenactment and momentary gratification for the analysand and analyst.

But Freud does not follow his non-analytic contemporaries in deducing from these beliefs about affect that it should be inhibited and avoided throughout life. Precisely because of its power to influence thought, affect becomes a critical element in analytic therapy. Here we find a further paradox in his writings. While pure thought is identified as the securest form of thought process, Freud is also clear that mere thought, without the presence of affect, is insubstantial and unable to effect real change in the individual's difficulties. At the beginning of his analytic career, while the trauma theory is dominant, Freud, (1893–1895) writes: "Recollection without affect almost invariably produces no result" (p. 6). Freud suggests that remembering trauma, without a currently felt reaction to that memory, will not have therapeutic efficacy. The insistence on affectively charged reproductions of the traumatic event stems from a belief that the curative process depends on the opportunity to discharge or abreact the suppressed energetic reaction to it. The toxic fluid must be drained. The expression of emotion in response to difficult events, then, represents a more adaptive, more conscious response than the formation of neurotic symptoms.

While Freud ultimately abandons the cathartic theory of therapeutic action, he retains a belief in the necessity for an affectively charged experience. In his later work, he argues for the importance of the analysis of the transference because its emotional impact is the only route through which the analysand gains conviction about the truth of analytic interpretations. He (1905a) writes: "Transference cannot be evaded, since use is made of it in setting up all the obstacles that make the material inaccessible to treatment, and since it is only after the transference has been resolved that a patient arrives at a sense of conviction of the validity of the connections which have been constructed during the analysis" (p. 117). Here Freud ventures an important distinction between the accuracy and the conviction of perception. While thought may be most efficient and unbiased when freed from practical aims and the press of emotion, this mode of thought does not have the weight of certainty that more affectively charged experiences offer. Our map of the interpersonal world is shaped not by abstraction, but by the emotionally significant events that touch us. It is emotion that offers the "indication of reality." Durable change, then, does not occur through pure understanding. The intellect is a relatively weak player in the theater of the mind. We may know something about ourselves, about the world—we may have read it, or been told about it, or even deduced it—but unless this knowledge penetrates below the surface of consciousness it will be ephemeral and will not change either the course of our actions or the pattern of our symptoms. Affect serves as fertilizer, driving deep the roots of knowledge.

Not only is affect critical in producing substantive therapeutic change, it also provides vital guideposts in the search for the unconscious determinants of suffering. In the defensive work of the mind, the original wishes and experiences, and the ensuing conflict that conditioned the neurotic suffering, are obscured by symptom formation and distortion. In the language of dreams, the dream work that sets about purifying the wish to make it acceptable to consciousness leaves a confusing map to trace to its source. Objects are condensed, symbols substituted for the original, wishes inverted, leaving no definite trail to follow, and no determinate cipher to decode these transformations. The analyst, in setting about the interpretive reconstruction of the latent dream thoughts, needs some starting point for her endeavors. In *The Interpretation of Dreams* Freud suggests that affect may provide that small piece of firm ground on which to orient the enciphered elements of the dream. While the thoughts and images of the dream may easily be transmuted, affect stays more constant. "It will be noticed," Freud (1900) writes, "that the affect felt in the dream belongs to its latent and not to its manifest content, and that the dream's *affective* content has remained untouched by the distortion which has overtaken its *ideational* content" (p. 248). And again: "The *affects* are the constituent which is least influenced and which alone can give us a pointer as to how we should fill in the missing thoughts" (p. 461). In the analytic enterprise, the unconscious becomes the essential, looked-for reality, and the conscious elements become the surface of appearance. In the language of dreams, ideas have been severed from the ground of unconscious reality, and so are unreliable. Affect, however, pierces through the dividing barrier between unconscious and conscious, like a plant with a root and stalk that connect the subterranean with the surface. Affect provides an access to the world of the unconscious and, in this case, the intrasubjective, the more real ground of meaning. Freud (1909b) returns to this view of affect as a route to intrasubjective reality in his case history of the Rat Man. "On the contrary, the physician says: 'No. The affect is justified. The sense of guilt is not in itself open to further criticism. But it belongs to some other content, which is unknown *(unconscious)*, and which requires to be looked for'" (p. 176). Here the viscous nature of affect, in contrast to the electrical patterning of thought, is useful: While affect may be less flexible because of its fluid nature, that quality is precisely what makes it less readily transmuted by the distorting effects of unconscious defense. However, the contents of thought–

ideas and symbols—are easily displaced and rearranged, and so are less reliable to the analyst in searching out the reality behind the false front of the symptom. The reliability of affect in pointing the way to the unconscious is a theme that informs Freud's analytic technique and epistemological views throughout his writing.

In assessing the value of affect, Freud even goes so far as to suggest that the capacity to feel affect is an essential component of health. In children, impulses immediately become action. This can be action manifested in response to hallucinatory perception, as is the case with the infant, or merely unfettered pleasure-seeking that does not facilitate reality testing or the aims of civilization. In neurotics, there is a similar kind of immediate venting of impulse, although in these cases the impulse is discharged through the convoluted form of the symptom. In both cases, however, there is a failure of inhibition. If the neurotic remained conscious of the thought processes behind the sequence of symptom formation, the action of the symptom would be replaced by affect. "If this inference were capable of entering consciousness," Freud (1900) writes, "it might possibly give rise to a *fear* of having the same kind of attack. But, in fact, the inference is made in a different psychical region, and consequently results in the actual realization of the dreaded symptom" (p. 150). Affect, in this model, is the normative state, a state that represents a higher developmental achievement. When the unconscious thought process becomes accessible to consciousness, the process of symptom formation is replaced by affective reactions.

This second view of affect as a phenomenon transitional between the realms of action and symbolic thought is brought into sharper focus in Freud's final theoretical model of emotion. In "Inhibitions, Symptoms, and Anxiety" (1926), he explicitly abandons his view that emotions are the product of dammed-up or repressed libido. In its place, he proposes that emotions are reactions to early traumatic experiences that function as signals to the individual about impending situations of danger. He writes: "We may legitimately hold firmly to the idea that the ego is the actual seat of anxiety and give up our earlier view that the cathectic energy of the repressed impulse is automatically turned into anxiety" (p. 93). This is a radical shift. Emotions, no longer seen as libidinal residue, take on the role of signal and information. By placing their origin in the ego rather than the id, they become part of the individual's executive functioning. The ego, Freud states, is the organized part of the id; it is the structured mind. If affect belongs to ego, it too must be part of structured experience, part of the realm of meaning. Affect is a form of communication from the ego to the id about an impending situation of danger that if experienced would evoke displeasure. Its aim is to promote action to ward off the danger. When the individual is unable to formulate action in the real world to avoid the danger, the result is a reversion to making internal changes. In response to anxiety that we cannot change, we change ourselves so as not to have to feel the negative affect. This attempt to avoid negative affect is the starting point in symptom formation. In this new conception, affect becomes critical to proper functioning, and the source of misadaptation in illness. The individual, and presumably the analyst, in health, must remain conscious of affect and be able to react to its signals in adaptive ways.

This final account of affect, however, comes late in Freud's career when he has already turned his attention away from technical questions. The idea that affect provides information, is a form of cognition, comes too late to inform his writing on the countertransference. But to suggest that Freud ever fully embraced affect as a positive force would be to falsify the record. Even in his final writings on affect, there are glimmers of his earlier, more pessimistic accounts of it. In a discussion of the "actual neuroses" he (1926) writes:

> It might still be true, therefore, that in repression anxiety is produced from the libidinal cathexis of the instinctual impulses. But how can we reconcile this conclusion with our other conclusion that the anxiety felt in phobias is an ego anxiety and arises in the ego, and that it does not proceed out of repression but, on the contrary, sets repression in motion? There seems to be a contradiction here which it is not at all a simple matter to solve [p. 110].

Affect is a paradox for Freud that he realizes he cannot readily resolve. Given the complexity of affect's status in his model, it is not surprising that he ultimately recommends that the analyst avoid or eliminate any countertransferential response.

Objective Thought and the Location of the Real

Freud, then, in the complexity of his thought, recognizes that objectivity is not simple. His cognitive-epistemological model takes into account affect's contradictory nature, its capacity to obscure as well as reveal truth.

When removed from these subtleties, however, he returns to a more conventional view of knowing. For Freud, as for his contemporaries, the capacity to rise above need-based affective pressures is the hallmark of critical thought, and the basis of the capacity to perceive the world objectively. The capacity to separate ourselves from practical aims is the necessary first step for accurate perception. Only when free from this hallucinatory pressure can we begin to sort through our perceptions and distinguish between those that are based in reality and those that gain their semblance of reality from a wish.

For Freud, the most certain means we have for innoculating ourselves against the prejudicial effect of the wish, is to turn to pure thought. This view affects his understanding of both the analysand's pathology and the effectiveness of the analyst. Throughout his work the necessary goal of thought must be to overcome the pull of the pleasure principle and align oneself with the rationality of the reality principle. His insistence that the countertransference be overcome is a direct correlate of this early theory. Countertransference would interfere with the capacity to engage in thought freed from practical aim.

The problem of knowing, however, has two parts. If the first question of epistemology is the method of knowing, the second concerns the nature of what is to be known. We must ask after the location of the real. This is already a dualistic framing of the problem; it points to a gap between the object in consciousness and the object in the world. Philosophy, in its skeptical suffering, has mourned the difficulty of attaining the thing-in-itself. Freud continues this tradition in his account of the difference between reality-based perception and wish-driven hallucinatory perception. In the process of trying to know the external world, the conscious mind lies above the unconscious in its accuracy of perception. While the unconscious is unable to separate fact from fantasy, the conscious mind, allied with the inhibitory powers of the ego, offers a more secure route to truth. The unconscious is unable to play by the rules of epistemology. Consciousness, on the other hand, is the seat of the reality principle. It is able to distinguish between internally and externally generated perception, and can hold back the distorting coloration of the wish. This championing of the conscious mind, the rational mind, places Freud firmly in alliance with Platonic dualism and Western rationalism.

Despite his intended loyalty to these ideals, however, Freud quickly provides kindling for the opposite view. His cognitive–epistemological model is primarily concerned with the capacity to perceive and know the external world. But he is not a doctor to the external world. His theater is the intrapsychic—he probes after the internal reality of the individual. In this internal realm, the traditional dualism is inverted and everything is stood on its head. While Plato draws the contrast between the real and the apparent in our knowledge of things and concepts, Freud extends this dualism inward. Until Freud, the intrasubjective had been protected from dualistic skepticism. Descartes, in his Cartesian philosophy, suggests that the awareness of self is the only certainty in human experience and is the basis of all knowledge. Freud overturns this by positing the existence of the unconscious. In the analytic enterprise, consciousness is the surface and the unconscious is the essential depth. He (1900) writes: "The unconscious is the true psychical reality; *in its innermost nature it is as much unknown to us as the reality of the external world, and it is as incompletely presented by the data of consciousness as is the external world by the communications of our sense organs*" (p. 613). When the analysand enters the analytic context, he presents to the analyst through free association the contents of the conscious mind. But these associations, the analysand's conscious account of his difficulty, act to conceal the true neurotic conflict and forbidden fantasies. Consciousness, in the internal realm, is mere appearance. The thing-in-itself, within the mind, is the unconscious. The id is what counts, what drives consciousness and determines its manifestations. That is what is searched for by the analyst in her epistemological striving. By making the unconscious the ground, the real self, Freud demotes consciousness to acting only as a surface coating, or at best a weak manager of the stronger forces of the unconscious id.

By extending Platonic dualism to the interior of the self, Freud threatens to overturn it. The epistemological structure has been undermined. Nothing remains certain, and Descartes' certainty about the location and existence of the self is overturned. In contemporary terms, two variables are covariant, the self and the world, and there is no outside observer to see which is which. If consciousness is no longer the ruler of its own domain, then the whole field of observation, introspection, and the possibility of knowing objectively are called into question. These are all activities that belong to consciousness, and that realm has become shaky, threatened by rebellious forces. If the observer can no longer be certain of herself, we can no longer trust the imagination's inclination to posit a realm of being opposed to appearance. When all variables covary, we can no longer discern what causes what, and the idea of a linear path of causation from being to perceived appearance becomes untenable. The presence of internal dualism sews further seeds of paradox into Freud's work. While he wants to champion the ideal of the objective self, both in the analysand and in the analyst, the existence of the unconscious muddies the water. It demands that the irrational, the affective, and the passionate be granted pivotal roles in the epistemological process.

Health and the Connection to Reality

As Freud turns to his clinical work with patients, he brings with him his epistemological view of human functioning. Embedded within this model of cognition is a nascent view of health and pathology. According to this scheme, health depends on the epistemological capacity to discover elements that will meet the instinctive needs of the self. We are healthy when we see the world accurately, ill when we distort it through hallucinatory wish. Again Freud has carried over the Platonic connection between the good and the real, although in keeping with the Darwinian influence he adds an evolutionary twist. Now the good is defined in relationship to biological needs and the capacity to preserve the organism's life. Since the pleasure principle is insufficient to sustain life, we require a capacity to turn away from the immediate conditions of pleasure, and so gain the capacity to see and act clearly. Even after Freud has fully consolidated his mature theory of neurosis, he holds to this model of health. In his Clark lectures (1910a) he writes: "The energetic and successful man is one who succeeds by his efforts in turning his wishful phantasies into reality" (p. 50). The ability to act on reality, to convert it to one's wishes, is the cornerstone of health.

If health is dependent on our capacity to know and alter reality, illness proceeds from our retreat from it. While earlier we spoke of pathology in terms of disruption to the processes of gratification, we can now enlarge on this and describe pathology as a disturbance in the process of knowing. While under the sway of the seduction theory, Freud viewed pathology as a fracturing of the capacity to perceive the present. In the face of traumatic events and inexpressible emotion, repression is brought to bear and the affective reaction is suppressed. This reaction, however, is incomplete; the affective reaction continues to exist in dissociated form in the economy of the mind. The effect of repression, then, is that it acts to break up the continuity of mind. The repressed impulse is now removed from the sphere of consciousness, and becomes alien to the ego. This is the first breakdown in the epistemological integrity of the individual. She ceases to know or perceive parts of herself as herself.

This first act of dissociation, however, leads to further degradation in epistemological processing. The repressed memory and affective reactions, through their energetic value, continue to make demands on the ego. In their dissociated existence, they begin to act as suggestive influences. They create symptoms without the patient's awareness of their influence, just as the patient is influenced to perform acts under hypnosis without awareness of the hypnotist's influence. In this process of symptom formation, the perception of time breaks down. What was in the past, and should belong to the province of memory, is converted into action in the present in the form of the symptom. This is the core of the transference; the past, through the act of repression, cannot be known as memory, and so insists on manifesting itself in the present. The present is misperceived as a recapitulation of an unknown past.

As Freud moves away from the seduction theory and embraces the developmental model of sexuality and its vicissitudes, he preserves the belief that pathology stems from a breakdown in reality testing and that the connection with reality is the key element in health. In his mature theory, however, the epistemological pathogen is seen as frustration rather than trauma, and the nature of the rupture is more fully elaborated. People fall ill because they are unable to procure adequate gratification in the sphere of the real, and turn, out of frustration and weakness, back toward the pleasures of hallucination. He (1910a) writes: "We see that human beings fall ill when, as a result of external obstacles or of an internal lack of adaptation, the satisfaction of their erotic needs *in reality* is frustrated. We see that they then take flight into *illness* in order that by its help they may find a satisfaction to take the place of what has been frustrated" (p. 49). In the real world, problems require action and effort to resolve. The neurotic feels unable or unwilling to take on that task, and takes the easier course of altering the internal world. The neurotic lacks the stamina to perceive the real, regardless of the discomfort: "Neurotics turn away from reality because they find it unbearable—either the whole or parts of it" (1911a, p. 218). The turn toward illness is pressured by the experience of pain.

This brings us back full circle to the question of gratification and the operation of the reality principle. While in his earliest work Freud views pathology as an interruption to the normally adequate functioning of the perceptual field, he later comes to see health, the capacity to perceive reality accurately, as a developmental achievement. At birth the individual is dominated by the pleasure principle and ruled by the component, perverse sexual instincts. The infant satisfies these libidinal urges in autoerotic activity and finds pleasure in sucking, defecating, and masturbation. These pleasures allow the infant to use himself as an object, to make a narcissistic object choice, and so remain free of the necessity of making changes in the external world in order to procure gratification. But these autoerotic pleasures have limits. We need real food, not just sucking, real people with genitals, not just our hands. These objects from reality are required for survival and procreation. To achieve adequate functioning, to ally oneself with the real, two steps must be accomplished: the separate libidinal zones must be integrated under the genital, and the world of fantasy (masturbatory activity) must be given up for the attainment of real objects, actual people rather than imagined. Freud (1905b) writes: "The sexual instinct is now subordinated to the reproductive function; it becomes, so to say, altruistic" (p. 207). Freud has coupled a Darwinian sensibility about the value of reproduction with a metaphysical faith in the virtue of the real. The teleological aim of the human organism is to progress through the phylogenic stages of evolution. Ontology must follow phylogeny. In practice this entails that the diverse libidinal zones, primitive and pleasure-seeking, are integrated into genital activity, and that this whole organization is brought into consciousness and governed by the reality-testing capabilities of the inhibitory ego. Animal becomes scientist, and in this transformation civilization is served. This represents, for Freud, the highest form of virtue.

We are successful as organisms when we link gratification with reality. We fall ill when under the press of frustration we turn away from reality back to the regressive[3] substitutes of autoeroticism and hallucinatory perception. The problem of masturbation can now be seen more clearly. Freud (1912b) writes:

> He falls ill of his attempt to adapt himself to reality and to fulfill *the demands of reality*—an attempt in the course of which he comes up against insurmountable internal difficulties. . . . His task is to exchange one kind of satisfaction for another, and he breaks down from his inflexibility. . . . A young man who has hitherto satisfied his libido by

[3] Regressive in both its perceptual and developmental aspects.

> means of phantasies ending in masturbation, and who now seeks to replace a régime approximating to auto-eroticism by the choice of a real object . . . [falls] ill from the most laudable effort, if the earlier fixations of [his] libido are powerful enough to resist a displacement [pp. 233–234].

Masturbation is a more primitive form of gratification that fails to connect the individual to reality. Its reliance on fantasy constitutes one part of its epistemological toxicity. The second aspect of this rupture, however, is reminiscent of the seduction theory. The libido is fixated on past, internalized objects, and is unable to leave them behind for the pleasures of the present. In other words, the internal images of the satisfying parent, the first love, are too attractive, and cannot be put aside for new lovers. Once again the past, which no longer exists in actuality, is brought forward into the present, leading to a distortion in the perception of time. The fixation of the libido, coupled with its capacity to subvert reality testing, leads the individual to be unwilling to trade the hallucinatory satisfaction of masturbatory activity for the less predictable realm of reality.

Restoring the Real: The Analytic Attitude and the Analysand's Connection to the Real

We are now in a position to see more clearly the roots of Freud's technical prescriptions. Pathology, he argues, stems from disruption to the analysand's connection to reality. The restoration of health, therefore, must depend on the analyst's capacity to restore the real. The analysand is cured, according to this view, through the strengthening of his epistemological processes. This is another way of viewing the analytic attitude—it is formulated to compel the analysand to abandon the hallucinatory dominance of the pleasure principle and move toward the sometimes painful, but ultimately more nourishing, realm of reality. Freud's insistence on analytic neutrality and his injunction to avoid gratifying the patient both stem from his concern that suggestion and gratification will lead to a tendency to debase the real.

The first part of this, the analyst's neutrality, has its roots in Freud's earliest therapeutic experience. After his initial ventures in employing authority-based suggestive influence, he turns away from the use of direct influence. Hypnotism depends on faith and complicity. While it may alter the shape of the analysand's symptoms, it cannot inoculate him against further difficulty because it fails to strengthen his relationship to reality. In keeping with this sensibility, Freud turns away from more direct therapeutic approaches, suggestion and the pressure technique, toward the more abstinent technique of free association. Free association, a process that helps the analysand explore the unknown regions of his own mind, relies on the exploration of truth, rather than on compliance with authority. It asks the analysand to take responsibility for himself, to become a full participant in the search for truth.

In Freud's earliest theory, the curative factor in analysis concerned the retrieval of memory as memory. When the awareness of the temporal is restored—when we know past as past and present as present—the symptoms are cured. We have argued that in the seduction theory the pathogenic factor stems from repressed memory acting as suggestive influence. The key to overcoming this suggestive influence is to bring back into the continuous realm of consciousness the repressed impulses or memories. Again, connection with the real, in this case the reality of internal memory, brings about the cure. By remaining neutral, the analyst allows the analysand to engage in the explorative process in a way that strengthens the analysand's objectivity.

The importance of neutrality in supporting the analysand's epistemological autonomy continues throughout Freud's work. What is strengthened in the turn toward the drive theory, however, is his awareness of fantasy's tenacity. Now, rather than recovering memory of an actual trauma, the therapeutic task is to uncover the buried fantasy and expose its unreality. But this is not an easy task, for the analysand's tie to fantasy has shaped a strong marriage: "Neurotics are dominated by the opposition between reality and phantasy. If what they long for the most intensely in their phantasies is presented to them in reality, they none the less flee from it; and they abandon themselves to their phantasies the most readily where they need no longer fear to see them realized" (1905a, p. 110). Freud now sees that the rupture in the analysand's epistemological capacity is not merely inability, it stems from choice. Neurotics have come to fear reality, to fear its tangibility, and choose instead to occupy the realm of fantasy where omnipotent control can be maintained.

Yet while Freud states that neurotics choose fantasy precisely because they recognize that it avoids bringing about change in the external world, change that could be dangerous, at other points he suggests that the core of neurotic difficulty stems from the inability to distinguish between the properties of fantasy and reality. The neurotic fails to see that fantasy exists only in the mind, not in the world, and in this epistemological error he is controlled by internal phantoms. Freud suggests that in the case of Little Hans, it was the developmental inability to distinguish between fantasy and reality that led to his symptom formation, and the subsequent development of this capacity that ultimately leads to his cure. Freud (1909a) reports a conversation between Hans and his father about his wish that his little sister might drown:

> *I:* That was why you thought when Mummy was giving her her bath, if only she'd let go, Hanna would fall into the water . . .
> *Hans* (taking me up): . . . and die.
> *I:* And then you'd be alone with Mummy. A good boy doesn't wish that sort of thing, though.
> *Hans: But he may* THINK *it.*
> *I:* But that isn't good.
> *Hans: If he thinks it, it* IS *good all the same, because you can write it to the Professor.*[1]
>
> [1]Well done, little Hans! I could wish for no better understanding of psycho-analysis from any grown-up [p. 72].

In his footnote to this exchange, Freud states that the cornerstone of analytic value, analytic cure, is the capacity to reliably know the difference, both epistemologically and ethically, between thought and reality. When Hans comes to know that his aggressive fantasies do not constitute actual violence, he is released from his obsessive symptoms.

The analytic attitude, then, must take into account the pull of fantasy, and seek to lessen its influence. It must uncover the difference between thought and reality, and strengthen the ego's capacity to resist regressive perception. Anything that strengthens the tendency to indulge in fantasy, that leads to a regression along the sensory pathways to hallucinatory satisfaction, is harmful. Reality is imperfect, and is only partially contoured to meet our needs. When we engage in fantasy, it lessens our appetite for it. Fantasy is like eating dessert before the main course; it is sweet and readily chosen, but it spoils our appetite and fails to sustain us.

Freud's therapeutic aim, then, must be to help his patients overcome the dominance of fantasy, to aid them in creating an identity between mere wish and tangible reality. But this task, from the beginning, is saturated with paradox. Freud's intention is to lead his patients away from their fantasy attachments and toward real objects, to connection to real people. This transition is to happen in the context of the therapeutic relationship. To Freud's mind, however, this relationship is at least partially artificial; it is not a genital relationship between two adults seeking mutual pleasure and procreation. The analytic relationship is a refuge from the real world, and is conditioned by the financial terms of the agreement. Therefore, if the patient comes to sort through the obstacles to gratification solely within the analytic relationship, he has merely substituted one form of fantasized autoerotic activity for another. We can compare such a success with recovery in an institution. Freud (1912a) writes: "For, from the point of view of recovery, it is a matter of complete indifference whether the patient overcomes this or that anxiety or inhibition in the institution; what matters is that he shall be free of it in his *real* life as well" (italics added; p. 106). Gratification in the analytic relationship, a relationship that stands apart from the real world, can only constitute another version of masturbation. It protects the patient from the impingement of displeasure from the world that might prod him toward recognizing the real. This, above all else, is why the doctor must refrain from any countertransferential pull to indulge the erotic demands of the transference. Freud (1915a) writes:

> For the doctor, ethical motives unite with the technical ones to restrain him from giving the patient his love. The aim he has to keep in view is that this woman, whose capacity for love is impaired by infantile fixations, should gain free command over a function which is of such inestimable importance to her; that she should not, however, dissipate it in the treatment, but keep it ready for the time when, after her treatment, the demands of real life make themselves felt. He must not stage the scene of a dog race in which the prize was to be a garland of sausages but which some humorist spoilt by throwing a single sausage on to the tracks. The result was, of course, that the dogs threw themselves upon it and forgot all about the race and about the garland that was luring them to victory in the far distance [p. 169].

The garland in this analytic race is a relationship with someone outside of the treatment environment. In keeping with his Platonic sensibility, Freud prohibits gratification because it leads to a degradation of the analysand's connection to reality.

Again, we are returned to the paradox that we have been tracing. In this model, frustration is the motive for the turn away from reality. Yet this same force, frustration, is also the key element, when applied correctly, to turn the individual back toward reality. In this way it is like the blade of a knife: it can function as weapon to injure, or scalpel to heal. Frustration is necessary because it provides the energetic force to overcome the fear of reality and the gravitational pull of fantasy. In recognizing the energetic workings of the unconscious, Freud (1913a) must turn away from any mental version of therapeutic action:

> It is true that in the earliest days of analytic technique we took an intellectualist view of the situation. We set a high value on the patient's knowledge of what he had forgotten, and in this we made hardly any distinction between our knowledge of it and his. We thought it a special piece of good luck if we were able to obtain information about the forgotten childhood trauma from other sources—for instance, from parents or nurses or the seducer himself—as in some cases it was possible to do; and we hastened to convey the information and the proofs of its correctness to the patient, in the certain expectation of thus bringing the neurosis and the treatment to a rapid end. It was a severe disappointment when the expected success was not forthcoming [p. 141].

Again we see that while Freud ultimately champions the mind and objective perception, he sees that by themselves they are weak allies in the battle against fantasy and neurotic symptoms. Analysis must be willing to make pacts with the forces of pleasure to bring about structural change.

The first step in this process is the activation of the transference. The transference, Freud feels, is an unreal relationship, based on projections from the analysand's past. But at the same time, the transference acts to bring the intrasubjective fantasy out into the open and connects it to an actual person, the doctor. In this sense transference acts to continue the paradox we have been discussing. It is part fantasy, part reality. Freud (1914a) writes: "The transference thus creates an intermediate region between illness and real life through which the transition from the one to the other is made" (p. 154). Now Freud might defend himself against critiques that in making use of the transference he has compromised his epistemological purity, by stating that the analyst stays neutral in regard to the unreality of the transference; the analysand constructs the transference by himself, plays at it by himself, while the analyst merely watches and interprets. At times this does seem to be his line of defense. Yet it is a line that cannot be held. He has already retreated from the intellectual approach and acknowledges that analysis must do more than merely observe the energetic fantasy of the transference; he sees that it must be employed. While he is clear that analysis no longer uses the force of suggestion to obscure truth and forbid the symptom, this does not mean that suggestion has been completely expelled from the analytic repertoire. Instead, the analyst now draws on the force of the positive transference, a force based in unreality, to motivate the analysand to work through his resistance and continue the analytic exploration, the analytic search for reality. He (1916b) writes: "This work of overcoming resistances is the essential function of analytic treatment; the patient has to accomplish it and the doctor makes this possible for him with the help of suggestion operating in an *educative* sense" (p. 451). This statement that suggestion is used in analysis, although only to affect the resistance, not the symptom, stands in marked contrast to Freud's claim that the analyst should act as a mirror. If the analyst does use suggestion, regardless of its object, she must interject some of herself; she must demonstrate that she values something, has preference in regard to the analytic relationship. This preference, a preference that the analysand embrace reality, would seem to constitute an inescapable countertransference by the analyst. This is a critical point that we will return to later. What we must see for now is how Freud's technical prescriptions are conditioned by his understanding of the epistemological functioning of the analysand. Abstinence and neutrality are required to shore up the analysand's connection to the real. But even here there are countercurrents, and Freud hints at the necessity for greater involvement by the analyst to mobilize the forces of change.

The Analyst's Epistemological Process

The analyst, in shaping her technical demeanor, has more to consider than the analysand's epistemological process. She must also seek to position herself as an observer in a way that permits objectivity. If the analysand is cured by truth, not suggestion, then the analyst can only be effective when she has established a means for knowing the truth, for divining reality. Again, neutrality and abstinence seem to come to Freud's rescue. The analyst must avoid the countertransference, must remain abstinent, in order to ensure that her perception is not colored by wish. By relying on free association, Freud feels he has removed the contaminating influence of practical aim and can observe the manifestations of neurosis from an objective perspective. Free association, Freud (1925) writes, "exposes the patient to the least possible amount of compulsion, it never allows of contact being lost with the actual current situation, it guarantees to a great extent that no factor in the structure of the neurosis will be overlooked and that nothing will be introduced into it by the expectations of the analyst" (p. 21). Freud's experience with the seduction theory has reinforced his belief in the importance of analytic abstinence as a means of achieving objectivity. Countertransferential affect, in this epistemological model, can only serve to heighten the analyst's practical aims and so compromise the efforts to secure knowledge. The analyst's objectivity, then, depends on her capacity to inhibit herself. To this point Freud seems quite conventional, and it is this aspect of his thought that has been stereotyped. Freud's vision of the analyst is quickly described as a relic of nineteenth-century science. Yet to remain here is a disservice to his legacy, and Freud's struggle to define the ground of analytic objectivity contains many levels of complexity. In part this is the product of his years of work; but even from the beginning the seeds of complexity are present. In the *Project*, Freud does suggest that accurate perception depends on the process of inhibition. Yet this is only one side of the equation. To gain knowledge, in this model, the mind also needs the freedom to try out the full range of associations. The inhibition, then, must remain partial. It must keep the energetic charge of the associations below the threshold where it would activate hallucinatory perception, but still allow enough energy to flow for thought to be expansive. This tension between inhibition and freedom augurs Freud's struggle to find coherent ground for objectivity in the analytic endeavor.

As Freud confronts the inherent uncertainty of the unconscious and the difficulty of finding firm ground in the analytic enterprise, cracks begin to emerge in his solid positivist stance. By driving dualism inward, he has multiplied the number of variables—the analysand's and the analyst's conscious and unconscious each demand attention now—and in this multiplicity has uncovered a field where meaning shimmers, like light in desert heat. When Freud writes the first edition of *The Interpretation of Dreams* (1990), in the moment between the collapse of the trauma theory and the reemergence of a narrative theory based on the Oedipus complex and infantile sexuality, he moves to the verge of adopting a constructivist epistemology. In this way of understanding, reality does not stand fixed, apart from the act of perception, but is conditioned precisely by the act of being perceived. In this context we can say that

Freud is a post-Nietszchean philosopher because he recognizes that the mind shapes its perception of the world, and that this shaping is due to motivating factors. The wish is the determining force in the creation of the dream, and, while less consistently potent in the waking state, it also shapes daytime perceptions. But this interpretive view is frightening, and only insecurely grasped. While Freud discusses phenomena that have constructivist implications, this never leads him to abandon his positivist language. He remains convinced throughout his work that he has preserved his objectivity as an observer. When the relativist implications of his work become clear, and are seized upon by his critics, Freud reacts by turning away from these observations to buttress the apparent objectivity of his new science. Although Freud admits fragments of this discovered constructivist frame, he does not pursue their implications, or reformulate his positivist values. Constructivism, as we will see, is a perspective that Freud ultimately rejects.

But this rejection cannot reverse what Freud has discovered about the mind and perception. By recognizing the role of fantasy and wishful impulse in the creation of thought, Freud urges us to take responsibility for our perceptual acts. Traditionally when we notice a feeling in ourselves, we look around for its cause, and we assign the cause to an external factor. We say: "He made me do that," or, "You made feel as I did." In this reliance on external events as the determining force in our affective life, we abrogate responsibility for our emotional world, and so become victims of our internal states, rather than their agents. Freud reverses this, and rescues our affective life and the transference from the myth of linear causation. He denies that the way we feel toward the interpersonal world is determined solely by the press of that world; he denies that the analysand's emotional reaction to the analyst is determined by the analyst's actions. Instead, through the distorting lens of unconscious motivation, the perception of the present, of the analytic relationship, is colored by the past.

Freud's recognition that reality is not static, does not remain immobile outside of the act of perceiving, takes further shape in his theory of dream interpretation. In contrast to previous methods of dream interpretation, Freud insists that the meaning of a given dream can be understood only in the context of the dreamer's associations. Previous works on dreams had tried either to discount them as meaningless, or to uncover a fixed means of deciphering their meaning. This attempt to fix the translation of the dream's meaning can be seen in the symbolic approaches to dream interpretation. Here, the theorist tries to formulate a Rosetta stone that will allow the language of the dream to be reliably translated into the language of awakened thought. Meaning in this approach is fixed, waiting only for the necessary key to be translated. "If I consult a 'dream-book,'" Freud (1900) writes, "I find that 'letter' must be translated by 'trouble' and 'funeral' by 'betrothal.' It then remains for me to link together the key words which I have deciphered in this way and, once more, to transpose the result into the future tense" (p. 98). In the same vein, other writers had tried to establish the absolute connection between dreams and physical states of the body during sleep. Pressure on the hand during sleep, for instance, might lead to a dream of being trapped. Meaning in dreams, under this view, is independent of the dreamer's particular subjectivity.

Freud, however, rejects these static modes of interpretation. He insists that dreams must be interpreted in the context of the dreamer's thoughts. In this procedure, a given dream element can take on multiple meanings not only between individuals, but within a given individual on different occasions. What is critical in determining meaning are the associations of the dreamer, not the intrinsic connections between symbol and latent dream content. This is a radical position for a positivist to adopt. It suggests that there is no absolute meaning to events separate from the relationship of the perceiver to the perceived, or at least the dreamer to the dreamed. If we stop here and consider the implications for analytic technique, we are faced with questions about the possibility of the analyst's objectivity. Freud, if he is to make plausible his objectivist theory of reality and knowing, must provide us with criteria that indicate the distinction between false belief and genuine knowing in the analytic exploration. If meaning is determined contextually, rather than intrinsically, where can the analyst stand that allows her to know the analysand separately from the analysand in relationship to herself? Freud will ultimately argue that this can be handled by the analyst adopting a posture of abstinence. By controlling the behavior of the analyst, that pole is kept constant; the analyst is a non-participant in the creation of the shape and meaning of the transference relationship. But if we extend the method of dream interpretation and its implicit epistemology to the analytic setting, it becomes clear that the meaning of abstinence is also an element of the dream content that cannot be placed outside the associative web. Furthermore, the meaning of abstinence will be displaceable not only for the analysand, but for the analyst as well. Just as a given symbol can take on different meanings for a dreamer at different times, so too must the meaning of abstinence for the analyst.

But Freud ultimately retreats from this fully contextual approach to dream interpretation, and he avoids extracting the full implications of its significance for objectivity. In later editions of *The Interpretation of Dreams* (1990), Freud begins to reverse himself and hints that psychoanalytic exploration may reveal a more fixed relationship between specific symbols and their unconscious meaning. Staircases come to be translated as the act of intercourse, and pieces of wood as the female sexual organ. While Freud continues to insist that the use of universal dream symbols will never be adequate apart from the technical rules of dream interpretation he has formulated, he does move away from the chaotic tumult of possible meaning implicit in this transitional position. This trend to resystematize meaning gains firmer organization as Freud formulates his developmental theories. With the recognition of the Oedipus conflict, he begins to venture interpretations that are formulated in accordance with an a priori theoretical narrative and are less dependent on the specific associations of the analysand.

Freud's retreat from the specter of relativist epistemology is quickened by the growing attacks on the scientific foundation of his work. Throughout his career, Freud is buffeted by critics who dispute the validity of his findings. Initially these come from theorists outside the analytic community who seem disquieted by Freud's sexual theories. To defend against these voices that insist his findings are more a reflection of his own peculiar fantasies than an indication of reality, Freud feels he must realign himself with positivism. For Freud, accepting relativism would be equivalent to admitting that his work was groundless. In defending the validity of his sexual findings, Freud (1905b) writes: "My recollections, as well as a constant re-examination of the material, assure me that this part of the theory is based upon equally careful and impartial observation" (p. 133). He insists that anyone who repeats his procedure with patients will observe the same phenomena and, if clear of personal bias, reach the same conclusions.

But Freud's reassertion of his positivist foundation soon runs into difficulty from another front. As he gains followers, these new analysts, employing the analytic method, also begin to question Freud's theories. Jung, Adler, Reich all come to dispute key positions in Freud's theoretical edifice, and eventually leave the analytic fold. It becomes clear that merely employing free association as a therapeutic technique is not enough to insure the repeatability (a key to verification) of Freud's findings. Relativism is now used by his opponents within the analytic world to dispute the universal applicability of his work. They suggest that analytic findings are relative to the observer, and that this should permit them to venture away from Freud's strict sexual findings. Once again, Freud strives to preserve the possibility of objectivity. This can be seen in his attack of Adler's use of relativity in his theory. In *On the History of the Psychoanalytic Movement*, written as a defense against critiques from the defectors Jung and Adler, Freud strives to recover the objectivity of analytic findings. He (1914b) writes:

> The stress on arbitrary personal views in scientific matters is bad; it is clearly an attempt to dispute the right of psychoanalysis to be valued as a science. . . . Anyone who sets a high value on scientific thought will rather seek every possible means and method of circumscribing the factor of fanciful personal predilections as far as possible where ever it still plays too great a part [pp. 58–59].

Freud's positivist orientation has reasserted itself to fight back the challenge to his theory. While Freud knows only too well from his early mistakes with the trauma theory that the investigator can be misled, he is determined to hold on to the possibility of objectivity. Freud restates his objection to relativistic critiques at the end of his career. At this time Einstein's theory of relativity has gained recognition, and has threatened the foundation of knowledge based on objective observation. Freud (1933), answering the voice of a fictitious critic, writes:

> 'Probably you are just as right as we are. After all, who can possibly know who is right? In spite of our antagonism, pray allow us to represent your point of view in our publications. We hope that you will be kind enough in exchange to find a place for our views which you deny.' In the future, when the misuse of Einstein's relativity has been entirely achieved, this will obviously become the regular custom in scientific affairs [p. 144].

While Freud clearly does not embrace constructivist sensibility in his understanding of epistemology, his rejection of it is less straightforward than we might imagine. This ambiguity stems from the necessity for verification. If there is a basis for knowing that rises above the personal predilections, we must ask what allows the individual to recognize when conclusions are objective, rather than merely subjective.

The difficulty Freud's positivist epistemology faces become clearer when we consider the problem of certainty. In creating an analytic epistemology we must ask not only, how is knowing possible (an issue Freud addresses through his neurological account of perception), but how can we ascertain when we have met those conditions of knowledge? To have any confidence in our analytic action we must have some way of knowing that we know; we must be able to differentiate with some reliability whether our inferences about the analysand are correct, grounded in reality-based perception, or merely hallucinatory or non-penetrating projections. There are two aspects to this problem of certainty. The first problem the analyst faces is finding a criterion for evaluating whether her internal processes have functioned adequately, or whether they have been disrupted by the distorting pressure of need. Freud, if his proscription of the countertransference is to be sensible in practice as well as theory, needs a method for determining when the countertransference has been "overcome." If the countertransference is unconscious, then how do we know whether it has been overcome, or merely overlooked?

Our problems with certainty do not end here. Even when we have successfully cleared our perceptual apparatus as an analyst, we still face the multiple levels of intrasubjective existence in the analysand. Freud, having postulated the existence of the distorting influence of the unconscious, needs criteria for determining when this veil has been successfully drawn. How do we know when our interpretations have penetrated the surface of consciousness, through the distorting symptoms, and reached the real ground of the analysand's unconscious?

Freud early on in his work encounters the difficulty of ascertaining the certainty of his objectivity. To overcome these internal obstacles, Freud turns his analytic method toward himself and he begins his self-analysis. The result of this self-analysis, however, is more extensive than Freud had imagined when he undertook it. As he probes his emotional world and its network of motivation and fantasy, he discovers that, at least in his case, the childhood seduction was imagined, rather than actual. Through this act of self-purification, Freud feels he has recovered objectivity, and gained the ability to perceive his analysands without distortion. Yet Freud's self-analysis involves a suspicious brand of bootstrapping:

he seeks to perfect his method of observation and cure, and to do this he brings to bear the analytic method, a method that was created out of his pre-analyzed self. How can the subjectively contaminated give birth to the objectively pure?

Freud is not unaware of this difficulty. In a letter to Fliess (1887–1904) he writes: "My self-analysis remains interrupted. I have realized why I can analyze myself only with the help of knowledge obtained objectively (like an outsider). True self-analysis is impossible; otherwise there would be no (neurotic) illness. Since I am still contending with some kind of puzzle in my patients, this is bound to hold me up in my self-analysis as well" (p. 281). Here Freud states that the boot-strapping operation of the self-analysis cannot be carried out in isolation. In order to get some traction in the attempt to raise himself he must bring in other relationships. He suggests that in looking outward we may have better success in preserving objectivity than we can in looking inward at our own complexes. This seems to make some sense. In Freud's model, we can look clearly when we free ourselves from practical aims. Our investment in analysands whom we do not know outside of the treatment context should be less than our investment in ourselves and the outcome of the self-analysis.

The intrinsic difficulty of self-analysis becomes apparent to Freud as his science gains followers who, as they stray from the theoretical doctrine, he sees as falling prey to countertransferential difficulties. In 1910 Freud still holds to the possibility of adequate self-analysis, but it is a conviction that is receding. The problem of the analyst falling prey to her own unconscious thought processes drives Freud (1919b) to write:

> We have become aware of the "counter-transference," which arises in him as a result of the patient's influence on his unconscious feelings, and we are almost inclined to insist that he shall recognize this countertransference in himself and overcome it. Now that a considerable number of people are practicing psychoanalysis and exchanging their observations with one another, we have noticed that no psychoanalyst goes further than his own complexes and internal resistances permit; and we consequently require that he shall begin his activity with a self-analysis and continually carry it deeper while he is making his observations on his patients. Anyone who fails to produce results in a self-analysis of this kind may at once give up any idea of being able to treat patients by analysis [p. 145].

Self-analysis, however, is particularly prone to incompleteness; due to the press of displeasure, the temptation to stop short in the face of the critical resistances is too great. The difficulty of making progress in self-analysis, a problem Freud seems to feel is more substantial in his followers than it was in himself, leads him to begin insisting that prospective analysts go through a training analysis of their own. With the help of an external observer, greater perspective is gained, and progress is more certain.

Freud has changed his position about the conditions of certainty regarding objectivity and the analytic observer. Isolated from others, we cannot be sure that our self-analysis is complete, and that our interpretations are any more than projections from our own unexamined unconscious. Freud (1912d) writes:

> But if the doctor is to be in a position to use his unconscious in this way as an instrument in the analysis, he must himself fulfill one psychological condition to a high degree. He may not tolerate resistances in himself which hold back from his consciousness what has been perceived by his unconscious. . . . It is not enough for this that he himself should be an approximately normal person. It may be insisted, rather, that he should have undergone a psycho-analytic purification and have become aware of those complexes of his own which would be apt to interfere with his grasp of what the patient tells him. . . . I count it as one of the many merits of the Zurich school of analysis that they have laid increased emphasis on this requirement, and have embodied it in the demand that everyone who wishes to carry out analyses on other people shall first himself undergo an analysis by someone with expert knowledge [p. 116].

In seeking to ensure the objectivity of the analyst by prescribing the training analysis as a necessary precondition, Freud has implicitly recognized the interpersonal nature of reality and knowledge. Knowing, in contrast to believing, concerns the process of reaching agreement with others. Freud would certainly dispute this constructivist interpretation of his conclusion. Instead, he would argue, the interpersonal does not create reality. It creates the necessity for acknowledging it. The tangibility of others, the impossibility of affecting them through hallucinatory perception, insists that we abandon perception based on the pleasure principle for more objective modes of knowing. Yet the constructivist position is not truly overcome. The criteria for certainty regarding one's own objectivity becomes the judgment of the senior analytic community. But this senior community acquired whatever objectivity they have through the process of self-analysis. Ultimately the Causa immanens (the self created) cannot be escaped. The inescapability of the personal, as we will see, causes increasing friction in the emerging analytic community.

While Freud is clear about the dangers of the countertransference and the obstacles it poses to objectivity, he fails to provide clear criteria for recognizing its presence. We can guess that affect or libidinal impulses would certainly constitute one set of markers, but even this is not explicit in his writings. Furthermore, since repression, when deeply effective, banishes the affect as well as the action, the possibility of unrecognized unconscious influences on the analyst seems palpable. Again, we are thrown back upon the collective opinion of the analytic community as arbiter. The persistence of subjectivity, despite self–analysis or a training analysis, makes certainty for the analyst elusive. Freud recognizes the impossibility of acquiring an immutable objectivity when he suggests that self-analysis must be ongoing. He (1937) writes: "Every analyst should periodically—at intervals of five years or so—submit himself to analysis once more, without feeling ashamed of taking this step" (p. 249). Lengthy experience has taught Freud that complete "purification" of the analyst is unreachable. The best we can hope for is greater clarity and a strengthened ability to resist projection.

The difficulty of certainty, however, extends beyond the analyst's relationship to her own unconscious. Even if personal biases are brought under control, we still face the need to establish criteria for recognizing when we have adequately located the unconscious ground of the analysand. Given the ability of the unconscious' ability to produce defensive distortion, and the presence of resistance and its willingness to deliberately camouflage the id derivatives just as the analytic enterprise draws close to discovery, how can the analyst discern whether her interpretive understanding has reached the essential core of the analysand's neurotic conflict, or whether it has only discovered a new level of distortion? Freud is deeply sensitive to this difficulty, and does not underestimate it. The first platform Freud turns to is a corollary of the pleasure principle. While the surface, consciousness, may seem to pursue increases in excitement, or willingly engage in unpleasurable activity, the ground, the unconscious, must necessarily obey the dictates of pleasure. Correct interpretation, then, can be distinguished by its capacity to account for this fact.

But the presence of the wish, while necessary in an adequate interpretation, is not sufficient. This is clearest in regard to dream interpretation. The dreaming reality is multilayered, and merely penetrating the surface of the dream does not ensure that its depths have been reached. Freud (1900) writes:

> It is only with the greatest difficulty that the beginner in the business of interpreting dreams can be persuaded that his task is not at an end when he has a complete interpretation in his hands–an interpretation which makes sense, is coherent and throws light upon every element of the dream's content. For the same dream may perhaps have another interpretation as well, an 'over-interpretation,' which has escaped him. It is, indeed, not easy to form any conception of the abundance of the unconscious trains of thought, all striving to find expression, which are active in our minds. Nor is it easy to credit the skill shown by the dream-work in always hitting upon forms of expression that can bear several meanings [p. 523].

Again Freud shows wariness about the ease with which the analyst can be misled to a false confidence about her findings. When we consider the generativity of the unconscious, it becomes clear that the term "dualism," when applied to the inner world, fails to capture the manifold complexity of the self. Locating the latent wish, then, cannot satisfy our need for an indication of certainty, and we must look elsewhere.

Freud offers several other indicators that might give weight to the conclusion that an interpretation is adequate. These rely on the proposition that the mind, including the unconscious, is sensible, that it follows laws of reason and meaning. Freud believes that there is a determinate meaning to be discovered in the intrasubjective world. At first glance, this stands in direct contradiction to the idea that the unconscious is insensible and ignores reality. How are these to be reconciled? Freud is clear that within the unconscious there is no capacity to separate reality from wish-driven fantasy. But it is not *that* failure in reality testing that prevents us from knowing the unconscious. Instead, it is precisely because the pleasure-driven id comes into conflict with the demands of civilization, the demands of the intersubjective reality, that it must be disguised, and these processes of concealment are coherent. While unconscious defense and its derivatives distort the unconscious wishes and conflicts, that distortion is not random. Even that which appears absurd, when decoded, is utterly sensible.

Freud's premise that the unconscious and its workings are sensible, an assumption much like Einstein's remark that "God doesn't play dice with the universe," gives him a patch of firm ground from which to locate the intrasubjective reality and to appraise the adequacy of interpretation. The first of these brings us back to the question of affect and the justification for its level of intensity. As we have stated, Freud saw affect as relatively less mutable than thought in the dream work. The solidity of affect provides an entrance point for uncovering the unconscious reality. If the dream work has transmuted the content of the latent thought into more acceptable or commonplace events, but left the affect undisturbed, than the result will be an incongruity between the intensity of the dream affect and the dream situation. We might dream that we walk into a room and suddenly are consumed by anxiety that is out of proportion to the objective situation. This breakdown of proportion in the conscious sphere is a critical clue to the unconscious. If the unconscious is sensible, then there must ultimately be a sensible origin to the extreme affect. Any adequate interpretation will reconstitute the relationship between affect and content, and make this connection conscious. Freud makes this clear when he discusses the breakdown of proportion between affect and content that is also present in hysterical symptoms. The hysteric vomits and feels extreme disgust over ordinary food; the vomiting strikes us as too extreme. Freud (1896c) writes:

> Tracing a hysterical symptom back to a traumatic scene assists our understanding only if the scene satisfies two conditions; if it possesses the relevant *suitability to serve as a determinant* and it recognizably possesses the necessary *traumatic force.* Instead of a verbal explanation, here is an example. Let us suppose that the symptom under consideration is hysterical vomiting; in that case we shall feel that we have been able to understand its causation (except for a certain residue) if the analysis traces the symptom back to an experience which *justifiably produced a high amount of disgust*—for instance, the sight of a decomposing dead body. But if, instead of this, the analysis shows us that the vomiting arose from a great fright, e.g. from a railway accident, we shall feel dissatisfied and will have to ask ourselves how it is that the fright has led to the particular symptom of vomiting. This derivation lacks *suitability as a determinant* [pp. 193–194].

The correct interpretation, then, can be measured by its ability to account for both the force and the quality of the affect. This epistemological arbiter, however, depends on the assumption that affect contains within itself an intrinsic value scale. Freud suggests that the nature and intensity of our affective experience is determined in an a priori fashion, so that everyone should respond similarly to similar affective events. And when this principle seems to fail, it is only because additional, unconscious meaning has been attached to the events. We may question, however, whether this scale of affective value is as unambiguous as Freud suggests. While basic threats to life may hold this clarity of meaning, other traumatic events are determined interpersonally. Political scandal, sporting triumph, gain their magnitude by the collective system of belief.

The mind may be sensible, but the nature of this sense does not easily disclose itself. Ultimately, Freud must turn away from these indicators of intrasubjective reality and, like a true empiricist, turn toward the utility of his treatment as an indication of his theoretical accuracy. The final arbiter of the accuracy of interpretation is whether it effects change in the patient. Freud (1916b), writing in response to criticism that his findings are merely the result of suggestive pressure, states that the accuracy of the analyst's interpretive activity is safeguarded by the need to make therapeutic progress:

> But you will now tell me that, no matter whether we call the motive force of our analysis transference or suggestion, there is a risk that the influencing of our patient may make the objective certainty of our findings doubtful. What is advantageous to our therapy is damaging to our researches. This is the objection that is most often raised against psycho-analysis, and it must be admitted that, though it is groundless, it cannot be rejected as unreasonable. If it were justified, psychoanalysis would be nothing more than a particularly well-disguised and particularly effective form of suggestive treatment and we should have to attach little weight to all that it tells us about what influences our lives, the dynamics of the mind or the unconscious. That is what our opponents believe; and in especial they think that we have 'talked' the patients into everything relating to the importance of sexual experiences—or even into those experiences themselves—after such notions have grown up in our own depraved imagination. . . . The doctor has no difficulty, of course, in making him a supporter of some particular theory and in thus making him share some possible error of his own. In this respect the patient is behaving like anyone else—like a pupil—but this only affects his intelligence, not his illness. After all, his conflicts will only be successfully solved and his resistances overcome if the anticipatory ideas he is given tally with what is real in him [p. 452].

Freud is still haunted by his early work with suggestion, although now, rather than doubted, its effects are seen everywhere. He knows, however, that the power of suggestion has limits and cures are not readily come by through its influence. But Freud has gone further than merely defending himself against the charge that his findings are the result of suggestive influence–he has made a claim about the relationship between truth and efficacy. The neurotic, he claims, will be cured only when the analyst is able to form an interpretive understanding that mirrors the intrasubjective and unconscious basis of the suffering. The link between cure and truth provides the analyst with an unambiguous test of the validity of his knowledge. If the analysand recovers, the interpretation was accurate. Yet this epistemological cornerstone, under closer inspection, conceals further uncertainty. False interpretations might provide comfort and help sustain marginal functioning. Clearly this is how Freud viewed religion–it provided a false explanation of the mind, but was still of some help. We can also imagine, and certainly those who were morally offended by Freud's view of sexuality did imagine, that having our intrasubjective reality revealed could be damaging. Even if we accept the proposition that recovery is dependent on validity, we still are left with the task of measuring recovery. How do we know when the analysand's conflicts are solved? We might answer that we recognize recovery when the presenting symptoms are removed–the hysteric is better when the paralysis of her arm is dissipated. Yet Freud himself has moved beyond this criteria of symptom relief and come to recognize the mutability of pathology. The paralysis may be lifted, but it is replaced by a neurotic transference. The problem of what constitutes health and how it is to be recognized, suggests that Freud's solution to the epistemological conundrum has merely transferred the difficulty of certainty to another realm, resolving the transference rather than overcoming it. He is involved in a circle of justification–we are cured by the truth, but we know that our position is true when it leads to cure. We cannot escape the necessity of value in the construction of our vision of health. For Freud that value concerns the capacity for genital gratification and the progression of civilization.

The Therapeutic Environment, Gratification, and Reality

Having ventured into remote territory in Freud's thought, we can now return to our starting point, the therapeutic environment and analytic action. Having developed our understanding of his views of gratification and epistemology more fully, we are in a better position to see both the roots of his technical conclusions and to evaluate how we should treat this inheritance. The breakdown in functioning that occurs in neurosis, according to Freud, occurs from the inability to complete the developmental progression toward the genital organization of libidinal energy, an organization that brings the pleasure principle under the regulation of the reality principle. The task of therapy is to detach the fixated libidinal cathexis from the internal realm of fantasy and hallucination, and reorient this energy to the external world and reality. Freud, in his therapy, hopes to draw analysands back to the world of real relationships, where actual satisfaction can occur. In this endeavor, the transference is the critical battleground, the only ground where real transformation may occur. To succeed in this work, the analyst must first control the possibility of mutiny within herself; she must bring the countertransference into check.

Perhaps above all, Freud's capacity to recognize the transference as fertile ground rather than therapeutic disaster marks his genius. Transference, then, is first distinguished by its utility for therapy. In that sense, transference is substantial. Yet what allowed Freud to embrace the transference, rather than flee from it, was his recognition of its unreality, his recognition that transference is phenomenologically continuous with the process of neurotic symptom formation. In this sense, transference is insubstantial, a mirage in the hot sand of analysis.

To understand the foundation of Freud's conviction of the transference's unreality, we must see how he framed the analytic situation. Trained as a doctor, Freud continues to see this as his essential identity even as he moves further away from the realm of biology, and toward the subjective world of the mind. His relationship to the patient, then, is clinical rather than human. At the turn of the century, the medical community regarded itself as removed from the normal emotions and passions that dominate human existence. The young girl should feel no modesty when asked to undress in front of her physician. The physician has assumed the attitude of the scientist, and so has left behind any propensity toward sexual titillation that might justify shyness. The professional identity is complete, and it transcends the personal or the passionate.

Freud feels that the therapeutic context is, in actuality, governed by the same principles. Therapy is an unreal framework for an actual relationship; it is conditioned by the principles of treatment, not relatedness. As a clinical context, its reality does not call for emotional reaction on the part of the analysand. The analyst is a doctor, not an interpersonal other, and certainly not a potential object of gratification. The analytic situation calls for no reaction other than cooperation with the scientific endeavor. The clinical identity of the analyst is guaranteed by her abstinence; she shows detached curiosity, but not affective presence. The analyst sits behind the patient and so underscores treatment's separation from ordinary life. Freud (1913a) writes about his motive for sitting out of view: "I insist on this procedure for its purpose and result are to prevent the transference from mingling with the patient's associations imperceptibly, to isolate the transference and to allow it to come forward in due course sharply defined as a resistance" (p. 134). While not directly stated, Freud suggests that by remaining invisible he can control the actual meaning of his presence, so that whatever occurs in the patient comes from projection rather than actual perception.

In normality, then, Freud expects that the patient would enter treatment with the same detached curiosity as the analyst and they would act together as scientific colleagues, bound by intellect and the desire to know. But the analysand is not normal and he needs treatment; the difficulty that constitutes the core of neurosis is precisely the inability to maintain detached curiosity. The analysand suffers because his reality testing has broken down, and the routes toward gratification are blocked. This is the seed that leads the analysand to misperceive the analytic context and relationship. Freud (1912a) writes:

> Now, our observations have shown that only a portion of these impulses which determine the course of erotic life have passed through the full process of psychical development. That portion is directed towards reality, is at the disposal of the conscious personality, and forms a part of it. Another portion of the libidinal impulses has been held up in the course of development; it has been kept away from the conscious personality and from reality, and has either been prevented from further expansion except in phantasy or has remained wholly in the unconscious so that it is unknown to the personality's consciousness. If someone's need for love is not entirely satisfied by reality, he is bound to approach every new person whom he meets with libidinal anticipatory ideas; and it is highly probable that both portions of his libido, the portion that is capable of becoming conscious as well as the unconscious one, have a share in forming that attitude.

> Thus it is a perfectly normal and intelligible thing that the libidinal cathexis of someone who is partly unsatisfied, a cathexis which is held ready in anticipation, should be directed as well to the figure of the doctor [p. 100].

As we saw in the discussion on epistemology, the unconscious is governed by the pleasure principle, and does not concern itself with the shape of reality. It wants what it wants, wherever it can get it. Under the press of the libidinal aim, the image of the doctor is entwined with past gratifying objects, and this perception is given the indication of reality. The analysand comes to misperceive the doctor as a potential source of gratification, rather than accurately perceiving her as a treatment source and scientific colleague.

While the analyst, when situated behind the analysand, observing, can clearly see the breakdown in reality testing that lies at the core of the transference, the analysand is unable to view it in this way. Instead, and this is the basis of his suffering, the analysand has the strongest conviction that the transference is real. He feels convinced that his love of the doctor, or his hate, is founded on the doctor's actual attributes, and that the only resolution to the transference that would provide satisfaction is for the transference feelings to be acted on. The hysteric insists that the analyst return his advances, the paranoiac, that the analyst acknowledge persecutory intent. The analyst's task is to assist the analysand in penetrating this erroneous attribution of reality and in coming to see that the transference is a projection from past, repressed wishes.

We are now in a position to make fuller sense of Freud's technical recommendations. The analysand has fallen ill from a breakdown in reality testing due to frustration; the developmental progression toward genital organization and accurate perception of the other has been arrested. By remaining abstinent, the analyst accomplishes two key points. First, by denying gratification the analyst avoids supporting the analysand's masturbatory tendencies. Because the analytic relationship is not real, to allow gratification would be to allow sexuality to continue to be consummated in relationship to a fantasized object. By frustrating these libidinal needs in treatment, the analyst creates a dam, and the energetic charge, denied an outlet in action, builds up until it can break through the repressive barriers and into consciousness. Abstinence, then, is dictated by the need to frustrate—only through frustration can the libidinal derivatives enter consciousness and the realm of representation.

Abstinence and frustration, though, have further work assigned to them. While the progression from action to representation is significant, it is still insufficient to bring about systematic change in the organization of the individual. These represented needs still falsely attribute reality to their cathected fantasies and project them onto the current perception of the world. The analysand must be aided in overcoming this misattribution, and in seeing the transparency of transference. This last step is the most difficult. Freud (1926) writes that the process of convincing the patient that he is "*repeating* in the form of falling in love with the analyst mental experiences which he has already been through once before" (p. 227) places the greatest demands on the physician. It is here where the "gravest" mistakes can be made. By remaining abstinent, however, staying out of view, striving to serve as a blank screen, the analyst minimizes her actual participation in the analytic relationship, and so sharpens the contrast between her neutral reality and the analysand's highly charged transference. This attempt to polish the analytic self so it reflects clearly is critical. Transference, when free of the grossest distortion, strives to make its case sensible. Freud (1905a) writes that transference feelings take advantage "of some real peculiarity in the physician's person or circumstances and [attach] themselves to that" (p. 116). By remaining silent, by avoiding emotional entanglement, these peculiarities are taken out of play, and the distorting element in the transference is revealed.

When considered at this level of analysis, the prohibition of the countertransference, the call for analytic abstinence, the view of epistemology and gratification, all seem congruent. The analytic relationship is unreal, and the hallucinatory gratification must be blocked in order both to motivate the analysand to find real sources of satisfaction and to help correct the deficiency in reality testing that has made this impossible. Yet throughout this section we have repeatedly confronted the complexity and paradox that weave through Freud's work. It would be surprising if that paradox were to suddenly terminate in such rich ground as the transference. While Freud often describes the transference as an unreal relationship (and this seems to be his core view of its epistemological status), he recognizes that the question of transference's reality is more complex. We have already seen the beginning of this recognition in his statement that transference feelings take advantage of a "real peculiarity" in the analyst's personality. The transference, then, seems to be some unspecified mixture of reality and fantasy. It exists halfway between the fantasy-based world of neurosis and the reality of health. He (1914a) writes: "The transference thus creates an intermediate region between illness and real life through which the transition from the one to the other is made" (p. 154). The "intermediate" is a point halfway between two points, but the real and the fantasized, at least in positivist terms, are utterly discontinuous. Freud (1915a) is aware of this difficulty and acknowledges that the unreality of the transference cannot be glibly accepted. He writes:

> I should now like, however, to examine these arguments with a critical eye and to raise the question whether, in putting them forward to the patient, we are really telling the truth, or whether we are not resorting in our desperation to concealments and misrepresentations. In other words: can we truly say that the state of being in love which becomes manifest in analytic treatment is not a real one? [p. 168]

He answers this question by admitting that transference love, while abnormal as a mental process, is a genuine love. To Freud's mind, all loving admits some abnormality: because it indicates diminished reality testing, is blind to the actual value of the loved object, and dismisses negative consequences. What is left to set transference love apart from other forms of loving, is its capacity to serve the resistance and the manner in which it is engendered by the treatment situation. To the extent that desire is the natural state of the organism, and the sole motive force, we must expect that this desire will be transferred to the analyst, if for no other reason than that she is the only one present. The only other option would be complete autoeroticism.

If transference has some greater connection to reality than we previously acknowledged, how does this affect Freud's technical views concerning abstinence and non-gratification as instruments for restoring reality testing? When we read his work more closely, it becomes apparent that the therapeutic relationship requires more than the dispassionate interest that has initially been described. While the goal of therapy remains the strengthening of the reality principle, Freud recognizes that reality, when held only in cognition, lacks the force to overcome the adhesion of fantasy.

Lifting repression leads to a reexperiencing of past traumas and internal conflicts. This is painful, and the ego, if left alone, has no choice but to pull away from it. The balance between pleasure and pain must be righted. Freud (1916b) is clear that what allows the ego to surmount the negative affect that is engendered by analytic exploration is the pull of the positive transference:

> At this point what turns the scale in his struggle is not his intellectual insight—which is neither strong enough nor free enough for such an achievement—but simply and solely his relation to the doctor. In so far as his transference bears a "plus" sign, it clothes the doctor with authority and is transformed into belief in his communications and explanations [p. 445].

Reality can be approached only through the intellect, but insight alone offers insufficient magnetism to draw the analysand close. The transference is the necessary affective ingredient for surmounting the displeasure self-exploration evokes. While Freud has abandoned the use of suggestion for the direct suppression of symptoms, he acknowledges that it is still in play in the therapeutic environment. Through the force of the positive transference, the analyst is able to introduce suggestions that the resistance not be heeded. In the early use of suggestion, its function was to strengthen the patient's capacity to deny his symptoms, in essence to deny the reality of his suffering. Now, however, the same process of influence is utilized to bring the analysand closer to reality. It provides the courage necessary to undertake the difficult intrasubjective exploration.

We must ask how abstinence can be reconciled with this notion of utilizing the transference as a suggestive force to overcome the resistance. The first question we face is, how is the positive transference possible in the face of an abstinent therapist? Freud is clear that the transference is the product of the unconscious. For a positive transference to exist genuine pleasure must exist in the analytic situation. This pleasure must arise either from actual factors in the analytic relationship and be based on reality, or from autoerotic satisfaction generated by the fantasy life of the analysand. Now Freud is clear that autoeroticism plays an important role, but if it is the only factor behind the positive transference, then the fate of analysis is bleak. As the analysand benefits from treatment the utilization of autoeroticism will diminish, and thereby lead to a parallel diminution of the positive transference. With this decrease, the energetic force to overcome the resistance will be sapped, and the analysis will have to come to a standstill. If, on the other hand, the positive transference has some basis in the real relationship, then the analyst's abstinence cannot have been complete.

The paradox of abstinence and the transference is even more complicated. To use suggestion is necessarily to exhibit a preference. The analyst wants the analysand to move through the resistance to a restoration of uninterrupted free association and so toward an increased capacity to know the real. Not only does the desire to cure reveal preference, but it also unmasks compulsion. The analyst actively strives to change the analysand's behavior. To the extent that influential powers are brought to bear on us, whether they be benign or coercive, affective reactions seem called for. To the extent that we benefit from this influence, we should love; and to the extent we are controlled or injured, we should hate. Through these actions the analyst becomes a real object and the demand for abstinence is not as unambiguous as it might seem on first encounter.

Countertransference and Analytic Objectivity

Having explored Freud's foundations we are ready to complete the circle and reconsider the countertransference. He refers to it by name only twice in his collected works—an extraordinary paucity. In both these instances, he prohibits the countertransference. He first writes (1910b): "We have become aware of the 'countertransference,' which arises in him as a result of the patient's influence on his unconscious feelings, and we are almost inclined to insist that he shall recognize this countertransfer in himself and overcome it" (pp. 144–145). And in a similar vein, Freud (1915a) writes about the danger of mistaking the transference for something real: "For the doctor the phenomenon signifies a valuable piece of enlightenment and a useful warning against any tendency to a countertransference which may be present in his own mind" (p. 160). In these passages, Freud is unequivocal about the need to resist the countertransference. How should we understand the nature of this prohibition? For Freud, the countertransference is literally the counterpart to the transference. In his mind, as we have seen, the transference is based on a breakdown in reality testing; it is an unreal relationship. The countertransference, then, is the parallel process in the analyst. If the analyst comes to believe that the transference is a real attraction to her person, an attraction that may be returned with sexual advances, the analyst has misperceived the nature of the transference out of the pressure of her own libidinal needs. She has fallen into unreality.

Here we must first make sense of the purpose of Freud's writings on the countertransference. He writes his technique papers at a critical juncture in the development of psychoanalysis. He has moved through the lean years when his work was largely disregarded, and he has now begun to attract general interest from the medical world and has developed a group of followers. In his technical writings, then, he has two concerns. The first is to protect the field from naive appropriation by casual readers of his theoretical work. He is concerned that doctors, reading that hysteria is caused by libidinal frustration, will justify their own search for gratification in treatment by claiming that it is in the best interest of the patient. But Freud is equally concerned about the directions taken by analysts who have trained with him. Jung has an affair with a patient, and Ferenczi has fallen in love with another. The prohibition of the countertransference is written in response to these more dramatic experiments in analytic technique. The strong phrasing, perhaps, is chosen to turn his followers away from such rash maneuvers, rather than to capture the full subtlety of Freud's own thinking about the analytic attitude.

In Freud's mind, then, the countertransference constitutes the reactivation of the analyst's unconscious, frustrated libidinal fragments in reaction to the analysand's transferential feelings. This reactivation necessarily compromises the analyst's objectivity. As we saw in the section on epistemology, the energetic presence of needs endows wishes and memory with the indication of reality, and engenders hallucinatory perception. In the realm of primary process, the self-referential desire for pleasure undercuts the possibility of gaining perspective. To the extent that the countertransference is activated, the analyst will venture interpretations not out of a correct perception of the analysand, but out of reference to herself; she will behave egoistically. Interpretations will be formed from projections or reactivated memories of the analyst's own parental imagoes; thus, therapeutic action will be conducted to gratify the analyst, not to cure the analysand.

The difficulty with countertransference remains even if we expand our definition of it. The first meaning of "countertransference" refers to the analyst's erotic response to the patient's transference. Acting on this response, consummating the transference affair, is clearly exploitive and is predicated on the self-deception of the analyst. If we expand the concept of "countertransference," however, to include the whole compass of the analyst's emotional reaction to the analysand, the necessary breakdown of objectivity remains. For most of his career, Freud views affect as arising from the backing up of libidinal energy. Affect, therefore, necessarily reflects the pressure of the analyst's sexuality on her analytic attitude. It is the primitive vestige of our evolutionary origins.

Freud (1912d) is clear that even the presence of countertransferential feelings must be overcome. To act on these feelings or to expose them to the patient constitutes only further error. He writes that the analyst, in the course of working with patients who suffer unduly from self-recrimination, may be tempted to employ self-disclosure as a way of lessening the analysand's suffering. To act on this sentiment, however, is a mistake:

> Young and eager psychoanalysts will no doubt be tempted to bring their own individuality freely into the discussion, in order to carry the patient along with them and lift him over the barriers of his own narrow personality. It might be expected that it would be quite allowable and indeed useful, with a view to overcoming the patient's existing resistances, for the doctor to afford him a glimpse of his own mental defects and conflicts and, by giving him intimate information about his own life, enable him to put himself on an equal footing. One confidence deserves another, and anyone who demands intimacy from someone else must be prepared to give it in return. But in psychoanalytic relations things often happen differently from what the psychology of consciousness might lead us to expect. Experience does not speak in favor of an affective technique of this kind. Nor is it hard to see that it involves a departure from psychoanalytic principles and verges upon treatment by suggestion. It may induce the patient to bring forward sooner and with less difficulty things he already knows but would otherwise have kept back for a time through conventional resistances. But this technique achieves nothing towards the uncovering of what is unconscious to the patient [p. 118].

To employ self-revelation is to make use of the analyst's personality and convey permission to circumvent the resistance. The analysand's ego is made stronger, more willing to expose its thoughts, by being yoked to the analyst. But this easing of the analytic strictures cannot furnish the tension necessary for impelling unconscious materials to gain the energetic charge to overcome the power of repression. For the analyst to expose herself in this way only serves to gratify the analysand, and so takes away the motivation for genuine analytic exploration. Freud continues:

> It makes him even more incapable of overcoming his deeper resistances, and in severer cases it invariably fails by encouraging the patient to be insatiable: he would like to reverse the situation, and finds the analysis of the doctor more interesting than his own. The resolution of the transference, too–one of the main tasks of the treatment–is made more difficult by an intimate attitude on the doctor's part, so that any gain there may be at the beginning is more than outweighed at the end. I have no hesitation, therefore, in condemning this kind of technique as incorrect. The doctor should be opaque to his patients and, like a mirror, should show them nothing but what is shown to him [p. 118].

To allow the patient access to the analyst's countertransference, because doing so provides gratification, feeds the greediness of the pleasure principle, further undermining the felt necessity for living life under the reality principle. To avoid this dilemma, the analyst must consistently frustrate the analysand's diverting desire to know the analyst's unconscious and countertransference. Here Freud frames his strongest prescription of abstinence when he writes that the analyst must be "opaque," like a mirror. In this prescription, Freud plants the seed for analytic rigidity in his followers, the rigidity that has been mocked in conventional portrayals of analytic technique–the analyst who sits silently, stoically, saying nothing but "hmm," or "what does that bring to mind."

The analyst who fails to see the validity of this line of reasoning, Freud might argue, has fallen prey to the resurgence of childish exhibitionism. The mature analyst will have controlled this desire to expose herself. Any successful attempt to argue for the utility of the countertransference and the possibility of revealing it to the analysand, then, must answer to Freud's charges. First we must provide an account of how the presence of countertransference does not necessarily entail the break down of analytic objectivity. Then, if that necessity can be met, we are obliged to answer the charge that revealing the countertransference is not motivated solely by the analyst's need to gratify herself, and that this exposure will not undercut the motivation of the analysand to press forward with the uncovering of the unconscious.

While in his explicit writings about the countertransference (those that mention it by name), Freud is unambiguously condemning of it, in his larger body of work he speaks about the analytic method and the conditions of childhood development in ways that are more auspicious for countertransference's value. To see this we must reconsider the range of reference he intends when he speaks about "countertransference." While what we have argued above gives good reason to believe that Freud would be suspicious of any emotional reaction in the analyst, it ultimately seems more tenable to think that he intends a narrower range of meaning. It is true that Freud strives to be a positivist, and his account of affect, on the whole, frames it as an obstacle to objectivity. But this is only part of the story. Freud also sees informational value in affect, talks about the analyst using her unconscious as a tool for interpretation, and reveals his own affective response to patients. When taken together these points must modify our understanding of Freud's view of the analytic attitude.

We will begin our exploration of these countercurrents with a consideration of the role of affect. As we have seen, while Freud frequently speaks of affect as the by-product of the pathological damming up of libido, he also sees affect as a form of information, and its presence as a higher developmental outcome than symptom formation. When affect is blocked from expression, the result is pathology. To prohibit emotion in the analyst, then, would be to insist on re-creating the strangulation that generates symptoms. Now he might argue that suppressing emotion is unhealthy, but this does not affect his technical recommendation regarding the prohibition of the countertransference. The well-analyzed analyst should no longer react to the productions of the analysand with emotions, so there would be none to suppress. But even this defense can be criticized through reference to Freud's own writings. In *The Interpretation of Dreams* (1900), he writes that dreams may suppress affect in the manifest content as a way of disguising the unconscious meaning: "If I then turn back to the dream, it not infrequently appears colourless, and without emotional tone of any great intensity. The dream-work has reduced to a level of indifference not only the content but often the emotional tone of my thoughts as well. It might be said that the dream-work brings about a *suppression of affects*" (p. 467). If the task of uncovering the dream's reality requires the resurrection of the suppressed affect, why would we assume that the same process would not apply to the analyst? In the interpretation of a dream, Freud suggests, we should be suspicious when it appears colorless. If the analyst is colorless, is opaque like a mirror, why wouldn't we have this same suspicion? We can wonder if the training analysis has purified the analyst of the need for affect or, instead, merely strengthened the defensive processes that lead to the suppression of affect.

If we now bring up Freud's second theory of anxiety and affect, where emotion acts as a signal of danger situations, we have further cause to question the prohibition. When viewed as a signal, rather than as merely an energetic buildup, affect takes on a more cognitive dimension. We have to ask, then, why wouldn't the countertransference, when defined as the affective reaction of the analyst, be fertile ground for the formation of analytic interpretation? The analyst's affect could be seen as a way of knowing about the analysand. This line of reasoning is not entirely foreign to Freud. While he adamantly rejects the countertransference, he nonetheless suggests that rational thought alone is inadequate to form a full analytic understanding of the analysand. This is surprising from a positivist, one who has written that pure thought is the most reliable way of knowing reality. But it should not be unexpected given his writings about the process of self-exploration. To form a deep understanding of the analysand's unconscious, the analyst, Freud (1913c) writes, must turn to her own unconscious: "I have had good reason for asserting that everyone possesses in his own unconscious an instrument with which he can interpret the utterances of the unconscious in other people" (p. 320).

Freud suggests that the empathic connection between individuals is formed through the ties of the unconscious, a form of instinctual knowing of the other. Now if the unconscious of the analysand acts on the unconscious of the analyst, how is the analyst to become aware of this effect? Certainly not directly through the rational voice. The unconscious does not know that language. What is the signal then? I suggest it must be in affect. The unconscious, the id, is instinctual in energy and makes itself felt through feeling states. The unconscious speaks in the voice of desire, of frustration, of love and anger. If this is true, we must find a way to reconcile Freud's prohibition of the countertransference with his suggestion that the unconscious is a fertile source of interpretation.

Perhaps the most consistent way of accomplishing this reconciliation is by narrowing the definition of countertransference. We must, however, do this with caution and uncertainty. Revisionist accounts always bend the truth. When he writes about the countertransference, Freud seems to be speaking about somewhat circumscribed therapeutic actions. He is concerned about analysts taking sexual advantage of their analysands, or confusing projection with actuality. If we narrow the definition of countertransference so that it refers to the erotic response of the analyst to the analysand, a response that engenders a lapse in the analyst's reality testing, we may be closer to Freud's intent.

The task for the analyst, under this definition, is not to avoid affect altogether and be purified of human subjectivity, but to modulate these energies. The analyst must find a way to keep her affective reaction within bounds, so that it may serve as a signal rather than act as an energetic pressure generating hallucination, or displeasure that necessitates repression. If contained, affect provides the point of entry to the analyst's unconscious, and her unconscious has means of perceiving the analysand that are not available to her conscious thought.

For Freud to prohibit all emotion in the analyst would also expose him to charges of inconsistency. Not only is the absence of libidinal or unconscious processes impossible under his theoretical scheme, his experience with patients provided him with ample opportunity to observe his own countertransferential reaction. In his work with patients, Freud repeatedly struggles with both positive and negative countertransference. He voices frustration, distaste, sympathy, and moral judgment. In the section on epistemology we saw how Freud sees "practical aims" as the critical threat to the pure objectivity of the observer. When we strive to move in a particular direction, the wish is activated and misperception through emotional pressure readily ensues.

At the beginning of his career, Freud is brimming with practical aims. He needs to make a living, he has dreams of becoming famous, and he wishes to prove his worth to unreceptive seniors. As his work gains recognition, these goals are largely met, and recede. To the degree that the clinical project matters to him, however, he cannot completely escape the press of practical aim. To work with patients, and to care about doing it well, is to hold to the practical goal of helping the patient. Freud is motivated to be of use, and this provides the fuel for emotional reaction. When patient's resist treatment, adhere to their neurosis despite Freud's best efforts, he is affected emotionally. We can see this in Freud's (1909b) work with the Rat Man: "I had revealed the element of revenge against me and had shown him that by refusing to tell me and by giving up the treatment he would be taking a more outright revenge on me than by telling me" (p. 281). For the Rat Man to deny Freud the opportunity to bring the treatment to a successful completion is an act of hostility, an act that causes him to suffer. This same sense of being wronged by the patient is evident in even more dramatic form in his work with Dora, who, feeling Freud's lack of empathy, flees treatment. Freud experiences this as a painful frustration. Discussing Dora's negative transference and aggressive motive, Freud (1905a) writes: "For how could the patient take a more effective revenge than by demonstrating upon her own person the helplessness and incapacity of the physician?" (p. 120). The patient, when all else fails to move the analyst, can force countertransferential affect by frustrating the one irreducible analytic motive, the motive to help. Freud tries to mitigate the effect of this countertransference at the end of treatment when he tells Dora that he has forgiven her for her vengeful behavior: "I promised to forgive her for having deprived me of the satisfaction of affording her a far more radical cure for her troubles" (1905a, p. 122). But this very forgiveness belies the presence of his wounded feelings. There can be no cause for forgiving where no damage has been done.

Freud's own countertransference can be seen in his statements about the frustration he feels when treatments become stuck and about the difficulty the analyst encounters in managing the transference. But perhaps most dramatic are his writings on the relative moral value of analytic patients. His capacity to extend neutral understanding to patients has limits. He (1893–1895) writes: "I cannot imagine bringing myself to delve into the psychical mechanism of hysteria in anyone who struck me as low-minded and repellent, and who, on closer acquaintance, would not be capable of arousing human sympathy" (p. 265). This is a sentiment he repeats ten years later when he states that analysis is only appropriate for valuable characters (1904, p. 254). The difficulty of treating patients, of helping them work through the resistance, often leads Freud to write about the process in military terms. The analytic situation, in his mind, is comparable to a battle ground, with the analyst opposing the forces of the analysand's unconscious. In his work with Dora, Freud clearly struggles to force her to accept his interpretations. In his (1914a) technical paper, he continues to describe the treatment process as fraught with struggle; the negative transference makes it inescapable: "From then onwards the resistances determine the sequence of the material which is to be repeated. The patient brings out of the armory of the past the weapons with which he defends himself against the progress of the treatment—weapons which we must wrest from him one by one" (p. 151).

Clearly, in Freud's experience, the analytic relationship is not peaceful. It is difficult to imagine the analyst maintaining the calm demeanor of the objective scientist in the midst of such pitched battles.

Freud's view of the countertransference, I have argued, is founded on paradox. When we look beyond the surface, we find exception and complication: this is its richness. In concluding this section on Freud, then, it seems appropriate to end with a final paradox. Freud's proscription of the countertransference, his insistence on analytic abstinence, his edict that the analyst remain opaque, reveal nothing, all stem from (although in ways are countermanded by) his view of gratification and epistemology. In his writings about the vicissitudes of development, however, Freud repeatedly talks about the emergence of curiosity in the child. Children are driven by a kind of epistemological instinct, a need to know. He first writes about this drive in his *Three Essays On the Theory of Sexuality* (1905b) and later expands upon this discussion in his case history of Little Hans in his (1908c) paper on children's sexual researches. Hans, he states, strives to make sense of his own genital makeup. He wants to know the difference between men and women, and how this difference is connected to the creation of babies. This emergent sexual curiosity is the basis of the more generalized thirst for knowledge. In essence, children begin life as positivists, as empirically-based observers. When adults dissemble in front of children, however, this natural tendency toward rational investigation is damaged. The child is caught between his love of truth and his love of the parent. Given the child's dependency, the object love triumphs over the epistemological, and the drive toward truth is sacrificed.

This sacrifice is critical in preparing the soil for neurosis. Symptoms and character disorder, Freud (1905b) argues, arise when fantasy supplants reality; a connection to the real is subverted by masturbatory pleasure. When the child's epistemological striving is frustrated, it leads to permanent damage: "It therefore follows that the efforts of the childish investigator are habitually fruitless, and end in a renunciation which not infrequently leaves behind it a permanent injury to the instinct for knowledge" (p. 197). In response to habitual frustration, the ego comes to anticipate the displeasure that will follow from investigative searching and renounces this instinctual drive, settling for hallucinatory pleasures in its place. When parents dissemble with children, tell them false stories about sexuality, not only is the epistemological instinct damaged, but the relationship with the parent is undermined. He (1907) writes: "The customary answers given to the child in the nursery damage his genuine instinct of research and as a rule deal the first blow, too, at his confidence in his parents. From that time on he usually begins to mistrust grown-up people, and to keep his most intimate interests secret from them" (p. 136). The concealment perpetrated by the parents creates the motivation for the child to harbor secrets of his own.

We must ask, then, given Freud's acute awareness of the damage done by concealment to curiosity and reality testing, why he insists that the analyst enact a parallel process. When the analyst remains opaque, when she refuses to acknowledge her own unconscious or countertransferential reactions, why would this be any less damaging to the analysand than the original traumatic events in childhood? I suggest that analytic abstinence, in its strong form, is a re-creation of this initial blow to the instinct for knowledge. By remaining opaque we further stress the analysand's reality testing, force him to create false explanations for his intuitive sense of our emotional state, undermining the analytic alliance and creating more distrust and secretiveness in the analysand. The parallel between these early developmental events and the analytic situation does not go unnoticed by Freud, yet he draws the opposite conclusion. He (1914a) explicitly draws the comparison when he writes about the management of the transference. In the transference, memory of the past is represented by action in the present: the patient "does not remember how he came to a helpless and hopeless deadlock in his infantile sexual researches; but he produces a mass of confused dreams and associations, complains that he cannot succeed in anything and asserts that he is fated never to carry through what he undertakes" (p. 150). Freud sees the re-creation of the past in the present, and the frustration the analysand feels. Yet rather than seeing this as an argument for self-disclosure by the analyst, he views it as further justification for abstinence. The analysand transfers his frustrated epistemological feelings onto the analyst, but the transfer is misguided and inappropriate, another example of the distortion in reality testing. By remaining abstinent the analyst can draw more clearly the separation between the analyst's reality and the patient's projection. Freud, despite the evidence from his own emotional reaction to patients, despite the thrust of his theoretical work, maintains that the analyst can overcome the pressure of the unconscious, and achieve a position of genuine neutrality and objectivity that is free from affect.

Again, however, we must turn to Freud's own work to argue with him. He argues for the necessity of the transference—only through the transference can the analysand gain an emotional experience of his unconscious that will give him a felt sense of the interpretations' reality. The transference, when worked through, provides the conviction that gives an analytic cure durability, a durability that suggestion lacked. He (1912a) writes:

> It cannot be disputed that controlling the phenomena of transference presents the psychoanalyst with the greatest difficulties. But it should not be forgotten that it is precisely they that do us the inestimable service of making the patient's hidden and forgotten erotic impulses immediate and manifest. For when all is said and done, it is impossible to destroy anyone *in absentia* or *in effigie* [p. 108].

He suggests that nothing can be done "in absentia." The transference is critical because it makes things present. Freud's drive theory and the stress it places on the wish-driving fantasy, lead him to believe that what must be present in the analytic situation is the wish, not the object. Yet to the extent that we admit interpersonal as well as intrasubjective forces as the determinants of our character and suffering, an alternative reading of these passages—a mistaken one in terms of Freud's intent—may not be without substance. For the complex to become activated, to be present, the critical object must also be present. We cannot change our relationship to central objects only within our head—they must become present. When we have lived with cruelty or manipulation, we cannot gain faith in other possibilities when they are represented only in effigy. We need a real relationship that does not stop at the false front of the therapeutic persona. We need analysts who do not practice in absentia.

We began this chapter by remarking on the brevity of Freud's technical papers, a brevity that seems to leave them suspended above the rigorous argument of his theoretical papers. In this chapter I have tried to demonstrate the basis for those papers and their connection to his larger theoretical work. In part, Freud prescribes abstinence and proscribes the countertransference out of his cultural context. He comes from an academic community grounded in positivism and a social community wrestling with sexuality. The image of the analyst as a reserved scientist protects the credibility of the field. Yet Freud's technical recommendations are also conditioned by his early therapeutic experiences and his theoretical positions regarding gratification and epistemology. His work with suggestion and catharsis gives Freud firsthand experience of the danger inherent in therapeutic activity. It increases the intractability of the resistance and obscures the separation between fantasy and reality. Furthermore, to act in the therapeutic environment is to risk gratifying the analysand's unconscious wishes. When gratified, the pressure to become conscious is removed, and the motivation to work through difficult resistances is undercut. Finally, his theory of perception leads Freud to adopt an epistemological view that by aligning himself with "pure thought," thought uncontaminated by practical aim, he could achieve a genuine objectivity. While we may disagree with Freud's conclusions, we must admire his rigor and breadth. Before we too easily adopt a more permissive view of countertransference, we must be willing to address these questions.

CHAPTER FIVE

The Evolution of Psychoanalytic Technique after Freud

In the existing literature on countertransference, the interval between Freud's (1911–1915) *Papers on Technique* and the resurgence of interest in countertransference in the 1950s tends to be spoken of as a kind of latency period for the development of countertransference theory. Langs (1918), in his encyclopedic collection of papers, *Classics in Psychoanalytic Technique,* writes that after Freud's dismissive comments on countertransference, there "was therefore a rather long hiatus, during which little consideration was given to this subject in the psychoanalytic literature" (p. 137). Given the apparent accuracy of this statement–virtually nothing was said about countertransference in the published journals and texts during those forty years–it might seem sensible to move directly to the current literature on the countertransference. This intermediate period in psychoanalytic history, however, is more than just a fallow one and to ignore it would be a mistake. In a field formed from the clinical encounter, this historical material is our data. I argue that this record demonstrates the untenability of abstinence. The clinical papers from this time, even when not speaking overtly of the countertransference, reveal the struggle analysts faced in trying to make sense of their emotional reactions to the analytic encounter. These papers chart the technical difficulties and clinical failures that exerted evolutionary pressure on the analytic method. They reveal that patients were not readily cured of their difficulties and that they required more than interpretation and abstinence on the part of the analyst. What is missing in the current literature on countertransference is a discussion of how the clinical events during the time between Freud's *Papers on Technique* (1911–1915) and the 1950s propelled psychoanalysis toward the eventual recognition and acceptance of countertransference.

Clinical experience, I argue, demanded revision in the understanding of countertransference. The capacity to make complete sense of this experience, however, was not immediate. Analysts always see their patients' behavior through the lens of theory. The progression in the understanding of countertransference, then, proceeds more like a game of leapfrog between theory and clinical practice—first one, then the next, leaping over the other. As theory changes, patients can be seen in new ways, and as patients refuse to cooperate with analytic expectation, pressure mounts for theory to change. In the inching-forward process of countertransference theory there were two primary seeds of change. First, there was the growing influence of Freud's structural theory. The structural theory, with its emphasis on early experience, identification, aggression and the informational function of affect, acts to focus attention on the relational aspects of the analytic process. It calls attention to the real effects analysand and analyst exert on each other, and ultimately, through the mediation of object-relations and interpersonal theory, lends theoretical weight to revisionist countertransference positions. Second, there was the growing body of clinical experience: the patients who were encountered and the difficulties they posed to technique upset complacency. Patients, through their resistance, demanded that psychoanalysis mature in its clinical technique.

Charting the historical sequence in a field as complex as psychoanalysis is a difficult task. The evolution does not adhere to a steady chronological progression. Psychoanalysis does not simply move from drive and abstinence toward relationship and provision. Instead, as it moves forward it must constantly balance the tension between gratification and abstinence, between provision and stillness. The historical narrative is inherently circuitous and to establish a coherent argument for the countertransference we will need to elucidate the central themes behind the progression of psychoanalytic theory and technique. First, however, I want to provide a brief overview of the chronological sequence in psychoanalytic history.

The progression of analytic theory and technique gains momentum as Freud's work attracts an expanding group of followers. These first analysts—Abraham, Ferenczi, Nunberg (1915–1926), among others—try to implement Freudian technique in a fairly literal way. Through interpretations based on the narrative of drive, they translate the analysand's symptoms. It is an intellectual approach to analytic practice and it leads to sterile encounters. In response, analysts bring forward more affectively active approaches to the analysand. We can see this in Ferenczi's (1919b) experiments with active techniques and mutual analysis, and in Reich's (1933) work on character analysis. These methods are successful in arousing a more engaged response from the analysand, but they create iatrogenic impasses. The excessive activity by the analyst clouds the transferential waters and reveals an attempt to compel or seduce the analysand to change.

These impasses lead to a second round of analytic revision. In the work of the ego psychologists, Freudian technique reaches its maturity. Writers such as Anna Freud, Glover, Fenichel, and Sterba (1938–1952)—through their critique of manipulative and gratificatory practice—reassert the necessity of neutrality. In their accounts of analytic technique, however, the understanding of neutrality is formulated on more subtle and durable lines than were the previous, simplistic methods of rigid abstinence. It is only when this new version of neutrality has been understood, made a solid part of the clinical repertoire, that a new understanding of countertransference and its potential can emerge. At the same time that ego psychology comes to the fore, however, Klein's (1932–1964) and Winnicott's (1947–1971) work in England give rise to the object-relations school and the middle school of thought. In addition, Sullivan's work in the United States (1924–1964) initiates the interpersonal school of analysis. These schools take an explicitly more relational approach to development and the problems of clinical technique. During the last three decades relational models have increasingly dominated the field of psychoanalysis. They have paved the way for a more extensive consideration of the intersubjective forces in the analytic encounter, and for an appreciation of how the countertransference can function as a source of information and action.

Roughly speaking, then, the progression in the field moves from Freud's drive model to modern relational accounts of motivation (Greenberg and Mitchell, 1983), from the prohibition of countertransference to its recognition as being central to the clinical palette. Increasingly, the analyst's capacity for pure objectivity and the necessity for strict abstinence have been questioned. The criticisms of classical theory and technique are now well established and new paradigms for practice have emerged. These new approaches to clinical work, however, are still taking shape. It is not an easy process to step past what is archaic in the field while struggling to grasp what is essential in the history of psychoanalytic understanding.

Freud's Unfinished Legacy (1915–1939)

Although Freud's *Papers on Technique* (1911–1915) were completed by 1915, he continued to revise his theory of development and mental functioning until his death in 1939. This gap between the theoretical foundation for his technical recommendations and his mature theory left it to those who followed to realize the technical implications of his later work. In his last two decades, Freud developed the structural theory, revised his understanding of affect, and changed his view of motivation to include the primacy of aggression. These revisions each had a profound effect on the field, and changed how analysts perceived their patients. By changing what could be seen, Freud's mature theory changed how analysts understood the therapeutic process and the curative factor and, finally, how they experienced themselves and their countertransferences.

After his technical papers Freud's first major revision to his theoretical structure is the creation of the structural model. In his tripartite model Freud moves beyond the simple vertical division between conscious and unconscious, and maps out the more complex horizontal division among the id, ego, and superego. The structural model, with its emphasis on introjection and early Oedipal experience, necessarily directs attention to relational factors in development and pathology. It represents a shift away from an exclusive focus on id energies and libido. Under this model the nature of suffering becomes more complicated. Although Freud initially understood suffering to stem from the experience of frustrated desire, he now sees it in more variegated form. We suffer not only from the repression of instinctual wish, but from the internalization of external prohibition as it takes shape in the superego. The superego adds guilt to frustration as another source of suffering. The patient, then, is not only libidinous in the transference, but self-punitive in anticipation of the analyst's reprisals. The structural theory—although Freud would not agree with this implication—reemphasizes the significance of trauma in the development of pathology. The superego becomes the repository of civilization's vicissitudes, the imprint of family cruelty. While Freud ultimately returns to a more constitutional model of personality development, the appeal of this environmental model continues to exert influence on the psychoanalytic field. This emphasis on relationships and how they influence the course of personality development, has decisive effects on the next generation of analytic practitioners. It leads them to ask how they participate in the introjective experiences that shape the superego, and to consider how analysis can modulate its punitive tendencies. If relational experience had created its harsh injunctions, then perhaps a new relationship could revise it. This is an idea that subtly reopens the issue of abstinence in analytic technique.

The second critical change in Freud's theory, a change that had been implicitly working its way to consciousness, coalesces with the publication of his (1926) *Inhibition, Symptoms, and Anxiety.* In this work, as we have outlined, he moves away from his original view of affect as the toxic residue of undischarged libido, and grants it a more pivotal role as an informational signal. Anxiety is now seen as a signal of danger; it provides information, processed by the unconscious, about the world and emerging id impulses. Affect is thus transformed: It is no longer merely an obstacle to accurate cognition; it becomes a potential guide to correct action. With the advent of signal anxiety, the ego—formerly the weak mediator between the id and the external world, between the id and the superego—takes on greater strength. It now has the energy of affect through which to exert its influence. If affect plays an informational role for the patient, consistency demands that we question what information affect might provide to the analyst. Freud's more positive view of affect creates a perspective from which his followers eventually rework their understanding of countertransference. Analysts eventually come to see the countertransference, the analyst's affectivity, as more than subjective residue; they come to see the countertransference as an avenue of perception, another means of knowing the analysand.

The last major change in Freud's work concerns his view of motivation and the primacy of aggression. Early in his work, Freud sought to explain conflict by placing the id impulses of the libido against the self-preservative drives of the ego. This opposition, however, failed to provide adequate explanation for the growing body of clinical observation. Patients regularly developed negative transferences, resisted the rule of free association and the clinical process, and showed negative therapeutic reactions. To explain these results, Freud revised his model of motivation, and substituted Thanatos for the ego instincts in opposition to the libidinal instincts. This emerging focus on aggression and the negative transference led analysts to pay increasing attention to the resistance in the analytic process. The act of attending, however, is not neutral, and tends to heighten the expressed intensity of the negative reaction. Patients begin to show more and more overt hostility to the analyst. Now analysts, rather than struggling with the demands of the erotic transference, must confront the rigors of hate. Analysts begin to feel attacked. Positive emotion is more readily modulated than negative emotion. While we are the objects of a positive transference, we are likely to feel flattered or needed. The countertransferential response to this transference is more easily contained, and in its modulated form is less insistent on recognition. In the face of the negative transference, however, we more readily react with fear or rage. These negative countertransference responses have sharper edges, and are less easily modulated. They insist that we recognize them. The analysts who come after Freud, paying attention to the negative transference and signs of resistance, have a harder time ignoring the reality of the countertransference. They can no longer defend the metaphor of the analyst as surgeon and this leads them to ultimately rework their understanding of the significance of the countertransference.

In Freud's mature theory, his view of health and pathology becomes more complicated. Increasingly, it no longer is tenable to view health simply as the absence of repression. Abend (1989), in his paper on the evolution of countertransference theory, writes that these changes in theory were critical in laying the foundation for a new theory of countertransference:

> One factor that I believe should be regarded as an essential, albeit indirect antecedent of the alteration of our view of countertransference is the introduction of the structural theory. . . . Though it would take all of thirty years, or perhaps even longer, to be acknowledged, the intellectual nucleus was put in place for a revised, improved conceptual grasp of the relationship between normality and pathology, of character traits and symptom formation, of adaptation, sublimation, object relationships, and psychic development. The view that Freud held at the outset of his research that neurosis is a sequestered area of abnormality in an otherwise healthy personality, which held us in its appealing grip for so long, would eventually have to yield to the more realistic assessment of the complex and variable functioning of the psychic apparatus, in analyst and patient alike, that holds sway today [p. 377].

Freud's mature theory implicitly includes a view of health that is based on the developmental acquisition of skill and structure. The capacity to procure gratification in the sphere of reality is no longer simply dependent on the absence of repression. It requires the formation of a tempered superego, the capacity to utilize signal affect, and the creation of adaptive ego defenses. The subtlety of health in this mature view is captured in Nunberg's (1928) catalogue of the effect of psychoanalysis: "The energies of the id become more mobile, the superego more tolerant, the ego freer of anxiety and the synthetic function of the ego is restored" (p. 204). This move to an active view of health opens the analytic field to a new understanding of therapeutic action. The task of analysis is no longer simply to remove an obstacle to health, to lift repression; instead, it must somehow aid the analysand in correcting the internal structure of her personality, in gaining the skills that are the prerequisite for adequate functioning. The analyst who takes this seriously must consider the question of supplementation. The field must finally ask is there something we must give to analysands, and if the answer is yes, then what is the nature of that provision? Freud's increasingly sophisticated view of health ultimately leads the field to reexamine the question of abstinence in technique. How is this attempt to provide active help to be reconciled with the technical insistence on abstinence leading to insight? The effort to answer this question plays a critical role in shaping the development of analytic technique. If supplementation plays a role in analytic cure, then the use of the analyst's affectivity, his countertransference, becomes plausible.

These changes in Freud's theoretical position lay the foundation for the continuing evolution of the analytic movement. Freud's followers draw on this work as they attempt to understand patients and develop a therapeutically effective technique. They focus on superego development, pay attention to affect and aggression, and struggle with the resistance. It is this next generation of analysts that we must now consider.

The Impact of Applied Technique (1919–1926)

Psychoanalysis, for all its forays into theory, cannot escape the return to the consulting room; the analyst must sit down again with his patients, try to be of help, listen to their complaints. No matter how elegant the stories we tell ourselves through theory, no matter how plausible our technical recommendations, they have no durability if they fail to provide the working analyst with a sense of efficacy. The question of efficacy, however, is not simple. Analysts are conditioned for the long haul; clinical theory predicts resistance and reversals on the road to recovery. We expect, then, to have to endure periods without apparent progress. But these caveats cannot change the necessity of experienced efficacy. Eventually, to tolerate the demands of the analytic setting, we must feel that we know what we are doing and have confidence that we are proceeding toward a better outcome. The modern analyst can endure much—can sit with raging clients, endure long periods of disconnection, even tolerate uncertainty and confusion—because he has a sense of the meaning of these activities, and has a belief in how the current process will eventually lead to change. When that confidence is lost, however, the analytic situation becomes unbearable. If the analysis is not proceeding toward cure, then it is not proceeding as it should, and the human tendency in the face of lurking failure is to look for an object to blame. The analyst, caught in the grip of failing expectations, has limited choices in assigning blame. He can hold the patient responsible, blame her for refusing to get well, for not following the therapeutic contract; he can hold himself responsible, question his understanding of psychoanalysis, examine his personality for limitations or, finally, he can question his inherited theory and technique. This final choice is the act that leads to revision in psychoanalysis. I suggest that to trace the evolution of psychoanalytic history and technique is to see how it is driven forward by analysts' reaction to the painful countertransferential feeling of the failure of cure.

After years of working in relative isolation, kept company only by Fliess and an increasingly estranged Breuer, Freud, with the beginning of the Wednesday Psychological Society in 1902, began to attract a cadre of followers. The movement grew from this nucleus as Freud's texts gained notoriety and attracted adherents in more distant European towns. These early followers of Freud began practicing as analysts with an extraordinary paucity of information or training. Some, like Stekel, had undergone short analyses with Freud and had participated in the Wednesday seminars. This marked the upper end of analytic preparation. Those who lived in foreign countries had even less training. Some physicians began conducting "analyses" on the basis of having read only a few of Freud's texts. These first analysts often took a literal understanding of Freud's work to their practice. They expected patients to bring in dreams for analysis, and the analyst to then provide the translation that would uncover the unconscious significance. The physician's cognitive presentation of the unconscious, they expected, would lift the repressive barrier, drain off the disturbing cathexis, and restore the patient to health. But not remarkably, this expectation was not matched in reality. This kind of simplistic understanding and practice of psychoanalysis led Freud to undertake his *Papers on Technique* (1911–1915), and led to greater awareness of the need for affectively engaged clinical interaction and for a period of working through.

During this initial period in analytic history, the first generation of analysts after Freud had to catch up with his understanding. Abraham (1919) and Ferenczi (1919a & b) joined the analytic fold, and after a decade of study began publishing their own papers on technique. In reading these papers, what becomes clear is that these analysts (and, it seems safe to assume, their peers) were struggling with patients who failed to meet the expectations engendered by the analytic contract. For these early analysts, analysis cured through the process of interpretation and reconstruction of genetic material. But for the analyst to proceed with this work, the patient had to fulfill her commitment to free associate. These analysts informed their patients in the first session of the fundamental rule: they were to say everything that came to mind. In return, and here the bargain moves from the explicit to the implicit, the analyst agreed to remain implacable and to interpret the unconscious, libidinal transference that they fully expected would develop. In essence, the analyst, through interpretation, would correct the patient's misperception of the analyst and would help the patient see the analyst as a present, professional object, rather than a past, parental object. But patients, less cooperative than proper in bourgeois society, failed to honor this bargain. They developed negative transferences, showed resistance, and found manifold ways to oppose free association. In breaking the fundamental rule, patients quickly threw analysts back onto feelings of disorientation and uncertainty. Abraham (1919) describes this difficulty:

> When we begin to give a patient psycho-analytic treatment we make him acquainted with its fundamental rule to which he has to adhere unconditionally. The behaviour of each patient in regard to that rule varies. In some cases he will easily grasp it and carry it out without particular difficulty; in others he will frequently have to be reminded of the fact that he has to make free associations; and in all cases we

> meet at times with a failure to associate in this way. Either he will produce the result of his reflected thoughts or say that nothing occurs to him. In such a situation the hour of treatment can sometimes pass without his producing any material whatever in the way of free association. . . .
>
> Whereas in most of our cases we meet with a resistance of this kind which appears and disappears by turns, there is a smaller group of neurotics who keep it up without interruption during the whole of their treatment [p. 83].

Those patients who consistently fail to free associate, a group that comes to be labeled "narcissistic," upset the expectations and complacency of the early analysts. In Abraham's view, they have refused to provide material for the analyst to operate on.

Part of this confusion between analysts' expectations and analysands' actions stemmed from the significance each group assigned to free association and the analytic relationship. As we traced in the section on Freud, the analytic community saw itself as the representatives of science, not as part of the interpersonal weave of the human community. The relationship between doctor and patient was professional, and so there was no rational cause for modesty. Under this understanding, the request to free associate was the moral equivalent of a doctor asking his patient to "open wide and say 'ah.'" It was value-neutral, merely a method of research. But for the patient, free association (and here we move to a more modern conception of it) is a demand to place oneself at the mercy of another, and it requires a full measure of vulnerability. For these patients, implacability on the analysts' part was not fair compensation for vulnerability on their own.

In reaction to this imbalance, patients invent elaborate means to circumvent the fundamental rule. They speak without pause, arrange their material to present themselves in a better light, or even jump up from the couch (Abraham, 1919). With Ferenczi, always a more permissive analytic presence, patients stretch the analytic contract in even more flamboyant ways. In his article "On the Technique of Psycho-analysis," Ferenczi (1919a) describes patients who resort to producing only senseless associations or meaningless sounds, claiming that this is what comes to them in free association, or another patient who acts out her free association (with a show of logical consistency that reflects the very insistent quality in which the fundamental rule was first described to her) by jumping up and kissing Ferenczi. And finally, in the clearest sign of the hate engendered by the oppressive weight of the analytic contract, there are the patients who ask "What, though, if it occurred to them to get up suddenly and run away, or to maltreat the doctor physically, to kill him, to smash a piece of furniture, etc.?" (pp. 92–93).

The early analysts, in trying to master a difficult task, reified Freud's technical recommendations. Freud's recommendation for analytic abstinence, one filled with complexity and exception as we have seen, is taken at face value. The analysts strive to actually behave like a blank screen. What has happened, in part, is that Freud's technical recommendations—initially designated to protect the patient—have become a kind of rigid abstinence and demand for exposure that act as a source of humiliation for patients. Regardless of the particular form of resistance, however, what is clear is that the analyst and analysand have failed to form an alliance that allows them to penetrate the defensive surface. This failure leads to analytic sterility. These early analysts failed to attend adequately to the conditions that foster a sense of safety, and in their eagerness elicited strong resistance that was not easy to bear.

From this perspective we can say that all of these early analysts are implicitly describing their own countertransference. While on the surface Abraham and Ferenczi write about their patients' behavior and manifestations of resistance, if we pay closer attention we can sense that this form of resistance captures their attention because it evokes a strong countertransferential response. They are struggling to avoid an uncomfortable feeling of incompetence. The most direct route to self-protection is to project the blame back onto the patient. Abraham (1919) shows this tendency in his description of the narcissistic patient who refuses to free associate. Rather than sensing the fear in the patient, he sees the resistance as a sign of self-indulgent gratification: "The tendency to regard a curative measure merely as an opportunity for obtaining pleasure and to neglect its real purpose must be regarded as a thoroughly childish characteristic" (p. 84). In designating the resistant patient "childish," Abraham has stumbled away from neutrality and compassion, and resorted to moralistic perception. We can see how the transcendent view of morality persists in his view of gratification. This reversion to moralism deserves our understanding and asks us to remember the difficulty the early analysts faced. But understanding does not preclude questioning how this negative countertransference manifested itself in the analytic situation.

Abraham concludes his article by saying: "I certainly have the impression that it is easier to overcome such narcissistic resistances now that I make known to these patients the nature of their resistances at the very beginning of the treatment" (p. 88). While we cannot recover the words with which Abraham framed these explanations, we can only guess at his range of tact and expect that some of his disdain for the patient's childishness made itself felt.

The tendency to blame the patient for frustrated analytic ambitions takes even clearer shape in statements that the impasses in analytic therapy stem from the patient's desire to remain ill. Reich (1933), in a pivotal work on character analysis, describes this tendency to resort to blame in the face of a patient who refuses to free associate: "And finally, almost always, the idea—which was used as an alibi—that the patient simply did not want to get well or that he was 'all too narcissistic'" (p. 258). What Reich points out is that the obstacle to collaboration in the patient, the resistance, rather than being seen as something from which the patient suffers, rather than being treated analytically, is seen as something selfishly willed by the patient and is treated moralistically. In the face of resistance, understood under this reprobative shading of the transcendent, the analyst has few choices. He can resign or he can confront the patient with her fault. This move to confront can be seen in Nunberg's (1926) paper on "The Will to Recovery":

> Another patient, who was abused, tormented and humiliated by his wife and yet could not leave her, wished that analysis, which he underwent submissively, should bring him to the point of resolving to get a separation. When, however, it was revealed that he was excessively passive and had strong fantasies of being beaten and bound, he ceased to come for treatment [pp. 190–191].

In this passage, Nunberg seems to be utterly unmoved by the patient's flight from treatment. It is as though he feels that he did what he could; the patient died, but that lies in the hands of God. What is clear in these earliest technical papers is that the analytic process, as it was understood from Freud, had notable limits. Patients came for treatment, analysis was begun, but change did not occur. Abstinence and interpretation as practiced led to resistance rather than cure. And in the face of these emergent negative transferences on the part of patients, the press of a negative countertransference was difficult to resist.

The absence of success in these early cases, coupled with the forbidden presence of the negative countertransference, pressured the field to move from blaming the patient to questioning technique. The field had to reexamine its understanding of neutrality and abstinence. It is this pressure that leads Ferenczi to embark on his experiments with technique.

Ferenczi's Humanistic Experiment (1919–1932)

In a field that begins with Freud, a Ferenczi was bound to follow. Freud, for all his courage and intellectual integrity, retains a core of propriety and adherence to authority that draws an unseen boundary around technical exploration. He shows a formality of technique that preserves distance between analyst and analysand. Yet even more critical in the shaping of his technique is the inaugural character of his efforts. As the progenitor of analysis, the role of the analysand must remain a stranger to him. Freud analyzes himself, but he does not know the vulnerability of being analyzed by another. Here, Ferenczi—Freud's heir, antithesis, and remedy—enters the analytic field. Innately more affectionate than Freud, more wounded in his self-esteem, Ferenczi is in the position of the one who comes second. He was analyzed briefly by Freud and for the rest of his life wrestles with his relationship to Freud and struggles to find some form of closeness to his former analyst. In this sense, Ferenczi is the first analyst who remembers his affinity with the analysand, remembers his own analysis and its difficulties. The memory of his struggle with Freud, coupled with his own innate sensitivity to the analysand and his acute desire to be of help, lead Ferenczi to undertake radical experiments concerning the limits of the analytic relationship and the reciprocity between analyst and analysand. With the publication of Ferenczi's clinical diary in 1988, it has become apparent that Ferenczi explored issues in the use of the countertransference far in advance of his era. These experiments—his use of both active and passive techniques, his use of mutual analysis with the patient RN—point out both the perils and potential of an active use of the countertransference. By taking up Ferenczi's work here, we begin to establish more clearly the position antipodal to Freud's and lend force to the dialectic.

Ferenczi's nature keeps him acutely sensitive to the progress of the analysand. In the face of a therapeutic impasse, he cannot retreat into an explanation that the patient misbehaves or wants to remain ill. The patient's suffering is too clear to him to resort to blame that ends in resignation. This sensitivity, painful as it is, is the source of his insight, the reason he practices innovation. At the beginning of his work, Ferenczi, like the other early analysts, encounters analytic impasses through resistance to the fundamental rule—patients fail to free associate. Or, perhaps it is more accurate to say that patients fail to free associate correctly, at least as far as these analysts are concerned. But this is a peculiar statement—the juxtaposition of "free" and "correctly"—that harbors contradiction. The patient is ostensibly free to say whatever comes to mind, but at the same moment, the analyst clearly has strong views of what constitutes a genuine exercise of that freedom. The sense of therapeutic paralysis in the face of resistance to the fundamental rule initially leads Ferenczi to become more pedagogic. Ferenczi (1919a) resorts to explanation and compulsion:

> In one case I was forced, in direct contradiction to the psycho-analytic rule, to insist that the patient should always complete any sentence he had begun. For I noticed that whenever a sentence took an unpleasant turn he never completed it, but switched off in the middle with a 'by the way' on to something unimportant and beside the mark. It had to be explained to him that the fundamental rule did not, it is true, demand the *thinking* out of an idea, but certainly the complete *utterance* of what had been thought. He required many admonitions, however, before he learnt this [p. 92].

Ferenczi clearly has the feeling that the analysand isn't playing by the rules of the game. It is as though he were involved in a chess match with a player who consistently violates the rules of movement—the bishop is moved horizontally, the knight attacks in semicircle. Ferenczi, who knows the ordinary rules of chess, cannot proceed meaningfully in this game; he must either leave the table or reach agreement about the rules. His first impulse is to be more precise in explanation, to say that free association requires a particular form of freedom to be of use to the analytic process. Explanation, however, is not adequate to overcome the difficulties.

When explanation fails to establish the necessary freedom of association, Ferenczi, along with his contemporaries, begins to see that the impasse stems from active resistance, rather than from a failure of understanding. In his effort to counter this resistance, Ferenczi again turns to Freud for answers. Building on Freud's work with the Wolf Man, Ferenczi begins to enforce more active abstinence to gain leverage over the resistance. Even before his first publications on the active technique, the seeds are present. Ferenczi (1919a) writes:

> If explanations have no result, it must be assumed that the patient wants to beguile one into detailed instructions and explanations and in this manner to obstruct the work. In such cases it is best to encounter the patient's silence with silence. It may happen that the greater part of the hour passes without the doctor or the patient having said a single word. The patient finds it very difficult to endure the doctor's silence; he gets the impression that the doctor is annoyed with him, that is he projects his own bad conscience on to the doctor, and this finally decides him to give in and renounce his negativism [p. 91].

While Ferenczi describes his silence as simply silence, silence which the analysand then projects her bad conscious on, it is clear that his silence is actually coercive silence. It aims to force the analysand toward free association. The development of abstinence as a means of gaining therapeutic leverage becomes more clear with the publication of his work on the active technique. Ferenczi proceeds from setting an arbitrary termination date, to prohibiting forms of masturbation that reduce the motivation necessary to bring the unconscious into consciousness. In the development of the active technique, Ferenczi (1919b) pushes abstinence to its extreme. He writes: "I was compelled in this case to give up the passive part that the psychoanalyst is accustomed to play in the treatment, which is confined to the hearing and interpretation of the patient's ideas, and had by active interference in the patient's psychic activities to help over dead points in the work of the analysis" (p. 116). By exaggerating abstinence, Ferenczi indirectly exposes the hostility it can conceal. He talks about the "dead points" in analysis. Or, more starkly, he (1919a) states that the analyst should not feel guilty when he falls asleep listening to a patient–sleeping is only a reaction to the "emptiness and worthlessness of the associations" (p. 92). Again, Ferenczi reacts to the negative transference with his own negative countertransference. He assigns responsibility for the failure to the analysand. What sets him apart from the other early analysts, however, is that he ultimately comes to recognize his own contribution to the impasse, and seeks to take responsibility for his countertransference.

While Ferenczi scores some early successes with the active technique, it is quickly exposed in its limitations. Although he manages to push patients to present previously withheld material, these acts of revelation are insufficient to bring about more substantive change. The active technique, like suggestion, depends on compulsion and compliance to function, and patients are resourceful in finding ways to circumvent compliance. This point is critical. While the resistance takes shape out of the core of the patients' neurosis, it simultaneously represents the heart of their sanity. The resistance marks both the tenacious clinging to the past and dysfunctional modes of satisfaction, and the refusal to sacrifice the authentic self. We have already made this point in regard to the manifestations of hysteria in Victorian culture; it holds equally true in regard to the manifestations of resistance in the analytic setting. The rigidity of the analyst's posture, the unnatural attempt to function as a blank screen, and the relentless interpretation of the transference fail to establish an environment of safety; resisting this "cure" demonstrates a form of sanity. The resistance, then, becomes the patient's means of insisting on a more fundamentally correct technique. The patient knows something about what is necessary for cure and withholds collaboration and associations as a bargaining chip in the negotiations. To the extent that these negotiations proceed and analytic technique evolves, the patient should be given credit (in the tradition of Anna O) along with the analyst for refining the analytic method.

When Ferenczi extends abstinence to its extreme, patients respond with new forms of resistance that ultimately force him to recognize its limitations. Demonstrating a perverse, taunting consistency, an analysand asks Ferenczi whether he should give up eating and breathing as well. Unless Ferenczi wants to claim that the only good analysand is a dead one, he must acknowledge the necessity of some gratification in the analytic process. Ferenczi learns, as Freud learned with suggestion, the shortcomings of activity and coercion. And in his willingness to recognize sanity in resistance, Ferenczi undergoes a shift in his perception of the Gestalt of the analytic situation. He begins to see how the transference, rather than necessitating analytic abstinence, may in fact be caused by it. In his diary Ferenczi (1988) writes:

> The modification of his therapeutic method, becoming more and more impersonal (levitating like some kind of divinity above the poor patient,

> reduced to the status of a mere child, unsuspecting that a large share of what is described as transference is artificially provoked by this kind of behavior), one postulates that transference is created by the patient. . . .
>
> A patient is quite justified in describing part of the behavior of such an analyst as crazy. Certain of the doctor's theories (delusions) may not be challenged; if one does so nevertheless, then one is a bad pupil, one gets a bad grade, one is in a state of resistance.
>
> My active therapy was a first, unconscious assault directed against this situation. By exaggerating and exposing this sadistic-educative methodology, I came to realize clearly that it was untenable [pp. 93–94].

Ferenczi has begun to see the iatrogenic effects of abstinence in the analytic situation. To withhold empathy in the face of traumatic memories hides the analyst's sadism. To unwaveringly insist that all associations refer transferentially back to the analyst displays a kind of "narcissistic delusion" (ibid., p. 95). To remain coldly authoritarian and impersonal is not a neutral act; it has meaning and the patient reasonably reacts to this behavior with resistance. The analyst is not without motive in assuming the analytic attitude, and cannot function merely as an objective scientist in the analytic relationship. "Analysis offers to persons otherwise somewhat incapacitated and whose self-confidence and potency are disturbed an opportunity to feel like a sultan, thus compensating him for his defective ability to love" (p. 194). The analyst's subjectivity and his own incomplete self-curative needs condition his responses in the analytic setting, and in turn condition the analysand's transference.

Ferenczi has begun to recognize the logical consistency of reversing the causal sequence between analyst and analysand. In his initial work, Ferenczi perceived the analyst's abstinence as sane and the patient's resistance as crazy. This perspective felt appropriate, or in Freudian terms, it was accompanied by the subjective indications of reality. But now, after the shift in the Gestalt, that perspective is turned inside out, and abstinence becomes crazy as the patient's resistance becomes sane. This perspective, also, carries the subjective indications of reality. In undergoing this shift between two mutually exclusive but individually convincing realities, Ferenczi (1988) has an intra-analytic experience of constructivism. His epistemological sense of reality begins to change. In a note to himself from his diary that echoes Hume, he writes:

> I think: the dog is barking
> In reality: I see—the dog } Simultaneously and from the
> I hear—barking } *same direction.*
> Thereupon I neglect the subjective element and feel justified in regarding (recognizing) "dog" and "is barking" as "really" existing, even without my subjective evidence [p. 112].

Here Ferenczi points out the phenomological independence of visual and auditory perceptions. He points out the way we construct, rather than directly perceive, the identity of the object and our understanding of the material world. This emerging view of reality and the nature of analytic epistemology leads Ferenczi to approach the analytic relationship with greater flexibility. Sensing the fluid aspect of phenomena, he is less willing to impress his views on the analysand.

Now Ferenczi, always one to take ideas to their logical conclusions, abandons the active technique and endorses passivity in its stead. The key to this reversal, in addition to his growing awareness of the potential sadism involved in abstinence, is Ferenczi's realization that although hysterics may lie about their childhood, this dissembling does not preclude the reality of trauma. He has gained a more multifaceted understanding of the nature of truth. While more careful in his published writings, in his diary Ferenczi returns to the seduction theory to recycle the formative role of environmental assault in the creation of suffering. He (1930) writes:

> To-day I am returning to the view that, beside the great importance of the Oedipus complex in children, a deep significance must also be attached to the *repressed incestuous affection of adults, which masquerades as tenderness...* The premature forcing of genital sensations has a no less terrifying effect on children; what they really want, even in their sexual life, is simply play and tenderness, not the violent ebullition of passion [pp. 299–300].

The factors behind Ferenczi's return to a traumatic theory of etiology are complex. In part he revisits this first theory as a result of how he listens to his patients. His empathic presence is such that he cannot stay simply separate from his patients' accounts of how they were injured; he feels it too immediately. But his capacity to empathically join with his patients around their childhood suffering is equally determined by his own past. In his diary he alludes to traumatic events in his own upbringing. While these are not specified, it is clear that Ferenczi feels they are responsible for his own wounded sensibility. Regardless of the final significance of the personal factor, Ferenczi's acceptance of traumatic etiology has critical ramifications for his technical approach to analysis. In adopting a view that suffering is the by-product of narcissistic parenting, of parenting where the child's needs are disregarded, he commits himself to exploring the possibility that cure is dependent on the analyst's willingness to meet those needs.

Ferenczi, in the second phase of his therapeutic experimentation, begins to explore the use of indulgence with patients in the attempt to use supplementation as a method of cure. But this is not merely a naive attempt to supply the missing "milk"—he is driven toward indulgence by a kind of relentless logical consistency. Ferenczi states that if he accepts the reality of trauma, he betrays this acceptance through analytic neutrality. To remain silent and stoic in the face of traumatic memories is to violate the human standard of affectivity. Freud has suggested that the key to dream interpretation is to locate the latent content of the dream that brings the intensity of affect in line with objective causes. Ferenczi travels the same route in regard to the analyst's behavior. For the analyst to meaningfully convey his belief in the analysand's traumatic story, the objective scale of affective value demands that the analyst be visibly moved. He (1988) writes:

> It appears that patients cannot believe that an event really took place, or cannot fully believe it, if the analyst, as the sole witness of the events, persists in his cool, unemotional, and, as patients are fond of stating, purely intellectual attitude, while the events are of a kind that must evoke, in anyone present, emotions of revulsion, anxiety, terror, vengeance, grief, and the urge to render immediate help [p. 24].

While Freud did not doubt the reality of trauma, he felt that in the normal course of things grief would be abreacted through the process of mourning. When that abreaction fails to occur it is because the analysand has reaped secondary gains from the grieving process. The recollection of grief, then, is not merely the report of a tragic event; it represents a covert attempt to gain gratification in the transference situation. Abstinence, under this view, is not lack of sympathy for the real pain of the past events, but an attempt to block the covert avenue of gratification that prevents the factors which perpetuate the grief reaction from reaching consciousness. Ferenczi, however, reverses the motivation behind the preserved grief. Echoing the seduction theory, he suggests that the trauma remains active because the child had to suppress her reactions out of fear of further reprisal from adults. In Ferenczi's mind, fear rather than desire is the force that perpetuates the damaging effect of the traumatic reaction. To react to the recollection of traumatic memory with analytic stoicism, under this understanding, is to repeat the lack of empathic consideration for the analysand that permitted the original adult to perpetrate the crime.

Ferenczi comes to believe that analytic warmth and responsiveness are necessary elements of cure; they are what permit the analysand to differentiate between the present and the past, and so begin to release outmoded adaptations. As a result of his clinical experience, he feels he must break with Freudian technique, at least as he understands it. Now, in contrast to the principle of abstinence, Ferenczi begins to extend himself to his patients. While he continues to withhold consummated sexual gratification, he allows patients to touch him, to kiss him, to accompany him on vacation, to extend their sessions to two hours. He engages his natural warmth and compassion. These changes lead Ferenczi to alter his view of therapeutic action and the effects of psychoanalysis. Rather than stressing adaptation to reality, Ferenczi underlines the capacity for inhabiting the authentic emotional self. He becomes concerned with the experience of wholeness, with undoing fragmentation and lifelessness. He (1988) speaks of patients' feelings of "inner emptiness" (p. 142), and strives, through the process of regression and empathic joining, to help patients refind their spontaneous feelings and affective vitality. Here, Ferenczi both anticipates Winnicott's work on the true self and revisits the original vision of psychoanalysis: the awakening of full orgasmic capacity. In this stage of his work, the pendulum swings from the adaptation to reality back to the capacity for gratification. Paralleling the shift in his epistemological position, Ferenczi moves from the morality of abstinence and discipline, toward the value of relaxation and developmental provision. "If we succeed in gaining insight into the psychic life of a child who as yet has been spared pain and suffering," he writes (1988), "then we come ultimately to the assumption that man becomes passionate and ruthless purely as a consequence of suffering" (p. 151). The innate goodness of the individual emerges naturally in the presence of caring. Morality, then, is reestablished on a developmental rather than transcendent basis.

While Freud rendered sensible the paradox of abstinence curing frustration, Ferenczi untangles the paradox of the acceptance of distortion as a route to reality. In working with more severely disturbed patients, Ferenczi finds that their retreat from reality is motivated not only by the narcissistic gratification found in the self, but by the lack of responsiveness in the interpersonal matrix. The analyst, by accepting the potential reality of hallucination, can reverse this trend. Ferenczi (1988) writes that if analysts do "not reject a priori the possibility of the psychic reality or otherwise real nature of their [the analysands'] observations, we will be rewarded in turn by the partial return of their interest in ordinary reality" (p. 32-33). This is a key passage in his work because it points to the emergence of a new epistemological paradigm. By empathically accepting the patient's claim of a traumatic past, Ferenczi gains a sense of the perspectival nature of reality. He both promotes the genuine accuracy of the psychotic's perception in the phrase "otherwise real nature of their observations" and demotes the privileged status of the analyst's perception or conventional reality by calling these "ordinary" reality. Here we are at the end of Ferenczi's published thoughts. He does not systematically extend his thinking about epistemology and the analytic situation, but we can see the emerging pressure on the field to move away from the objectivist epistemology that formed its Freudian foundation. Analytic progress, Ferenczi finds, is dependent on moving beyond sequestering reality in the hands of the analyst. The objectivist's stance can only serve to recapitulate the traumatic events of childhood, when the child's sense of assault was obscured by the adult's claiming that incestuous actions were mere tenderness.

Ferenczi's experiments with relaxation, then, lead to two key discoveries. First, coming to see the sense in the analysand's resistance, Ferenczi is brought to the verge of a constructivist epistemology. Second, he suggests that some form of indulgence is necessary to help ameliorate the patient's fragmentation and restore a sense of affective vitality. But these are not isolated discoveries and Ferenczi begins to see the relationship between gratification and reality in a new light. When the analyst shows empathic warmth, this gratifying behavior, rather than freezing the patient in hallucinatory outlets, allows the patient to sense the reality of past traumatic events, and in this reacceptance of the past, the analysand regains confidence in her perceptive capacity in the present. When the relationship is no longer conditioned by embattled struggles over authorship of reality, then the analysand, knowing her sense of conviction will not be stripped away, is free to examine other modes of seeing.

Yet indulgence, as we have come to expect in a field impregnated with paradox, is not without problems. While empathic response and caring action overcome some of the difficulties that stemmed from the latent sadism inherent in abstinence, they create new therapeutic impasses that demand further revision. As Ferenczi begins to practice supplementation as a route to cure, patients begin to increase their demands. They seem to reason (or perhaps just feel) that if cure will come from receiving what they missed as children, and if they are still suffering, then the solution must lie in further giving by Ferenczi. The progression here is predictable. He (1988) writes: "I gave in to more and more of the patient's wishes, doubled the number of sessions, going to her house instead of forcing her to come to me; I took her with me on my vacation trips and provided sessions even on Sundays" (p. 97). But this level of extended care remains inadequate, and the patient begins to demand that the analysis be extended to twenty-four hours a day. In making this impossible request the patient once again serves as educator, exposing the untruth in the method. If cure is possible, it must rely on more than the doctor's efforts at caregiving and affection.

Ferenczi, if he wants to proceed further with analysis, must acknowledge the impossibility of full relaxation in technique. He can no longer maintain the illusion of unlimited analytic kindness. He (1988) writes about the progression in technique:

> a. Original catharsis and precautions arising in consequence of it, and the development of an impersonal attitude.
> b. Failures and incomplete successes, demands for change: increase in tension (active therapy); adverse effects of excessive strictness. Experiments with passivity, relaxation; as extreme consequence, loss of authority, provocations ("when will his patience snap"), "ad-absurdum" feeling.
> c. Confession of artificiality in the analyst's behavior; admission in principle of emotions such as annoyance, unpleasure, fatigue, "to hell with it," finally also libidinal and play fantasies. Result: patient becomes more natural, more affable, and more sincere [p. 10–11].

Ferenczi senses that patients find his passivity inauthentic, and in response develop a negative therapeutic reaction. They become increasingly crazy and demanding, emphasizing their own pathology, in an attempt to prove the falsehood lurking in his analytic demeanor. He is forced to recognize the inherent paradox in the analytic situation. The patient, while made ill by deprivation, cannot be cured by any quantity of love, and while theoretically deserving complete compassion, tugs at his hate. Merely surrendering to the patient's subjectivity and hunger leads to further impasse. This forces Ferenczi to set limits in the analytic setting and to admit the force of his negative feelings. When Ferenczi finally acknowledges the reality of his own negative countertransference, the patient is able to surrender her extreme behaviors, and become more sane.

As Ferenczi (1988) points out, though, the analyst is not the only observer in the room, and the analysand has the capacity to see through our presentation, to see beyond our words, and to detect our countertransference regardless of our attempts at concealment or management. He writes:

> The experiences I have gathered since then have led me to suspect that it is no use, or not much use, to show more friendliness toward the patient than we really feel. Subtle, barely discernible differences in the handshake, the absence of color or interest in the voice, the quality of our alertness or inertia in following and responding to what the patient brings up: all these and a hundred other signs allow the patient to guess a great deal about our mood and our feelings [pp. 35–36].

Ferenczi reasons that if analysis is founded on the ethic of truthfulness, on the idea that only through the full acknowledgment of reality can we live sensibly, then to obscure the presence of the countertransference displays a betrayal of this principle. How can the analyst ask the patient for honesty while simultaneously engaging in concealment? This critique is pivotal; it must be addressed by any analyst who advocates a more conservative handling of the countertransference and its disclosure. This admission, however, lends weight to the patient's demand for further technical experimentation. Ferenczi's patient, RN, having ferreted out the countertransference, having exposed the impossibility of pure analytic neutrality or unlimited compassion, claims that, in the interest of her safety, she has the right to subject Ferenczi to analysis before she can risk further self-exposure. The analyst must be further perfected before he can serve adequately as the instrument of cure. In response to this demand, Ferenczi, always extreme in his consistency and daring in his method, begins the most courageous and perhaps (some would argue) misguided experiment in the utilization and exploration of countertransference on record, and subjects himself to mutual analysis with RN. He begins to split his analytic sessions in half, spending half the time on the couch as patient, and half the time in the chair as analyst.

As Ferenczi enters into his mutual analysis he finds the technique is productive for the analytic process. The first gains, nicely enough, are in his own self-understanding and functioning. He begins to see that the practice of analytic relaxation stemmed in part from a reaction formation against his fear of being devoid of genuine concern. We might say that Ferenczi had formulated a defense against his own unintegrated aggressive tendencies. He sought his niceness as protection against the fear that acknowledging his aggression would overwhelm his decency, leaving him merely cold or rapacious. Showing a vestige of this fear he (1988) writes: "Could it be that my entire relaxation therapy and the super kindness I demand from myself toward patients are really only an exaggerated display of compassionate feelings that basically are totally lacking?" (p. 86). But this concern, although never extinguished, abates, and Ferenczi begins to see his real compassion and its limits.

As Ferenczi makes this internal leap, his understanding of the therapeutic process and the nature of cure move forward as well. By placing himself under the analytic gaze of RN, Ferenczi exposes the presence of his own neurosis, joining RN in the ranks of the mad, and steps down from the pedestal of authority. This move, rather than aborting the analytic process, provides help in overcoming the therapeutic impasse. RN no longer needs to see herself as the only one who suffers, as the only bad one. If neurosis is universal, then it no longer is cause for shame, and in the absence of shame the difficulty can be explored more freely. Furthermore, as the analyst is seen more clearly, the analysand's tendency to idealize is diminished. When the analyst is seen through the transference as an omnipotent other, the analysand logically presumes that cure has to flow from the analyst. The task of the analysand, under this view, is only to convince or cajole the analyst to part with the necessary caretaking supplies. But this wish to be cured absolutely, to be made free from all bad feelings, is impossible. Real help comes only when the patient comes to terms with the imperfect necessities of the world. Ferenczi writes: "It is my hope that with tremendous patience and self-sacrifice on our part, after hundreds of instances of enormous forbearance, sympathy, the renunciation of every authoritarian impulse, even acceptance of lessons or help from the patient, it will be possible to make the patient renounce that colossal wish-fulfillment and make do with what offers itself" (p. 68). The analyst, as a result of mutual analysis, can now be seen in his mortality, as someone who could help despite his flaws. When the limits of the analyst are recognized, the patient must accept the necessity for participating more fully in the curative process.

Ferenczi's experiment with mutual analysis is an experiment in the limits of analytic honesty and equality. He sets out to hide nothing behind the screen of the analytic attitude, to preserve no artificial hierarchy between patient and doctor. In part the experiment is a success. RN moves through her therapeutic impasse and begins to show a more trusting attitude in the analytic context, and to show more flexibility in her extra-analytic life. Yet experiments in limits are bound to reach their own, and the inconsistencies in mutual analysis are exposed, once again, by the patient. If the analysis is genuinely mutual and Ferenczi is receiving help, the patient reasons, then he should pay a fee to the patient. Ferenczi, however, is unwilling to make this reversal and sacrifice his livelihood, and so rejects RN's suggestion. Mutual analysis runs into further difficulty around the issue of inter-patient confidentiality. If Ferenczi is to participate fully in the analytic process he must say everything that comes to mind. As he lies on the couch, however, he begins to have associations to his work with other patients. To report this material would violate these patients' confidentiality. Ferenczi must therefore withhold associations from RN. Finally, mutual analysis demonstrates its impossibility around the issue of tact. Ferenczi has clearly seen the necessity of safety in the development of trust. Without trust in the analyst, analysis is defeated. Complete honesty in mutual analysis, however, collides with the necessity of safety. For Ferenczi to report his affective reactions to the patient without editing, to include all of his hostile or judgmental thoughts, precludes the possibility of tact and undermines the establishment of trust. "Can and should the analyst," Ferenczi (1988) writes, "analyzed in this way, be completely open, right from the beginning? should he not take into account the patient's reliability, capacity to tolerate, and understanding?" (p. 11). Telling the patient he finds her repulsive, Ferenczi concludes, will not facilitate the analytic process regardless of whether it leads to an increase in truthfulness.

Claims for Neutrality, the Lure of Activity (1925–1933)

As we have charted, the first generation of analysts found that analysis and analytic neutrality failed through the stalemate of unproductivity.

Patients entered analysis, failed to free associate either through silence or planned speech, and the analyst's interpretations skimmed over the surface without touching the patient affectively. Reich (1933), in his work on character analysis, writes that this tendency to interpret intellectually leads only to "the typical hopeless picture of an analysis rich in interpretations and poor in results" (p. 250). In the face of these poor results, analysts, as we have noted, turned to pedagogic measures, resorted to prohibitions, and rationalized their negative countertransference. These actions were not helpful–they drew the analyst away from the analytic attitude and neutrality. Out of the recognition of the failure of both the initial vision of neutrality and of these engaged responses, comes revisionist hopes. In the works of both Alexander (1925) and Reich (1933) there is an attempt to reformulate the meaning of neutrality, to claim that the failure of the early analysts stemmed from a poorly wielded neutrality. For Alexander the key to effective neutrality lies in the analyst's relationship to the analysand's superego. The analyst acts to replace the irrational and punitive prohibitions of the superego with the more modulated, reality-oriented voice of the analytic interpretation. Reich, on the other hand, sees the key to effective neutrality in maintaining interpretive activity in the face of character resistance. The analyst must, at the moment of impasse, persevere with neutrality and interpret the function of the resistance. Yet, in both of these writers' claims to have extended neutrality there lie concealed points of allegiance and hostility. Out of these subterranean alignments emerges the lure of activity, and both Alexander and Reich resort to direct action in the attempt to change the analysand.

When the analyst, in the interest of neutrality, limits his contact with the patient to the cognitive realm, the lack of affective involvement fails to bring about a mediated end to the patient's (and the analyst's) difficulties. The analyst and the patient, however, both expect change to occur. This expectation slowly draws the analyst into the conflict and the analyst becomes aligned. Once drawn into alignment, there are only two positions for the analyst: he must enter into the war on one side of the conflict or the other; he must align himself with the patient's pain or against it. Ferenczi, successively, uses both of these approaches, first, with the active technique, squaring off against the patient and her neurosis, and then in his passive technique switching allegiances, joining the patient and her pain. The tension between these two sides is extended in more dichotomous form in the works of Alexander and Reich. Alexander, in his theory of the therapeutic action of analysis working to ameliorate the superego, aligns himself sympathetically with the patient. Reich, on the other hand, by focusing on the penetration of character armor, places himself in a more antagonistic role. These engaged positions, for both analysts, act to undercut their claim to pure neutrality, and in the end lead to renewed pressure on the field to develop a more sophisticated understanding of the necessity of neutrality.

Alexander, responding to Freud's development of the structural theory, suggests that the aim of analysis, rather than simply uncovering the repressed material, must be to disassemble the superego. The superego, he reasons, is an atavistic organ. Developed out of the primitive cognition of childhood, it fails to adequately assess the demands of reality. It unwarrantedly prohibits behaviors that would be both id-gratifying and ego-syntonic, while simultaneously allowing "auto-plastic" gratification through the mediation of self-punishment. He (1925) writes: "The super-ego behaves, in short, like a dull-witted frontier guard who arrests everyone wearing spectacles, because he has been told that one particular person is wearing spectacles" (p. 100). In the move toward the structural theory, Alexander has embraced an implicitly more environmental model of the pathogenesis of suffering. The superego, as Alexander sees it, is an imprint of the past relationship between child and parents. It is made up of commands and prohibitions that are imbued with a critical affective tone. This punitive aspect interferes with adequate functioning, and must be reversed.

In response to this understanding, Alexander implicitly reframes the meaning of neutrality. If originally neutrality, concerned with the id, entailed the avoidance of gratificatory entanglements, now, focused on the superego, it must entail the avoidance of punitive interactions. In the analytic context, the patient develops a transference to the analyst that re-creates the conditions under which the superego was first formed. "By means of the transference he [the analyst] gains the patient's confidence and produces the original childhood situation during which the superego was formed" (p. 103). Once this re-creation has solidified, the analyst is in a position to inhabit the role originally played by the parents–the analyst takes over the role of the superego. In the transference, the demands of the id are brought into relationship to the analyst rather than the superego, and through this process the analysand can begin to reshape her relationship to her instinctual base and the external world. This change can occur because the analyst, in contrast to the parents, is a more rational, more modulated voice. In the analytic setting, Alexander writes, "the demands of reality are, however, not communicated by means of orders and prohibitions, as previously happened under the sway of the superego, but by a 'super-personal' method, by logical insight, by accurate testing of reality" (p. 104). Neutrality, in this context, comes to mean avoiding allegiance with the punitive superego. While Alexander is not explicit about his technique, we can imagine that his view of the analyst as a benign superego led him to present a gentler front to his analysands.

While Alexander speaks the language of neutrality and presents a picture of the analyst as the calm voice of science, his therapeutic theory contains an essential move toward action and engagement. The analyst, positioned through the transference as a parent, becomes a new object for the analysand, a presence that communicates necessity out of a concern for the patient's well-being. In this way, the analyst aligns himself with the patient against the harsher voices of her past as encapsulated in the superego. While still speaking the voice of adaptation to reality, Alexander has taken on a vision of cure through supplementation and endorses a concept of the analytic process based on the principle of reparenting. He strives to give to the patient something that was missing in childhood.

In taking this position, however, Alexander squarely sides himself against the superego in favor of the ego and the id. In taking sides, he abandons neutrality and seeks to become a reparative good object for the analysand. As a result, his patients are unable to work out the internal splitting between good and bad objects and must seek to preserve the protective relationship with the analyst; under Alexander's care patients regress and seek to avoid terminating the analysis. He (1925) writes:

> In bidding good-bye to his superego he must finally take leave of his parents, whom by introjection he had captured and preserved in his super-ego. He has indeed been ignominiously hood-winked in analysis. The analyst seduced him into giving up the introjected parents, by himself taking over the rôle of the super-ego, and now he wants to saddle the patient with the burden. The latter protests and attempts in return to score off the analyst by sending him in the long-since-closed account for his birth, and this often by way of somatic symptoms [p. 107].

By stating that the patient is "ignominiously hoodwinked" by the analyst, we can sense how Alexander's analytic procedure begins to unwind. Deception has never been long palatable to the analytic process. By aligning himself with the patient as the benevolent object, Alexander has merely cast himself in the role of the split-off good object. The essential paranoid split between the malevolent and benevolent object remains, and must be defended against, in this case by a regression to somatic symptoms. The analysand, still living in a world of bad objects, finds termination too dangerous. Alexander's active attempt to replace the superego, an effort that successfully circumvents the first level of encountered resistance, ultimately leads to a forfeiture of neutrality that stymies analytic work.

While Alexander focuses on his role as benevolent object, Reich turns his attention to the adversarial quality of the transference relationship. The resistance, Reich points out, rather than merely acting as an obstacle to analytic progress, is the cornerstone of the analysand's neurosis and character. Characterological resistance is the necessary front of analytic work, the most fertile soil for interpretation. This understanding marks a key advance for analytic technique. When patients enter analysis and fail to obey the fundamental rule—withhold dreams, limit their affect—Reich is no longer at a loss. These behaviors provide the material for analytic interpretation. He (1933) writes:

> Rarely are our patients immediately accessible to analysis, capable of following the fundamental rule and of really opening up to the analyst. . . . It is a difficulty which has been termed "narcissistic barrier." There are, in principle, two ways of meeting this difficulty, in especial, the rebellion against the fundamental rule.
>
> One, which seems the usual one, is a direct education to analysis by information, reassurance, admonition, talking-to, etc. That is, one attempts to educate the patient to analytic candor by the establishment of some sort of positive transference. . . .
>
> The other way is more complicated and as yet not applicable in all patients, but far more certain. It is that of *replacing the pedagogical measures by analytic interpretations* [pp. 232–233].

Rather than trying to persuade the patient to abandon the resistance, the analyst must interpret the meaning and purpose of the resistant behavior. For Reich, the key to effective neutrality is the capacity to remain interpretive in the face of the resistance and the negative countertransference it can elicit. The prolonged silence, the mumbling voice, the obscure manner of speech are formed along the same architecture of more overt symptoms, and can be analyzed in the same manner. They are the disguised manifestations of the analysand's fear and hate of the analyst. In this focus on aggression we can see again the effect of Freud's mature theory. In contrast to the first analysts, Reich is not thrown off stride in the game when the analysand makes a move contrary to the rules of analytic chess. He can begin playing right away without the need to educate, or at least without the need to educate through the abandonment of the analytic attitude. He doesn't need the analysand to surrender the resistance before proceeding. Instead he sets about pointing out the resistance and its relationship to the analysand's symptoms. Having clarified these connections, the analyst must leave it to the analysand whether this awareness is utilized to alter her character and her pattern of resistance. He calls this "education to analysis *by* analysis" (p. 241). By pointing out the possibility of analyzing the resistance, by illuminating how interpretation can replace suggestive compulsion, Reich restrengthens analytic neutrality.

But to simply call Reich an advocate of neutrality (at least in the modern sense) would be a misstatement. In this way he is an ambiguous figure in the development of analytic technique. For while Reich avoids the pedagogical lapse from neutrality, his interpretive attitude is forceful and tends to be marked by antagonism. This is his countertransference, and he uses it directly in the analytic relationship. In interpreting the resistance, Reich is relentless in drawing attention to the subterranean motive, the bad faith in the patient's behavior. He tells patients that their behavior is designed to ward off material that is threatening. In this way he sets about stripping patients of their defensive "armor." But in war, stripping away the opponent's armor is not an act of neutrality; it understandably elicits violent attempts to guard oneself against the ensuing naked vulnerability. This tendency to forcefully remove the analysand's protective measures is evident in Reich's (1933) presentation of his work with a bank employee: "This time, however, I went a step further in the resistance interpretation. I told him that not only was he distrustful of the analysis; that, furthermore, by his behavior, he pretended the exact opposite" (p. 269). Reich embarks upon this interpretive line without regard to the strength of the analytic alliance. The analysand is involved in deception, and Reich is determined not to be party to it. The patient, in response to Reich's breaching interpretation, responds dramatically:

> 1. He thrashed around with arms and legs, yelling: "Let me alone, don't come near me, I'm going to kill you, I'm going to squash you!" This action often changed into another:
> 2. He grabbed his throat and whined in a rattling voice: "Please let me alone, please, I'm not going to do anything any more!" [p. 269].

To Reich, these charged responses are good news. He feels that his technique of resistance analysis provides the key for breaking through analytic sterility and intellectualism. I will not debate that he succeeds in this goal; his analyses were colored by crisis and affective upheaval. Reich knows how to get traction in the therapeutic mud that stranded the first analysts, but this success over sterility comes at the cost of safety. This patient's response is not an isolated event in Reich's therapeutic practice. In another case the analysand sees him as masculine and brutal. Nor is Reich ashamed of this tendency to elicit violent reaction; he sees it as a mark of his courage and efficacy:

> In this connection another fact must be mentioned: character-analysis creates in every case violent emotional outbursts and often dangerous situations, so that it is important always to be master of the situation, technically . . . The means of character-analysis, the consistent emphasis on the character-resistance and the persistent interpretation of its forms, ways and motive, are as potent as they are unpleasant for the patient [p. 260].

In this passage Reich provides convicting testimony for his method. In his insistence that the resistance need not lead to an analytic impasse requiring education, Reich advances the field's awareness of neutrality. He helps move analysis more firmly away from the simple analysis of symptoms to a more comprehensive approach to character. But in his relentless method lie seeds of sadism and contempt that undermine the analytic alliance, seeds that show themselves more clearly in the title of his book *Listen, Little Man!* The changes Reich observed in his patients, perhaps, result more from fear than from insight.

The Resurrection of Neutrality (1936–1953)

In a political climate stretched by multiple factions, the possibility of establishing neutrality is complicated. The analytic situation, conditioned by the contending voices of id, ego, and superego, by the internalized objects and the history of analysand and analyst, creates similar difficulties for the analyst. Staying out of this internal war requires delicate negotiation and skillful compromise. The first analysts, however, had to learn this lesson in practice. They read Freud with the naive eyes of inexperience and expected that silence coupled with interpretation would secure their status as a non-aligned party. But their behavior, rather than neutralizing the conflict, instigated patients to mass their armies on the analysts' borders. I choose this martial metaphor intentionally; it mirrors the language that was spoken in these first post-Freud papers on technique. Abraham (1919) and Nunberg (1926) speak of the neurosis as a hostile force that seeks war with the analyst and they strive to overcome the resistance. Rather than remaining neutral, these early analysts are pulled into the battle, and pit the forces of analytic understanding and technique against the resources of the resistance. As is always the case with war, victory for either party comes at a high cost. There are too many casualties: the analysis fails, the patient's autonomy is sacrificed, the suffering continues. These casualties lead analysis toward a more refined understanding of neutrality's demands. The movement toward activity in the work of Ferenczi, Alexander, and Reich, while initially undermining neutrality, ultimately acts to reveal the temptation and dangers of allegiance in the analytic context. In this unknowing act of revelation, these first writers pave the way for the next generation. In the second wave of analysts, writers like Fenichel (1938), Sterba (1953), and Anna Freud (1936) develop a better articulated understanding of neutrality, a neutrality that takes into account the multiple aspects of the analytic context, a neutrality that is not so easily toppled in the face of analytic passions.

Initially, Reich's method of character analysis magnetizes followers. It seems to offer a solution to therapeutic impasse and to provide the analyst with surer means of accessing the affective core of the analysand. But the charismatic effect of Reich's presentation is transitory, and the hostile aspect of his method becomes increasingly clear. Now even many of his followers turn away from this approach and, in their critique of

Reich, begin to formulate a more subtle understanding of neutrality. Fenichel points out that Reich's approach constitutes an aggressive shattering of the patient's defenses. The negative reaction in response to this therapeutic attack is justified and cannot reasonably be spoken of as a negative transference. Furthermore, the shattering of defenses does not necessarily entail meaningful characterological change. Informed by Freud's revised theory of masochism and the economics of pleasure, Fenichel (1938) writes: "The 'shattering of the defense armor' is masochistically enjoyed by many patients, and specific transferences can hide behind such enjoyment and escape discovery" (p. 272). While character analysis may cause strong affect to erupt to the surface, this revelation of magma may cover over other critical aspects of the neurotic's self.

Even Sterba, initially an ardent follower of Reich, although still recognizing Reich's contributions, eventually comes to renounce his methods. The heart of Sterba's criticism concerns Reich's unwillingness to acknowledge the validity of the positive transference. When the patient's positive feelings toward the analyst are constantly questioned and reframed as an obfuscation of hostility, the patient must begin to feel persecuted. Analysis, as practiced by Reich, leads to iatrogenic effects:

> Under the impact of his technique, which is conditioned by the mistrust in the patient's positive transference reactions and by the disbelief in the genuineness of initial and even later transference-love, the patient must necessarily feel unaccepted and constantly questioned as to the truthfulness of his positive feelings toward the analyst, so that he finally has to develop negative reactions out of his feeling of being frustrated and rejected. If these negative reactions finally manifest themselves in dreams or otherwise Reich is triumphant because it proves to him that the initial transference was not genuinely positive [p. 279].

In focusing on the iatrogenic effects of Reich's approach, Sterba calls attention to the dynamic character of analytic reality. From Reich's perspective, his insistent approach serves to ferret out the truth of the negative transference; he uncovers a preexisting reality. From Sterba's vantage point, however, Reich's searching activity has meaning and through its force sacrifices neutrality. The aggressively charged character of his interpretations objectively registers on the affective scale of value, and so must create real (rather than transferential) effects in the analysand. Sterba, in conjunction with the other ego psychologists, still holds that there is a solution to this difficulty. By reining in the self, subduing the manifestations of subjectivity, the analyst can return to neutrality and separate the observed more clearly from the observing process. Nonetheless, each of these emerging realizations of the iatrogenic character of the analytic context gradually moves the field closer to adopting a constructivist epistemology.

The emerging understanding of how sensitive the analysand is to the analyst, how easily influenced the patient is by the analyst's movements, culminates in a more refined articulation of neutrality. Having encountered the real patient rather than the imagined, analysts can no longer content themselves with the hope that mere silence and reserve will by themselves serve to secure neutrality. Rigidity of this kind leads to resistance. But the field is not yet ready to abandon the ideal of the analyst as the objective scientist, as the holder of reality. The Platonic sentiment runs too deep. The key, these critics of activity suggest, is to avoid entanglements that would cloud the transferential nature of the analysand's perceptions. The increased sensitivity to the iatrogenic response leads them to redouble their efforts to remain only interpretive. What is needed for success in this task is a more complex understanding of the multiple forces involved in the analytic relationship, an understanding that is made explicit in Anna Freud's work.

Neutrality is resurrected through Anna Freud's deployment of the structural theory in her description of ego psychology. Under the governance of the topographic model, of id psychology, neutrality could be understood as remaining uninvolved in the analysand's strivings for libidinal gratification. The unfolding of the structural model, however, multiplies the parties involved in the conflict. In addition to the id, the analyst must consider the ego and the superego. The claims of libido, conscience, and reality are all vying for the analyst's allegiance. Each of the components–id, ego, and superego–represents a necessary function for the individual, and if their aim is not respected, the analysand, according to the affective scale of value, should protest. It is this understanding that leads Anna Freud (1936) to shift the definition of neutrality from simple avoidance of gratifying behavior, to the more complicated notion of equidistance:

> It is the task of the analyst to bring into consciousness that which is unconscious, no matter to which psychic institution it belongs. He directs his attention equally and objectively to the unconscious elements

> in all three institutions. To put it in another way, when he sets about the work of enlightenment, he takes his stand at a point equidistant from the id, the ego, and the superego [p. 28].

The analyst achieves neutrality by finding the position that is equidistant from each of the psychic agencies. Anna Freud speaks of this refined version of neutrality in positivist terms. She speaks of bringing the unconscious into consciousness, of acting "objectively," and in this language reveals that she is still operating in an objectivist epistemology. This is the growing thrust of ego psychology—the aim of analysis is to bring the analysand into greater adaptation to reality. Ego psychologists speak of the neurosis and the pathogenic thinking of the analysand being corrected by the standard of reality. The idea of equidistance, however, contains within itself a subtle shifting in tone. In Freud's original view, neutrality was maintained through avoiding gratification and distancing oneself from affective pulls. It is the neutrality of the Victorian scientist. Neutrality understood as equidistance, however, implicitly evokes the question of value. To stay equidistant from each agency is to suggest that each aspect of the analysand is valued equally; the claims of one institution are not placed above the other. While the analyst may not agree with the methods adopted by any one component of the personality—he may disagree with the punitive, exclusionary stance of the superego, the distorting defenses of the ego, or the impatience of the id—he remains sympathetic to the intent of each. Gratification is necessary, restraint is prudent, and protection of self-esteem unavoidable. Although the language of the ego psychologists preserves the positivist framing of the analytic stance, it lets in through the back door a vision of neutrality that is aligned with compassion. It is not the simplistic sympathy of the sentimental, a surface-level grieving for another's pain; instead, it is a compassionate extension of care to the totality of the other that recognizes the inevitable difficulties of life. This evolution in the definition of neutrality is a critical shift. The new understanding contains an awareness of neutrality's difficulty, the difficulty in not affecting what is observed. Modern attempts to modify analytic technique, attempts to argue for the utility of analytic activity, would do well to reference this period of analytic history. To merely resurrect the virtue of activity and a more forceful use of the countertransference, either positive or negative, would seem to me to only be again snared in the difficulties that met Alexander and Reich.

CHAPTER SIX

The Move to Modernity

The Changing Patient Population (1890–1975)

Psychoanalysis was cultivated in the bed of medicine and took shape out of the effort to treat a disorder, hysteria, that hovered between the somatic and the psychological. For this group of patients, hysterics, the medical model seemed appropriate. As the practice of psychoanalysis gained in reputation, however, it began to attract a broader class of patients, patients whose suffering was less clearly demarcated. Now the field began to trespass on territory that had belonged to religious and moral disciplines. The impetus for change in psychoanalysis during this period was spurred on by analysts' encounters with these patients. Analysts began to work with patients who were simply unhappy or who suffered from deficits in self-esteem, with children and with psychotics. These patients, while widely different in presentation, all required a more engaged mode of contact with their analyst, and put pressure on the field to refine the theoretical underpinnings of analysis.

As analysis became widely recognized it began to magnetize the hopes of the simply unhappy. People began to seek analysis who had no clear-cut symptoms, no dramatic oddities that separated them from their peers or their analysts. The first of these patients, it seems, were those, like Ferenczi, who came seeking analytic training as a route to happiness. Later, this cover of professionalism was not as necessary, and patients came to analysis reporting only that their life was not as they would wish. Reich (1933), in his work on character analysis, described one of these patients: "A man 30 years of age came to analysis because he 'didn't get any fun out of life.' He did not really think he was sick but, he said, he had heard about psychoanalysis and perhaps it would make things clearer to him" (p. 242). The diffuse quality of this complaint makes it both more subtle and more pervasive than the tightly focused hysterical paralysis or obsessional ritual.

These patients, rather than developing dramatic symptoms, suffer from conflicted or impoverished relationships, and they feel divorced from their spontaneity. Feeling under valued by the world, they are acutely sensitive to the analyst's attitudes. They try to see through the analyst's silence, and are attentive to the vicissitudes of her compassion and attention. These patients relentlessly monitor the analyst's countertransference, and in so doing turn a mirror back on the analyst. This scrutiny by the analysand puts pressure on analysts to acknowledge their own affective sensitivity, their perturbability during the analytic session. These patients' perceptions cannot be so readily disregarded as the projections of the mad. Furthermore, these patients, so ready to feel slighted, require more attention to the analytic alliance. This group of patients, I suggest, when not looking for punishment, actively elicit caretaking responses from the analyst. They seem to require softer handling before an alliance can be forged and their longing for support leads analysts to increasingly question the blanket necessity of abstinence.

The problem of abstinence or analytic non-participation was further underscored by the movement toward treating children. While the advent of child analysis was marked by the case of Little Hans, it was a beginning at a distance. Freud conducted the analysis primarily through the mediation of Hans' father, and so was not faced with the child's inability to free associate. Yet Freud expressed hope that psychoanalysis would have an impact on the principles of child rearing, and this hope began to take more tangible form in the efforts of Anna Freud and Melanie Klein. These analysts realized that they had to retool psychoanalysis to conform to the needs of child patients. It is clear that asking children to lie on the couch and speak fluently is a losing proposition. Children will not even pretend to comply with such a request. For these analysts inactivity is untenable; they have to play with children if they want the relationship to proceed. In working with children we are one step less removed from the maternal impulse. While we may expect adults to care for themselves, "to clean up their own mess," we feel more willing to take a child's hand. The nurturant quality of the relationships with children is both easier and more apparent; their needs underscore the potential utility of the supportive countertransference. It is this aspect of child treatment that leads Anna Freud (1936) to write that with children, at least, the analyst cannot be seen merely as a transferential object; the analyst, in fact, acts as a new object in the child's life. The analyst cannot imagine herself as abstinent because she must contribute to the child's development; she plays a key role in the child's initial development of psychic structure. Working with children provides a glimpse into the possibility of using more active techniques as part of the therapeutic tool chest.

These two groups of patients, children and those suffering deficits in self-esteem, are closer to normality. Their normality underlines the continuity between physician and patient. This continuity undermines the analyst's privileged position of psychic authority and focuses analytic attention on the countertransference. The final group of patients, however, the psychotics, moves in the other direction on the spectrum toward increased abnormality. They show more extreme symptoms and greater distortion in their reality testing. Paradoxically, however, this move to extremity has the same effect as the earlier move toward normality. It underscores the inescapability of analytic participation. Initially, analysts concurred with Freud and saw psychotics as untreatable by analysis. According to the classical formulation, psychotic individuals suffered from a narcissistic cathexis of libido. Their libido was turned back on themselves, and so was unavailable in the context of treatment. These patients were unable to form a transference, and this made analysis impossible. The historical direction of psychoanalysis, however, has always been towards greater inclusion and reach, and eventually analysts began to venture into these difficult realms of treatment. As analysts began working with schizophrenics, it became clear that these patients were not suitable for classical treatment. When faced with a merely interpretive analyst, these patients respond regressively, and their hallucinations become more vivid and their affect more disturbed. To work effectively with these patients, the analyst needs to soften her approach. Landauer (1924), a predecessor of Reich, draws attention to this necessity when he writes:

> My first analyses were attempts to treat psychoses along the lines of the 'early Zurich school': translations from psychotic language into normal speech. This was work exclusively on the part of the physician; if he was lucky enough to have found an interpretation, he would fling it in the patient's teeth; a descriptive performance. One could not help noticing that, with this procedure, almost regularly the patient's condition grew worse [p. 179].

Not only must the analyst be more delicate in her analytic presence, it begins to become clear that the location of reality must be questioned. This realization strikes Ferenczi when he speaks of the utility of attending to psychotics' reality as a way of reenlisting their interest in conventional reality. By granting respect to the hallucination, Ferenczi clears a path to therapeutic alliance. Yet respect, when genuine, gives way to understanding, and analysts begin to see that psychotics' hallucinations are not without substance. Although the surface form of the hallucination seems nonsensical, within this distortion lies accurate perception. This is what Searles (1975) comes to see. He realizes that schizophrenics are dramatically altered by subtle shifts in his own countertransferential state, and that buried within their hallucinations are psychotherapeutic strivings directed at the analyst. Searles writes about a patient who helped shape this understanding:

> Then, she talked, and I felt she was giving me a tremendous working over by saying many caustically deprecatory things in a highly delusional way. I had long since realized that everything she said, no matter how delusional, consciously or unconsciously alluded to something in the immediate situation. She repeatedly implied, 'if the shoe fits, wear it.' I was often aware, through feelings of guilt, inadequacy and self-condemnation that the shoe fit all too well [p. 115].

For Searles, schizophrenics not only speak some part of the truth, but it is a truth that demands that the analyst consider her own countertransference. Paradoxically, it is the schizophrenics, the patients who suffer from the most dramatic distortions in reality testing, that put pressure on the field to abandon the objectivist epistemology.

Ego Psychology, Object Relations Theory, and Interpersonal Psychoanalysis (1925–1960)

During the late 1920s and early 1930s, as Freud reaches an advanced age, a new generation of analysts emerges to take over intellectual leadership in the field. The growing body of clinical experience and the changing patient population has strained psychoanalysis' theoretical foundation; it needs revision to support the changes that are underway in clinical practice. It is during this time that Anna Freud, Melanie Klein, D.W. Winnicott, and Harry Stack Sullivan come into prominence and bring their divergent views of human functioning into contention. All of these authors, through their clinical insight, act as catalysts for separate schools of analytic thought; they mark the beginning of ego psychology, object-relations psychology, the British middle school, and interpersonal psychoanalysis.

The emergence of these four schools of thought and the growing split between them is critical to our concern with countertransference. These schools are the leading voices of the contemporary analytic dialogue, and each has come to hold a different view on how the countertransference is best conceptualized and managed. Ego psychology, on one end of the spectrum, with its focus on the adaptation to reality and the management of neutrality through "equidistance," comes to speak against the countertransference as a tool for analysis. It continues to champion the more conservative vision of countertransference as an obstacle to analysis. It understands countertransference as the product of the analyst's unanalyzed, idiosyncratic self. Klein, although she preserves Freud's focus on the intrapsychic origin of sexual and aggressive drives, turns her attention to earlier phases of infant development. She sees how the infant seeks to manage overwhelming affective experiences through projection. Her focus on projective identification opens the door for subsequent theorists in the Kleinian tradition to consider how this process evokes feelings in the mother and the analyst. It is object-relations theorists who first see how the countertransference may be evoked by the analysand (rather than produced by the analyst's underanalyzed unconscious) and so serve diagnostic functions.

Winnicott also turns his attention toward the earliest phases of infantile development. His emphasis on the holding environment and the integration of the authentic self, however, paints a less aggressive portrait of the infant and allows him to see the empathic role of the countertransference. The middle school recognizes that the countertransference can serve as an affective mode of knowing and making contact with the analysand. It provides the basis of the analyst's concern. Finally, the interpersonal school, claiming the other end of the spectrum, questioning the whole assumptive underpinnings of objectivity and abstinence, speaks for the most active use of the countertransference in the clinical setting. Authors from this rank are the most willing to argue for the utility of the countertransference and the use of disclosure. These opposing views of countertransference, however, do not spring up arbitrarily; they are intimately tied to broader theoretical positions in each school. Ego-psychology, object-relations, middle-school, and interpersonal theorists split on the question of countertransference because they hold different visions of the nature of motivation and health, the composition of reality, and the therapeutic action of psychoanalysis. Bringing attention to these less visible influences in the evolution of countertransference theory helps bring clarity to the current debate on countertransference and strengthens our capacity to reach judgment on how to settle the dispute.

Motivation, Drives, and Relationship

Perhaps the most well-charted point of disagreement among the four schools of psychoanalysis concerns their understanding of human motivation. Greenberg and Mitchell (1983) point to the emergence of object relations, the British middle school, and interpersonal psychoanalysis as a key point in the evolution of analytic theory. These schools begin to move away from the drive model, and embrace a more explicitly relational view of motivation. While the ego psychologists continue to rely on the language of drive and libido, these other theorists suggest that non-libidinal needs play a critical role in shaping character. Klein, while still overtly speaking of sex and aggression, points to the role of primitive anxiety and the dramatic security operations it engenders. Winnicott, extending his developmental view to early infancy, suggests that the libido is only one component of the infant's instinctual structure. Sullivan, even more radical in his point of view, contests the whole conceptual framework of instinct. The divergence amongst the four schools in their understanding of motivation exerts a governing effect on their evolving views of the countertransference.

Ego psychology, in keeping with Freud's adamant prescription to stay faithful to the primacy of sexuality, continues to focus on the driving force of the id, even as it seeks to expand understanding of the ego and the superego. It sees the individual as motivated by the search for pleasure. Anna Freud (1936) writes: "Different instinctual impulses are perpetually forcing their way from the id into the ego, where they gain access to the motor apparatus, by means of which they obtain gratification" (p. 6). This language strongly echoes Freud, and it is a theoretical stance that focuses on sexuality and aggression. By framing the ground of human activity in such stark terms, these theorists wed themselves to a particular view of the therapeutic process and the nature of health. For the individual to function well, these raw id impulses must be brought under the constraints of the reality-based processes of the ego. The individual must find a way to discipline these instincts without sacrificing their integrity. In the analytic relationship, according to these analysts, the same motives are operative. If the needs that drive the analysand are sexuality and aggression, it is hard to imagine how they could be adequately gratified in the analytic relationship. Unless they were well sublimated (a situation that would forestall the need for analysis), gratifying these instinctual motives would be equivalent to consummating the sexual affair or submitting oneself to murder. Gratification in the analytic relationship necessarily undermines the pressure toward consciousness and change. This instinct-based framing of motivation, then, must also be applied to the analyst. The positive countertransference can only stem from the analyst's sexual needs, and for the analyst to make use of her emotionally-founded nurturant impulses would be to capitulate to the fantasized relationship. The negative transference, under this understanding, is generated from the analyst's aggressive needs, and to lend it reality is to confuse inner world with external reality. Ego psychologists, then, remain more firmly committed to abstinence in analytic technique. To submit to the pull of the countertransference, a force that can only spring from the analyst's unconscious, would be to become further entangled in the web of these problematic motives.

Klein begins her career loyal to Freud's conception of endogenously determined drives. In her arguments with Anna Freud, Klein stresses that she takes Freud's theory of the conflict between Eros and Thanatos seriously. Her focus is to extend the study of these drive structures and their operation to the earliest periods of infant development. While Klein retains the language of drive, her description of infantile fantasy makes it clear that she understands these drive structures as inherently relational. The infant comes into the world ready to imagine breasts, penises, good and bad objects. Klein draws attention to how the infant's world is dominated by experiences with the object, both satisfying and frustrating. She sees how the infant responds to these experiences with love and hate. The experience of frustration and the hate it engenders, however, is overwhelming to the infant, and the infant responds by projecting the hate and the persecution it attracts into the mother. Klein's focus on the relational elements inherent in the drives and her portrayal of splitting and projective identification leads to a reconceptualization of the analyst's role. Now rather than serving as the neutral interpreter of reality, the analyst comes to be seen as a container for the analysand's projective processes. The analyst must be able to withstand the analysand's hate and help the analysand reclaim his projections. To realize this task, Klein's followers argue, the analyst must be open to the countertransference; it is there that the projections are registered. The analyst's task is to process these affective communications and render them workable through the process of symbolization and understanding. In the Kleinian tradition, the analyst is no longer seen as operating above the realm of affect. However, within this tradition the emphasis remains on containment and understanding. The countertransference is to be known, made use of, but not acted upon. This understanding of the analyst as container provides shape to a different version of analytic neutrality and abstinence.

The interpersonal and British middle schools, however, increasingly question this technical stance. By focusing on pre-oedipal issues, Winnicott begins to move away from the sexual and aggressive themes that dominate the oedipal stage. The newborn, helpless away from the mother, is not easily described in terms of sexual motivation. The basic needs—hunger, holding, breathing—are too strong in their own right to readily undergo the translation into libidinal language. Winnicott (1963) writes: "In early psycho-analytic days adaptation could only mean one thing, meeting the infant's instinctual needs. A great deal of misconception has arisen out of the slowness of some to understand that an infant's needs are not confined to instinct tensions important though these may be" (p. 86). He suggests that in the first phases of life, the infant's need is not solely for gratification experienced as pleasure, but for caretaking that allows him freedom from the press of internal and external impingements. Winnicott (1965b) states that he needs a relationship that can hold him:

> Only if there is a good-enough mother does the infant start on a process of development that is personal and real. If the mothering is not good enough then the infant becomes a collection of reactions to impingement, and the true self of the infant fails to form or becomes hidden behind a false self which complies with and generally wards off the world's knocks [p. 17].

By stressing the nurturing rather than sexual aspects of these first relationships, Winnicott develops a new portrait of the developmental pathways to health. Health is more dependent on good-enough adaptation from the environment than on adequate internal control of the instincts. This reconceptualization of the developmental process leads to a parallel shift in the understanding of the analytic process. While gratifying sexuality in the analytic relationship seems problematic, meeting the need for a holding environment, for adequate empathic understanding, does not arouse the same uneasiness. It is easier for the analyst grounded in this kind of relational perspective to imagine providing these goods to the analysand. Winnicott writes:

> In our *therapeutic* work over and over again we become involved with a patient; we pass through a phase in which we are vulnerable (as a mother is) because of our involvement; we are identified with the child who is temporarily dependent on us to an alarming degree; we watch the shedding of the child's false self or false selves; we see the new beginning of a true self, a true self with an ego that is strong because like the mother with her infant we have been able to give ego support [p. 19].

For Winnicott, the analyst is not only permitted to but must utilize her emotional drive toward nurturance. She must provide ego support. Once the ground of human activity is reframed in relational terms, the analyst's own countertransference no longer seems so threatening. Her emotional base is conditioned not only by sexual and aggressive cords, but by the responsive instincts of the good-enough mother.

The move away from drive theory is even more pronounced in Sullivan's interpersonal theory. While he continues to acknowledge the inherited portion of our nature, Sullivan is more impressed by the role of culture and upbringing in the development of the individual. He (1953) writes:

> Briefly, I shall proceed by examining one hypothesis after another, selecting those which seem to be the best theoretical formulations now available as to how, from birth onward, a very capable animal becomes a person–something very different from an animal; and as to how this transformation of a very gifted animal–who is always there but who cannot be defined because he is constantly being transformed–is brought about, step by step, from very, very early in life, through the influence of other people, and solely for the purpose of living with other people in some sort of social organization [p. 5].

For Sullivan, libido and aggression are not the central organizers of development. The human animal is above all else a social animal, and it is the necessities of interpersonal living that condition our development.

We are motivated by the need to be connected to others, and it is the impulse toward connection that determines our health and pathology. To even speak of human instinct is misleading. The developmental pathways are not so rigid:

> It is likewise clear that the inborn potentialities which thus mature over a term of years are remarkably labile, subject to relatively durable change by experience, and antithetic to the comparatively stable patterns to which the biological concept of *instinct* applies. The idea of 'human instincts' in anything like the proper rigid meaning of maturing patterns of behavior which are not labile is completely preposterous [p. 21].

Here Sullivan distances himself from the Freudian biological tradition. What drives development is the need to be connected to others and to adapt to the social context. The analytic situation, then, is best seen not as a theater of libidinal or aggressive gratification but as a moment of connection between two individuals. The task is not to ferret out the hidden drive forces but to examine the conditions of the relationship. What are the forces that facilitate or obstruct the capacity to be together? Sullivan's disavowal of instinct leads him to move away from prescriptions of technical abstinence. The analyst must help the analysand locate a feeling of security before the obstacles created by anxiety can be explored. As a result he is more willing to consider the analyst's tenderness as a necessary component of analytic practice. The analyst's activity cannot be seen simply as an entanglement in sexuality. Instead, it is part of the movement toward or away from relationship. The countertransference will be conditioned more by the terms of the analyst's anxiety and security operations than by the workings of sexuality and aggression.

Trauma and Choice

In approaching the origins of our suffering we quickly encounter the question of responsibility. We ask: are we the agent of our suffering, do we create it through our actions and choices, or are we the object of our suffering, do we receive it through the misministrations of our family and culture? The answer, of course, must be that we are both, but the route to this balanced reply may vary. The second thematic split amongst the four schools concerns the emphasis each places on the locus of responsibility. Ego psychology and object relations, with their focus on the endogenous tension between the sexual and aggressive drives, the necessarily conflicted position of the Oedipus complex, begin by stressing the agency of the individual. Analysands create their pathology as protection and as substitute gratification. Middle-school and interpersonal theorists, on the other hand, as they increasingly focus on the question of developmental provision, begin by stressing the role of the individual as object. The analysand, in his genealogical origins, suffered from failures in the holding environment, from contagious anxiety in the mother. His adaptation to these failures cannot reasonably be described as a choice–it is a reaction by an as yet unformed person. While this polar description of the split unquestionably fails to account for the real complexity in each school's position and the way each considers both trauma and choice, it is a simplification that still holds some value in our consideration of the development of countertransference theory. I suggest that ego psychology's and object-relations theory's greater emphasis on the analysand's agency in creating suffering leads these schools to retain their allegiance to abstinence in the therapeutic environment; abstinence or the containment of the countertransference, in this view, is the key to demonstrating how the analysand's agency operates. The middle-school and interpersonal theorists' emphasis on the analysand's initial objectness, however, leads them away from tradition. They expand their focus to include how the environment's and the analyst's real failings contribute to the analysand's suffering. Analytic technique must pay attention not only to how the analysand currently creates his suffering, but to how the traumatic action of environmental failure operates on the analysand as an object. Part of this accounting requires that the analyst consider how her countertransferentially mediated action (or lack of action) genuinely impacts the analysand.

Ego psychology, standing more firmly in the Freudian tradition, stresses the analysand's constructive shaping of his experience. The analysand, as an infant or child, in the effort to avoid pain, chooses defensive measures that distort reality. Now, rather than passively and accurately receiving stimuli, the analysand begins to act upon the perceptual process, changing its meaning. The stress on agency, in part, is a derivative of the Oedipus complex. The oedipal child is an active player in the family drama. With the surge in genital interests, the child begins to reperceive the family situation. What was a relatively neutral, loving, triangular environment, is now conditioned by the child's loving and hating. From within the child comes the desire to copulate with the mother, the urge to kill the father. These are the child's desires and out of them the child acts upon the world. The process of distortion and defense, however, divorces the child from this agentive aspect of experience. As an adult, this same analysand enters the therapeutic situation having concealed his agency from himself. The analysand turns to the analyst in the transference and claims that she is the cause of his perceptions, his suffering. The core of his pathology is that he disavows his desire, and claims the world has created his character for him, has traumatized him in a way that necessarily causes his particular defenses. To break through this defensive denial of agency, the analyst must avoid acting. Non-action is the key to alerting the analysand to the discrepancy between his denial of responsibility and the actuality of the analytic situation. By remaining abstinent, by remaining without countertransference, the analyst secures the possibility of showing the analysand how he projects and constructs his experience.

Klein and her followers, while taking a more relational view of instinct than the Freudians, continue to stress the analysand's strong agency in creating his own suffering. They view the infant as dispositionally endowed with a particular degree of aggressive and libidinal drives, with a specific capacity for tolerating frustration. When an infant is endowed with high levels of aggressive drive and low tolerance for frustration, he is prone to attack the frustrating object and to project outward his own distonic experiences. These aggressive maneuvers carried out in fantasy, while momentarily keeping the infant from felt danger, establish a realm of objects that resent their mistreatment and so take on a persecutory relationship to the infant. In essence the infant, through projection, loses track of the endogenous, agentive origin of aggression, and comes to inhabit a paranoid world where he is the victim of persecutory objects. Within the analytic setting, the analysand reenacts these same splitting and projective processes. The analyst's task is to tolerate the projections, receive them without being persuaded by them. By remaining steady in the interpretive stance of understanding, the analyst strives to help the analysand take back the projections and acknowledge more fully how his own fantasy processes have structured his adaptation to reality.

The middle school moves in a different direction. Having seen the iatrogenic difficulties that occur when the analysand feels blamed by the analyst, this school moves toward a position that is implicitly more in line with Freud's seduction theory of pathology's ontogenesis. While the aim of middle-school analysts remains to bring the analysand to an increased experience of his own agency, to allow his true self to emerge and take over authorship of his life, they take a different route to accomplishing this end. Rather than stressing the analysand's agency in the creation of experience, they instead emphasize the analysand's initial complete lack of agency. Winnicott (1962) suggests that the newborn can not yet be considered a center of will. The newborn is a collection of reflexes and motilities that require adequate maternal provision to be gathered into a center of going-on-being:

> It can be said that good-enough ego-coverage by the mother (in respect of the unthinkable anxieties) enables the new human person to build up a personality on the pattern of a continuity of going-on-being. All failures (that could produce unthinkable anxiety) bring about a reaction of the infant, and this reaction cuts across the going-on-being. If reacting that is disruptive of going-on-being recurs persistently it sets going a pattern of fragmentation of being. The infant whose pattern is one of fragmentation of the line of continuity of being has a developmental task that is, almost from the beginning, loaded in the direction of psychopathology [pp. 60–61].

Winnicott stresses that the infant's response to holding failures is a "reaction"; it cannot be described as a choice. While the oedipal child is already an integrated self, the newborn does not operate from a unified center of will, and his reactions cannot be described as a form of agency. The infant's relationship to the mother comprises a state of "double dependence": the infant is absolutely dependent on the mother for his well-being, but is utterly unaware of this dependence. As the infant begins to coalesce into a subjective center, he mistakenly, omnipotently assumes that his experience comes into being as the result of his own wishes and thoughts. This error is the exact reverse of the error the ego psychologists are concerned with. The infant takes agentive responsibility for his experience when he is in fact only the object of the familial events swirling around him. This error in assignment of responsibility is so pervasive that it comes to permeate the infant's perception of himself. He begins to formulate a false self based on reactions to impingements, and mistakes this shadow and artifice for his actual core.

Analysis, then, before it can operate on the agentive aspects of the

Oedipus complex, must first undo this more primary distortion in the perception of the self as object. To restore the analysand to health, the traumatic and uncontrollable aspects of infancy must first be recognized as outside of the analysand's control. What is re-created in the transference is not simply the impossible libidinal expectations of the oedipal child, but the essential needs of the newborn. The analysand, if he is to regain his authentic self, requires a holding environment. What is critical in the analytic project is for the analyst to empathically adapt herself to the analysand in such a way that the true self can emerge without the threat of annihilation. The understood meaning of abstinence has undergone an implicit shift. In this theoretical world abstinence, rather than the simple avoidance of libidinal gratification, comes to signify the effort to avoid impinging on the analysand's subjective core. The analyst must monitor how she acts upon the analysand as object. In contrast to the abstinence of discipline and morality, this new abstinence evidences a more gentle aspect. And it is an abstinence that does not rule out action beyond interpretation in the therapeutic context. To the extent that the analyst can avoid impingement or magical mothering, there is room for caretaking. To provide soothing functions may be useful in allowing the analysand to begin to reestablish himself on a more authentic foundation, may pave the way for these functions to be internalized.[1] This reframing of the therapeutic context admits a revised relationship to countertransference. If analysis calls for a soothing analytic presence, then we can see how the analyst's affective response becomes critical. The analysand needs to be met emotionally as well as cognitively. The analyst's countertransference, her subjective capacity to mother, plays a critical role in the provision of these key therapeutic actions.

For Sullivan, the critical factor in the development of health and pathology is the mediation of tenderness and anxiety in the family environment. At birth the newborn is utterly dependent on his parents. In a well-functioning system, when the baby signals his needs through his affective distress, this elicits a feeling of tenderness in the parents. The experience of tenderness leads them to reliably meet the child's needs and gives the baby his first experience of connection. When the family

[1] This discussion takes us into the territory of self psychology mapped out by Kohut. His work, however, belongs to a later period in the development of the field, and I will take it up more explicitly in chapter seven.

system is compromised, however, the urgency of the baby's needs, rather than eliciting tenderness, causes anxiety in the parents. This anxiety is empathically communicated to the baby, and it leads to serious disturbances in functioning. Sullivan (1953) writes:

> The not-me is literally the organization of experience with significant people that has been subjected to such intense anxiety, and anxiety so suddenly precipitated, that it was impossible for the then relatively rudimentary person to make any sense of, to develop any true grasp of, the particular circumstances which dictated the experience of this intense anxiety [p. 314].

In agreement with middle-school theorists, Sullivan stresses how the incursion of difficulty is an experience that occurs outside of the analysand's actions. The infant does not yet have the integrative capacity to make sense of the mother's anxiety. He cannot fathom what causes it or what might alleviate it. Because the mother's anxiety is resistant to the infant's comprehension, the whole experience must be dissociated and forms part of the "not-me." The analysand, in the present, continues to find those kinds of interpersonal experiences a source of unmanageable anxiety, anxiety that prohibits new experience from registering. Mere abstinence on the part of the analyst, then, will be insufficient to change the paralyzing effect anxiety has on the analysand's cognition. The analyst, if she is to be effective, must provide some assistance to the analysand in modulating the unmanageable anxiety. Not only must the analyst draw on her countertransferential affectivity to shape a tender response, she must be willing to explore how her actual participation in the analytic setting contributes to the onset of anxiety. The analyst is a participant in the analytic relationship and exerts real interpersonal influence through the mediation of the countertransference. This emphasis on the analyst's real effect on the analytic relationship leads theorists of this school to be more willing to examine and disclose their countertransferential participation.

Reality and Creativity

The lure of "reality" is compelling in the analytic dialogue. It provides the hope of an independent and absolute arbitrator for technical disputes; it offers the analyst hope for some authority greater than a precarious subjectivity. Ego psychology, with its focus on the mechanisms of defense, increasingly is concerned with the adaptation to reality. Pathology, in this model, originates from the distortion of reality to avoid affective suffering. Anna Freud (1936) writes: "For some years the infantile ego is free to get rid of unwelcome facts by denying them, while retaining its faculty of reality testing unimpaired" (p. 83). As the child ages, however, the reliance on denial begins to fray the connection with the actual, and reality testing suffers. Truth is sacrificed to the demands of immediate affective well-being. As illustration, Anna Freud describes a child she worked with in play therapy. When the child notices that Anna Freud is more skillful with the pencil, he disavows his pleasure in drawing and renounces the activity in order to avoid the displeasure that is aroused by his felt inadequacy (p. 94). While the renunciation is successful in warding off the experienced threat to self-esteem, it comes at the cost of whittling away a piece of reality, a domain of activity. With time and further threat, more and more of the real is abandoned, leaving the child with an impoverished world in which to operate. The analysand, then, is kept in this impoverished world through the atavistic assertion of these distorting tendencies. Now, suffering, originally instigated by the press of the real, comes about by the denial of the real.

Analysis seeks to correct the distorting tendencies of the analysand. The analyst's abstinence provides a context where the discrepancy between the analysand's affective experience and the analyst's actual nonbehavior can bring awareness to the distortion. The analyst's interpretive activity, then, acts as a dose of reality for the patient. Sterba (1953) writes: "Each separate interpretation reduces the instinctual and defensive cathexis of the ego in favour of intellectual contemplation, reflection and correction by the standard of reality" (p. 366). The world of subjectivity is set apart from the more durable standard of the real, and it is this impersonal presence that leads to cure. In ego psychology, reality testing becomes the benchmark of health, and the analyst becomes the standard bearer of reality through the avoidance or management of countertransference's impinging presence. Ego psychology's faith in objective reality is a key factor in its disdain for claims that countertransference might have value. Countertransference belongs to the realm of subjectivity and wish, and as such it must exert a distorting influence on the analyst's behavior and perception.

The object-relations school, however, approaches the analytic situation from a different view of development and health. Rather than focusing on the mechanisms of defense, Klein (1932) is concerned with the role of fantasy in perception. The world is never first perceived directly; from the beginning of life the external world is grasped through the mediation of fantasy; we reach out to perceive objects with our imagination, not just our eyes. The infant feels aggression and projects this into the breast to discover a persecutory object. He feels love and weaves this into his perceptions to create the good mother. Furthermore, these external objects, shaped by fantasy, are not static. The infant then reintrojects these objects, further coloring his affective world and shaping his future perceptive possibilities. The analyst's role is to help the analysand see how fantasy has governed his relationships to the world. While the countertransference has a role in gaining access to the analysand's governing fantasies, it must be strongly contained in order to prevent further damage to the capacity to perceive reality.

As the circular process between perception and construction becomes clearer, the idea of an independent standard of reality becomes more remote. The act of perception and its effect on the perceived are too closely tied. While Klein sees the potentially destructive aspects of this process, Winnicott is more keenly aware of how health, too, is dependent on the capacity to generate fantasy. He is concerned less with how the individual comes to adapt to reality, than with how reality adapts to the child. To his mind, the key to health is the family's capacity to form a holding environment for the child. When caretakers are able to provide good-enough mothering, they act to protect the child from both internal and external impingements. Within this protected zone the child has periods where he is protected from the necessity to react. In Winnicott's terms, he is left in a state of "ongoing-of-being." Freed from the need to attend to the external world (and Winnicott would include the press of instinctual need as part of the external world at this stage of development), the infant can turn inward to his own emergent subjectivity. From within this space arises the possibility of the spontaneous gesture–the act unconditioned by external pressure or internal reflex. He (1965b) writes: "The innate creative impulse withers unless it is met by external reality ('realized'). Each infant must re-create the world, but this is only possible if bit by bit, the world arrives at the moments of the infant's creative activity. The infant reaches out and the breast is there, and the breast is created" (p. 12). The true self exercises its creativity when the world adapts to its vision.

I suggest that this idea of the spontaneous act arising out of the true self is conceptually parallel with Freud's earlier views of the orgasmic completion of the reflex arc. Both signify the unfettered expression of the organism's somatic intent. They value the energetic press of subjectivity over the constraining impression of society. This vision of health supports a different view of the therapeutic process. Rather than demanding an objective analyst, one who refrains from imposing subjectivity in place of the real, it calls for an analyst who can nurture the unfolding of the sequestered core of subjectivity. The middle school's emphasis on the authentic exercise of subjectivity leads it to embrace more readily a constructivist view of reality, and to place greater faith in the analyst's subjectivity and in the countertransference as an important source of analytic skill.

The reframing of health and objectivity is even more pronounced in the interpersonal school. Sullivan, immersed in the intellectual culture of pragmatism, approaches the field informed by a markedly different philosophical background. He begins by questioning the assumptions that underlie objectivism. Psychiatry, although it aspires to operate as a science, is conditioned by confusion. Sullivan (1953) writes: "Psychiatry is the preoccupation of psychiatrists; it is all that confounding conglomerate of ideas and impressions, of magic, mysticism, and information, of conceits and vagaries, of conceptions and misconceptions, and of empty verbalisms" (p. 13). In this scathing critique of psychiatry, Sullivan begins by asking his reader to question the limits of what can be known. He suggests that psychiatrists are not privileged observers; their activity is deeply conditioned by the terms of their culture. Here Sullivan shows the influence of Ruth Benedict's cultural anthropology. It has made him aware that all activity proceeds from a ground of cultural experience, and because of the pervasiveness of that culture, its influence tends to operate outside of the psychiatrist's field of vision. When this is understood, we become aware that there is no escape from the influence of our culture and prejudicial experience: "The events which contribute information for the development of psychiatry and psychiatric theory are events in which the psychiatrist participates; they are not events that he looks at from atop ivory towers" (1953, p. 14). The psychiatrist must always act as a participant observer in the analytic process; the task is not to overcome this participation (an impossibility), but to become more fully aware of how this participation makes itself felt. Interpersonal psychoanalysis, then, is grounded in a fundamentally more constructivist epistemology. It begins with an awareness of the inevitable subjectivity of the analyst, and so it can make no sense out of a claim that the analyst must overcome her countertransference. To overcome the countertransference would be to lose one's humanity, a task as impossible as it would be harmful to the patient. The countertransference, rather than being an obstacle to objectivity, forms part of our empathic knowing. It is what allows us to know each other as human and it must be made use of in the analytic relationship. In this view health cannot be seen as alignment with reality; there is no reality to be located separate from the human community's connection to perception. Instead health must be reframed as the skillful capacity to live in community, to adapt to the various demands of relationships. This has been an under-recognized necessity: "But no one lives in anything like the highest style of the art; and it is very disconcerting to notice how badly one lives in the sense of the extent to which fatigue and other discomforts are connected with one's most important dealings with other people" (p. 3). For Sullivan, health must be understood more as an art than a science. It is concerned with our creative capacity for relationship and perception, rather than the allegiance with an independent reality.

Complications and Overlapping Ideas

We have suggested that ego psychology, object relations, the British middle school, and interpersonal psychoanalysis diverge along central thematic concerns and that this divergence plays a critical role in the development of countertransference theory. Yet the deeper complexity of each school is easily lost in the broad brush strokes that I have used to portray them and to suggest that this split is unambiguous would be an error. While the dictates concerning length make it unreasonable to draw out the interplay between the schools more fully, I do want to sketch out briefly, particularly in relationship to ego psychology and the middle school, some of the complexities surrounding their views of objectivity and subjectivity. The difference between their positions is not as unambiguous as it might seem at first glance. In Anna Freud's work, the foundation of ego psychology, lie seeds of the constructivist position. In Winnicott's writing there are claims concerning objectivity. To recognize these additional layers of complexity is to be reminded of paradox, and this awareness of ambiguity leads us more firmly toward the present.

While Anna Freud speaks in objectivist language, there are moments in her writing when the subjective tense breaks through. As we have stated, the primary thrust of ego psychology is concerned with correcting the distorting tendencies of the analysand by the "standard of reality." But reaching agreement with the analysand about the location of this standard is not easy. In part this difficulty is a correlate of the revisions inherent in the structural model. With the development of the tripartite model, Freud moves away from a simple split between conscious and unconscious perception. Now, the ego, formerly the unvarnished venue of accurate perception, is partially submerged in the unconscious. The ego, on the one hand, is the location of the reality principle and, on the other, it is a source of defense. It is this reworking of the ego that leads Lacan (1953) to write: " . . . the ego is structured exactly like a symptom. At the heart of the subject, it is only a privileged symptom, the human symptom *par excellence,* the mental illness of man" (p.16). The ego is no longer the Cartesian core of reality, its proof, but an ambiguous extension of neurosis. With this revision, the capacity to know the real is compromised. For the analysand, his ego-based defenses, rather than feeling crazy, seem to be in accord with the standard of reality. Anna Freud (1936) writes that in contrast to the analysis of libidinal transferences, transferences of defense are not easily felt as distortions by the analysand:

> The interpretation of the second type of transference [transference of defense] is more fruitful than that of the first type [transference of libido], but it is responsible for most of the technical difficulties which arise between analyst and patient. The latter does not feel the second kind of transference reaction to be a foreign body, and this is not surprising when we reflect how great a part the ego plays—even though it be the ego of earlier years—in its production. It is not easy to convince him of the repetitive nature of these phenomena. The form in which they emerge in his consciousness is ego syntonic [p. 19].

While Anna Freud will proceed to argue that the core of the transference of defense analysis is to secure the conditions that will allow the analysand to recognize the unreality of the defense, an unreality that would be readily recognized by any neutral observer, she has still drawn attention to the difficulty of agreement with the analysand. Reality is not undisputed.

The traumatic aspect of this dispute is drawn out more clearly in Anna Freud's discussion of childhood development. Her work with children has made clear to her the normative aspect of fantasy. The young child naturally remakes the world into a vision that is affectively concordant. The adults in the child's life, however, may not find this remaking tendency to be in accord with their needs. While the child's fantasy that he is a horse or an elephant may be enjoyed for a period, as soon as this fantasy interferes with the adult's needs, this amiable tolerance is short-circuited: "The indulgent attitude of the [adult] toward the child's mechanism of denial vanishes the moment that he ceases to make the transition from fantasy to reality readily, without any delay or hitch, or tries to shape his actual behavior according to his fantasies—to put it more exactly, the moment his fantasy activity ceases to be a game and becomes an automatism or an obsession" (1936, p. 86). Again, Anna Freud is careful to stress the fantasy aspect of the game, the way the remaking of the world through fantasy can become an obsession. But at the same time, by stressing the abruptness of the parent's attitude change, she reveals the potentially traumatic and self-absorbed character of the parent's action. Insisting that the child (and so by analogy, perhaps the analysand) accede to our reality, we may do damage. She writes: "The real point at issue is how far it must be the task of education to induce children of even the tenderest years to devote all their efforts to assimilating reality and how far it is permissible to encourage them to turn away from reality and construct a world of fantasy" (p. 85). The language of the real and the fantastized is preserved and kept separate here. Anna Freud, in contrast to more radical constructivists, feels clear about the difference between the two. But to even question the value of imposing reality on a child is to break with the Platonic tradition, which holds to the real as equivalent to the good; it is the ultimate tonic. She has subtly opened the door to a questioning of the immediate accessibility of reality. It leads us to consider the necessity of exploring the conditions of our agreement with the analysand. These are questions that lead toward constructivism.

Ego psychology, then, is not unacquainted with constructivism. The middle school does not abandon objectivism. While, as we have outlined, Winnicott's emphasis on fantasy and subjectivity moves toward an implicitly constructivist position, he simultaneously begins to shape a revised view of objectivity. In his model, objectivity, rather than stemming from the capacity to transcend emotion, is based on the empathic capacity to connect with the roots of our affectivity. Affect is now no longer merely the atavistic resurgence of our animal nature, a resurgence that must interfere with our more evolved cognitive capacities, but a mode of interpersonal communication to ensure the well-being of the newborn. Winnicott (1965b) writes:

> We notice in the expectant mother an increasing identification with the infant. . . . In my view this is the thing that gives the mother her special ability to do the right thing. She knows what the baby could be feeling like, No one else knows. Doctors and nurses may know a lot about body health and disease. But they do not know what a baby feels like from minute to minute because they are outside this area of experience [p. 15].

The healthy mother objectively makes use of her intuition to read the baby's affective state, to sense his needs. The baby objectively responds to the presence or absence of care through the unveiling and masking of his true self. In this model the foundation of objectivity stems from our affective core, a theme we are familiar with from Freud, and it provides the affective scale of value to inform our judgments and technique. This sense of affect's solidity seems to be at the root of Winnicott's technical recommendations. He (1947) writes that in working with psychotics we must be willing to risk bringing our objective hate to bear. The psychotic, filled with terrifying introjects, cannot help but torment us. And nor is this marshaling of torment carried on outside of his awareness. He hates us, in part, and knows that he has behaved in ways to elicit our hate. If we fail to respond with objective affect to this pressure, then we turn the real analytic environment into a dreamscape where nothing can be trusted, where the real is unreachable. Unless the psychotic can access our genuine hate, Winnicott writes, he will be unable to trust that he can access our genuine love; he is thrown into a state of hopelessness and further divorced from the possibility of adequate reality testing. The middle school's sense of an objective scale of affect plays a critical role in the emerging debate on countertransference. As we will see, it permits them a sense that entering the murky waters of the countertransference does not entail a turning away from all reference points.

Health as a Skill (1919–1960)

The evolution in psychoanalytic theory through the 1940s leads to a pivotal shift in the field's understanding of the nature of health. In this revised understanding, health is no longer understood simply as the absence of repression, as the automatic state of the organism in the absence of pathological interference. Instead, psychological health, the capacity to perceive the world and the self accurately, comes to be understood as the end result of specific developmental experiences that lead to the development of key psychological skills. Health is now seen as the active exertion of the affective and cognitive capacities of the self. This shift in understanding has important implications for the technical understanding of abstinence. If health depends on the presence of non-automatic skills, as well as on the absence of distorting tendencies, then we must ask how psychoanalysis acts to facilitate the development of these missing skills in the analysand. Clearly one reasonable answer is that the analyst acts to provide psychological supplementation. To the extent that this supplementation falls in the emotional realm, it would seem that the analyst must engage her own affectivity. In bringing the analyst's emotional self into the mainstream of therapeutic action we are implicitly asked to reconsider our relationship to the countertransference. The countertransference becomes the medium of supplementation.

Freud began with a negative model of health. Health required the absence of repression, the avoidance of compromise formations. When the active interference with accurate perception was lifted, health would automatically make itself manifest. His belief in the automatic character of health had key ramifications for his technical position. To Freud's mind, the ego is naturally synthetic; in the absence of obstacles, its associative nature leads it to draw connections and piece together a coherent picture of reality. When the resistance is conquered, memory is immediately recovered, and the transferential power of the past alleviated. His faith in the recuperative powers of the self can be seen in his address to the psychoanalytic congress in Budapest (1919a). Freud suggests that the first phase of analysis acts to disassemble the pathological defensive formations in the analysand. It is a period of undoing and taking apart. But does this period of undoing have to be followed by a period of active reassembling? The analysand, Freud argues, does not require the assistance of the analyst to reintegrate himself after a course of analysis:

> In actual fact, indeed, the neurotic patient presents us with a torn mind, divided by resistances. As we analyze it and remove the resistances, it grows together; the great unity which we call his ego fits into itself all the instinctual impulses which before had been split off and held apart from it. The psycho-synthesis is thus achieved during analytic treatment without our intervention, automatically and inevitably [p. 161].

The synthetic powers of the ego, freed from the restraint of anticathexis, will fill in the missing pieces just as water floods a valley after a dam is breached. The analyst can only err if she succumbs to the temptations of supplementation.

The influence of the four schools of psychoanalysis, however, has diminished the faith in the automaticity of health. The advent of the structural theory (Abend, 1989) has led to an increasingly active and positive view of health. Analysts can no longer hold to the idea that their task is only to unravel pathology, to undo repression; their awareness of the active skills that are required in health is too clear. For ego psychology the task of analysis must in part be the strengthening of the ego. It must become better able to tolerate tension and utilize affect as a source of information. The ego must learn how to mediate skillfully between the urgency of the id and the punitive restrictions of the superego. For Klein, health requires that the individual develop a resilient capacity to occupy the depressive position. The individual must relinquish splitting and integrate his ambivalent feelings. The capacity to temper hate and make reparation needs to be developed. Given the active skills required for health, I argue, the ego or the object-relations psychologist must question how abstinence, by itself, will lead to the creation of the missing skills.

Within the British middle school and interpersonal school this problem is experienced even more acutely. At the core of Winnicott's and Sullivan's work is the idea that the child is critically dependent on the adult. The reliance on the parent for developmental supplies does not stop at birth. The holding environment provides the material from which the infant will construct internal structures. Pathology, in this model, arises not only from the distorting press of defense, but from the failure of development. The suffering adult has never had the experience of an adequate holding environment that would allow him to organize the subjective core of his true self. Health is dependent on the presence of internal structure that can be created only in the context of particular emotional experience. The goal of analysis, then, must be twofold. The analyst must not only interpret defense but act to provide missing experience. The analyst must act as a holding environment, must provide a remedial relationship. These changing views of health and pathology lead to a parallel shift in the understanding of therapeutic action.

Therapeutic Action (1950–1999)

The growing focus on the nurturant environment of childhood, coupled with the recognition of the skills essential to health, leads to attempts to broaden the background theory of therapeutic action. Analysis acts not only through the force of interpretation, but by its capacity to shape a new relationship, a relationship not conditioned by the traumatic pressures of the infantile past (Winnicott, 1956; Loewald, 1960; Mitchell, 1993). In this new relationship, developmental adaptations that have become ingrained in obstructive ways are reopened. The analytic situation fosters a regression to previous developmental stages, and through contact with the maturer presence of the analyst, these stages can be reworked. This metaphor of reparenting can be seen both in Anna Freud's statement (1936) that the analyst is a new object for the analysand and, perhaps even more strongly, in Balint's (1953) suggestion that analysis offers a new beginning to the analysand. The idea that the analyst acts as a new parent for the analysand is most clearly stated by Winnicott (1965b): "My thesis is that what we do in therapy is to attempt to imitate the natural process that characterizes the behaviour of any mother of her own infant. If I am right, it is the mother-infant couple that can teach us the basic principles on which we may base our therapeutic work, when we are treating children whose early mothering was 'not good enough,' or was interrupted" (pp. 19–20). These emerging ideas on therapeutic action, however, trespass on dangerous ground. To suggest that the analyst actually provides something new to the analysand, something beyond the pure reality of interpretation, is to venture into the realm of suggestion.

Suggestion demands that the therapist cast her lot behind particular changes and set herself against the resistance. Alexander (1946), in forwarding his theory of the "corrective emotional experience," seems to take these ideas on therapeutic action to a logical extreme, but in passing this way he fails to give adequate concern to the specter of suggestion. Alexander argues that the therapeutic effect of psychoanalysis is dependent on the analyst's capacity to function as a new object for the analysand. In particular, the analyst must distinguish herself from the emotional climate established by the parents during childhood. If the parents were critical and emotionally cold, the analyst needs to separate herself concretely from this transferential past by displaying praise and warmth.

In this attempt to separate the present reality from the transferential past we can see the echos of Alexander's earlier views on superego analysis. Change occurs through the analysand's realization that the present no longer requires the self-punitive adaptations that were evolved to cope with a difficult past. Alexander's theory, however, called forth an avalanche of criticism. The most concentrated criticism was leveled at the idea that the analyst should consciously manipulate her presentation in order to evoke certain reactions or realizations in the analysand. To suggest that the analyst should deliberately dissemble not only flies in the face of accepted ideas of abstinence but also insults the ethic of truth that underlies analysis. Furthermore, to deliberately play a benevolent role in the analysand's psychic economy is to run into difficulties–we risk instituting or reviving a manic defense. Our merely acting as a split-off good object cannot help the analysand move to the more integrated depressive position. Despite this well-founded barrage of criticism, the idea of analysis acting as a corrective emotional experience does capture something about the evolution of the field at that time, and it is an idea that is not without merit. When we are concerned with establishing an atmosphere of safety, when we try to avoid vicious cycles in the transference-countertransference interaction, we are working to provide a particular kind of emotional experience for the analysand that we believe will be of use. The question, and it is a question we will have to return to in later chapters, is not whether the therapeutic action of psychoanalysis is dependent on a corrective emotional experience, it is how we structure the analytic situation to best provide that experience. As analysts, how do we change ourselves to provide an atmosphere of safety without sacrificing our authenticity? How can we make ourselves felt as an integrated object, a real object, rather than an omnipotently good object? These questions are critical for how we eventually decide to make use of our emotional response, our countertransference.

The Reemergence of the Countertransference (1942–1960)

The period from Freud's *Papers on Technique* (1911–1915) to the reemergence of countertransference in the literature in the 1950s, I have tried to show, cannot be seen merely as a latency period for countertransference theory. To do so is to misrepresent the complexity of the underlying forces that paved the way for the changing attitudes toward countertransference. During this period the field underwent essential change in its understanding of neutrality and the untenability of conventional objectivism. The field's view of pathology became refined and there was a growing sense of the multiple skills required for health. But at the root of all of these changes was the enduring pressure of the clinical situation, the necessity to be of use. Analysts had more churning within them than surgical contemplation. In the struggle against resistance, analysts experienced a wide range of feelings. But these facts were not easily contained in the strained theoretical edifice of psychoanalysis.

At first theorists strove to preserve the traditional prohibition of the countertransference by stretching the boundaries of the old model to include the new findings. This accommodating trend can be seen in the work of both R. Fliess (1942) and K. R. Eissler (1953). Both theorists redefine the role of the analyst, while preserving the vocabulary of the traditional model. Fliess, in his article "The Metapsychology of the Analyst," is concerned with the basis for the analyst's interpretive activity. Benefiting from the experience of previous analysts, Fliess is clear that interpretations must be grounded in the affective life of the analysand if they are to be effective; the analyst must avoid the trap of conducting a merely cognitive, non-penetrating analysis. This awareness, however, poses a challenge to the understanding of neutrality. How can the analyst secure an emotional understanding of the analysand without sacrificing her neutrality and objectivity? Fliess (1942) responds that the analyst can secure her objectivity by visiting the emotional realm under controlled conditions. He writes:

> On what does the so called born psychologist's keenness in sizing up his object's utterances depend? Essentially on his ability to put himself in the latter's place, to step into his shoes, and to obtain in this way an inside knowledge that is almost first-hand. The common name for such a procedure is 'empathy'; and we, as a suitable term for it in our own nomenclature, should like to suggest calling it *trial identification* [p. 220].

The analyst, in the course of working with the transference, must introject the patient as an object. Through this introjective process, the analyst can gain a taste of what it is like to perceive the world as the patient does. Then, with this experiential knowing secured, the analyst discharges the introject through projecting it back onto the analysand.

The introjection must be transitory in order to protect the analyst from sacrificing the free play of her associative capacity. This account of the analyst's process is in part a radical departure from the historical account of the analyst. Fliess has acknowledged that the analyst is transformed by the analytic encounter; she does not remain implacable. In this sense we can see how Fliess anticipates Racker's (1968) work on the countertransference. Fliess has suggested, although without speaking the word, that the countertransference is a source of knowing the patient.

Yet, while Fliess moves awareness forward, the omission of reference to countertransference is significant. Fliess seems uncomfortable with the more subjective term "empathy" and substitutes the more technical-sounding "trial identification." Fliess is careful to speak of the trial identification as a carefully controlled procedure. He describes the process as though it was a laboratory experiment. We set the timer, enter the chamber of our affectivity, and then emerge to towel off the subjective dew. The analyst visits her subjectivity; she does not live there. The analyst's identification process is not owned, it is only a trial run, a kind of test drive without commitment. By admitting the process of trial identification, Fliess actually works to forestall the recognition of countertransference's inevitability. He has created a language that allows the analyst to describe the troubling findings of the analytic encounter, without abandoning the inherited model of technique.

Eissler (1953), in his well-quoted article: "The Effect of the Structure of the Ego on Psychoanalytic Technique," falls prey to this same fault. He struggles to preserve the classical notion of abstinence, while simultaneously admitting its limits. Eissler writes out of an awareness of the failures that stemmed from the practice of the basic model: "Early experience demonstrated that the basic model technique had led to a stalemate" (p. 400). Phobias demanded more than interpretation to succumb to analysis. For moments, at least, the analyst needs to issue commands to the analysand that he approach the phobic situation in order to heighten the available quota of affect. The demand for activity can also be seen to underlie the difficulties later analysts faced. Patients with poor ego strength may not be able to cope with the abstinent character of the analytic situation. In the early stages of analytic work they may require greater support. Eissler's concern is that if the analyst permits herself forays into activity, she may surrender the capacity to demonstrate to the analysand the transferential nature of his convictions. Through this activity, the analyst runs the risk of deeding too much reality to the analysand's perceptions. But by holding back, the analyst runs the risk of sterile stalemates. Eissler tries to avoid this dilemma through the introduction of parameters. Under certain conditions, he suggests, the analyst may introduce parameters into the analytic situation that extend beyond interpretive activity. These parameters of technique, however, should be seen as deviations from the pure metal of analytic action. Eissler, stressing the ultimately undesirable necessity of parameters, writes:

> (1) A parameter must be introduced only when it is proved that the basic model technique does not suffice; (2) the parameter must never transgress the unavoidable minimum; (3) a parameter is to be used only when it finally leads to its self-elimination; that is to say, the final phase of the treatment must always proceed with a parameter of zero [p. 400].

By demanding that analysis complete itself with a phase devoid of parameters, Eissler underscores the dichotomy between genuine analysis and compromised analysis. Parameters may be necessary to move the analytic relationship forward, to be able to reach true analysis, but they are in no way desirable in and of themselves. By underscoring the necessity of going beyond pure abstinence, Eissler creates greater permission in the field to explore the analytic needs of patients who have more pronounced personality difficulties. But these explorations, when understood as parameters, must necessarily be appendages to analytic theory.

It is theoretically more elegant and more satisfying if the whole field of analytic technique can be governed by a unified theory. The "diversions" required by more disturbed patients, rather than sidebars to pure analysis, should be reconceptualized so they can be brought back into the analytic fold. It is this push for a more unified theory of analytic technique—a unification that does not require a radical split in the understanding of the patient's and the analyst's subjectivity, that does not require a fundamental split in the methods for characterologically disturbed versus neurotic patients—that leads the field to reconsider its relationship with gratification, subjectivity, and countertransference.

The Rehabilitation of the Countertransference (1947–1999)

This account of analytic history has brought us to the moment when the term "countertransference" reenters the clinical dialogue. At the end of the 1940s and the beginning of the 1950s, Winnicott (1947), Heimann (1949), Tower (1956), Little (1951), Racker (1968), and others, almost simultaneously, began to write about the countertransference as not only an inevitable but potentially useful component of the analyst's psychology. It had become clear to these writers that sanitizing the analyst's subjectivity is not feasible; the pressures of the clinical environment are too pervasive to allow the eradication of the countertransference. The question they must grapple with, then, is how the unavoidable presence of the countertransference can be integrated into the body of analytic technique. For the Kleinians the emphasis is on how the analysand's fantasy registers on the analyst's unconscious through the process of projective identification. The countertransference, for these writers, comes to be seen as an extended part of the analyst's objectivity. For others, the pervasiveness of the countertransference leads to a more radical challenge to the traditional understanding of the analytic situation and the role of objectivity. These writers recognize the interpersonal nature of the analytic situation and come to see how the analyst can not avoid her subjectivity. To remain ostensibly implacable, while in fact subtly affected, is to subject the analysand to a mythical account of the analyst's reality. The insistence on the analyst's objective purity has become a traumatic imposition on the analysand. To refuse to meet developmentally appropriate needs can only lead to a further stalemate. These changing views of objectivity and gratification lead to a new willingness to consider the function and use of countertransference.

During the fifties a rush of articles are published detailing the potential use and misuse of the countertransference. It is at this point that other surveys on the history of countertransference theory begin to take up the subject in depth. Tansey and Burke (1989), Slakter (1987), and others have thoroughly documented this period. The work we are now detailing belongs to the modern period, and as such must be addressed in any current account of how the countertransference is to be understood and utilized. In the following chapters I will return to some of this work to consider the arguments in more detail, but I want to explore here the main thrust of theoretical development and controversy concerning the countertransference.

The first step in the reemergence of countertransference is the final coalescent recognition of classical neutrality's untenability. While the difficulties inherent in the metaphor about the surgeon have long been recognized, its Lazarus-like character has kept it in the center of analytic debate. After each apparent death, to this point in analytic history, it has reformed itself to recapture the analytic imagination. At this point, however, this resurrective capacity seems to wane. These new critics of analytic technique are not content merely to revise the vision of abstinence and neutrality–they want to overturn it. They begin to turn the critique of subjectivity against itself. Rather than suggesting that the presence of countertransference marks the eruption of the egocentric, they suggest that the demand for the absence of countertransference is itself determined by unconscious countertransference. The denial of the analyst's subjectivity is based on fear. Racker (1972), perhaps the most dedicated champion of the countertransference during this period, suggests that the durability of the surgeon metaphor has been dependent on the inadequate and collusive nature of the training analysis:

> The lack of scientific investigation of countertransference must be due to rejection by analysts of their own countertransferences–a rejection that represents unresolved struggles with their own primitive anxiety and guilt. These struggles are closely connected with those infantile ideals that survive because of deficiencies in the didactic analysis of just those transference problems that later affect the analyst's countertransference. These deficiencies in the didactic analysis are in turn partly due to countertransference in the didactic analyst, as I shall show later. Thus we are in a vicious circle [p. 179].

Here Racker suggests that the countertransference is a source of anxiety for analysts; it is a reminder of our too human past, of our fallible subjectivity. As a result, analysts have denied its existence and perpetuated its denial in each successive generation of analysts through the narrowing of the training analysis. Tower (1956) echoes this same theme when she discusses the shame that has surrounded acknowledgment of the countertransference; the subtle implication has been that "for analysts to discuss their countertransference reactions in public would be somewhat indecently self-revealing" (p. 131). The capacity for denial, however, has slowly worn away, and Racker, awakened to his irreducible subjectivity, will not capitulate to the restrictive power of this shame. He (1972) suggests "We must begin by revision of our feelings about our own countertransference and try to overcome our own infantile ideals more thoroughly, accepting more fully the fact that we are still children and neurotics even when we are adults and analysts" (p. 179). The analyst, Racker argues, cannot be placed on a discontinuous plane from the analysand.

Having turned the critique of the countertransference on its head by questioning the neurotically determined motivation to avoid it, Racker opens the door for a more sustained questioning of classical technique. Increasingly, what is plainly stated is the significative character of the classical analytic attitude. Inherent in this attitude is the assumption that by avoiding speech, the analyst can remove herself from action, and so secure her impressionless ambiguity. Analysts, however, have increasingly felt the difficulty connected with claiming that the patient's feelings about the analyst's inactivity is merely projection. Now Racker (1968) speaks to this implicit feeling directly: he suggests that "the analyst's *silence is a form of acting.* To interpret also is to act" (p. 36). To describe the analyst as non-active, then, makes no sense. The analyst is always acting–the only question is, what is the nature of that action, and how might we expect the analysand to react to that action? In certain cases with which we have become familiar, silence reasonably elicits iatrogenic effects. Revealing the impossibility of non-behavior by the analyst again restrengthens the trend toward analytic responsibility. Analysts now realize they cannot just blame the analysand for the resistance. The resistance, whatever its neurotic character, is tied to the analyst's acting (silent or otherwise), and the analyst as the presumably more adaptive member of the dyad must be willing to change herself. Winnicott (1956) writes:

> In these phases of analytic work resistance or that which would be called resistance in work with neurotic patients always indicates that *the analyst has made a mistake,* or in some detail has behaved badly; in fact, the resistance remains until the analyst has found out the mistake and has tried to account for it, and has used it [p. 417].

The analyst, rather than assuming her sanity and the patient's insanity, must be ready to question how she has participated in the transference matrix through the influence of her own countertransference.

But the recognition of the latent countertransference and its potential iatrogenic effects on the analysand does not entail further attempts to withdraw from the subjective. The increasing awareness of the analysand's emotional pressure leads to an increasingly solid recognition that countertransference, rather than being a necessary sign of the analyst's dysfunction, is a normative part of the analytic process. Winnicott (1947), in his article "Hate in the Countertransference," suggests that analysands behave in ways that objectively call for an emotional response on the part of the analyst. When patients act in difficult ways, when they provoke us, we naturally respond: "What we as analyst call the countertransference needs to be understood by the psychiatrist too. However much he loves his patients he cannot avoid hating them and fearing them, and the better he knows this the less will hate and fear be the motives determining what he does to his patients" (p. 195). At times, the analysand will act in self-destructive ways, ways that so thoroughly destroy the analyst's helpful intentions and acts, that the affective scale of value calls for analytic hate. The objective response in these cases is hate, not indifference. The situation is the same as that with an adopted child:

> It is notoriously inadequate to take such a child into one's home and to love him. What happens is that after a while a child so adopted gains hope, and then he starts to test out the environment he has found, and to seek proof of his guardians' ability to hate objectively. It seems that he can believe in being loved only after reaching being hated [p. 199].

Unless the analysand can reach our hate in these moments he will be unable to trust that he can access our genuine love. Racker takes this a step further by proposing the "law of talion": that every positive transference evokes a positive countertransference and every negative transference must evoke, at some level, a negative countertransference. For Racker the interaction between transference and countertransference is inevitable and is governed by clear principles.

This emerging sense of the affective objectivity in the countertransferential response opens thought to its epistemological value. In the work of Heimann, Little, and Racker, among others, there is a sharpening focus on the analyst's affective response as a method of knowing. They suggest that the countertransference, when adequately attended to, provides critical information about the analysand's object world, his projective and introjective experiences, and his effect on others. Heimann (1949) writes: "My thesis is that the analyst's emotional response to his patient within the analytic situation represents one of the most important tools for his work. The analyst's counter-transference is an instrument of research into the patient's unconscious" (p. 140). Increasingly, the analyst's affectivity is seen as more than merely subjective residue. It comes to be recognized as the innately human responsiveness to the analysand's presence. Extending Klein's (1946) theory, Racker (1968) implicitly redefines projective identification. He begins using "projective identification" to signify the actual rather than the fantasized effect that the analysand has on the analyst. This redefinition takes hold, and "projective identification" comes to suggest the affective influence the analysand wields on the analyst. To the extent that the countertransference is determined by the analysand rather than by the idiosyncrasies of the analyst, it becomes a reliable means of knowing the analysand. In part, this suggestion that the countertransference can function as a source of analytic insight is simply a return to Freud's statement that the analyst must turn his unconscious toward the patient as a receptive organ. But to see only the continuity with Freud is to overlook the significance of language. By describing the countertransference as the analyst's source of affective knowing, these analysts begin to disassemble the analyst's epistemological privilege. With this revised understanding, the classical opposition between cognition and emotion is mediated. Objectivity is no longer dependent on the ability to levitate above the emotional realm. Instead, the analyst must draw on the emotional aspect of herself as a genuine source of immediate knowledge of another human.

The recognition of countertransference as a source of knowing, however, cannot be seen simply as the triumph of constructivism. While on the surface the acceptance of the analyst's subjectivity as part of the capacity to know seems to undermine traditional notions of objectivity, it simultaneously acts as a lifeboat for certainty. If objectivity is dependent on the capacity to "overcome" the countertransference, then the eruption of countertransference would require the analyst to abandon claims to objectivity. These theorists aim to rehabilitate the analyst's objective capacity by reframing the significance of the countertransference. Both Heimann and Racker suggest that the countertransference, rather than necessarily being the idiosyncratic property of the analyst, is actually the creation of the analysand. Heimann (1949) writes: "From the point of view I am stressing, the analyst's counter-transference is not only part and parcel of the analytic relationship, but it is the patient's *creation,* it is part of the patient's personality" (p. 142). The analysand, through the process of projective identification, unconsciously but deliberately injects the countertransference into the analyst. While Racker is careful to disclaim the necessary veracity of the countertransference, to caution that the countertransference must be made an object of awareness and processed further, he still preserves the conceptual separation between subjectivity and objectivity. The countertransference, through this understanding, is purified and freed from the potential degradation of the analyst's subjectivity. The analyst, when she reaches a correct understanding of the countertransference, can reclaim the mantle of objectivity.

This rush toward the countertransference, however, is driven by more than the epistemological revisions in the field; it is a resurgence that draws part of its strength from the changing views of gratification. The analysand needs to make real contact with the analyst in order to become well; and the necessary point of contact is through affectivity. The analyst, if she is to be helpful, must allow her countertransference to become manifest; it is the vehicle of her reality and caring. Without the opportunity to access the analyst's affective subjectivity, the analysand cannot recognize the analyst as a real other. Only when the analyst participates more fully as a subjective other, can the analysand gain any hope that this may be a new kind of relationship, that the world actually holds possibility. The analysand, in order to rework his damaged relationship to himself, to believe in his own goodness, must first have a believable experience of being found valuable by another. Winnicott argues that the analysand must be able to locate more than the analyst's professional self–he must be able to feel the analyst's actual self. When the analysand is acting antagonistically he needs to be able to experience our objective hate in order to gain trust in the reality of our responses. While Winnicott is careful to caution that the analyst needs a well-developed capacity to sustain affect without acting, he has suggested that there are moments when we must act on our affectivity if we are to be helpful.

This sense of the necessity of some analytic affect also seems to be behind Tower's (1956) work on the countertransference. In her account (see chapter one) of how she forgot and missed a session with an abusive client, Tower implies that her unwillingness to subject herself to further abuse is not only reasonable, but helpful. When she acts out her countertransference, the patient gains some sense that she can affect Tower, that she matters. For these analysts, supplying this kind of affective presence, when it is grounded in the actual felt core of the analyst, is a form of necessary gratification rather than a seductive pull into substitutive gratification.

As Ferenczi argued in his clinical papers, the analysand needs to experience the analyst as fully human. Only when the analyst's failings are integrated with her strengths can the analysand move beyond fantasies of rescue. This is Little's (1951) argument when she suggests that the analyst must be willing to offer explanations for her analytic mistakes:

> Such explanation may be essential for the further progress of the analysis, and it will have only beneficial results, increasing the patient's confidence in the honesty and goodwill of the analyst, showing him to be human enough to make mistakes, and making clear the universality of the phenomenon of transference and the way in which it can arise in any relationship [p. 148].

Unless the analyst is willing to admit to her human participation in the analytic relationship, the analysand is left with the difficult feeling that he is the only one with neurotic impulses. The shame of being the sole author of the transference reaction acts to restrict the analysand's willingness to explore these difficult waters. Through the disclosure of the countertransference, Little argues, we help the analysand develop better reality testing and greater tolerance for his own humanness.

It is at this point in the argument for the use of the countertransference that division begins to occur in the ranks of the revisionists. While these analysts seem to be in agreement about the use of the countertransference as a mode of knowing the analysand, and even to agree about the necessity of not claiming objective purity, they disagree about whether the countertransference should be directly communicated to the patient. Winnicott (1947) suggests that the countertransference must be borne for a long period in silence (p. 198). Racker (1972) argues that while there may be moments when countertransference disclosure is helpful, in general "the purposes sought by communicating the countertransference might often (but not always) be better attained by other means" (p. 200). The hesitation surrounding countertransference disclosure stems from a concern that it may injure or impose a burden on the analysand. Heimann (1949) suggests that the countertransference, while useful in gaining insight, should not become a point of discussion. The countertransference "is his private affair, and I do not consider it right for the analyst to communicate his feelings to his patient. In my view such honesty is more in the nature of a confession and a burden to the patient" (p. 142). When the analyst discloses a countertransference response, she has subtly imposed a constraint on the analysand. If the analyst says she was upset during a session when the analysand raged, she makes it more difficult for the analysand to explore that territory in the future. The analysand will tend to restrict himself out of concern for the analyst or the possibility of retaliation. The countertransference disclosure has placed reality as an obstacle to free association. Those who defend disclosure, however, might reply that this restriction in free association, this assumption about the analyst, can now productively become the new front of analytic exploration.

While the beginning of the 1950s sees a surge in more positive accounts of the countertransference, these revisionist claims are not without critics. Led by Annie Reich (1951), analytic purists seek to retain the division between the analyst's empathic responsiveness and her countertransferential reactions. While Reich admits that the analyst will experience a limited range of emotional response to the patient, she argues that this cannot be properly labeled countertransference. The analyst, she writes, must have some relationship to the patient:

> We expect him [the analyst] to be interested in the patient, to have a friendly willingness to help him. He may like or dislike the patient. As far as these attitudes are conscious, they have not yet anything to do with counter-transference [p. 154].

Reich, without notice, is verging on contradicting the surgeon metaphor. The analyst, she admits, has human emotions in reaction to the analysand. But when the analyst is well analyzed, this reaction will be well contained; the emotion will remain within a narrow band of intensity and will avoid intrusion from the unconscious. This self-control is necessary for the analysand to be able to use the analyst as a screen for the transferential projections:

> The analyst has to remain neutral in order to make this transference possible. He must not respond to the patient's emotion in kind. He must be able to tolerate love and aggression, adulation, temptation, seduction, and so on, without being moved [p. 154].

In this passage, Reich clearly aligns herself with the classical view of abstinence, neutrality, and the countertransference. The analyst must remain uninvolved to secure her objectivity, her capacity to distinguish authoritatively between the patient's distorted transference and her own clear abstinence. The perseverance of this more conservative voice underlines the controversy in the field concerning the countertransference. The acceptance of the countertransference, after so many years of prohibition, does not come easily.

To suggest that the field has reached any unanimous decisions concerning the countertransference would be an error. The conservative forces find too much eloquence in the classical model to abandon it outright. Writers like Brenner (1985) continue to speak of the countertransference as a compromise formation. Under this concept the countertransference is seen as the product of drive derivatives and unresolved internal conflict. It cannot be understood as synonymous with intuition or empathy. When countertransference is the product of pathological compromise formations, it "interferes with the conduct of an analysis or makes it impossible altogether" (p. 449). Here countertransference continues to signify the analyst's unresolved personality difficulties, and as such it is a pervasive threat to the analyst's objectivity and skillful handling of technique. In this case the presence of the countertransference must be dealt with by further self-analysis. Yet even Brenner is no longer willing to defend the claim that the analyst must be without countertransference. He writes: "Countertransference is a ubiquitous phenomenon, a set of compromise formations comprising the analyst's transference to the patient(s). . . . We all agree, from the writings of many colleagues on the subject, that countertransference is not necessarily harmful or disadvantageous" (p. 449). Brenner concedes that the analyst, like any other, cannot shed her humanity.

This view of countertransference, however, has been increasingly overshadowed by the totalist camp (Kernberg, 1988). The primary thrust of analytic writing has moved toward a broader definition of countertransference, a definition that includes the full range of the analyst's emotional reactions. Within this wide majority (Mendelsohn et al., 1992) the force of opinion has come to accept the use of the countertransference as a diagnostic tool. The countertransference is recognized as an essential means for assessing the state of the analysand's internal object world and interpersonal relations. Emotional impact is neither random nor necessarily undermining of objectivity. As Schafer (1992) writes: "*In place of the analysis of resistance, we may install the analysis of countertransference alongside the analysis of transference and defensive operations as one of the three emphases that define a therapy as psychoanalytic*" (p. 230). The countertransference is now regularly spoken of in clinical papers, and the question no longer seems to be whether the countertransference holds informational value about the patient, but rather how best to decipher this information. This position is well represented by Tansey and Burke (1989) in their book *Understanding Countertransference.* They strive to outline a procedure for converting raw countertransference experience into the more considered form of analytic empathy.

While the storm surrounding the informational use of the countertransference has subsided, the same cannot be said concerning the communication of the countertransference to the analysand. Seventy years after Ferenczi first ventured into the difficult waters of mutual analysis, the field at large continues to regard countertransference disclosure with suspicion. To reveal the countertransference to the analysand, this reasoning suggests, is to cloud the transference and burden the analysand with responsibility for the analyst (Schafer, 1992; Brenner, 1985). Countertransference disclosure, it is argued, works to stifle exploration; it lends the appearance of reality to the transference and obscures the capacity to uncover the projective nature of perception. The temptation to reveal the countertransference is determined by the *unconscious* countertransference (understood in the classical rather than totalist sense), and as such is motivated more by the analyst's urges for gratification than by the analysand's needs. Rather than correcting psychic reality through disclosure, the analyst better serves analysis by interpretation and exploration of the analysand's unconscious beliefs and wishes.

Yet this conservative, centrist position is not without debate, and increasingly analytic writers have come to question the taboo against disclosure. In many cases this questioning is a cautious one. Writers like Mitchell (1993), Spezzano (1993), and Tansey and Burke (1989) underline the phobic quality of the technical prohibition against countertransference disclosure. They suggest that while interpretation should remain the first choice, there may be moments when countertransference disclosure, despite the dangers it entails, may be effective. But these writers, perhaps wary of the field's rancor, say little about the positive uses of countertransference disclosure, and do not provide detailed decision procedures for evaluating when to employ disclosure. At the more radical end of the spectrum are writers like Bollas (1987) and Ehrenberg (1992) who suggest that there are moments when the analyst's willingness to bring the countertransference into the analytic discussion is critical to circumventing therapeutic impasse. Ehrenberg, perhaps the most extreme in the active disclosure of the countertransference, regularly speaks of her subjective states as part of the analytic process. To her mind, the willingness to reveal the countertransference plays a critical role in building trust and helping the analysand perceive the analyst more accurately.

To adequately understand countertransference and its use, we must explore how we currently understand analytic epistemology and the role of gratification and abstinence in the analytic context. Only by addressing these two facets of neutrality can we reasonably begin to move beyond assertion and reach a more considered conclusion to the countertransference debate. It is these issues that I take up in the remainder of this work as we more systematically explore recent writings on the countertransference.

CHAPTER SEVEN

KNOWING AND ANALYSIS

Analysis claims that it is a therapy based on understanding. Change unfolds through the process of understanding. The question of what constitutes understanding, then, must be addressed as we try to sort out the significance of the countertransference. In the analytic context, epistemology is critical to the problem of countertransference both in the effort to make sense of the analyst's understanding and in the analysand's connection to the real. The way we understand these issues will exert a governing effect on how we view the countertransference. It is necessary to take up the problem of epistemology to clarify how the countertransference hinders or facilitates our knowledge of the analysand. The conclusions we reach will determine how we imagine the therapeutic process and its effect on the analysand's reality testing.

Epistemology, regardless of our wish for foundational thought, though, is never a first question. Rather, it is a question that emerges only in the middle of conversation. We are going along in conversation, a claim is made, and we want to ask, "How do you know?" or, more to the point, we disagree and so the question of "Who knows?" arises. We make an interpretation and the analysand asks, "Why do you believe that to be true?" The question of epistemology, then, is always derivative of experience. Before we become philosophic skeptics, we must first learn the language to phrase the question; we must have entered into disputes with our siblings and peers to experience the urge to prove, the worry of doubt. Knowing is always an embedded act. It takes place in a community of discussants and it cannot, and should not, escape the realm of value and choice. These are necessary guides as we move to fix Gestalts and reach agreements that form the basis of interpretive activity. I will argue that analysis has been poorly served by an objectivist epistemology. Our analytic experience has driven us toward a constructivist epistemology, but our understanding of this evolution's implications remains incomplete. This chapter seeks to make the process of knowing more available to our understanding, and to draw out the significance of this theme for our work with the countertransference.

Freud's prohibition of the countertransference, we have argued, stemmed in part from his fear that it would undermine the analyst's ability to see clearly. The activation of the analyst's affect would exert energetic, hallucinatory pressure on his perceptive process. We have seen, however, that the weight of analytic history has undermined this view of perception. When we move from an objectivist to a constructivist epistemology (Hoffman, 1983) we can no longer defend the idea of a non-subjectively mediated access to a singular reality. The analyst's epistemological authority, then, cannot proceed from the capacity to rise above subjectivity. What I want to argue is the reverse: to gain objectivity requires a movement toward our subjectivity. The occurrence of affect in the analyst, rather than posing an inevitable obstacle to objectivity, can in fact serve as an instrument of understanding. Under a constructivist epistemology the countertransference becomes a critical source of our knowing. It helps form the promontories and buttes from which we gain perspective on the analytic relationship. Does the acceptance of constructivism imply an abandonment of objectivity? I am suggesting that it does not, but to make sense of this we need to revise our understanding of truth and verification. In part this is the question of how we decide when our countertransference is idiosyncratic and potentially harmful, and when it is revealing and a source of skillful therapeutic action.

Epistemology also gains significance in relation to the effort to strengthen the analysand's connection to the real. Freud cautions against the countertransference, we have argued, because he feels it must involve the analyst in a gratificatory web that would deplete the impetus toward reality. When we move to a constructivist epistemology, however, reality loses its unambiguous quality. The epistemologically corrective experience of analysis, then, cannot be understood simply as the discarding of fantasy and the acceptance of reality. That view of the therapeutic process requires reality to be singular and accessible asubjectively. But reality is always narratively mediated (Schafer, 1992) and it admits multiple perspectives. Our view of the epistemologically corrective experience of psychoanalysis, then, must be revised to come into accord with the more fluid view of reality inherent in constructivism. The influence of psychoanalysis cannot be to persuade the analysand to abandon fantasy for reality; it must be to help the analysand gain greater flexibility in her perceptive process, to allow her to move between perspectives, and to see how these perspectives are connected and influenced by affective states.

I will suggest that when we understand the sense of constructivism, it leads to a more active use of the countertransference in our relationship to the analysand. Our countertransference can help us form interpretations that lead the analysand toward a more flexible perceptive process. There are even moments in the psychoanalytic process, I will argue, when speaking about our countertransference may provide help to the analysand in understanding perspectives that were formerly too threatening or unimaginable. In this view of analysis, the countertransference plays a critical role in strengthening the analysand's relationship to constructivist reality.

The Death of Objectivism

To speak of objectivism's demise, while once a provocative act, has become commonplace in the analytic literature. Positivism has lost its privileged place in the analytic community, and is now regularly strapped to the board and thrashed like a discredited intellectual in China's Cultural Revolution. The possibility of uninvolved observation is disavowed and the scratches and burrs in the analytic mirror have been well charted (Schafer, 1983; Hoffman, 1983; Mitchell, 1993; among others). The undermining of objectivism has become so thorough that Donnel Stern (1991), in his article "A Philosophy For The Embedded Analyst," writes: "So few analysts are willing any more to defend the blank screen metaphor of the analyst's role, at least in its stark form, *sans* qualifications, that to attack it has become a gratuitous act, useful only as a kind of chest-beating" (p. 51).

The overturning of objectivism has so thoroughly permeated the field that even the ego psychologists, those who were most ready to speak about "adaptation to reality," have been affected. This is perhaps most clear in the case of Roy Schafer. Trained in the traditions of ego psychology, he (1992) has become one of the most eloquent voices for the necessity of wedding psychoanalysis to constructivist epistemologies:

> It is especially important to emphasize that narrative is not an alternative to truth or reality; rather, it is the mode in which, inevitably, truth and reality are presented. We have only versions of the true and the real. Narratively unmediated, definitive access to truth and reality cannot be demonstrated. In this respect, therefore, there can be no absolute foundation on which any observer or thinker stands; each must choose his or her narrative or version [pp. xiv–xv].

Here Schafer has offered a radical critique of objectivist epistemology. Not only does he question the traditional image of the analyst as a mirror-like presence, but he also qualifies the practical nature of reality. For Schafer, reality is not a thing-in-itself that exists outside of our narrative constructs.

As a community, on the whole, we are ready to state our disbelief in objectivism, but we have failed to free ourselves from its ceremonies. In reading modern analytic literature, I am struck by how the language of objectivism tends to creep back into speech as it moves away from the overtly epistemological discussion. We can see this tendency in Bird's (1972) work. In the space of two paragraphs Bird both recognizes the inevitability of the analyst's subjectivity and falls prey to the hope that this subjectivity can remain quarantined:

> Under this arrangement every feeling of warmth, pity, sadness, anger, hope, excitement, even interest; every feeling of coldness, indifference, disinterest, boredom, impatience, discouragement; and every absence of feeling, should be assumed to contain significant elements of the analyst's transference as focused on the patient. This would mean, essentially, that everything arising in the analyst about his patient is assumed to be a part of the substance of analysis, that nothing represents merely the analyst's "real" reaction to his patient, and that especially when something seems most real it can be counted on to contain important aspects of the analyst's transference.
>
> Were the analyst to take this rather imperative view of his own transference potential, he might be much more likely to remain abreast of the personal, neurotic meanings of the myriad but often subtle reactions and attitudes he develops toward his patient. This in turn might make it possible for him at least to keep his transference out of the patient's way and hopefully to use it to further the analysis [p. 66].

Bird holds out an understanding of the analyst's embeddedness, and then immediately surrenders it to the hope of resurrected analytic purity. If the analyst's reactions are inevitably conditioned by his transferential subjectivity, and the degree and location of this conditioning cannot be reliably determined, then awareness of this inevitability cannot serve as an inoculation. When Bird suggests that awareness might help us keep our transference "out of the way," he has realigned himself with objectivist hopes. Through awareness we might change the impact of our transference on the analysand, but we cannot avoid it.

The tacit retreat to objectivism and foundationalism is a tendency that claims even the most sophisticated writers on the subject. Roy Schafer (1992, 1983) and Jay Greenberg (1992), both remarkably sensitive thinkers about analytic metapsychology who are deeply aware of the limits of objectivism, revert at times to objectivist hopes and understanding. Schafer has inherited a language to describe the analytic relationship that he has not yet fully updated to bring it into accord with his wider epistemological stance. Describing the analyst's ability to enter into trial identifications, Schafer (1992) writes: "The analyst will not participate in this empathic way in order to implement or enforce any particular value other than the health-value of knowing reality inside out, as it were, for it is this kind of knowledge that helps the analysand work out less costly and painful solutions or compromises than those with which he came into analysis" (p. 126). Given Schafer's earlier statement that there can be no narratively unmediated access to reality, how can we make sense of the claim that the analyst participates only to promote the value of "knowing reality inside out"? What reality is this? If Schafer is consistent then it must be a reality that *is* mediated, and that mediation must involve a narrative that is chosen by the analyst. The analyst must choose his narrative foundation through some kind of value system. To suggest otherwise, to suggest that one narrative line is objectively more true than another, is to surrender his previous argument.

This move to distance the analyst's interpretive process from the specter of value and choice can also be seen in Greenberg's (1992) *Oedipus and Beyond.* Greenberg, working from a partially interpersonal perspective, is well aware of the untenability of the traditional view of the analyst. He writes: "Theorists who disagree on many other issues unite in insisting that the analyst inevitably participates, inevitably reveals himself, inevitably influences the course of treatment and the evolution of the transference" (p. 214). He goes on to suggest that transference is better understood as a transference of conviction rather than a transference of impulse. He argues that in making this shift, it becomes less plausible to easily dismiss transference as a distortion of reality testing. There is plausibility in the analysand's perception of the analyst and the analyst's countertransference, and this must be respected. Analysis works, under this model, not by asking the analysand to renounce her convictions, but by broadening her perceptive field to admit other ways of viewing the situation. Greenberg writes:

> Transference can be optimally creative only when the patient can be playful with it—only, that is, when he can experience any particular reaction as reflecting but one part of a vast range of possibilities. This depends on the freedom to be aware of as many transference paradigms as possible. . . .
>
> Furthermore, although new transference paradigms do emerge as analysis proceeds, I don't think that what is therapeutic is that a "less realistic" paradigm yields to one that is "more realistic." This, again, would be the version of things in the classic model of transference resolution. But who is to judge which of the paradigms is realistic, especially at any given time? [p. 239].

In this account of therapeutic action, Greenberg suggests that the curative aspect of psychoanalysis proceeds in part from its effect on the analysand's epistemological capacity. The analysand moves from an implicitly objectivist view of the world, a view where only one framing of phenomena is accepted, to an overtly constructivist position. The analysand gains the capacity to hold the reality aspects of multiple perspectives; she gains flexibility and playfulness in her cognitive outlook.

Yet earlier in his book, when he tries to explain his concern with reworking Freud's drive model, Greenberg seems less willing to stay with this constructivist view of reality. Instead he seeks to locate an epistemological foundation for the analyst's interpretive activity. This desire seems to be behind his implicit critique of Loewald's (1971) revisionist work on drive theory. If drives, as Loewald suggests, are conditioned by experience, then the possibility of locating a foundation for interpretation is undermined: "[If] an impulse—any impulse—acquires its particular characteristics over time, as a consequence of its history, . . . [then] there is no one place that a particular piece of analysis can stop, no interpretive bedrock on which everything else is built" (1992, p. 66). Yet Greenberg (1991) seems to suggest that analytic practice requires such an interpretive basis. It is the capacity to locate this ground that allows the analyst to offer interpretations to the analysand that extend beyond the analysand's previously held understanding:

> Perhaps more important, multiple-drive and mixed-model theories put the analyst in the position of listening with what is essentially a kind of naive atheoretical or pretheoretical empathy. Theory supplies the guidelines–the basic rules of procedure–to support the idea that one mental content is inevitably a transformation of some other mental content. Without these, the interpretation never gets beyond what the patient is saying. The interpreting analyst needs some construct that gives warrant for assuming that the patient's experience is more than it seems to be [pp. 126–127].

For Greenberg, the justification for interpretation is provided by the construct of the dual-drive theory. Substituting safety and effectance for libido and aggression, he develops his own account of a dual, endogenous drive theory that allows the analyst to account for both environmentally driven frustrations and internally generated conflicts.

Greenberg's revisionist drive theory provides a critical reworking of metapsychology. In reading his work, however, it is difficult to understand exactly how he stakes out the epistemological ground. In holding that the interpretive warrant should rest on a revised theory of drive, is Greenberg claiming that he has uncovered the analytic foundation, the unconditioned ground? Or is he merely arguing that drive theory provides the most useful starting point for therapeutic interpretation? While there may be reason to be sympathetic to the appeal to biology as the source of epistemological adjudication (an argument I will return to in my treatment of affective knowing and verification), to claim that drive theory could provide an unconditioned bedrock is to slip back toward an insupportable objectivism. Central to Greenberg's argument is the distinction between preexperiential drives and drives conditioned by experience. To accept that drives are conditioned by experience, he argues, is to fall into the abyss of relativism. If drives gain their shape only through interaction with the conditions of living, then the door is opened to a multitude of possible drive formations. The analyst can no longer say what came from the child and what came from the world. There is no way to pin down the analysand's participation in the creation of her neurosis.

The preexperiential drive, however, locates the biologically given in the self. It is the starting point of the person and it allows the analyst to authoritatively construct how the analysand was motivated in the family, how the events of her life might have affected her. The preexperiential is a source of confidence for the analyst, yet this confidence must remain provisional. Even if we accept the idea of preexperiential drives—drives that retain their form, immune from the indentations of experience—we cannot merely appeal to their grace to justify our interpretive authority. By dividing the preexperiential from the conditioned experience, Greenberg has reconstituted the split between appearances and the thing-in-itself. The drive that is conditioned by experience functions in the world of appearance: it is uncertain and difficult to pin down and it provides no sure guidance for action. The preexperiential drive, however, is secure in its being, untouched by the mediation of our subjectivity—it is a thing-in-itself. As soon as we make this differentiation, however, between the pure and impure, the conditioned and unconditioned, the thing of perception and the thing-in-itself, we are fated to lose what we most value. The thing-in-itself, the real thing, becomes severed from the possibility of knowing. If the preexperiential drive is the essential ground for interpretation we must mourn its unattainability. While the drives may not be conditioned by experience, our attempts to know them are deeply conditioned. The way we imagine what safety means, what counts as effectance, has been conditioned by the terms of our life and our culture. The analyst's contact with the unconditioned must always be conditioned by his subjectivity. The hunt for the preexperiential drive cannot free us from the necessity of choice in the formulation of interpretation.

In this consideration of Schafer's and Greenberg's work, the tenacity of the objectivist pull becomes clear. Even among those who are most aware of constructivism, the tendency to lapse into accustomed habits of speech is strong. It is like the reformed cigarette smoker reaching for a match before remembering that she has surrendered that vice. Part of this regressive pull of objectivism stems from the force of history. Our language and our thinking about the mind have been conditioned by the weight of Western history, and the past, as every analyst knows, is not easily surrendered. Yet the difficulty of surrendering objectivist language goes beyond any historical conditioning. Radical skepticism, while intellectually defensible, does not accord with our ordinary experience. We know where we live, remember our address, and feel no need to question the solidity of that knowledge. We condemn child abuse and are free from ambivalence about it. In large portions of our life, the sense that reality is solid is strong. We cannot abandon that sense without doing violence to our epistemological sensibility. Yet the history of psychoanalysis argues persuasively that to accept objectivism naively creates iatrogenic obstacles in our clinical work. We need to find some way of bringing together simultaneously the recognition of constructivism's sense and the enduring sense of reality's solidity.

The Untenability of Objectivism

When we find ourselves repossessed by the desire to locate objectivity, to find greater certainty for our interpretive stance, one way we can help quiet our anxiety is by looking to the wider community of inquiry. During the last century the intellectual world has slowly moved away from objectivism. Physics, the philosophy of science, literary criticism, the psychology of perception, and anthropology have all participated in this evolution.[1] Within each field the static descriptions of reality offered by objectivist epistemologies have proven inadequate to encompass the facts of experience. The participants have come to see the malleable quality of reality, the impossibility of standing outside that which they would judge. These cross-discipline discussions have resulted in a consensus that pure observation of the observed is unattainable. We cannot disembed ourselves from the historical context, from the press of our human subjectivity, or shed our personal bias to become a sterile surface. While it is problematic to take the conclusions of these fields as necessarily weighing on the matters of psychoanalysis, this does not mean that they are without relevance. We should be clear that for psychoanalysis to embrace objectivism, in the face of this cultural concurrence to the contrary, would be to follow a lonely path.

Yet more vital in quieting our anxiety is the evidence from the clinical encounter in documenting objectivism's untenability. Objectivism cannot adequately describe the overlapping realities of the transference and countertransference, and the rigidity of the objectivist approach tends to engrain analytic resistance. In what follows, I will detail the clinical

[1] The trend toward constructivism in these fields has been well documented. To avoid unnecessary digression, then, I treat this theme here with only the broadest of brush strokes. See Gadamer (1960), Feyerabend (1975), Rorty (1982), Bernstein (1983), among others, for a more rigorous account of this epistemological shift.

encounters that have necessitated the adaptation of the new epistemological paradigm.

What sets psychoanalysis apart from philosophy or religion is the encounter between the analyst and the analysand. The necessity of finding some way to work together, the necessity of making life more than merely bearable, creates an empirical imperative. The press of this experience is as close as we can come to fact. The experiential facts of the clinical encounter are not well explained by the traditional objectivist epistemology. That frame of reference forces analytic thought to choose between binary options. It makes us ask whether it is the client or the analyst who sees clearly; it asks us to choose between mutually necessary realities.

When Freud abandons hypnosis in favor of free association, he sets in motion a retreat from the compulsion of epistemological authority. Suggestion is unconcerned with the patient's perception of reality. It asks the patient to sacrifice perceptions and accede to the therapist's will. The therapist says, "The snakes you see are not real; let those perceptions dissipate through in attendance." In this framework the therapist is not only the holder of the real but the arbiter of health and correct action. The patient is not asked for her understanding, is told to not contradict the suggestion. As Freud begins to make use of the cathartic technique, however, this changes. While the analyst retains his authority, the analysand is now admitted as a partial participant in the process of knowing. She must provide the missing memories. With the abandonment of hypnotic trance for the pressure technique, and then the discarding of pressure for free association, the compelling character of the analyst is incrementally reduced. In each step of the progression, the patient's resistance challenges the analyst's ability to impel the patient to accept a particular vision of reality, and leads to a reduction in the use of influence. While this retreat from authority begins as a practical measure and is seen as a concession to necessity rather than truth, it slowly takes deeper root in the psychoanalytic consciousness and asks analysts to consider the genuine sense in the analysand's perceptions.

The enduring presence of resistance in the face of objectivist-inspired technique has driven the field to slowly abandon influence and epistemological absolutism. Seen from this angle the resistance can be understood as the struggle between analysand and analyst for authorship of reality (Spezzano, 1993). When the analyst behaves in such a way as to impose his view of reality on the patient he undercuts the analysand's sense of safety. This assaultive practice works to reinforce rather than alleviate the analysand's difficulties. Greenson (1971), in an article on the "real relationship" between the analyst and the analysand, writes: "By focusing constantly on the patient's transference distortions and ignoring the reality elements, we undermine his self-esteem and make him feel he is always wrong, sick, or crazy, beliefs which he has brought with him into the analysis" (p. 92). To avoid this difficulty the analyst must first work to enter empathically the analysand's perception of reality. This is Kohut's (1984b) critical realization when he suggests that the analysand has a right to demand that the analyst see it entirely from the analysand's point of view. He understands how critical it is for the analysand to first feel perceptively met by the analyst. This epistemological joining is necessary to shape the conditions of safety. Ornstein (1993) writes: "When transference longings are interpretively thwarted (by not being recognized or considered legitimate in the light of infantile or childhood experiences; or as a result of miscarried neutrality or abstinence) they tend to be transformed into resistances, instead of remaining the natural vehicles of understanding and cure" (p. 29). Self psychology is grounded in an understanding that the patient's reality concerning her felt needs must be given credence. This realization has increasingly come to permeate the field. Only after "taking up residence inside the [analysand's] apparently chaotic blaming story," Spezzano (1993) writes, can the analyst "effectively suggest useful narrative changes without evoking this sense of an alien voice trying to wrest authorship of the patient's psychic reality from him" (p. 124). To avoid unmanageable impasses the analyst must be willing to abandon the imperialism implicit in objectivist epistemologies.

This intimate link between safety and epistemology extends beyond the realm of interpretation. While the conflict over truth can be most readily seen when the declarative value of the interpretation organizes the analytic material in a way that cuts across the analysand's pattern of belief, it is a conflict that can pervade the therapeutic context. In regard to the management of the countertransference, this point takes shape in conflicts about the significance of the analytic attitude. For Freud, silence constitutes a key part of the analyst's neutrality. By not speaking, we avoid foisting ourselves onto the analysand's free-associative chain. The analysand, however, may feel threatened by this silence or experience it as a lack of attention. When the analyst avoids speaking about his own emotional participation in the analytic relationship, he may understand this omission as critical to providing the analysand transferential freedom. The analysand, on the other hand, may experience this avoidance as a form of dissembling or coldness. Clearly these negative transference reactions are an essential part of a thorough analysis. In part they belong to the projective impulse of the analysand and their analysis is what leads the analysand away from paranoid isolation. On this side of the Gestalt, these perceptions misrepresent the truth about the analyst; they are a distortion. But the Gestalt can shift, and if we reimagine the analyst as a holding environment or selfobject, then what was distortion becomes sane. From this angle the analysand is right to expect support and active care from the analyst, and the analyst's silence, in the face of the analysand's needs, does represent a form of abandonment. To disregard the sense in the negative transference can lead to its entrenchment. The analysand is left feeling too threatened, the alliance is undermined, and collaborative work cannot proceed. For safety to be restored to the therapeutic relationship, the historical evidence suggests, the analyst must be willing to join with the analysand, at some level, around her sense of reality.

The first force in the field's abandonment of objectivism, then, is pragmatic rather than purely rational. The primacy of the pragmatic, however, should not be seen as a poor method of discovery. Inherent in the nature of the discovered, the veracity of constructivism, is the intimate link between the pragmatic and the real (Dewey, 1929; James, 1907; Rorty, 1983). Constructivism rejects the view that truth is perceived directly by pure thought, through transcending practical aim. It suggests instead that truth is always embedded in the context of value and human necessity, and that this, rather than operating as a degraded form of truth, holds greater sustenance for human activity than truth that would deny its context and relationship to the human. Pragmatic consideration, then, forces open the epistemological door. Having entered the room of constructivism, however, psychoanalysis comes to perceive the logic of ambiguity. The process of joining–if the analyst is to retain his understanding of reality and to avoid the artificiality of dissembling–requires the analyst to hold the simultaneous reality of alternate perceptive frames. This is Greenberg's point (1992) when he suggests that the therapeutic process should not require the analysand to discard her initial transferential set but should instead help her gain the capacity to inhabit multiple perspectival vantage points. The analyst's truths and the analysand's truths, while not congruent, are still not contradictory. To understand this is to increase our understanding of constructivism.

When Freud first opened his clinical practice, the patients he saw held beliefs that were well-distanced from conventional reality. The hysterics had extreme physical symptoms and the obsessives were dramatic in their anxiety-driven practices. The Rat Man, Freud's most notable obsessive, insists that he must repay a debt to a colleague that he does not owe. He tortures himself with impossible train schedules and unlikely rendezvous in his quest to make good the fee for his spectacles. These obsessive acts seem clearly divorced from reality. In objectivist terms this failure in reality testing means that the Rat Man has imagined something to be the case that is not so. He creates a perception based on nothing. In constructivist terms, however, we must instead say that he is divorced from reality in the sense that the community of observers cannot understand why he behaves as he does. We cannot agree that his behavior is sensible. At this level of pathology the distinction between constructivism and objectivism seems more semantic than substantive. But obsessions can be grounded more firmly in the possible. When the fear of flying or the concern about our health become fixed and limit our spheres of action, we have found real trouble to serve as a more suitable binding for anxiety. Now the question of reality becomes less firm. Planes do crash, people do die of heart attacks—we cannot simply dismiss these fears as ungrounded, but we are not willing to accept them as fully reasonable fears. The real and the nonsensical coexist; that is their difficulty. This mingling of sense and nonsense is not limited to the obsessive style.

The narcissist both imagines and knows that she has been let down by the therapist and those she most counted on. On one hand the narcissist creates her suffering through the misperception of the present. Lacking an internal sense of her wholeness or value, she tries to extract reflections of goodness from the interpersonal world. This relentless striving for grandiosity keeps her from sensing other people's compassion or needs, and having driven others away, she remains empty. From this perspective the narcissist creates her suffering through her distorted perception. It is this side of the Gestalt that Kernberg (1988) frequents. He suggests that the analyst must resist the interactional pressure exerted from this distorted perception and not concede to the unreasonable demands of the patient. But our perception of this patient can be inverted, and rather than seeing the distorting trends, we can look through to the white space and see the real injury she has suffered in her family, and now suffers again in the analytic relationship. This is where Kohut (1984a) stands; he sees the validity in the narcissist's perception. The patient implicitly understands that life has not provided her with the critical experience that would allow her to create internal structure. She has not had the opportunity to internalize good self-objects. This patient cannot change without first receiving her due from the analyst. While we may be able to mediate on the practical level between these competing views–Kernberg's or Kohut's approach may be more useful in bringing about particular changes–we cannot declare one view the exclusive champion over the other in the contest for truth.

Even with schizophrenics, or perhaps particularly with these patients, the real and the imagined overlap. Schizophrenics speak gibberish and show acute sensitivity to the world around them. While they speak about the world in ways that seem absurd, when we pay closer attention to this apparent absurdity, sense tends to emerge. When one of Searles' (1975) long-term patients states "You see, my mother was my mind" (p. 113), we are first struck by the delusional quality of the remark. Yet buried in this remark is an accurate perception of the impinging force of the introjected mother. And even more deeply, Searles realizes, the statement contains a communication about his therapeutic presence. He comes to see that his insistence on free association, his therapeutic zeal, have overwhelmed her. Searles, on one level, has acted like this women's mother, and she, in her schizophrenic manner, is letting him know this. Her crazy language contains within itself moments of insight and truth.

The idea that transference is only the product of imagination, when considered in the light of the clinical evidence, is untenable. Not only does the patient in her transference accurately perceive aspects of the world, she also acts in ways to bring these perceptions into being. The emotional pressure of the transference acts on the analyst to evoke countertransferential response. This realization belongs to numerous writers: Ferenczi, Levenson, Giovacchini, Tower, Racker and others have all felt this pressure in their clinical experience. When the analysand, for instance, out of her sense of being cheated, responds with stingy withholding, the analyst must be affected. The analyst may begin by feeling compassion for the analysand's plight and her difficult past, but over time tends to be drawn into closer orbit with her by the gravitational pull of the transference. He reaches the moment where any way he turns he cannot avoid reenacting the moment when she felt cheated. If he speaks, he reveals his judgment of the analysand's hostile stance. If he remains silent he shows a refusal to give.

Levenson (1972) writes: " . . . whatever goes on in the family will be replayed in therapy. Moreover, it will not be *distortion* or transference but an actual isomorphic replay in which the therapist participates. The therapist cannot avoid it by being 'well-analyzed' or perceptive" (p. 174). While the analysand has transferentially misperceived the analytic relationship at some point in the process (or at least construed it along narrow, idiosyncratic lines), that misperception belongs to the past, and in the current analytic moment she perceives something actual in the analyst and his countertransference. The relentlessness of enactment, rather than indicating a failure in the analyst's self-control or an insufficiency in his training analysis, is indicative of the character of reality and knowing. Reality is not a static presence that can be observed from the distance of the analyst's chair. It is a dynamic field that is shaped by the participation of both the analysand and the analyst. Knowing, then, cannot be dependent on the ability to contact the perceived without influencing it through the act of perception. It must instead be a coming into awareness that holds in mind how the very effort to know impacts that which we would know.

These critiques of objectivism in psychoanalysis are shaped out of the growing history of analytic practice. Yet there are those in the psychoanalytic community who remain unconvinced. Zucker (1993), in an article called "Reality: Can It Be Only Yours or Mine?", attacks the constructivist position. For Zucker the defense of ambiguity and multiple reality leads to the collapse of the analytic project.

> Reality conceived as it was early in psychoanalysis lays the ground for a question like "Whose Reality Is It Anyway?" Many who raise the question acknowledge that reality is out there, but are dubious that we humans are equipped to grasp it. Through this question they are in effect asserting that reality is up for grabs, that it is whatever a particular individual makes of it. Reality is thus individually held and essentially subjective . . .
>
> Ambiguity would thus appear to be a fateful condition confronting psychoanalysis. Actually this position, if correct, spells the end of theory on the psychoanalytic interaction for theory originates in the attempt to explain facts. Ambiguity without end does not produce facts [pp. 480–481].

Zucker is concerned that if we accept the viability of ambiguity, we are drawn onto the impossible slope of relativism. If all perspectives hold some truth value, then we might as well go to fortune tellers to help us with the interpretation of dreams. Zucker seems to suggest that constructivism cannot be true because the consequences of its acceptance would be unbearable. Yet desire, at least within the objectivist frame, cannot be a criterion of validation. The acceptance of ambiguity may be the most sensible relationship to reality, regardless of whether or not we find that comfortable.

Zucker wants to suggest that there is an actual reality waiting out there independent of our subjective process of observation. In Zucker's mind, patients have a shape independent of the pressure of the analyst and this shape is susceptible to impartial description: "I would ask: Is reality inevitably a construction or are there meanings that derive so closely from reality that these meanings are less impositions than descriptions of that reality?" (1993, pp. 480–481). Objectivism is a tenacious opponent. Although constructivism has dealt objectivism decisive criticism, or at least criticism that seems rationally decisive, we are not willing to abandon it. With Zucker, we find ourselves turning away from the prospect of relativism. We want to insist on reality and our capacity to locate it. We want to map out the possibility of making our knowing certain. In the face of strong evidence of its unreasonableness, the tenacity of the objectivist impulse suggests that forces greater than reason provide its fuel. Like hand-washing in the absence of dirt, it has an obsessional quality that speaks to the presence of anxiety. Bernstein (1983) calls this fear the "Cartesian anxiety": the fear that without the capacity to secure knowledge on an absolute basis we are left with nothing and are destined to be victimized by the irrational and the relativistic. The Cartesian anxiety drives us to search for what we imagine would be a more solid foundation than constructivism. It is this same fear that once made the countertransference such a controversial subject in analytic literature.

The Shape of Knowing

While the abandonment of objectivism requires that we surrender the desire for absolute arbiters, it does not demand intellectual anarchy. Constructivism constitutes a distinguishable epistemological position and the radical upending of objectivism does not entail the decline into relativism. At the core of constructivism lies an understanding that while reality is perspectival, and understanding is a construction rather than a reflection, that does not mean that we cannot proceed further in argument than stated preference. The terms of our human subjectivity—our affectivity, our rationality, our desires—provide some ground for bridging the multiple perspectives that are reasonably available to understanding. To make sense of constructivism we must see how reason and affectivity meet to govern our understanding. In this union emerges a basis on which a community of discussants may come to mediate their disputes and reach tentative consensus about reality and knowing. The nature of this consensus, we should be clear, is not dependent on or capable of producing certainty. Constructivist knowledge must always rely on the strength of probability and justified belief.

At root, constructivism is derived from the same deep realization that gives birth to relativism. The struggle to pin down the subjectively unconditioned ultimately betrays its own cause—the Cartesian anxiety—and reveals the perspectival nature of reality. Our attempts to make sense of the world are necessarily embedded in our subjectivity, and our ideas are constructed rather than received. In our work with analysands, it becomes clear that we cannot locate one absolute reality that must govern the perception of both analyst and analysand. When we attend to the issue of safety and realize that we must be willing to enter the analysands' reality before we can ask to make authorial changes, it becomes clear that their reality possesses sense. Like Ferenczi, we can move from seeing the analysand's resistance as a sign of pathology to recognizing the reasonable act of self-protection it contains. In part it is a question of where we choose to enter the circle of causality. Is the analyst caused by the analysand, or does the analyst cause the analysand? In the face of this perspectival multiplicity, we can be tempted by democratic resolution. We may want to say that everybody is partially right and if we add up all the perspectives then we will find reality, the unvarnished truth. This leveling trend, however, does not do justice to the competing perspectives. Each perspective does more than touch only some part of the world; each one claims to describe the whole world as it makes itself felt from that perspective.

To make sense of perspectivism we need to move beyond an idea of reality and knowledge based on correspondence. Reality does not exist as a static set of independent objects and qualities. When we pay attention to the energetic nature of atomic structure or to the fluid presentation of an analysand, it becomes clear that reality is a dynamic process that is constantly determined by the interactive web of relationships. We are determined, as we are at any moment, through the press of our relationship to the world, to other people, and to ourselves. We bump into a wall and we experience pain; we see an old friend and we become affectionate; we imagine an old flame and we become aroused. What allows a chair or a character to evidence a more durable presentation than, say, nitrogen or water (both of which are readily reshaped by their contact with barriers or obstacles) are their relatively more stable internal relationships. The chair hangs together because the molecules of wood and glue actively adhere. A person presents an enduring personality, we might say, from the relatively stable relationship amongst drives, introjects, and defenses. This stability in identity must always be active. If the glue loses its adhesiveness, the chair will wobble and then collapse. When our defensive organization is challenged we may slip into the chaotic world of psychosis, or if the conditions are more salubrious, move forward into greater psychic flexibility. To ask whose reality is correct, under this argument, is to mistake the nature of being. Reality is not only perceived perspectively, it is also determined perspectively.

This account, radical though it sounds, reflects our own analytic experience. The analytic experience creates a new past and a new present. Mitchell (1993) writes: "The patient's dynamics and life history do not have an independent reality that can be uncovered or grasped from the outside—they exist in a state of complex potentiality and are actually co-created by the observer's participation" (p. 58). In the process of knowing we construct an understanding of the world that helps give it shape. The Kernbergian analyst discovers a different analysand than the Kohutian. But it is equally true to say that each analyst, through the relational determining of being, creates a different analysand. To ask who is the analysand apart from these relationships is to fall back into the mistaken hope that we could locate the analysand-in-herself. To know a person or a thing in its essentiality, then, is not to know it in its isolation, but to gain an idea of how we affect it and how it affects us. The countertransference is the tangible way we are affected by the energetic presence of the other.

Affect and Knowing

When we come to understand the perspectival quality of reality, we can no longer hope to achieve some kind of rarefied objectivity. The nature of being ensures that contact is always transformational; to open ourselves to knowing we must be willing to be changed by what we would know, and we must be clear that our attempt to come close will change what we observe. Observation without effect is impossible. What we must consider, then, is how this realization alters our relationship to affect. In a constructivist world, how should we regard the affects of the countertransference? What legitimacy do they hold in the analyst's epistemological process? Historically, we have argued, affect, in its insistent quality, has been seen as an obstacle to objectivity. Yet if we can agree that aperspectival objectivity is fictitious, then this criticism loses its strength. Affect may lead us from perspective to perspective, but the disclosure that perspective has been active in seeing has lost its scandalous implication. We can no longer discard affect out of hand as some poor cousin to the intellect. Affect, under this view, is not simply a patina that coats thought–it is a mode of seeing and understanding the world. It too is built out of and creates the symbols that comprise knowledge. To address the epistemological status of affect we must examine the nature of its perspectives and ask whether these are useful promontories for our seeing. I will argue that these affective promontories are both inescapable and vital modes of human knowing. Affect both shapes our perspectives and provides a scale of value that allows us to begin choosing between perspectival frames. To make sense of the countertransference we must reexamine the nature of affect in light of modern theory and make its role clear in the process of knowing.

Psychoanalysis, in one view, is a long narrative about the role of affect. Psychoanalysis emerges from the predominance of suffering and the not yet extinguished hope for happiness. It aspires to expertise on how emotion shapes human life and is reshaped through the process of defense and adaptation. Yet psychoanalysis' account of affect, perhaps because the field began with a theory of drives rather than affect, remains ununified. We speak of projective identification, empathy, drive, and defense without a systematic account of what constitutes emotion or how it is elicited. In this section I will try to sort through some of this complexity surrounding affect. When we consider our patients it is clear that affect forms the root of their suffering. As patients try to fend off anticipated affective discomfort they develop defensive strategies that give rise to the transference. Out of fear and bitterness, perceptive templates are formed that restrict the patient's capacity to see the present as a new beginning and not necessarily congruent with the past. In this sense the pressure of affect can lead to the restriction of perception. It forces us to live only within a narrow range of the perspectival possibilities.

Acting out of these restricted perspectives, people behave in ways that separate them from the possibility of coordinated action. Outsiders look on at the borderline individual's rage and see it as unjustified by the commonly observable conditions. On the whole they find it too much work to empathically enter the borderline's perspective on reality; they find too few opportunities for their own needs to be met. Nor is the analyst exempt from the threat that affect poses to perception. In the previous chapters we traced how the early analysts came to see their analysands as opponents in the therapeutic war. Struggling to preserve their own esteem, these analysts became angry and hid their aggression behind interpretations of resistance. While we may now be more aware of this danger, clearly this awareness does not grant us immunity. We can readily point to moments in our own work when we have at least momentarily misperceived our patients and the correct course of action due to emotional interference. Although constructivism suggests that framing the analysand's behavior as resistance is not less true than seeing it as an iatrogenically conditioned response, it does suggest that we may value one view over the other. The move away from positivism, then, leaves unchanged our view that affect holds distorting potentials. While we may no longer elect to call these affectively narrowed perspectives false, we can see their destructive effects and how they block out other modes of truth. Affect, then, cannot provide a transparent, unerring guide to knowing.

While affect may pose difficulties to knowing, psychoanalysis has increasingly come to see affect as a critical ingredient for significant understanding. In the previous chapter we traced how those very moments of affective difficulty in the countertransference, when given adequate consideration, gave way to new insight into the analysand. This marks the other side of the epistemological paradox of affect. The first generation of analysts after Freud could not escape the realization that merely presenting the facts of the unconscious is insufficient to establish characterological change. The conscious, non-affectively experienced learning of the psychoanalytic storyline is not deep enough to evoke transformation. This initial failure in analytic technique alerted these analysts to the necessity of the analysand's affective participation in the process of knowing. It is this insight that led Strachey (1934) to write:

> Every mutative interpretation must be emotionally "immediate"; the patient must experience it as something actual. This requirement, that the interpretations must be 'immediate,' may be expressed in another way by saying that interpretations must always be directed to the 'point of urgency' [p. 352].

When Strachey argues that interpretations must be emotionally immediate in order to give rise to an experience of actuality, he has profoundly inverted the traditional separation between intellect and affect. He suggests that analytic research reveals that affect is what allows us to experience a perception as real, as a solid fact of experience. Only when an idea becomes united with affect does it gain a substantiality that can change the perception of reality. It is affect that has the capacity to capture our attention, to energetically impress a mode of knowing on our consciousness.

The increasing awareness of the necessity of affective immediacy in analytic treatment led the psychoanalytic community to reexamine the analyst's use of affect as a source of knowing. Just as it is not enough for the analysand to know only through shallow cognition, it also becomes apparent that mere cognition is insufficient as a basis for the analyst's understanding and interpretive activity. The analyst, too, if he is to know the analysand deeply, to know her in a way that will be useful, must attend to his own affectivity. We can see this shifting understanding of the analyst's epistemological process when Reik (1933) writes:

> No great harm would be done if it were merely 'ridiculous' to interpret every association connected with an umbrella as the thought of a penis, or to 'unmask' the returning Oedipus wish behind any friendly impulse on the part of an elderly lady! . . . But such a schematic application of knowledge is wrong. In a large number of cases it might even conceivably be correct in point of content and yet wrong in point of technique. For an interpretation in itself correct might at that particular point be devoid of all significance. Here we have a specially clear instance of the crucial difference between the kind of analytic knowledge which I should call 'pigeon-hole' knowledge and the *knowledge derived from one's own unconscious* [p. 376].

Schematically derived understanding may hold some form of truth, but it is a truth without impact or significance. To access an understanding that touches the analysand, an understanding with a pulse, we must draw on our unconscious. But what can this mean if the unconscious, in itself, is unknown? To my mind, what Reik must be suggesting is that we attend to our affectivity. It is within affect that news from the unconscious is printed.

This insight is further articulated by Kohut in his writings on self psychology. For Kohut, "vicarious introspection," the ability to empathically enter the analysand's perspective, is the defining method of analytic investigation. It demands that the analyst do more than merely think about the analysand's position; he must in some way enter the analysand's reality fully enough so he can know what it feels like to be the analysand. Only this kind of affective knowing can overcome the impasses that arise in the face of objectivist knowing. Ornstein (1993), describing the difference between extrospective and introspective knowing, writes:

> This listening position from the outside will inevitably prompt him to use his theories as a bridge to the patient's inner life, instead of "entering" it. This is especially true, if the analyst does not use the two-step sequence of understanding first (and checking if the patient feels understood) and explaining later (and checking if the patient can, indeed, find his explanations valid and useful). I believe this process is accurately seen as having remained extrospective–i.e. focused on what is externally observable—even if the observer-listener perceives complex affective-cognitive states, but ends up, nevertheless, with experiencing himself as the target of the patient's feelings, wishes, needs, etc. and has not moved on to perceive how it feels to the patient to feel these feelings and what his subjective reasons are for feeling them [pp. 9–10].

The analyst can only really know the patient if he can come to listen from the inside, from a position where affect accompanies thought. He must be willing to feel what it feels to be the patient.

Within the current analytic literature, the direction of argument has increasingly come to the support of affect as a mode of knowing. When we take the temperature of the clinical dialogue it becomes clear that the emerging consensus holds that the analyst's countertransference provides critical information in the attempt to understand the analysand. Rather than seeing affect as an obstacle to knowing, analysts have begun to see that without the participation of our affectivity, we are condemned to a shallow understanding of the analysand. Giovacchini (1989) writes:

> I also wonder whether analysts who can act like surgeons and who can, without feeling, electronically decipher messages are able to integrate these capacities within their psyches because they lack other qualities that may be essential to reach the deeper recesses of the patient's inner misery. I am referring to constrictions of character that make it difficult to be in touch with primitive feelings and parts of the self [p. 13].

This understanding of affect as critical to essential knowing belongs to a number of authors: Ferenczi (1923), Heimann (1949), Little (1951), Tower (1956), Racker (1968), Bollas (1987), Kohut (1984), Kernberg (1988), Greenson (1971), Mitchell (1993), and Spezzano (1993), among others. Only by allowing ourselves to be affectively touched by our analysands, this line of thought holds, can we gain a deep understanding of their psychic processes. For many this statement may seem obvious, yet this does not release us from the necessity for explanation. What is it about affect that allows it both to threaten accurate perception and to provide essential insight for penetrating knowledge?

Affect lies at the border between the found and the created. In one sense, emotion is something that happens to us. When we are threatened, fear automatically arises. When we lose someone we love, we find ourselves feeling grief. We cannot merely will emotion into being or make it stop. Things move us or leave us cold, and this affective valuing emerges from strata deeper than the deliberate realm of consciousness. Affect's quality, its subterranean origin, speaks to its connection to parts of the self that are prior to any prejudicial beliefs we might have about who we are. Affect's relative immunity to the pressure of desire or belief grants it some trustworthiness as an indicator of psychic reality. We have already discussed how Freud sensed this characteristic. It is an idea that is more explicitly captured in Spezzano's (1993) work:

> Structural concepts gain clinical immediacy and relevance when they are understood as labels for each person's unique blend of abilities and tendencies to generate and regulate those feelings that then become the key indicators of the state of one's psyche. This key role of affect leads us to agree widely that what we feel is a more reliable clue at any given moment to what is going on "inside of us" unconsciously than what we think [p. 71].

Spezzano suggests, and this is a conclusion that he feels is validated by consensual analytic experience, that affect is the critical indicator of the status of the unconscious. It draws its nutrients more directly from the deepest levels of the self. This penetrating quality of its roots leads us to place greater faith in affect than thought as a source of knowing.

As we pursue the source of this psychoanalytic intuition concerning affect, we are drawn back toward biology for an heuristic explanation. When we take an evolutionary perspective on human functioning, it seems that affect involves a mode of adaptation that precedes pure cognition (Frijda, 1986). Emotion is something we share with other mammals, and it depends heavily on evolution's earlier brain structures in the limbic system.[2] It seems reasonable to suppose that these emotional modes of behavior are more directly tied to key organismic goals, more closely related to survival and reproductive needs. In this sense affect seems to arise out of our biological ground.[3] It is our inborn reaction to critical situations that demarcate human existence. It is this innate, preexperiental

[2] The biology of emotion is not readily simplified. The limbic system does play a critical part in the activation of emotion, yet it would be a mistake to imagine that emotions can be neatly located in only one part of the brain. The crying response, for instance, is mediated at a number of evolutionary levels in the brain. Lesions in the basal ganglia, the thalamus, the hypothalamus, and certain areas of the frontal cortex can lead to diminished or excessive emotional crying (Duke-Elder & Scott, 1971; Records, 1979). What this suggests is that emotions cannot merely be seen as primitive functions. They are intimately dependent on the participation of the cerebral cortex, evolutionarily the most recent part of the brain. While emotions tap into the most elementary facets of our biology, this does not entail, as we will see, that emotions are separate from thinking.

[3] To speak of the "biological ground" or the "pre-experiential" aspects of the self is a delicate matter in a discussion on constructivism. At this point we risk falling back to an essentialist account of reality that would contradict the conclusions about perspectivity we have outlined. In turning toward biology and the question of authenticity I want to be careful to make clear that I am not arguing for a determinate "thing-in-itself" of the body. The idea of the inherited body, remains an idea. I think of it as determining a set of possibilities, rather than existing as a singular "true self"; in all of these lived possibilities affect plays a key role. In speaking of a "core self" or "authentic experience;," then, I do not want to suggest that these are found qualities that are recognized irrespective of the process of subjectively-conditioned valuing. These concepts instead refer to aspects of experience that have a felt quality of depth. They are moments within living about which, when they arrive, we tend to say, "That mattered." To speak about the levels of reality and the way some hold greater significance than others, without lapsing into language which evokes objectivist connotations, is a difficult task.

quality of affect that leads Spezzano (1993) to place it at the center of psychoanalytic practice, to suggest that it plays a critical role in our epistemological capacity:

> Psychoanalysis is psychoanalytic–because it emphasizes the ways in which "wired-in," preexperiential *affective* meaning categories are immanent in all immediate human experience. One might say that what distinguishes psychoanalysis from hermeneutics is that where hermeneutics tends, in general, to point first to culture and language as the major preexperiential mediums for the basic constitution of human experience, psychoanalysis points first to affects [p. 211].

Affects serve as the categories of human existence that exist prior to conscious thought. While far from inflexible, affects mark the boundary of what modes of behavior can be meaningfully utilized by our species. They are what shape our scale of value. Affects are vital to psychoanalytic epistemological strivings because they serve as a conduit to the deepest recesses of the self. They point the way to authentic experience.

The analytic view, however, while recognizing the centrality of affect, has resisted the naive faith that comes with being enamored. Psychoanalysis clearly sees how strongly our thoughts affect our emotions, and in this sense we recognize that affect can be created as well as found. The rage of the narcissist is deeply tied to her belief that she has been unfairly slighted. The analysis of the transference, in part, is a process of unraveling the tacit belief structure that chronically ignites unwelcomed affect. The daytime talk shows have become populated by people who feel their anger and misery are unshakably valid, a fact of experience more solid than Descartes' *cogito ergo sum*. Yet we may see the hysterical element in their presentations and how much they stoke their affect as a form of defense. What we focus on and how we frame the situation changes how we feel. Again, Spezzano is relevant here. He (1993) writes: "Perhaps the most crucial proposition–on the phenomenological level–of our psychoanalytic theory of affects is our assertion that patients do not always know what they are talking about when they tell us how they feel" (pp. 39–40). We should mark the apparent contradiction here: we feel that affect is more reliable than thought about what is occurring in us, while recognizing that patients may be deluded in their reports about their feelings. Patients, through the distorting processes of defense, may ward off awareness of anger and attend only to their sadness. We may even say that patients actively substitute one feeling for another. Affect, then, forms a kind of transitional space between who we are, and our mode of action that creates what we are. We have already outlined how affect can both distort and sharpen perception. Now we must also underline how affect is both genuine and assumed.

We have to ask, what is the source of this paradoxical duality surrounding affect? As psychoanalysis tries to answer this difficult question it turns to an account of affect that underlines its functional and relational qualities. Psychoanalysis has come to recognize that affect serves both as a mode of goal-seeking action and as a form of relational connection and communication. In part, affect serves functional goals for the individual. It helps us reach certain aims or reorder our internal economy. Freud (1917) points to this functional character of affect in his study of mourning. Sadness, in this account, works to decathect the loved object. He describes it as a piece of psychic work. The same functional aspect can be seen in fear or anger. We see rage as a reaction to frustration. We rage to remove obstacles. In the Oedipus complex, the child's fear is designed to help him curtail his amorous strivings that would elicit retaliation (castration) by the father. From this point of view, affect helps orient and energize us for the necessary work of human life. Our affects are biologically-grounded sets of action strategies that are in the service of our most basic drives and needs. When we become aware of their presence, we sense that they hold information about this core part of ourselves. It is here that the affective scale of value that we discussed in the chapters on Freud becomes operative. The relation between affect and function leads us to hold a tacit sense of what emotion, and in what intensity, is called for by a given situation. From our own experience we have strong intuitions that a child with an unreliable but charismatic father is likely to feel more toward this man than the unambivalent love that she claims. We imagine that the frustration and disappointment engendered by the father's unreliability must elicit some anger, but that this anger has been disavowed out of a fear of its consequences. Affect, then, can serve as a more reliable indicator than thought of our internal states because it is has a more direct connection to our central needs; but it can also serve as a false front to more genuine affect when we become afraid that the spontaneous manifestations of emotion will fail to accomplish their intended function.

As psychoanalysis has moved toward more relational perspectives, the role of affect in communication and relationship has captured increasing attention. Affect, under this view, acts to help shape human relationships; it conditions our interactions, bringing us into violent confrontation, passionate embrace, and nurturing parenting. Through affect we discover the tempo of the different dances of human life; we discover the complementary roles, both antagonistic and cooperative, that allow us to move in coordinated action. We can see this shift toward a relational view of affect in Winnicott's work. When Winnicott (1960) speaks about the mother-infant unit he repeatedly underlines the need for connection. During the course of pregnancy, the mother begins to identify with the growing infant, and this identification forms the basis of maternal empathy: "By and large mothers do in one way or another identify themselves with the baby that is growing within them, and in this way they achieve a very powerful sense of what the baby needs" (p. 53). We have to ask, what is the nature of this "sense" within the mother of the newborn? Clearly the baby has not communicated verbally. And Winnicott is clear that the mother does not arrive at knowing the baby's needs through an intellectual process. Instead, the baby feels things, and this feeling registers in his body. His muscle tone changes, his facial expression shifts, and perhaps, more obvious, he cries. These shifts in the baby's energetic state act as the communicative text of the baby's needs. These symbols are not read consciously. The mother doesn't deliberately note the dilation of the eyes, the alteration in respiration, or consciously decipher the underlying emotion. Instead the mother reads her baby's emotion and needs through her own affective states. The mother, with receptive intentness, finds her own feelings changed, and these shifts form the foundation of her empathic understanding and action. We can see this mode of affective knowing in the process of nursing. My sister, speaking about her own experience as a mother, says that when her baby became agitated, began to kick and squirm and make "ehh-ehh" noises, this created her own growing discomfort, and before deliberate thought, she would find herself standing, picking up her child, and beginning to move. If she hadn't nursed in a while, she would notice that her milk began to move into the nipple, and this internal prompting would remind her to feed the child. In describing this process of mothering, I do not mean to suggest that thought is absent or that discovering the right course of action is automatic. The mothering adaptation is a heuristic process that balances intuitive impulses with deliberate thought. But without this affective participation, the mother is bound to misread her child. This felt sense of being ready to feed is a way that she biologically knows her infant's needs. Affect is a primary medium through which the mother knows the newborn. It is what allows her to instinctively do the right thing in her caretaking. Countertransference provides the analyst with a similar mode of knowing the analysand. "More often than not," Bollas (1987) writes, "we are made use of through our affects, through the patient generating the required feeling within us. In many ways this is precisely how a baby 'speaks' to its mother" (pp. 203–204). Affect, he argues, serves as a mode of communication about fundamental human needs. As analysts we must be willing to listen to these messages.

Affect both represents a way we affect others and forms a channel of reception through which we are affected in turn. This relational view of affect lies at the core of projective identification theory. Although in Klein's original formulation projective identification is an internal fantasy process, the meaning of the term was quickly co-opted to refer to concrete relational processes. Projective identification, write Tansey and Burke (1989), "represents an interactional phenomenon in which the projector, by actual influence, unconsciously elicits thoughts, feelings, and experiences within another individual which in some way resemble his own" (p. 45). The relationship between the projective action and the introjective reception exhibits a kind of lawfulness that allows the analyst to make use of this affective effect to deepen his understanding of the analysand.

Part of affect's function is to bind people together and to alert them to the other's need. In the skeptical philosophic tradition the question is asked how we can know whether other people have thoughts and feelings like our own. This is the problem of "other minds." The skeptics argue that we can never be sure of our sense that we actually know what takes place in someone else's mind. From the analytic perspective that we have presented, however, it would seem that this philosophic anxiety can only arise through the denial of affective communication. When we begin to recognize the tangibility of this affective mode of knowing another person, we have to see this skepticism as an attempt to distance oneself from the affective vulnerability of the self. What is implicit in all these psychoanalytic perspectives is the idea that affect is a fundamental mode of communication and knowing.

The Skill Theory of Affect

Within academic psychology the research on emotion has been driven by a number of defining questions. The first of these concerns the nature of emotional experience. There are two parts to this question. First, we have to ask what it is about affective experience that distinguishes it from ordinary or non-emotional experience. But the necessity for demarcating emotion experience goes further. We must also ask what it is that distinguishes between different varieties of emotional experience? What makes the experience of fear, for instance, different from the experience of anger? As a first answer to these questions we might venture that affective experience is grounded more fully in the body. To feel something is to feel our body transformed. When we are captivated by emotion we undergo a number of physiological changes. Our eyes dilate or constrict, our blood pressure and our heart rate change, our digestion and adrenal levels fluctuate, among other effects. These physical changes provide the tonic ingredients to the felt quality of emotion. But this first level of answer does not yet answer our second question–what is it that distinguishes between specific emotion experiences? Historically, there have been a number of different views on this issue. In James' (1884) and Lange's (1885) view, emotional experience is determined by our behavioral response. We feel afraid because we run and tremble. Emotion, under this view, is more epiphenomenal. It follows, rather than determines, response. On the other side of the spectrum are theorists like Wundt (1903) and Titchener (1908) who hold that the subjective quality of emotional experience is central, and gives rise to particular modes of response. They suggest that it is our fear that makes us run and tremble. The debate between these two sides is long-standing, and has not yet reached a consensual decision. The question has some significance for the countertransference, however, because it touches on what information is conveyed by emotion.

This first issue in emotion theory is closely related to a second. To what extent is affect genetically determined (Ekman, 1984) or socially constructed (Harre, 1986b)? This dichotomy mirrors the split we discussed in the previous section in regard to affect's authenticity. Cross-cultural research on the facial expression of emotion (Ekman & Friesen, 1975), developmental studies of emotion talk in childhood (Bretherton, 1986), and other work seems to demonstrate that there is a core set of basic emotions. Researchers (Ekman, 1984; Izard, 1977; Shaver et al., 1987) using a variety of methodologies have consistently identified similar sets of basic emotions. Typically these include sadness, fear, anger, happiness, love, and, sometimes, interest, disgust, and shame as the basic emotions. These emotions evidence consistent facial expressions, show themselves relatively early in childhood, are part of children's speech, and give rise to particular forms of behavioral response. An angry baby in Japan will look much the same as an angry baby in America. If we show a picture of a Westerner with a sad face to members of an isolated rain-forest tribe, they will be able to specify the emotion and suggest the kinds of events that might elicit this expression. This concurrence of evidence suggests that the basic emotions are evolutionarily and biologically determined patterns of responsiveness to critical environmental challenges. It is these basic emotions that are wired into human physiology, and provide what we referred to above as the preexperiential meaning categories of our lives. They are the relatively universal aspects of human experience that make empathy possible.

When these basic emotions are elicited, our body undergoes physiological changes. These physiological changes that accompany emotion occur in the service of adaptive action. Frijda (1986), in his extensive overview of this literature, writes that these "physiological response patterns correspond to the functional requirements of dealing with the environment" (p. 165). When we feel angry, our body has changed itself to take action against obstacles. We become more ready to fight or argue. When we feel scared, we become prepared to freeze in hiding, or to run away from danger. Emotions, then, are genetically conditioned strategies to solve the critical difficulties in living. Again we can see the connection to the psychoanalytic dialogue: emotions serve a functional role. Frijda takes an inclusive approach in trying to answer the question we considered above about the nature of emotion experience. In part, he suggests, with Wundt and Titchener, that emotions are centrally determined response patterns. He sees them as biologically and evolutionarily mediated. The patterns of response connected to a given emotion, however, are malleable, and this malleability is part of what gives rise to the range of emotion experiences. Now Frijda aligns himself more closely with James and Lange. He suggests that the particular subjective quality or tone of a specific emotion is largely due to feedback from the physiological and gesticulatory changes it generates. When we feel an emotion, Frijda suggests, it conveys information about both how we perceive the world and how we are prepared to respond.

While it seems warranted to identify a list of basic emotions, this does not rule against the admission of socially constructed emotions. As we grow older the shape and expression of our emotions are changed by the constraints of societal mores and the pressure of our individual history. Some emotions like *accidie* (the subjective state of not caring induced by the physical regimens of the spiritual recluse) in medieval Europe (Harre, 1986a) or *amae* (the quality of filial devotion and love) in Japan (Doi, 1973), are not readily translated into other languages and seem to be the product of the particular culture. Other emotions, like contempt or patriotic pride, require the maturation of cognitive skills coupled with critical environmental experience. The emotions of the adult are not the same as those of a child. Even when we speak about regression and primitive emotional experience we are not dealing with exact equivalents of childhood experience. We may be beset by primitive rage or terror, but even in these desperate moments we respond differently than the newborn. We have learned language and developed expectations around environmental responses that impact the totality of our emotion experience. An adequate theory of emotion (and therefore of the countertransference) must provide an account of the relationship between the basic emotions present in infancy and the complex, socially and environmentally determined emotions found in adulthood.

The skill theory of affect (Fisher, Shaver, & Carnochan, 1989) begins with an outline of the process that governs the activation and expression of emotion. In agreement with the emerging consensus in the emotion literature, it suggests that emotions begin with the perception of notable change. Any change in the current status of events can set into motion an emotion sequence. Ongoing events don't lead to new emotions. This claim seems to be contradicted by the intuitive observation that if something negative goes on for too long we shift from discomfort to despair. In this case, though, we had thought that the negative event would come to an end sooner than it appears it will. Here the lack of change in the environment forces us to change our expectations. As analysts, when working with a difficult analysand, we may feel constantly attacked. And while being attacked, in itself, may not be enough to goad us into an emotion, may not yet upset our capacity for tolerance, if it becomes chronic it may come to impede the possibility of productive collaboration. Now the chronic quality of the attacking becomes the notable change that sets into motion the activation of the countertransferential emotion. When events lead to a perception of change or a violation of expectations, this acts as a signal to continue processing the input for its affective significance.

The second step in the appraisal process involves relating the event to concerns (Frijda, 1986). The term "concerns" refers both to the current needs and desires of the individual, and to his implicit goals. In this phase of processing emotion we evaluate whether an event has positive or negative implications for our concerns. Events that have negative consequences lead to negative emotions, while events that have positive consequences lead to positive emotions. This first level of emotion appraisal gives rise to the basic affective split between the good and the bad object that Klein traces to primitive experience. It is at this point in the processing model that we can begin to see the connection between affect and drives. We can understand concerns to be the product of our innate drives. Whether we endorse a more traditional drive model, and see our concerns as ultimately reducible to sexual and aggressive needs, or a more revisionist model like Greenberg's (1992), and identify the need for safety and effectance as central, affects are our response to how we see these concerns being served. The split between positive and negative emotions provides information about whether we feel our needs are being satisfied or threatened. To return to our imagined analyst, the emotional significance of the analysand's chronic attacks will depend on how this behavior interacts with the analyst's concerns. For each analyst these concerns will vary. We can expect that the analyst, as a human being, will evidence some concern around maintaining safe and positive interpersonal relations. We can expect the analyst to have some concern around maintaining positive self-esteem. And we may expect the analyst to have some range of more idiosyncratic or even neurotically determined concerns. All of these concerns, however, may be reasonably well modulated by the analyst, and so may not provide the primary charge to countertransferential affect. But every analyst, if he genuinely cares about his analytic work and the well-being of the patient, must focus some concern on the success of the analysis. While not ignoring the dangers of therapeutic zeal, the analyst, if he is to be more than a well-paid charlatan, must hold hope that the analysis will be of use. The chronically attacking analysand, by undermining the therapeutic alliance, thwarts the expectation for analytic progress, and the analyst's concern about being useful is undermined. The analyst, then, begins to experience negative emotion. The stalemate makes him unhappy; but the quality of that unhappiness is not yet determined. This level of processing is not yet sufficient to give rise to more specific emotional experience.

The selective activation of specific emotions, emotions that we have categorized as basic, depends on the appraisal of the change in relation to our coping potential. If, according to the appraisal, the events are desirable or going surprisingly well, the emotional reaction is joy. If he is able to find some other way of being with this analysand that breaks the repetitive cycle of attacks, the analyst is likely to feel the flush of happiness. If an event has negative implications for our concerns,[4] but we surmise that we have the resources to overcome that obstacle, the result is anger. Anger mobilizes energy to struggle with an obstacle. At the most primitive level, the analyst who feels stymied by the analysand's constant attacks, but still hopes to find some way to stop this pattern, is likely to become angry at the analysand. He may become more tempted to retaliate or utilize confrontational interventions. We can see this result in Nunberg's belittling interpretations that we described in the previous chapter. If events are dangerous and threaten a goal, and the individual feels little ability to directly block the events, the result is fear. Fear prompts us to try to avoid the negative events by hiding (the freezing reflex) or fleeing. The analyst may respond to the attack by feeling frightened. Because of this fear the analyst may retreat into himself and grow more silent, trying to avoid any action that will attract the analysand's rage. Or the analyst may be tempted to flee the analysand by missing appointments or referring the analysand to another analyst. Here, Tower's description (see chapter one) of her pivotal missed session with her analysand seems relevant. Finally, if events interfere with an important goal, and the interference is irreversible, the goal must be abandoned, and the result is sadness. The analyst, finding the impasse unworkable, may finally have to give up on the analysis, and grieve its failure.

These different emotions, evoked by a specific set of appraisals, can be seen as a set of patterned action tendencies (Frijda, 1986). Emotions are sets of tendencies to behave in particular ways. These action plans are sequences of behavior that are intended to bring about changes in our relationship to the environment. As emotions gain precedence, the body is prepared physiologically to take the indicated actions. But emotions

[4] The reader may object that the appraisal process for anger depends on more than merely checking to see whether an event has negative implications for a concern. When someone steps on our foot accidentally, we might be able to overcome this problem by angrily shoving the offender, but we are not likely to follow that emotional path. We usually withhold anger unless we see that someone has unjustly (and this usually includes an inference about intention) interfered with our concerns. This additional appraisal step, however, is not innate. We have to teach children to withhold retaliation for unintentional acts. I will return to this part of the appraisal process shortly.

are not unbendable. When we get angry we are drawn but not impelled to certain behaviors. Because of our anger we may be tempted to strike out, but instead merely raise our voice or stay tightly silent. Again, this is an aspect of how emotions lie in the transitional space between the found and the created. We use the term "action tendency" rather than a term like "action pattern" to underline the relative flexibility in these emotion dispositions. It is a flexibility that seems to be built into the biological base of emotion. The electrical stimulation of the monkey's mid-brain, central gray area, for instance, elicits aggression when the animal is surrounded by monkeys lower in the social hierarchy, and submission when it is surrounded by more dominant ones. But for these behaviors to be manifested the monkey must be in the presence of other monkeys (Delgado, 1967). The emotion behaviors are not sparked solely in response to the electrical stimulation, but require the presence of appropriate environmental conditions. With infants, the distinction between action tendencies and action itself is superfluous. For the infant, to feel is to act. With social experience and the development of cognitive capacity, however, children become able to represent action apart from acting, and so develop the capacity to modulate their emotion responses. Children come to be able to think about acting that leads to further feedback contributing to the subjective tone of feelings.

In studies of adults, such modulating tendencies have been referred to as coping or self-control efforts (Lazarus, 1984; Shaver et al., 1987). In the field of psychoanalysis we would call these attempts at adaptation either defenses or ego functions. In the emotion literature, these control structures are often portrayed as separate from the basic emotion sequence. To postulate separate control processes, however, is an unnecessary addition to the model. A more parsimonious account of the control of emotional behavior emerges if we treat the control processes as stemming from additional loops in the basic emotion process. The first pass of emotion experience leads to the generation of an action plan and a set of anticipated consequences for that plan. The evocation of this set of tendencies and expectations is an internal event that when monitored can become a notable event in its own right. The processing of these internal representations of action tendencies and their consequences leads to further emotions, and this emotion loop leads to emotions about emotions. Emotional regulation, in this account, stems from the action tendency of one emotion acting upon the action tendency of another emotion. It is a process that can account for both the maturational development of emotion and the ongoing processes of emotion modulation. We can see this more clearly if we consider the case of envy. In psychoanalysis, envy might be seen as part of the basic emotional repertoire. Under this model, however, while envy would be recognized as fundamental to human experience, it is not included in the list of basic emotions because it depends on the spinning process of emotion loops. We can see this looping process in Hanna Segal's (1967) description of envy:

> Envy aims at being as good as the object, but, when this is felt as impossible, it aims at spoiling the goodness of the object, to remove the source of envious feelings. It is this spoiling aspect of envy that is so destructive to development, since the very source of goodness that the infant depends on is turned bad, and good introjections, therefore, cannot be achieved [p. 367].

Envy is such a poisonous emotion partly because it constantly loops back on itself, denying the possibility of moving forward into new relationships. In this model, emotion loops are the motivational force behind developmental changes in emotion skills. Self-control stems from the possibility of having emotions about emotions. This capacity to modulate our emotions and reshape their innate action plans is what gives rise to the culturally determined emotions and the more complex and individual emotions of adulthood.

As we become older and gain in cognitive capacity, our ability to evaluate the consequence of our emotional action tendencies and to reenvision more complicated patterns of response grows. We begin to take into account not only the immediate consequences of our action, but the long-term and wider relational implications. As children we may begin by responding automatically to an accidental shove with a return shove. If we find that we are scolded when we retaliate, we are likely to begin responding to our own retaliatory aggression with fear. As a result we begin to incorporate an evaluation of intent into our emotional processing. But as we grow even older we may begin to notice more clearly the consequences of living with aggression. We see how the anger of others stems from their fear or hurt. Sensing this, we may feel some kind of love for them and direct this love at our anger, and so reach an experience of compassion. This is a much subtler affective state than the simple anger evident in childhood. As these emotion loops are repeated, the appraisal process that they are based on becomes increasingly automatic.

What was once conscious but slow, becomes unconscious but efficient. It is this rapidity of the appraisal process that leads us to sometimes overlook the complexity of cognition that is contained in emotional experience. The analysis of the transference and countertransference requires that we unpack this automatized appraisal process, and bring its basic components back into consciousness. It is a kind of unwinding of the emotion loops that have created the adult experience of affectivity.

The analyst who works to contain his countertransference is intimately involved in the process of emotion-loops through which we reach the analytic attitude. During the course of our analytic training we come to reshape our appraisal process about critical affective situations. We become more aware of the fear beneath our anger, or the anger beneath our fear; we start to see the motives of others more clearly, and begin seeing them acting less out of malevolence than a sense of being threatened. When we begin to understand the looping quality of emotion, the intimate link between thought and affect, it becomes clear that the countertransference is not an automatic or rigid response. How we feel is closely related to what we believe and, in the case of analysis, by what we believe about the correct course of an analytic treatment. Our psychoanalytic theory, then, has a direct impact on our countertransferential response. Stein (1991) makes this point about the overlapping effects of theory and practice: "The analyst's emotional reactions in the analysis depend on the analyst's theoretical convictions of what does and does not constitute good analysis. If the analysis is perceived as developing well, the analyst will feel favorably disposed towards the patient (a positive countertransference). If the work is felt to be going badly, the analyst feels disturbed" (pp. 326–327). We cannot, then, simply argue for a specific form of managing the countertransference based on its felt quality. That quality can be altered by changing our view of the situation. The strength of the negative countertransference in the early analysts stemmed from their idea that the patients were misbehaving in the analytic setting. In our time, the countertransference of a self-psychologist will differ from the countertransference of a more traditional analyst. While some might argue that the soothing presence of the analyst as selfobject is not genuine or too reminiscent of Alexander's corrective emotional experience, this argument overlooks the effect of the analyst's conviction. The self-psychologist who genuinely believes in the epistemological reality of the analysand's wounded world view, will actually feel as well as think differently about the demands placed on him by this kind of patient. "It is less frequently recognized," Ornstein (1993) writes, "that the analyst's theory–lack of adequate knowledge of it, the particular manner of its use, whether it enhances empathic entry or interferes with it, etc.–might also be a source of the analyst's countertransference response to the patient" (p. 33). Part of our question, then, must be not only what should we do with the countertransference, but what sort of countertransference should we strive for.

Having outlined this model of affect, we are now in a position to suggest how emotion functions as a form of knowing. At the center of this model is the idea that emotions are elicited through the interaction between events and our concerns. We begin to feel emotion when something touches on our need to feel secure, our need to be connected to loved ones, our need to feel valued, or any other key concern. This intimate relationship between affect and need is precisely what prejudiced objectivists against emotion. Need-based perception, it was held, exerted gravitational pull on the observer, dragging him out of his detached orbit and compromising his objectivity. The central thrust of our argument, though, has been directed at dismantling the myth of knowing, separate from perspective. In our experience, reality is not only known, but is determined perspectivally. From this understanding, we are forced to reframe emotional detachment as only one point of observation amongst many. The concerns that lie behind emotion, then, cannot be dismissed merely as pressures distorting perception. Rather, they must be seen as perspectival vantage points. Affects form perspectival positions that are fundamentally human. It is this quality that leads Spezzano to suggest that they form the preexperiential meaning categories of human existence. To know the world fully is to know it from many views. It is through affect that we are connected to need. We know someone else best when we know them as objects of our hunger, our lust, our need for intimacy, and so on. These concerns, rooted in our biology, are what makes us most fundamentally human. They are what shape meaning structures and the patterns of society.

In this model of emotion, concerns are connected to the possibility of coping. When we feel particular emotions, emotions that extend in complexity beyond the positive-negative split, we stand revealed in regard to our ideas about action. Each emotion is determined by appraisals about how the world will treat us, about the possibility of responsive action. Frijda (1986) writes: "The present hypothesis of correspondence between situational meaning structures and emotions requires that, for every different emotion as distinguished either by name or by action readiness mode, a unique situational meaning structure can be specified. It should be possible to present, for every emotion, a corresponding description of how the world looks to the subject" (p. 196). Our countertransference, then, is indicative of how we have been affected by the analysand. It provides us a kind of knowing that is antipodal to the aseptic quality of the objectivist stance.

Validation and Objectivity

To suggest that affect provides a vantage point for knowing is to walk on precarious ground. When wearing the spectacles of affect, an easy stumble or misstep can take us off the narrow edge into relativism and wild analysis. What prevents the acceptance of perspectivism and affective knowing from degenerating into a chaotic relativism? If truth is always embedded in perspective and grounded in the subjectivity of the knower, what are we left with to adjudicate between opinions? While the anarchists might welcome the collapse of epistemological authority, we should be clear that for the bulk of us that kind of mayhem is untenable, and if this is what constructivism entails, it will not long be welcome in the analytic community. Our ordinary experience speaks to us every day about the presence of reality, about the difference between truth and distortion. In our analytic work, while truth may be difficult to pin down, we can readily point out falsehood. We know something about the destructive use of the countertransference. An analyst who views the world through his anger and some notion of health through discipline might feel justified in berating his analysands like an officer on a British man-of-war. But we would look on this "therapy" with great doubt. While hard discipline served the King's navy well during war, and even the most empathic psychologist can see the manipulative or slothful aspects of neurosis, we remain more than ready to discredit this imaginary analyst's judgment. Our condemnation of this approach, we feel, stems from more than just the expected divergence of opinion in a democratic system. The approach is wrong and this analyst endorses his stand only by virtue of misperceiving the world. Analysands are not helped through harsh treatment; their difficulty should not be seen as a moral failing. If we are to honor this intuition of objectivity while not abandoning the recognition of perspectivism, we must remap the meaning of truth. From what I have already said, it should be clear that this verification cannot serve to secure certainty. But this does not entail abandoning estimates of probability. We must rely on standards that offer confidence about the truth value (and the value of that truth) of our observations.

When we accept a perspectival epistemology we move from a monadic to a pluralistic view of reality. As analysts we know from our interaction with analysands how many ways the world may be approached and constructed in thought. Yet to surrender to perspectivism and treat all of these constructions as equal is to abandon the possibility of analytic interpretation. If alternate perspectives are only different points of knowing, the analyst can only listen to the differences between them. As Greenberg (1992) points out, more is needed:

> The interpreting analyst needs some construct that gives warrant for assuming that the patient's experience is more than it seems to be. There must be something in our theory that allows us to interpret reported fantasies of self-fragmentation as reflecting fears of losing connections to an object, or castration fears as derivatives of concerns about the integrity of the self. But this also means that the analyst's interpretive system cannot be infinitely expandable. Multiple-drive and mixed-model theories do not support the analyst's having a perspective that is not the patient's. Without an alternative perspective, a cigar *is* just a cigar, at least so long as the patient says it is [pp. 126–127].

While I am not ready to accept Greenberg's claim that a dual-drive theory is necessary to avoid the relativist regression, he is correct in arguing that we must find some way to secure the boundaries of the interpretive system.

What provides the surveying stakes for this boundary is our affectivity. We choose between internally congruent perspectives on the basis of how it feels to occupy each view of the world. And this mode of valuing and choice, this affective scale of value, is not infinitely expandable, and can be mediated; it is grounded in the body and biology, and speaks to our innate drives or concerns. This should not be read as an implication that affect is inflexible or that it dictates one form of living, or one view of reality, over all others. To ask for that kind of adjournment of discovery is like asking what piece of music we should judge most perfect. We do not want to choose Mozart and then cease listening to Beethoven. But the acceptance of multiple compositions as beautiful still holds the possibility of discarding others. We reject the musicality of discordant banging on the piano and show some consensus in preferring Mozart to Salieri. Our aesthetic judgments of music are grounded, though not exactly determined, by the biology of hearing and the laws of harmonics and meter. I suggest that our judgments about human adaptation and interpersonal connection follow a similar path. The biology of our affectivity links us to our essential concerns and sets the parameters for evaluating different perspectives on reality and the forms of living they entail. We make aesthetic choices on the basis of affectively determined standards.

When we move from music theory back to psychoanalysis, there may be a tendency to balk at accepting the centrality of artistic judgments. Making this claim about the relationship between psychoanalytic truth and value breaks with Freudian tradition. But there is no viable defense to the claim that the analyst's neutrality consists in working for truth independent of value. We cannot hope for a source of truth transcendent to the human. The unavoidability of the subjective, however, does not entail licensing solipsism. Our affective judgments extend beyond the individual and provide a source of arbitration. "The state of psychoanalytic knowledge," Mitchell (1993) argues, " . . . is not anchored in enduring truths or proof, but rather in its use value for making sense of a life, deepening relationships with others, and expanding and enriching the texture of experience" (p. 65). We look at the thwarted, hateful world of the traumatized adult and can make sense of the truth in this way of looking at life; but the possibility of seeing its truth does not entail that we would choose to live there. We feel that psychoanalysis knows something about how to approach the world, about how to regard emotion and its roots, that when experientially grasped, when inhabited from the inside, leads to an expansion in our sense of meaningfulness. It is on the basis of this implicit system of values that we probe for repressed affect, endorse moving beyond manic defenses, and seek to increase the structuralization of the ego and self-objects. We feel that engaging in these modes of exploration and conversation, in occupying a new reality, we will move toward a more interesting and satisfying experience.

To identify affectivity as the arbiter of perspectival reality suggests that our relationship to the countertransference should not be governed by a hope to rid ourselves of our subjectivity. Instead we must ask, what is the effect of using our countertransference both as a mode of seeing and as a source of action? We must evaluate how using the countertransference changes our relationship to the analysand, and whether we find this changed relationship helpful. The use of the countertransference is something that the analytic community has rightfully come to value in the course of its history. This claim, however, can be assessed only in the context of an explicit set of values. The shape of the psychoanalytic value system is critical to our view of health and therapeutic action, and so its account is pivotal to how we understand and make use of the countertransference. This is a topic we will return to in chapters 9 and 10. But before we try to outline it more clearly, we must first say something more about how we confirm the validity of our choices.

To accept affect as the source of adjudicated decision does not imply that our affective judgments must possess some kind of immediate accuracy. While it might seem that if our affectivity is the source of adjudication between perspectives, who better than ourselves to know what feels correct, this appeal to hedonic intuition is misguided. Psychoanalysis' first insight is that we suffer because we lose track of the biological ground. While we know what we feel, we do not necessarily know why we feel what we feel, or what is required for us to feel differently. We find that our drives draw us into conflict, and we respond through distortion and repression. In these defensive acts, we lose track of our sexuality, our need for safety, and our interpersonal longings. The process of forming emotion loops draws us away from immediate affectivity. While our affects link us to our concerns, they are mutable, and the link may be convoluted. We cannot be certain that the manifest experience of an emotion offers a reliable guide to correct action. The result of this distorting process is that access to our authentic humanity is no more certain than our perception of the world around us. Constructivism, then, cannot be equated with hedonism. It knows too well that what feels good in the moment may bring a terrible hangover tomorrow.

We are clear in the psychoanalytic world that affect serves as a useful guide and mode of knowing only when we can suspend the temptation toward immediate action. The first wave of emotion is often egoistic; it aims to right the world so we can feel better. For an analyst this self-concern, while necessary, must be balanced with an awareness of wider goals and with concern for the analysand. Heimann (1949) writes:

> The aim of the analyst's own analysis, from this point of view, is not to turn him into a mechanical brain which can produce interpretations on the basis of a purely intellectual procedure, but to enable him to *sustain* the feelings which are stirred in him, as opposed to discharging

> them (as does the patient), in order to *subordinate* them to the analytic task in which he functions as the patient's mirror reflection [p. 140].

For Heimann the capacity to sustain emotion allows the analyst to form interpretations that more genuinely reflect the impact of the analysand. By holding the emotion the analyst can begin to see how the feeling relates to the analysand—does it reflect the analysand's predominate self-experience, how she customarily affects significant others, or is it more idiosyncratic to the analyst—and on the basis of this processed understanding generate a more skillful plan of action and interpretation.

If the successful use of affect in knowing is dependent on the capacity to sustain the emotion in thought, without the immediate need to take action, we must ask, what we hope occurs in the midst of that process? What does it mean to successfully process our affect for its useful meaning? Within the analytic field, the tacit suggestion is that we must try to distill the idiosyncratic reaction from the more objective emotional response. We want the emotion cleansed of its egocentricity. The countertransference should not be used for the analyst's self-protection or gratification, but for the benefit of the analysand. For Tansey and Burke (1989), the hallmark of successful utilization of the countertransference is when we are able to move from an experience of projective identification to a more nuanced empathic understanding. They identify three stages in this process. The analyst must first be able to contain his emotional experience and separate himself from its immediacy. This first step paves the way for the second: it allows him to begin studying his affective experience through his own and the analysand's perspectives. Finally, when all goes well, the analyst is able to form an empathic connection to the analysand, and comes to see how the world is seen from this perspective. Tansey and Burke's work is a useful account of the specific steps in the utilization of the countertransference.

Yet we need to go further in grounding the epistemological roots of this appraisal process. On what basis do we found our confidence in the result? Regardless of how we specify the approach to working with the countertransference, we must still ask how this is validated. Without some further corroboration we cannot distinguish between imagining we are being helpful and actually being helpful. Wittgenstein (1958) speaks to this problem when he writes: "And hence also 'obeying a rule' is a practice. And to *think* one is obeying a rule is not to obey a rule. Hence it is not possible to obey a rule 'privately': otherwise thinking one was obeying a rule would be the same thing as obeying it" (p. 81). When we carry out a practice in private we have no solid means of checking our objectivity, of deciding whether we are overcoming our egoism and our defensive adaptation.

Truth is not an end state or a mode of knowing that can be approached outside the web of human subjectivity. Thought is validated by its progressive movement, by the process of consensual support, and by its capacity to embrace the pluralism of perspectives. When we accept the inescapability of perspectival reality, we see that truth is not an endpoint to human inquiry. There are always further perspectives to inhabit. Instead, truth seems to operate as a progressive series. We move forward in our thought to increasingly more useful ways of speaking about reality. The first standard of truth rests on the principle of irreversibility. As we consider the world and ourselves, trying to approach an authentic mode of knowing each, we gain some confidence in our thought when it moves forward. We believe in our new mode of seeing because it feels more correct, it solves further problems in living than the perspective we inhabited formerly. We sense we are closer to a valuable truth because we no longer are tempted to go back to the previous understanding.

This is not to say that truth is whatever we want it to be. The process of judging progression is not arbitrary. It rests on the interlocking support of multiple criteria. We can point out the standards of parsimony, logical coherence, technological effect, and emotional impact as all playing a part in the judgment process. But none of these, the philosophy of science has pointed out, acts as a necessary or sufficient standard at all moments (Bernstein, 1983). We cannot escape the necessity of affectively determined valuing in the evaluation of theory. As analysts we accept the relational turn in analytic theory because it works better as a descriptor of the clinical findings. It helps us speak with our analysands more effectively. This same standard governs in the case of the analysand's analytic progress. While the analysand may never lose the capacity to reverse the Gestalt and view herself as damaged, the retreat to this mode of seeing seems increasingly transparent, and becomes subsumed under a wider understanding of her agency. To actively occupy one's agency feels better, ultimately, than to remain a victim. These subsuming movements in thought, the felt sense that this new mode of understanding is more complete, is the first indicator of increased objectivity.

What I am suggesting is that truth is pragmatic (James, 1907; Rorty, 1982). Truth is not a quality that exists in and of itself in our perception.

Things in their solitude are no concern of ours. What matters in knowing is how the world, its things and people, come to touch us. We seek to find understanding that works, that improves our relationship to the world. Countertransference is a necessary part of analytic technique, I argue, because when we make use of it, the practice of analysis works better and so feels better. Our analysands find the analysis more helpful and we are less likely to be mired in impasse. When we move beyond the global question of countertransference and approach specific moments of trying to make sense of a countertransference reaction, irreversibility remains relevant. In the self-analytic process we must ask whether our understanding of the countertransference is helpful; does it allow us to move beyond the difficult moments of analytic paralysis and provide a way to speak usefully to the patient about our understanding?

But irreversibility cannot stand alone. We can look at our experience and trace moments when we were gripped by a sense of progress in understanding, only to subsequently recognize that understanding's terminal qualities. The adolescent may fall in with a group of delinquents and feel that the rejection of conventional morality is a freeing, truer way of viewing the world. In part there is some genuine understanding in this embracing of delinquency; it senses the constructed quality of morality. Yet we look at this undoing of morality as misguided, as a misplacing of the affective scale of values, and hope that the adolescent, with time, will come to see the fallacy involved in delinquent thought. The individual on the verge of a manic break may be gripped by an intuition about the power of thought and set out to rescue the homeless through the power of his presence. He takes the homeless into his house, feeds them, gives them his clothes, and seeing their improved mood, is sure they are cured. For this individual his new mode of seeing and behaving feels much clearer than his previous, modulated activity. From the outside, though, we see the unrealistic and exaggerated quality of his hopes, the self-destructiveness of his behavior, and fail to concur with his sense of irreversibility in judgment. Measuring truth through the progression of thought is inadequate. In each of these cases the participants have an experience of moving from a lesser to a greater reality, but we look on and see this internal experience of progression as misdirected. As analysts trying to make sense of our countertransferences we too are vulnerable to errors in pragmatic judgment. Reich (1933) felt great confidence in his technique of character analysis, and while we may recognize his contribution to the field of technique, we are also well aware of the hostile impulses underlying his felt sense of advancement.

To secure objectivity the standard of felt irreversibility must be buttressed. To check whether our intuitions about truth are accurate, we must appeal to the arbiter of interpersonal agreement and subjectivity. We see the world in a certain way, and it feels true to us; it comes to govern our affective response, and now we must be willing to see whether this is idiosyncratic, or stems from a more authentic determination of our common humanity. If we accept the analytic insight concerning the operation of motivated, unconscious defense, then we must acknowledge that in solitude we have no certain method of ascertaining whether our view of reality is defensively determined or perspicacious. The only way we can measure this is if other people can see it in the same way, can feel it as we do, and having seen it this way endorse it as a more useful manner of approaching the world. Likewise in psychoanalysis we must turn to the other people who have engaged in this mode of inquiry and living. Mitchell (1993) writes: "Ultimately, it is the community of psychoanalytic practitioners who provide the crucial testing ground, in the crucible of daily clinical work, for the relevance and efficacy of all levels of psychoanalytic theorizing" (p. 65). The possibility of cutting through folly and delusion lies in agreement.

Now the objection might be leveled against this account that truth is greater than human prejudice. Copernicus, when he displaced Earth from the center of the galaxy, aroused strong disagreement. Are we to then say that while he was in the minority his view was false? No, the point is not immediate agreement, but the ultimate potential for agreement. We accept the truth of the Copernican view because, having looked at the evidence over a period of centuries, we all agree that this is the best account. The standard of agreement, then, must be weighed within larger historical periods. Human inquiry, over time, will correct itself and reach more useful modes of knowing.

The historical focus in this paper has been pursued as a way of tracing the evolutionary agreement that has emerged concerning the countertransference. The first strand that supports the necessity of the countertransference in analytic technique is this irreversible progression. The second strand is the historically driven agreement the field has reached. The countertransference is generally accepted now because analytic practitioners have agreed that to attend to it feels better, that this attention makes analysis more productive. Once we accept the utility of the countertransference, however, we are still left to develop procedures for its management. Within the analytic situation the verification of our understanding of a given countertransference reaction must depend on our capacity to reach agreement (eventually) both with the analysand and with the wider analytic community.

I have argued that within a constructivist perspective, objectivity is determined by the progressive, pragmatic movement of thought coupled with the validating force of consensual agreement. These first two standards of truth (irreversibility and agreement), though, do not capture the full scope of human knowing. The progressive movement of thought is also governed by the principle of inclusiveness. In a perspectivally determined world, we must look for modes of understanding that can hold the multiple vantage points for seeing. To avoid this multiplicity is to retreat from the insights of constructivism. The attempt to pin understanding to a singular perceptive position, to trample over the paradoxical diversity of human knowing, is damaging to the ecology of meaning and human adaptation. Constructivism values the capacity to nurture the full strata of understanding. It is from this kind of bridging perspectivity that objectivity emerges in a constructivist epistemology.

To make this claim is to present a value-determined argument. It is not forced upon us by the press of the world. There is nothing inherent about inclusiveness that makes it a more valid way of knowing than a more singular sight. The argument for inclusiveness, then, must rest on an account of why it is a more valuable way of knowing for human living. To understand the argument for inclusiveness as a standard of objectivity we must reconsider the action of the transference. The analysand seeks out analysis because of suffering. She suffers because she is trapped in a transferential paradigm that restricts her capacity to perceive other options or new beginnings. The transference, then, leads to an adhesiveness of perception that drives the anlaysand to repeatedly view the world from particular perspectives. In a sense we could say that the dysfunctional aspect of transference stems from its objectivist tendencies. It claims that its truths are the only ones, that reality is singular.[5] This singularity

[5] In describing transferential reality as singular, I do not mean to suggest that it is simple or straightforward. The analysand, within the transference, holds multiple and even paradoxical views of reality. I call it singular due to its lack of flexibility, its unwillingness to inhabit other perspectives.

of perception stems from the force of ingrained affective reactions. We feel something strongly and this becomes our promontory for perception. But, then, seeing the world in this way we react accordingly, and in this reactive gesture behave in ways to bring about the very conditions that would refuel the initial affective position. We feel resentment about the past, that we have not been given our due, and we fight to right the error; but in this angry grasping we instill stinginess in those around us. When we feel this stinginess in the world, the resentment draws new force. Or we imagine some point in our childhood prior to the fall from grace—a time of haven where we were loved unambiguously in our infantile dependence. Trying to regain that sweetness of relationship, we surrender our adult autonomy and seek caretakers rather than partners. But this regressive impulse fails to be met, thereby sharpening the sense that workable intimacy is unattainable. To make permeable these singular transferential perceptive sets, these affectively determined objectivist impulses, evoke feelings of threat and anxiety. It is these negative feeling states that keep us from moving toward more inclusive perception. We might say that the shame of who we have been becomes an obstacle to changing who we might be. To acknowledge that we contributed to our suffering is to risk feeling ashamed, and so we hold on to stale narrations about how the world operates even though it dooms us to dystonic repetition.

Part of the aim of analytic action is to begin softening this perceptive rigidity. To see this we must remember that the perspectival nature of reality necessarily makes truth uncertain and pragmatic. At any point our understanding may be limited in unseen and destructive ways. While we cannot escape those moments, we can avoid engraining them by remembering that truth is not static nor owned by authority. To hold this in mind is to develop a continual willingness to experiment with ways of viewing the world. The perspectival and provisional quality of truth suggests the virtue of flexibility and playfulness in perceptive activities. This idea of perceptive playfulness has increasingly come to pervade the psychoanalytic idiom. As we move to interpret and offer alternate views of reality to the transferentially determined perspective of the analysand, we should remember that this view cannot merely supplant the old. The old view of reality, while limiting and painful, cannot be seen as simply false. Greenberg (1992) makes this point when he describes transference as a transfer of conviction rather than impulse. He writes: "Transference can be optimally creative only when the patient can be playful with it—

only, that is, when he can experience any particular reaction as reflecting but one part of a vast range of possibilities. This depends on the freedom to be aware of as many transference paradigms as possible" (p. 239). Part of the aim of psychoanalytic practice, according to this view, is to strengthen the analysand's capacity to accept inclusive understanding. It helps us reach more pliable forms of perception. When we look at human development, it is clear that part of what sets the adult apart from the infant is the ability to hold multiple perspectives. This recognition lies at the core of Piaget's work. The adult has gained the ability to disembed himself from the perspectives formed out of immediate perception. The adult can put himself into the subjective shoes of the other, and through this ability can then perform cognitive tasks more skillfully. Inclusive perception is more objective because it leads to more positive adaptations. As we make interpretations we should keep in mind the multiplicity of reality. We work to expand the analysand's view of reality, rather than simply to exchange it for another.

Thought, as I see it, moves toward greater inclusiveness, in part, because it provides more durable forms of understanding, and this durability serves protective functions for humankind. When we align ourselves with a more singular view of the world we are constantly in danger of being unpleasantly surprised. At any moment another mode of seeing the world may break into our consciousness and upset the delicate balance. In part we include inclusiveness in the standard of objectivity because the durability it provides is helpful for human adaptation.

Yet durability of perception, by itself, will not support inclusiveness as a critical criterion of essential knowing. If the widened awareness of the adult leads only to resignation and bleak acceptance of the inevitable then we should look for blinders. But I do not think that this is the case. We have described affect as a series of perspectival promontories. Each emotional reaction represents a mode of knowing the world through our concerns. The adhesiveness of transferential perception that regenerates our suffering stems from the failure to keep in mind the paradox of perception. In Kleinian language, we might say that we fail to realize the deeply human contradiction of the depressive position and the redemptive force of the reparative gesture. Out of the restricted perceptive gaze, we are driven back onto polarized views of the world and ourselves. We come to believe that people are either good or bad, evil or virtuous, and we anxiously hope to find ourselves on the positive side of this linear scale or risk the collapse into negative self-esteem. It leads us to reject and condemn those who have let us down and assign them a spot on the devalued end of the continuum. When we begin to find the sense of safety and courage to move beyond the boundaries of the singular transference, the possibility of embracing more variant and nuanced positions unfolds. To wed inclusiveness with emotional knowing, then, is to hold within awareness the full range of our affectivity, and to remain aware of our fear and our loving in the midst of a moment of anger. It is to put ourselves in the position of the other even as that person evokes strong negative feelings in us. Inclusiveness of perception leads us away from a fixed belief in the singular self. We come to see that within our ongoing sense of identity we include multiple selves or self-states, and that these aspects of our being should not be collapsed into an artificial unity. Mitchell (1993), in a discussion of the singular versus the multiple self, writes:

> One of the great benefits of the analytic process is that the more the analysand can tolerate experiencing multiple versions of himself, the stronger, more resilient, and more durable he experiences himself to be. Conversely, the more the analysand can find continuities across his various experiences, the more he can tolerate the identity diffusion entailed by containing multiple versions of self [p. 116].

Analysis helps strengthen the analysand's epistemological capacity to know her paradoxical self and not be undone by the diversity. We can know ourselves as both poetic and dull, foolish and insightful, cruel and generous. When we free ourselves from the need to average this multiplicity to find its mean value, we no longer are left with the daunting task of trying to take the measure of our absolute worth. As we come to see this multiplicity of motivation and action within ourselves, we gain the capacity to reenvision the meaning of the other's behavior and intent. When we are confronted by another's coldness or punishing anger we can look beyond the surface of that behavior and develop some understanding of the painful predicament that has fueled these difficult behaviors. Seeing the fear and desire for good self-experience that underlie them, we begin to unravel the necessity of playing out the complementary emotional role. We no longer are so firmly bound to what Racker (1968) calls the law of talion, and can infuse our initial sense of indignation with a more caring understanding. When we develop an inclusive affective knowing, when we expand the looping quality of emotion, we develop another range of feeling. At this superordinate level, I argue, the outcome is compassion. Compassion is the emotional reaction of inclusiveness in perception. It is the derivative of all the different emotions and perceptions. To move beyond the partial perspective of resentment into generosity and compassion is an irreversible shift. We do not want to return to the old mode of understanding.

This compassionate mode of understanding is critical in the psychoanalytic arena. We hope our analyses culminate with analysands able to feel more empathy for their parents and their parents' mistakes. Mitchell (1993), discussing how a patient's expanded sense of his own multiplicity affected his understanding of others, writes: "As he became more able to contain other ways of experiencing himself, he came to be able to tolerate other dimensions of his parents and important people in his current life. Over the course of the analysis, other features of both parents emerged" (p. 120). This empathic understanding is critical in moving beyond the bitterness that fastens negative transferential perceptions in place.

In contrast to the objectivist premise of truth's singularity, the constructivist belief in the value of inclusiveness leads to an endorsement of the countertransference as an essential part of analytic technique. Within the countertransference lie further and necessary modes of knowing the patient. These emotional reactions provide further windows of insight than those afforded by thought alone. The standard of inclusiveness, though, also holds principles that suggest how the countertransference should be worked with within the therapeutic setting. When we first feel the growing press of countertransferential affect, attending to it provides us with one point of knowing the analysand. It leads us to know something about how the analysand has impacted our immediate concerns. But this is only a partial understanding. What we must then do is set about enriching this understanding by placing it in a more inclusive web of understanding. I suggest that the different descriptions of utilizing the countertransference put forward by people like Racker, Tansey and Burke, and others are all implicitly accounts of how to proceed in this widening process. They ask us to consider the emotions of the countertransference from multiple vantage points, and they suggest that this will enable us to move beyond reactive emotion into more compassionate understanding. Tansey and Burke (1989) write:

> Empathy is the optimal outcome that results from the successful processing of an identification and leads to emotional knowledge of the patient's experience. . . . We are widening the definition of empathy from an intrapsychic event involving only concordant identifications taking place within the therapist—either with or without the patient's influence—to an interpersonal process in which a series of steps leads to an empathic outcome in the therapist's understanding of the patient [p. 58].

They suggest that by working toward inclusiveness, even the initially negative countertransference reaction that is generated by a complementary identification can be transformed into an empathic and compassionate response. We see this same concept in Racker's (1972) work:

> Now the decisive moments arrive. The analyst, subdued by the patient's resistance, may begin to feel anxious over the possibility of failure and feel angry with the patient. When this occurs in the analyst, the patient feels it coming, for his own "aggressiveness" and other reactions have provoked it; consequently he fears the analyst's anger. If the analyst, threatened by failure, or to put it more precisely, threatened by his own superego or by his own archaic objects which have found an *agent provocateur* in the patient, acts under the influence of these internal objects and of his paranoid and depressive anxieties, the patient again finds himself confronting a reality like that of his real or fantasized childhood experiences and like that of his inner world; and so the vicious circle continues and may be reinforced. But if the analyst grasps the importance of this situation, if, through his own anxiety or anger, he comprehends what is happening in the analysand, and if he overcomes, thanks to the new insight, his negative feelings and interprets what has happened in the analysand, being now in this new positive countertransference situation, then he may have made a breach—be it large or small—in the vicious circle [p. 185].

In these accounts of the processing of the countertransference there is a tacit suggestion that by expanding understanding of a given emotional reaction, by moving toward greater inclusiveness, we can transform the negative or non-useful countertransference reaction into a more positive or compassionate emotional perspective that offers greater objectivity and the opportunity to overcome the destructive adhesiveness of the analysand's transferential perception.

CHAPTER EIGHT

Verification and Disclosure

The acceptance of an aesthetic or pragmatic view of truth can lead us to feel like the poor relative of our more successful cousins in the hard sciences. When we turn to these sciences–physics, chemistry, biology, and the like–we may think that they don't have to settle for such a debased form of knowing; they have not had to turn to affectivity as the standard of truth. Scientific truth seems to possess a rigor that extends beyond human valuing. We look at astronomy, for instance, and feel that it has proved that the Earth orbits around the sun, rather than the other way around. The movement of celestial bodies, dim theories of relationally determined being aside, are not influenced by human concerns, and the triumph of astronomy, we want to insist, is that it was finally able to brush aside human concern about our place in the universe to determine the actual state of celestial movement. But we must ask why this seems so objectively true. When we consider space, it becomes apparent that there is no fixed grid to which objects are attached. The sun, as much as the Earth, exists in a matrix of nothingness, and we make sense of their movement only through their kinetic relationship. If we choose, we could refix the Earth at the center of the universe, and describe the sun, the planets, and the stars as moving about it. While to accommodate this planetary centrism would require more arduous descriptive equations, and would force us to abandon simple elliptical orbits for more complicated patterns, there is no absolute reason why this retreat from Galileo couldn't accommodate all of the observational data. We endorse the Galilean perspective because our lives work better when we occupy this ground. The simplicity of the theory makes it easier to learn, and reduces the time required to work through predictive equations. We prefer the elegance of its spare lines and internal consistency. These scientific judgments, too, are aesthetically and pragmatically grounded.

Again, we may feel the temptation to object that while psychoanalysis may be forced to settle for verification through agreement, science knows a more transcendent relationship to the world. We sense that science is concerned with the state of the external world in its actuality, not with the terms of intersubjective agreement. But when we consider the method of scientific inquiry, we come against this same standard of objectivity. The experiment acts as a way of systematizing our efforts to reach agreement. Spezzano (1993) writes:

> Prior to the rise of the experiment as a convention, active critical argument was the foundation of truth, and the experiment never actually displaced such argument. There was, of course, a wish that it might, that we would be able simply to conduct experiments and hold them up for others to see, with no words required.
>
> Experiments, however, were just something else to observe and talk about [p. 7].

The experiment is a way of specifying the conditions that will allow us to agree about what we have seen. We fling particles down an accelerator, record the results of the impact, and then must try to reach an agreement about how best to speak about this outcome. Should we speak about quarks or some other kind of particle or event? In experimental psychology the operation of agreement is even more clear. We set up a behavioral observation and rate the interaction on a series of seven-point scales. The numbers that are generated are proof of our agreement. They say you and I, seeing the same thing, can behave identically, like synchronized swimmers. We watch a child in "the strange situation" and both speak the words "two" or "four" as we mark the rating sheet. When we reapproach the question of the countertransference, then, armed with this revised epistemology, it should be clear that our conclusions about its use will not be in accord with Freud's positivist conclusions. Psychoanalysis is not shackled to a less substantial epistemology than that which governs "hard" science. It should not feel diminished by the turn to constructivism.

Countertransference and Epistemology

We must try to draw out more explicitly the implications of constructivist epistemology for the understanding and utilization of the countertransference. There are two parts to this discussion. The first is, what is the countertransference about? What does it mean and how should we set about trying to extract its significance in the analytic situation? This part of the discussion concerns the epistemological process of the analyst. The second part concerns the utilization and disclosure of the countertransference. Here we move to concerns about the analysand's connection to the real. What is the nature of the analytic situation's reality, and how does speaking or not speaking about the countertransference affect the analysand's epistemological capacity?

The countertransference, as we have argued, is a critical part of the analyst's epistemological process. Our affects offer a way of knowing the analysand that reaches to the most fundamental or essential parts of our humanity. When we come to feel something during the analytic encounter we have been touched in some way by the analysand; our task is to bring organization to that feeling in a way that usefully informs our understanding and our capacity to act in the therapeutic situation. The current literature on the countertransference has done much to develop our understanding of this process. Heimann (1949), Little (1951), Tower (1956), Racker (1968), and, more recently, Giovacchini (1989), and Tansey and Burke (1989) have written important work on projective identification, complementary and concordant identification, and empathy. My intention here is not to retrace this work, but to try to articulate in more general terms how a constructivist epistemology speaks to our utilization of the countertransference.

In the chapters on Freud, we argued that he held a paradoxical view of affect. He writes about affect as both a source of confusion and as a trail marker on the path toward psychic reality. But in Freud this paradox is never explicitly spoken, and as such it must remain confusing to the analytic practitioner. The affect of the countertransference *is* a subjectively determined perspective on reality (as Freud suggests), but this subjectivity does not set it apart from cooler thought nor disqualify it from participating in the process of objectivity. The countertransference is a way of knowing the analysand, yet this is not enough in itself. To make the countertransference a useful part of analytic technique (part of Freud's free-floating attention, a means of turning the unconscious toward the patient) rather than a destructive one (an egocentric remaking of the patient into an object of gratification), the analyst must work to bring these moments of subjectivity under the more stable sway of considered thought. She must ask herself, what is the most useful or valuable way of holding this affective reaction? This is the turn to the affective scale of value. In this moment she tries to discover how the countertransference might contain insight that is useful in her attempt to be of help to the analysand. Whatever conclusions the analyst makes on the basis of her reading of the affective scale of value, they are not free-floating, unverifiable positions. The utilization of the countertransference as a source of knowing, while not without hazards, does not entail the abandonment of standards of judgement. The understanding of the countertransference gains clarity and confidence when it is subjected to the standards of irreversibility, agreement, and inclusiveness. Within each countertransferential occasion some part of us should ask: does this understanding move us forward in our capacity to be present with the analysand, to be of use; is this understanding something the analysand and other analysts can agree with; is this an inclusive understanding, and has it called to itself the more extensive range of affective positions and reached some level of compassionate empathy? It is this self-questioning process of the analytic community that allows us to secure some ground to stand on as we venture interpretations and judgments about what is of use. Whatever conclusions we reach about the significance of the countertransference, we should remember that our prejudices against it are grounded in tradition rather than in some kind of pure soil of objectivity. Human knowing is always provisional, subject to standards of confidence, not certainty.

In part, Freud's prohibition of the countertransference and gratification in the analytic setting stemmed from his concern with the analysand's connection to the real. After moving away from the influence of hypnosis, away from a reliance on authority and faith, Freud increasingly sought to cure through strengthening the analysand's epistemological capacity. The analysand, through the process of analysis, is brought into the realm of mature knowing. Analysis helps the analysand differentiate between past and present, fantasy and fact. The vehicle for the renovation of the epistemological structure is the analytic relationship. For Freud, the analytic relationship is a professional one, a relationship between doctor and patient, and the capacity to perceive this is the litmus test of cure. Initially, however, the analysand, due to the strength of libidinal impulse, misperceives the analytic situation as a gratificatory context modeled along past experience. This misperception is what the analyst, through interpretation, must correct. The analyst should not participate affectively in the analytic relationship because to do so would only further tempt the analysand to turn away from the sustaining but frustrating realm of reality back toward the easier but empty world of fantasy. To disclose elements of the countertransference (a countertransference that should not exist in the well-functioning analyst) could only serve to lend credence to the analysand's misplaced convictions. By remaining abstinent and rational, the analyst works to reinforce the operation of the reality principle in the analysand.

Once we have overturned the idea of a singular reality, however, the dichotomy between the real and the unreal becomes less neat. While the analytic relationship is certainly peculiar, that peculiarity does not reduce its reality, nor limit its actual significance to the professional. "In a superficial way," Mitchell (1993) writes, " . . . the analytic relationship could be defined as unreal, in contrast to real relationships in the rest of the analyst's life. Yet the unreal dimensions of the analytic situation often serve to make possible a much deeper, personally riskier, more profound experience than is possible in 'real' life" (p. 148). The analytic relationship is built on different premises than other relationships—it depends on a fee, it is asymmetrical, and it is focused on helping one member of the dyad—but these constraining premises cannot be called "unreal." They are constructed and maintained through the mutual participation of the analyst and the analysand, but this constructed quality, by itself, does not set it apart from other relationships or reduce its reality. Every relationship is constructed rather than found. Once we see this, we can no longer claim that gratification that is procured in the analytic relationship is hallucinatory, nor hold to a belief that we can approach reality through renunciation. The argument against analytic gratification and affective participation, then, if it is to be maintained, must rest on other justifications than this branch of epistemological concerns.

To argue against the dichotomized split between the real and unreal, however, does not entail an abandonment of Freud's concern with the analysand's epistemological capacity. Moving toward a constructivist mode of knowing, we have argued, is central to the analytic project. To reach some understanding of the constructed, multifaceted, and pragmatic quality of truth is critical in alleviating the adhesiveness of the maladaptive, transferential perceptive set. An implicit understanding of constructivism lies behind the capacity to be "playful" with the transference, to gain a flexibility in living. It is this kind of epistemological consideration that lies behind Mitchell's (1993) claim that "psychopathology might well be considered a failure of imagination, a life that is stuck because old constraints foreclose the possibility of new experiences, new states of mind" (p. 222). If we accept this idea that one root of analytic action lies in the unveiling of the constructivist capacities of the analysand, then we must ask again, what is required from the analyst to be of use in this project? Again Mitchell is relevant: "What the analysand needs includes a particular attitude toward knowing on the part of the analyst" (p. 78). The analysand needs the analyst to manifest an attitude toward knowing that will allow the analysand to move toward greater perceptive flexibility and an understanding of how value operates in truth.

In trying to make sense of this revised analytic attitude we can be clear that for the analyst to behave as the proprietor of an objectivist epistemology would be senseless. The analyst does not have an exclusively privileged access to reality that would allow her to immediately render judgment on the validity of the analysand's perceptions. The analyst cannot claim to have overcome her subjectivity, and to do so would only act to mislead the analysand about the nature of knowing. If truth is determined through the process of consensual agreement and is intimately involved with the process of valuing and affect, then the analyst must be careful not to devalue the analysand's capacity to participate in the process of determining meaning. Meaning and the right to weigh in on the question of reality are intimately tied up with the sense of safety and self-esteem. The analyst, according to Spezzano (1993), must work as a conarrator with the analysand in order to be able to "suggest useful narrative changes without evoking [the] sense of an alien voice trying to wrest authorship of the patient's psychic reality from him" (p. 124). For the analysand to develop a sense of how truth is created through the interpersonal and the subjective, the analyst must be prepared to grant the analysand equal epistemological rights from the beginning. In an epistemological democracy, change must come through persuasion rather than compulsion or authority.

The Use of the Countertransference

Not only is the analyst incapable of remaining affectless in the analytic situation, but this affect is a critical source of analytic knowing. The analyst will invariably need to experience and make use of her countertransference. We must ask, then, how this fact should enter into the analytic dialogue. Clearly the traditionalists would argue that it should not. The anonymity of the analyst is critical in providing an adequately clear medium on which the transference can be inscribed. The analyst does not speak about her family or private life, so why speak about the countertransference? The countertransference, under this argument, is part of the analyst's neurosis (the most conservative view), or an object for self-analysis and inquiry. To go beyond the internal processing of the countertransference, to begin speaking of it with the analysand, is to indulge oneself in rationalized forms of self-gratification that do not serve the analysand's best interests. The disclosure of the countertransference can only act to limit the analysand's ability to manifest his regressive perception in the transference.

This more traditional or conservative argument, however, quickly runs into difficulty. We have argued that the countertransference is a universal phenomenon and a central mode of knowing the analysand. Through our affect we come to know something about the affective states of the analysand. Yet if we are able to use our own countertransference to know the affectivity of the analyst, why would we assume that this mode of disclosure that operates underneath the verbal channel should transmit in only one direction? What keeps the analysand from using this same mode of knowing to know our countertransference? This is the question that Spezzano (1993) asks:

> We cannot claim to be able to identify disavowed affects in patients while simultaneously talking as if we were successfully hiding ours from them. There is no useful way for us to discuss affects without acknowledging, as we really have been doing all along, that they are knowable to the listener even when unknown to or hidden by the speaker; that is, that affects can be communicated in other than directly verbal ways [pp. 43–44].

The analyst's affects are perceptively available to the analysand. The expression of affect belongs to parts of the self that are preconscious. Even when we consciously set out to dissemble, these efforts are only partly successful. The polygraph depends on this insistence of the physical to root out the affects that accompany lying. We must admit, then, that the analysand, whether we speak of it or not, knows something about our countertransferential states. This realization, initially full of controversy, begins with Ferenczi (1988):

> The experiences I have gathered since then have led me to suspect that it is no use, or not much use, to show more friendliness toward

> the patient than we really feel. Subtle, barely discernible differences in the handshake, the absence of color or interest in the voice, the quality of our alertness or inertia in following and responding to what the patient brings up: all these and a hundred other signs allow the patient to guess a great deal about our mood and our feelings [pp. 35–36].

Over the course of the intervening years this observation has lost its scandalous quality. At this point in our development, the idea that the analysand knows something about us is not easily disputed.

If the patient knows about our countertransference and yet we refuse to include it in the analytic dialogue, it seems that this must act as a blow to the analysand's epistemological capacity. Our unwillingness to acknowledge what the patient has perceived, it would seem, can only act to throw off the epistemological chase, like an escaped convict doubling back through the stream to confuse the dogs. This kind of discrepancy between the acknowledged and the perceived must play some havoc with the analysand's reality testing. Here we should recall Freud (1907) and his writing on the childhood instinct for knowledge. He claims that the child naturally strives to discover the facts of sexuality, and that when this is blocked by "mystery making" on the part of the parents, the capacities of thought are damaged: "The customary answers given to the child in the nursery damage his genuine instinct of research and as a rule deal the first blow, too, at his confidence in his parents. From that time on he usually begins to mistrust grown-up people, and to keep his most intimate interests secret from them" (pp. 135–136). If our countertransference is a key source of our analytic insight, and yet we disclaim its presence, how can we expect the analysand to learn how to make use of his own affectivity? It is as though we were to introduce an apprentice to the silversmith trade, but refuse to show him the process of engraving. The writing on the silver would have to appear as though by magic. Not to find some way of discussing the countertransference is to surround it with mystification and taboo, and must lead the analysand to lose faith in his own subjectivity and in the analyst as a conduit of reality.

While the Freudian call for anonymity is powerful, to merely overlook the countertransference, to obscure it with silence or reflection is untenable. To do so is to germinate the seeds of inauthenticity and to weaken the analysand's capacity to know. In the face of this bind it can be tempting to invert the injunction and call for a radical honesty on the part of the analyst. This is the route that Ferenczi took in his work with

RN. He submitted himself to mutual analysis and attempted to tell all. But this radical promiscuity in countertransference disclosure is misguided and cannot be enlisted as an aid to strengthening the constructivist capacity of the analysand. To merely move from secrecy to confession is to preserve a naive distinction between truth and fiction, between the real and the unreal. While our emotions are critical to the process of knowing, they are not immediately reliable indicators of objectivity. They may be compensatory reactions that disguise more essential feelings. In this sense the mere presence of a given countertransferential feeling does not necessarily indicate the most salient aspects of what transpires within us. While it does indicate something about both the analysand and ourselves, it is not the whole story. To baldly confess our countertransference as a finished story, then, is to mislead the analysand about the nature of knowing and affect. Schafer (1992), while conceding the necessity of acknowledging the analysand's accurate perception of the countertransference, is clear about the danger of being lost in the actuality of events and merely confessing the countertransference when it has been registered by the analysand:

> Yet it does not follow from these points that, in this connection, analysts must shift the focus away from psychic reality more than temporarily. It remains essential that there be analysis of how and why the analysand elaborates further these results of unconsciously seeing, hearing, and understanding. In other words, analysts soon return to asking what the analysand makes of the analyst's seductiveness or cruelty, if these types of countertransference are in question....
>
> I am trying to bring out that analysts always employ a pluralistic view of what is real or actual. The events in the analysis, like all other events, are available only in versions then, and no one version states a significant fact in all its aspects [p. 215].

To simply confess the countertransference, without looking further, without considering what else might be occurring in the analyst, or why this means what it does to the analysand, is to abandon the insights of constructivism. This in turn can lead to a kind of tyranny of affect, a move to say, "I have to be true to my feelings" (with the covert claim that everyone else should be too), without realizing that our immediate feelings are only a partial and uncertain window to our concerns, and only one among many views of reality. The value of inclusiveness, irreversibility, and agreement are misplaced in this supplication to "affective authenticity." Mitchell (1993) points out the difficulty of deciphering what would constitute authenticity in disclosure:

> But how does the analyst know what he is feeling? If we want to locate authenticity in the analyst in his current affective state, how does the analyst who is conscientiously trying to be true and authentic, first to himself and then, when optimally useful, with the patient, decide which among his various feelings and reactions are most authentic? . . .
>
> Analytic reflection forces an attention to other features of the analyst's feelings about the patient than may be in the immediate forefront at any particular moment. Perhaps the rage or arousal is not the "truest" or most "authentic" feeling at all, but merely the one with the most intense immediate charge [p. 146].

For the analyst to speak about her countertransference in an unmodulated way can be more harmful to the analysand's epistemological capacity than silence. It portrays the analyst's self-awareness as immediately reliable and conceals the necessity for continual re-uncovering of reality.

To reveal the countertransference in this kind of simplistic, confessional way, then, is misguided. Rather than strengthening the analysand's epistemological capacity, it can only serve to weaken it. In addition to supporting a singular view of reality, it can act to inhibit the analysand in the process of free association. For the analyst to disclose her feelings to the analysand can act to burden the patient. The patient can begin to experience the analyst as needing care, and slowly refrain from speaking of negative transferences that he imagines might hurt the analyst. When this occurs the field of inquiry is narrowed, and the analysis will be less effective at exploring the plurality of self-states.[1] What becomes clear as we consider this difficulty is that just as the maintenance of anonymity can never be value-free, nor can the disclosure of the countertransference be carried out simply in the interest of honesty and authenticity. We must remain aware of which needs we serve in the act of disclosure. Are we warding off the analysand's rage? Are we seeking to distinguish ourselves from the non-empathic figures from the analysand's childhood? Greenberg (1992) cautions against disclosure on these grounds:

---

[1]Although we could argue that this restriction is actually another manifestation of self in the interpersonal realm that must be brought into the field and examined.

> Frequently, when personal information is given to the patient, unless it comes from a countertransferential outburst, it is given in the interest of promoting either trust or some kind of identification. These goals are generally incompatible with the establishment of a neutral atmosphere because they embody the analyst's decision that he should support or bolster one aspect of the patient's tendencies at the expense of another. Unsurprisingly, the effect of many personal revelations is to stifle feelings. The analyst who has told his patient that he, like the patient, becomes anxious when doing creative work such as writing may intend to promote, through identification, the patient's tolerance for his own anxiety in similar situations—but he will run the risk of making it difficult for the patient to express contempt for the analyst's nonproductivity [p. 221].

If we genuinely accept the relevance of constructivist insight, we must be clear that we cannot avoid the press of subjectivity and motive through open disclosure any more than we can through silent observation. Countertransference disclosure cannot act as a panacean stimulant for the emergence of a constructivist capacity in the analysand.

The Role of Disclosure

As we stumble after reality, a narrative reality, we seem caught between a lee shore and innavigable shoals. While silence cannot procure neutrality, nor can disclosure insure authenticity. The countertransference, at least at times, can seem to pose an impossible dilemma to the analyst. The untenability of this dilemma, however, gains its solidity only when we imagine that the answer to the question of disclosure should take shape along objectivist lines. If reality is paradoxical, why should the utilization of the countertransference be any different? There is no clear sailing in this area, but that does not mean that we must sink. To inhabit these paradoxical waters and to be of use to the analysand in his capacity to draw sustaining connections to the real, we must look for a solution to the problem of disclosure that is in keeping with the constructivist sensibility.

There appear to be two primary schools of thought about how this goal may be met. The first, somewhat more conservative, approach, holds that the analyst should remain open to the plausibility of the analysand's ideas about the countertransference, engage them as pivotal points of inquiry, yet generally refrain from overtly disclosing her own ideas about her countertransference (Greenberg, 1992). The second, more extreme, approach, suggests that the analyst must bring her countertransference into the analytic dialogue in order to facilitate the free-association process (Bollas, 1987; Ehrenberg, 1992). But, in contrast to the confessional approach, in this approach the countertransference is not disclosed as a fully known, authoritative entity. It too must be examined and pulled apart for its meaning to become evident. Each method has its advantages and choosing between them is not easy.

In the more judicious approach, the analysand's undeniable capacity to perceive facets of the analyst's affectivity does not imply that the analyst must respond to this perception with confirmation or obscuration. Rather than becoming entangled in the question of reality, being caught in the need to determine whether a given piece of countertransference exists or not, it is more helpful to explore what meaning this perception has to the analysand. If the analysand experiences the analyst as frustrated, what does this frustration entail? Does the analysand then imagine an irrevocable breach with the analyst? What keeps him from imagining other outcomes to the affective event? This is the approach that Greenberg seems to recommend: "I am not, in this connection suggesting that it is helpful either to confirm or to dispute any convictions the patient might express. At this phase of the work, the analyst must follow the often more difficult path of maintaining an openness to the patient's impressions and an awareness of their plausibility, even when doing so gets uncomfortable" (p. 248). In taking this approach, the analyst retains a willingness to explore all aspects of the patient's experience, and doesn't foreclose on the question of their validity. By staying open to the plausibility of the analysand's perception of the countertransference, the analytic dyad is more likely to reach an inclusive understanding of the situation's reality. Schafer (1992), arguing from a different theoretical background, supports a similar conclusion about disclosure:

> Analysts should not split off countertransference from acceptably accurate reality testing or soundly approved moral values; here the assumption of autonomous functioning does not preclude a more complex analysis. "Reality" is known to be a good defense. . . . Thus, in the clinical situation, even when it is recognized that the patient has correctly perceived a trait of the analyst's, even a countertransference manifestation, as a rule it is still best to keep the focus on the

> transference-significance of this piece of good reality testing. The timing, emphasis, mode of expression, and selectivity of whatever the analysand seems to have perceived correctly: All may signal significant transference and unconscious conflict. Truth, transference and counter-transference are not mutually exclusive [p. 232].

When we keep in mind the significance of constructivism, we will not be misled into assuming that a perception, even when it is in accordance with a consensually accessible reality, is strictly determined by that event. By not disclosing the countertransference we avoid falling into the trap of supporting a belief in a singular, non-affectively determined reality. This approach has a number of strengths. When we avoid confirming a given perception of the countertransference we keep open our receptivity to the full range of the analysand's transferential perceptions. For a given analysand it may be vitally important to see us as being withholding or outstandingly compassionate. These projections must be given room in the analytic process. Furthermore, by refraining from overt disclosure we may better avoid burdening the patient with our own affective vulnerabilities and needs. The disclosure of the countertransference can easily hide defensive maneuvers of the analyst. But perhaps this approach's strongest recommendation comes from the authority it leaves in the hands of the analysand. If we are swayed by object-relational accounts of development, then we must remember that part of what the analysand suffers from is a lack of confidence in his own perceptive capacity. By avoiding interjecting our own subjectivity too quickly into the analytic conversation, we leave more room for the analysand to try out the full range of his perceptive capacities. Our curiosity about this perception can bolster the analysand's ability not to give way in the face of the analyst's authoritative subjectivity. By remaining still we create space for the analysand to explore the tension between objectivity and subjectivity in perception. In the early stages of an analysis, I would argue, taking a more cautious approach to the problem of countertransference disclosure is warranted. While we can always move from silence toward greater self-disclosure in the analytic process, it is not a path we can easily tread in reverse. We cannot unspeak what has been said, or easily convince the analysand of our implacability once we have confirmed the presence of the countertransference.

In the second school of thought, by comparison, the countertransference is brought into the analytic dialogue not as a fixed entity but as a subjective state that needs to be unwrapped to reveal its genuine gifts (Bollas, 1987). Because this approach takes us further from Freudian proscriptions, we may feel greater reluctance to see its merit. It is easy to criticize this approach as a self-gratificatory maneuver by the analyst. To move past these initial condemnatory reactions, we must first see that there is nothing inherently more self-serving in this approach than in the more cautious one. Silence is as good a hiding place for nonhelpful countertransferential needs as disclosure. The justification of anonymity can free us from the need to take responsibility for parts of ourselves that we see as nonempathic. Furthermore, by not speaking directly to our countertransference, at least at some point in the analytic course, we keep our own epistemological process concealed. If the constructivist use of the countertransference is useful to our knowing, why shouldn't the analysand know this? This is the question Spezzano (1993) asks: "We have not considered in any rigorous way the alternative of analysts saying to themselves, to each other, and to patients that our main clue to what our patients feel is what we feel" (p. 46). The question we must struggle with, Spezzano suggests, is how this disclosure would affect the analysand's epistemological capacity. One could well argue that there needs to be a place in the analytic process for this kind of epistemological modeling, though it is best reserved for later in the analytic process, once the analysand has firmly recognized the workings of transference and the constructive and motivated aspect of perception. The analyst, by bringing her countertransference into the analytic discussion, allows the analysand to see how the analyst draws on her subjectivity in the process of knowing. Tansey and Burke (1989) write about the value of countertransference disclosure in this vein: "In addition to providing validation to the patient that his perceptions may be accurate, it also allows the patient the opportunity to observe the therapist as he applies the analytic method to himself in an effort to promote clarity and honesty within the therapeutic interaction" (p. 138). What is critical here is that disclosing the countertransference does not entail an abandonment of the analytic method. By talking about the countertransference as another object of inquiry, it provides a model of how the analyst understands the significance of affect. In the effort to make sense of this type of disclosure, Bollas (1987) has provided the most penetrating analysis. Bollas speaks about the necessity of using the countertransference in expressive ways:

> Because the analyst is the other patient, sustaining in himself some intersubjective discourse with the analysand, it is essential to find some way to put forward for the analytic investigation that which is occurring in the analyst as a purely subjective and private experience. It is essential to do this because in many patients the free associative process takes place within the analyst, and the clinician must find some way to report his internal processes to link the patient with something that he has lost in himself and enable him to engage more authentically with the free associative process [p. 205].

For Bollas, because the analytic process is essentially intersubjective, the discourse cannot be complete without the inclusion of the analyst's own subjectivity. Yet these expressive uses of the countertransference must be voiced in a way that reflect their subjective origins. If the analyst speaks about the countertransference as the creation and intentional impulse of the analysand, she obscures the workings of her own subjectivity. Or, if she presents them as completed facts, she misleads the analysand about the nature of the analyst's knowing and so, therefore, of knowing in general. Instead, the analyst must present these disclosures as ideas for further perceptive discovery and play. Bollas (1987) states:

> How is it possible to be so idiomatic in one's presentation of interpretations and not be traumatic to the patient? In my view, the answer lies in the way Winnicott regarded his own thoughts: they were for him subjective objects, and he put them to the patient as objects between patient and analyst rather than as official psychoanalytic decodings of the person's unconscious life. The effect of his attitude is crucial, as his interpretations were meant to be played with–kicked around, mulled over, torn to pieces–rather than regarded as the official version of the truth [p. 206].

The analyst, in bringing her own affectivity forward, remains helpful by speaking in a constructivist language. By remembering that truth belongs to an uncertain realm of consensual agreement, the analyst remains open to further discoveries about the significance of her own subjectivity. In this genuinely dialogistic process the analysand can rework his own relationship to knowing, and so come into closer contact with the real.

Knowing and Maturity

To the extent that this portrayal of epistemology and human valuing makes sense, I believe that speaking about the countertransference, at some point in the process, is an essential part of an analysis. To avoid this type of speech is to preserve a division between the analyst and analysand that prevents the analysand from becoming a full epistemological peer. Through a willingness to explore the analysand's perception of our countertransference and a willingness at times to speak of our affectivity, we offer assistance to the analysand in learning how to make use of his own affectivity as part of his ability to know. Part of maturity is recognizing the inevitably imperfect subjectivity of ourselves and those around us, and yet to not experience this imperfection as extinguishing value. It is this capacity to endure the truth of the human situation and the necessity of affective uncertainty that constitutes one indicator of readiness to bring an analysis to conclusion. Winnicott (1947) writes:

> If all this is accepted there remains for discussion the question of the interpretation of the analyst's hate to the patient. This is obviously a matter fraught with danger, and it needs the most careful timing. But I believe an analysis is incomplete if even towards the end it has not been possible for the analyst to tell the patient what he, the analyst, did unbeknown for the patient whilst he was ill, in the early stages. Until this interpretation is made the patient is kept to some extent in the position of infant–one who cannot understand what he owes to his mother [p. 202].

The countertransference must be brought into the analytic dialogue in order for the patient to know the world and how it adapts to him, without delusion. It is only when the analysand takes this step to know, and to bear knowing, the full mix of human interrelating, that he makes the transition from patient to cohort. Schafer (1992) writes:

> As termination approaches, the changes I have just been describing become particularly conspicuous in the transference. Analysands may become more and more reliable collaborators and even on occasion good supervisors–that is, participants who do not regress when the analyst seems not to have acted well. Instead, such analysands tend to find a way that is neither obscure nor self-injurious to let the analyst

> know what is disturbing the analytic work at one moment or another [p. 19].

When this stage is reached the analysand has gained enough confidence in his own epistemological capacity, and has freed himself enough from damaging constraints to expression, to identify that something has occurred in the countertransference that interfered with the collaboration. The analysand has reclaimed his ability to know as part of the human community.

the tonic quality of life is the arbiter

1
2. no imposition of virtue when using CT

human nature misconstrued
virtue constructed nature obscured
⇒ need diff. idea of virtue.

virtue depends on ability to dev. relationships & affect, ~~that~~ that in turn allow attainment of aims.

old ideas that are no longer acceptable
drive (leads to practice in which
analysand considered resistant --
& not fearful.)

repudiation of drive theory as possible but not necessary, and potentially damaging b/c it casts human inherently flawed (driven by, er, drives -- of sexuality & power.

C ~~wan~~ seeks a positive source for values,
sublimation doesn't cut it -
attacks transcendent & natural virtue

CHAPTER NINE

Stillness and Provision: Theories of Virtue in Psychoanalytic Practice

We now approach the question of virtue. While epistemology necessarily remains an unfinished question (at least from the constructivist point of view), we have said enough to move forward. When we wrestle with the technical problems of gratification and abstinence, neutrality and participation, we implicitly evoke deeper themes. The conclusions we reach are informed by how we understand the structure of health and the curative force of analysis. These issues are the foundational concerns of moral thought. Psychoanalysis, as a therapeutic endeavor, an endeavor that seeks to redeem us from suffering, is intrinsically a theory of virtue, and to reach a congruent theory of the countertransference we must first illuminate this implicit foundation.

We will do well to begin with basic questions here, questions that reach toward the teleological motivation of psychoanalysis. As analysands who have become analysts we should ask: what do we need? It seems we need to feel better. On the surface this is a tautology and it adds no new information. If it is suffering that pushes us toward analysis (and it is psychoanalysis' therapeutic claim that sets it apart from speculative philosophy), then there can be no other more immediate answer. But the answer's apparent obviousness masks controversy. The psychoanalytic field, grounded in Freudian views of psychic economy, knows only too well that the pleasure principle offers misleading guidance. The need to feel better draws us onto shoals; it leads us to linger in false pleasures, to find expedient but erroneous solutions to the difficulties in living. For psychoanalysis, merely feeling better does not seem to be enough. "Analysts would generally agree," Schafer (1992) writes, " . . . that among the forms of what they call resisting, there are flights into health, manic defenses, and transference cures, all of which may create false impressions of resolution of conflict and disappearance of symptoms in a lasting way" (p. 183). Psychoanalysis is wary of pleasure and from this concern comes what is perhaps the field's strongest technical injunction: the warning to avoid providing gratification in the transference. To gratify is to foreclose exploration and to short-circuit therapeutic motivation. This warning lies at the root of the proscription of the countertransference. While to engage affectively, to gratify, may lead to momentary reductions in suffering, it cannot provide the leverage needed for more permanent and essential characterological change.

If the lure of feeling better is such a source of danger to the analytic project, perhaps the tautology concerning need and the alleviation of suffering is less circular than it appeared. This question returns us to the debate between transcendent and naturalistic accounts of virtue. Do we require more discipline or greater freedom from restraint to achieve a virtuous life? While in the previous chapter we agreed that affect provides a scale of truth, we must also now recognize that it is affect that requires adjudication. The point of dispute concerns what we should best do with affect; should we cradle it and feed its needs, or be stern with our limits in order to break it of its spoiled demands? We should see, though, that while analysis may lead us to remain respectfully cautious in the face of feeling better, the determining force of happiness must eventually hold sway. We can distinguish between immediate gratification and more substantial forms of satisfaction, but the tonic quality of a life, we argued in the previous chapter, must act as the final arbiter in disputes. The question for psychoanalysis, then, is what will allow the analysand to feel better in an extensive and durable form. It is a question—a question about reliable value—that lies at the center of moral theory.

As Freud developed his therapeutic technique, he abandoned suggestion out of the realization that imposing values, while momentarily helpful, could not lead to secure change. At the core of Winnicott's developmental theory lies a recognition that impingement disrupts the child's well-being. Both of these analytic paradigms, drive and developmental arrest (Mitchell, 1993), are clear that psychic solutions, whatever their value, cannot be imposed on the analysand. To impose change is to risk both transferential submission and a deepening of the resistance. Schafer (1993) writes:

> Analyzing is not giving didactic instruction on how to be a "good" or comfortable analysand, nor is it teaching psychoanalytic generalizations about individual development or the way of the world. Certainly it is not giving advice and reassurance or issuing commands or prohibitions. As a rule, acting in any of these ways is neither analyzing nor preparing the way for interpretation. Most likely it is setting limits on what can be worked through later in the analysis. Consequently, such departures from the analytic attitude should be carefully limited. They may only be expressions of the analyst's narcissistically wishing to play guru. And the more the analyst plays guru, the more he or she reinforces the resistance to one important aspect of what remains to be analyzed more fully, namely, the analysand's presentation of a weak, empty, fragmented, "castrated," ego to the analyst in hopes of receiving his or her good ministrations [p. 11].

While developmental-arrest theorists might argue with Schafer's stern account of the analyst's presence, they are likely to concur with his argument that the therapeutic process is not served by the "issuing of commands or prohibitions." To seek change through didactic pressure can only add further layers to the false self. This shared recognition of the danger of imposing virtue forms the second pillar supporting the proscription of the countertransference as a source of action. To draw on the positive countertransference is to offer a palliative corrective emotional experience that cannot touch the underlying unconscious conflict. To enlist the negative countertransference in the issuing of prohibitions or exhortations is to rely on the force of personality; it may bring submission, but it cannot bring about more thorough change. To suggest that psychoanalysis constitutes a theory of virtue, then, may seem like a failure to have internalized these foundational insights. This attempt to distance psychoanalysis from the rhetoric of virtue, however, cannot hold. While psychoanalysis has learned well that virtue cannot be imposed, this conviction does not constitute an emancipation from the problem of value. Instead, it defines a theory of virtue. The psychoanalytic theory of virtue rests on the recognition that genuine virtue is reached only when action proceeds from the center of the agentive self.

The Moral Evolution of Psychoanalysis

We should see, then, that while the language of virtue may be a stranger to psychoanalysis, its concerns are familiar. The questions of insight and experience, gratification and abstinence, neutrality and participation, holding and facilitation–the narrative frame for the first century of psychoanalytic dialogue on technique–are all questions concerning the route to virtue. In endorsing insight, abstinence, neutrality, and holding, psychoanalysis has tried to build a therapeutic program that moves beyond assumed virtue. That conversation, in its sustained, progressive form, has assembled an extensive clinical structure. It is a structure that is useful in the therapeutic project; we seem to know something about the process of change, about how to help analysands feel better. The therapeutic frame, to the extent that it is effective, is shaped by genuine insight and should not be lightly overturned. But just as psychoanalysis has had to abandon its objectivist epistemological stance, in the realm of morality equally fundamental changes are necessary. In this chapter I will argue that psychoanalysis has been inadequately served by the transcendent and naturalist accounts of virtue that have governed its practice. These visions of virtue obscure its constructed quality and misconstrue the shape of human nature. As a result, they have failed to generate a fully coherent and robust structure for the analytic project.

In the evolution of psychoanalysis, Mitchell (1988) argues, three paradigms can be identified: the drive model, the developmental-arrest model, and the relational-conflict model. These paradigms correspond to the forms of morality that I have called "transcendent," "natural," and "constructed." He suggests that psychoanalysis, on the whole, has moved away from the metaphors of drive and developmental arrest. These metaphors have led to iatrogenic difficulty. In response, analysts have moved toward narratives of affect and relationship (Greenberg and Mitchell, 1983; Greenberg, 1991; Spezzano, 1993; Mitchell, 1993).[1] Psychoanalysis has accepted that the desire for attachment serves as a primary motive. It has come to speak about the centrality of affect, about the governing concerns of safety and vitality. In the current analytic dialogue, we tend to speak less about the derivatives of sexual drive or the need for reparative maturational supplies, than about the necessity for authentic con-

---

[1]This point will be argued more fully in chapter 10.

nection and spontaneous creativity (Bollas, 1987; Greenberg, 1991; Mitchell 1988, 1993; Spezzano, 1993). This shift in narrative structure marks the core of the emergent paradigm of constructed virtue. In tandem with the epistemological critique, it forms the second front in the upheaval of psychoanalysis. Mitchell (1993) writes: "Clinicians and authors who embrace the metatheoretical revolution without integrating into it the advances of the revolution in theory risk ending up with a methodology that floats in space" (p. 74). The conversation about psychoanalytic technique—to the extent it speaks about gratification and abstinence, neutrality and holding—implicitly refers to an outdated metapsychological and epistemological foundation. For the field to move forward we must work to clarify the structure of constructed virtue. Only through presenting the discourse of technique in the terms of current epistemological and metapsychological language, in terms of constructed virtue, can we hope to reach fully usable answers in the analytic encounter.

In this chapter I will argue that virtue does not lie in the capacity to locate a prenarrational reality nor in the realization of an innate biological program. Instead, both health and pathology are active structures that are best understood as adaptive reconstructions of our affective and relational action strategies. In this model, virtue depends on the construction of affective-relational skills that allow us to reach key motivational aims. While the theory of constructed virtue retains an awareness that virtue cannot be imposed, and remembers the danger of the submissive transference, it rejects the language of abstinence and neutrality. When we see that truth is a construction it becomes clear that the analyst—whether silent or speaking, reflecting or interpreting—is always acting and this action is inescapably informed by a theory of virtue. The conjunction between knowing and valuing implies that our affectivity permeates our therapeutic action. In some sense, then, we are always acting from the countertransference. We may mute our affectivity, try to quiet it, or even conceal it, but these are all forms of affective action. The question is not whether the countertransference has a place in analytic action, but what form it should best take. What kind of affective interaction is most useful in helping the analysand become unstuck from maladaptive transferential patterns and move toward more pliant and creative forms of living? To be helpful, analysts must bring to bear the same affective-relational skills they would offer the analysand. We can say with Freud that change cannot occur in abstenia, and that whatever is to be gained by analysis must first take shape within the analytic relationship.

Foundations for Virtue

While the transcendent and the naturalist accounts of virtue are antipodal in many of their positions, they share a common foundation. Both argue that the structure of virtue is preformed. In the transcendent view, virtue is determined by the architecture of reality. It is a destination that becomes immediately clear when the corrupting and distorting pull of incorrect desire is renounced. Within drive theory, this faith in preexistent virtue can be seen in the emphasis on "accurate reality testing." The analysand becomes well through moving beyond fantasy into an apprehension of the actual. Sterba (1934), describing the therapeutic action of interpretation, writes: "Each separate interpretation reduces the instinctual and defensive cathexis of the ego in favour of intellectual contemplation, reflection and correction by the standard of reality" (p. 268). The structure of virtue is embedded in and defined by reality. Within the naturalist account, while virtue is determined by the architecture of the body, it remains a predetermined structure. The germinal core of virtue is present at birth and, when free from traumatic imposition, will unfold naturally in adulthood. Within developmental-arrest accounts this faith in predetermined virtue reveals itself in the emphasis on the holding environment and the true self. The analysand becomes well by sloughing off the layers of false self and reasserting the developmental trajectory of the true self. The structure of virtue is embedded in and defined by the body. The narratives of drive and developmental arrest, then, while painting significantly different portraits of health, both suggest that its structure is preexistent, awaiting discovery. It belongs to reality and its shape is independent of subjectivity and choice.

The analyst, as the agent of "reality testing" or the "true self," is not personally implicated in structuring the therapeutic objective. This belief in the preexistent form of the therapeutic objective is intimately related to the psychoanalytic avoidance of moral theory. By equating health with the actualization of the real, the drive and developmental-arrest paradigms disclaim the operation of value. The sequestration of the countertransference, the prescription of neutrality, abstinence, and mirroring, are all corollaries of this obscuration of value. Within constructivism, however, the belief in an aseptically apprehended reality is an unworkable epistemological assumption. Value and understanding are always conjoined in the process of inquiry, and our account of technique, if it is to remain coherent, must make its values explicit rather than be cloaked in the fiction of impersonal truth. The narratives of drive and developmental arrest run aground in the therapeutic project, in part out of their mutual failure to recognize the necessary influence of value and the constructed quality of virtue. The drive model, in its transcendent tilt, and the developmental-arrest model, in its naturalism, I will argue, while grounded in real insight, are flawed narrative structures, and their limitations have led to difficulties in the clinical arena. To recognize the structure of these difficulties is to begin to make sense of constructed virtue.

Drive and the Limits of Transcendent Accounts of Virtue

We will begin with the drive model. To critique this paradigm, it might seem, is to critique the concept of drive. The difficulty with the drive model, however, does not stem from its reference to endogenous, preexperiential motivation. Relational models, with their emphasis on attachment systems and the innate need for human connection, also speak of a biologically determined agenda. To suggest that we are born with endogenous motives seems a necessary part of psychoanalytic explanation, but this should not be read as a retreat from constructivism. Instead, the difficulty with drive theory stems from its particular understanding of human motivation and its implicit alliance with transcendent accounts of virtue. Drive theory, in its understanding of the economics and aims of motivation, paints a bleak portrait of our biological base. It suggests that in their callow form our will is stagnant and our wants are rapacious. At bottom, our will is governed by the pleasure principle, and our motives are derivative of libidinal and aggressive energies. We exist in a state of original sin and to reach virtue this unmannered base must be transcended through the force of insight and reason. To become healthy we must relinquish unrealistic desires and establish a hegemony of the ego. The intuitive appeal of this narrative should not be overlooked. The image of the civilized beast speaks to the deeply conflicted quality of human existence, to the struggle between interpersonal adaptation and impulsive immediacy. Yet to view our precultured nature in reprobative terms, I argue, is to invite iatrogenic difficulty in the therapeutic context. Drive theory, through its critique of the callow and its call for transcendence, as we saw in the previous chapters, creates a subtext of shame and coercive struggle that limits its therapeutic effectiveness.

The first component in the transcendent moralizing underpinning of the drive model is its vision of the economics of will. While Freud is never simple or singular, in the main current of his thought he consistently argues that the operation of human motivation is governed by the pleasure principle. Humans are driven toward activity by the buildup of libidinal tension within the body, and their behavior is guided by the economic desire to reduce this tension to prearousal levels. The static quality of human motivation, according to the drive model, is what accounts for the difficulty of bringing about characterological change. We are always seeking out the lowest ground for tension relief. When we have found gratificatory outlets, even if they provide imperfect drainage, we are reluctant to surrender these known pathways. When the analysand comes to treatment, she is driven not by a desire for cure—a desire to find gratificatory relationships with real objects—but by a desire to avoid displeasure. The analysand, like Eve in the garden, suffers from a weakness of will. Given the opportunity, the analysand will subvert the analytic context through seeking hallucinatory pleasure in the transference; she will try to transform the therapeutic, mature, professional relationship into an infantile, gratifiying one. If the analyst succumbs to these transferential entreaties and provides such gratifiying experiences, the analysand will feel a momentary reduction in tension, and so lose the impetus that might drive her toward deeper discoveries about herself. The analyst, if he hopes to make progress, must firmly avoid the palliative effects of gratification, and hold steady in the interpretive course. It is only through insight that the channels of gratification can be rerouted and secure improvement achieved.

The assumptions about the economics of motivation in drive theory, assumptions that are congruent with transcendent virtue's understanding of will, lead it to adopt a view of therapeutic action and virtue that is based on abstinence. The reformation of the analysand's will requires the imposition of discipline and frustration. It is through the frustration of base desire that energy is lent to the awakening of insight. This vision of cure, however, predicated on the avoidance of gratification and the analyst's participation, creates difficulties in the clinical encounter with the analysand. When the analysand fails to make progress in the therapeutic process, it can lead the analyst to see the analysand as resistant rather than fearful. The analysand is seen as remaining ill from a lack of devotion, from an unwillingness to overcome indulgent habits. We can see this tendency in Nunberg's (1926) description of a patient who lacked the "will to recovery." While this morality-tinged attack on the analysand's motivation may have assuaged Nunberg's personal sense of failure, it seems to have offered little help to the analysand. The reprobative emphasis on the unmannered quality of will establishes an implicitly antagonistic, rather than affirmative, environment.

Drive theory takes a similarly dim view of the aims of human motivation. It suggests that human beings are caught between libidinal and aggressive drives. These drives are primary, and they bring us into relationships only in the interest of discharge. We seek out other people not as subjects, but as objects for our drives. Below our civilized exterior lies the more primitive truth of our libidinal and aggressive nature. Our generosity, our love—the traits we value—are merely disguises for the deeper, more selfish drives. According to drive theory, we become ill out of the innate conflict between these primary drives, from the pull between adaptive and impulsive urges. Our neurosis is a form of compromise through which we try to secure covert satisfaction for conflicted desires. To become well requires that we move beyond deluding ourselves about our intentions. In a kind of confession, we must first acknowledge the darker corners of the unconscious. Only through this courageous act of recognition can we begin to renounce the more problematic aims of the id and create lasting forms of sublimation. In the drive model, the accrual of virtue depends on the repudiation of degenerate impulses in favor of the conscious aims of the ego. Again, drive theory suggests that our callow nature, in aim as well as effort, is suspect. While this account of human motivation gains strength from its willingness to address the prevalence of violence and dissociated sexuality in human existence, its reprobative underpinning cannot provide an affirmative account of value. Having banished reference to God, drive theory must substitute the real for the divine as a destination for transcendence. But the real, in the objective view, is without numinous quality and cannot confer grace. In the real we can become aware of our churlish biological ground, and we can sublimate its impulses, but we cannot escape its grasp. It leaves us with sublimation as the cornerstone of virtue. But sublimation is a peculiar idea: it suggests that we are never directly connected to ourselves, that we act at a distance from ourselves, and that our virtue must remain derivative rather than radiant.

Schafer's Attempt to Rehabilitate Drive Theory

To disparage drive theory in this way, however, is problematic and somewhat imbalanced. Modern ego psychologists can reasonably argue that the explanatory rubric of drive theory does not need to be discarded to right the errors of reprobative analytic technique or correct its epistemological naiveté. It is here that Schafer comes to center stage. To my mind, his understanding of constructivism allows him to provide the strongest and most sophisticated defense of Freudian theory, and his work must be answered before we leave the paradigm of drive. Recognizing the cumulative empiricism contained in the history of psychoanalysis, Schafer (1992) warns us not to "make too free with theories and their histories and too free with the hard-earned methodology and interpretive resources of psychoanalysis" (p. 272). If analytic theory fails to meet challenges raised by new findings, Schafer's approach is to *"repair* the theory rather than replace it" (p. 273). Grounded in the insights of constructivism, he reconstructs the metapsychological and epistemological underpinnings of drive theory, while retaining its primary narrative lines. As a revisionist, he retains the "master narrative" of sex and aggression, and continues to stress the importance of neutrality and resisting the "seductive" entreaties of the analysand.

Schafer, in his account of narration and dialogue, has been at the forefront of the epistemological revolution in psychoanalysis. Perception, he argues, cannot be understood simply as a receptive act; it is always constructive. To see this is to recognize the inevitability of perspectivism. Schafer's foundational premise is that "narrative is not an alternative to truth or reality; rather, it is the mode in which, inevitably, truth and reality are presented. We have only versions of the true and the real. Narratively unmediated, definitive access to truth and reality cannot be demonstrated. In this respect, therefore, there can be no absolute foundation on which any observer or thinker stands" (p. xiv–xv). When we offer interpretations we cannot claim to offer the "truth" of the analysand's actions. Instead, we provide a retelling of the analysand's life within a new narrative structure. The terms of this transformational narrative are not imposed on us by reality. They do not present themselves in pure form through introspection. Schafer (1983) writes: "Subjective experience is to be viewed as a construction. Experience is not given or primary; it is not unmediated information or static information that is accessible through introspection and that serves as a court of last resort in settling questions of fact or truth" (p. 89). Nor can we argue that this narrative structure is determined by the associations of the analysand. What occurs in the analytic dialogue and how it is construed is determined constructively. We always bring to bear models of reality: "For the analyst the analysand is not someone who is somehow objectively knowable outside this model, whatever its nature. As an analyst, one empathizes with one's idea of the analysand" (p. 39). Throughout his writing–and it is a primary source of his polemic strength–Schafer demonstrates a pervasive understanding of constructivism, an understanding that protects him from the reductionism that plagued earlier drive theorists.

Yet despite this willingness to accord "constructivism and its corollary, perspectivism, an essential place in psychoanalysis" (p. 177), Schafer (1992) not only retains the narrative lines of drive theory, he also argues (at least by force of personal example) for their primacy (p. 77). While at times Schafer speaks of the value of diverse theoretical approaches (p. 191) he remains clear that theoretical pluralism is untenable. To work in a theoretically omnivorous way, is to rely more on flash than substance, and to be left with no ground under one's feet (p. 169). In order to gain some authority for the analytic project, the analyst must be willing to choose a theoretical base. For Schafer, as a self-identified Freudian, the master narrative of sexual and aggressive motivation remains primary. He (1983) writes: "As analysts we are always concerned to view actions in terms of infantile psychosexual and aggressive conflicts and the variations of these that the analysand has continued to fashion along with a suitable environment in which to enact them. *Above all*, the analyst is concerned with the versions of these conflicts that are presented in transference actions and resistant actions–the feeding, seduction, peeking, exposing, destroying, protecting, dirtying, withholding, impregnating, castrating, and so on and so forth that analysands enact, usually unconsciously, in the analytic relationship" (p. 91; italics added). If these narratives are not mandated by their privileged relationship to truth, why are they preferred "above all" others? What advantages are conferred by maintaining their primacy? To locate an answer to these questions we must inquire more deeply into Schafer's justification for maintaining the retellings of drive theory as a master narrative.

Throughout his writing, Schafer repeatedly stresses the need to maintain an affirmative attitude toward the analysand. In contrast to the derogatory attitude that we traced in the work of some of the early analysts, Schafer argues that the analyst must actively create an atmosphere of safety: "This affirmative constituent of the analytic attitude must play a great part in building the analysand's sense of safety, for it establishes that he or she is totally welcome in the analytic relationship and that the analyst not only sits but stands behind the analysand" (p. 28). By underlining the necessity of welcoming the analysand, Schafer opposes the tendency within transcendent virtue toward shame and antagonistic action. To even speak of "resistance," in this account, is problematic; it is to be caught up in the "wrong story." When the analysand opposes the work of the analysis, it is not an act of capricious desire; it is a reaction to a pervasive sense of terror: "The specific point to be appreciated is that when one is dealing with analysands, one must never forget that, unconsciously if not consciously, they are living in terror. They dread every kind of fantasized calamity, each of which is, in their psychical reality, as real as any objective danger and, owing to its infantile nature, far more terrifying" (p. 70). Analysands who draw the analyst into a negative enactment are operating in the best way they know how and their behavior expresses an attempt to solve a critical difficulty. To challenge this so-called "resistance" is to abandon neutrality and fall into an adversarial stance.

According to Schafer, then, the adversarial, reprobative posture is not intrinsic to drive theory. These errors of moralism do not stem from the prescription of abstinence, but from the breakdown in neutrality. He writes: "Because the analytic attitude, therefore, has no place in it for undue therapeutic or didactic zeal, it provides no *work-appropriate* opportunity for the analyst to feel frustrated, disappointed, or impatient. . . . It is therefore puzzling, to say the least, when one hears an analyst complain about an analysand while conveying no recognition of the fact that he or she is ventilating a countertransference reaction" (ibid, p. 12). The analyst who retains a firm sense of the affirmative attitude will avoid these intrusive outbreaks of negative countertransference.

Given Schafer's awareness of the untenability of objectivism and the iatrogenic dangers of lapsing into an antagonistic relationship with the analysand, we must ask both why he retains the language of drive theory as a master narrative and whether his reasons are convincing. As Schafer (1992) says, "...today we must always be prepared to argue the merits of our chosen position" (p. 155) and he cannot escape this accounting. The first level in Schafer's argument for the preservation of the Freudian storyline centers on the role of convention and ordinary speech. Psychoanalytic narratives are not invented out of whole cloth. Instead they owe their genesis to the structures of "refined common sense." Schafer (1983) states: "Refined common sense serves as the source of the precritical assumptions from which the psychoanalytic narrative structures are derived, and these structures dictate conceptual and technical practices" (p. 214). To speak of aggressive and libidinal motives, then, does not constitute an arbitrary retelling of the analysand's life. It reflects an understanding that is already part of our communal thought. When the analyst speaks of anal fantasy, for instance, it is not without corroborating evidence. Schafer (1992) writes:

> It is a well-established interpretation that people in general and particularly those who are emotionally disturbed, construe emotionality in the terms of anal fantasy. . . . They deal with emotions as with fecal matter–that is, both as dangerously sadistic expulsions or explosions and as shameful, dirty, messy incontinence. . . . We need not depend on the clinical analytic method to develop support for the claim that this equation is ubiquitous, for there exists an abundance of concordant anal jokes, colloquial sayings and metaphors, insults, rituals, myths, and fables of every kind. "I feel shitty" is a representative instance [p. 122].

The fabric of convention and ordinary language provides support–in constructivist terms, corroborative agreement–for the explanatory rubric of drive theory. At moments, Schafer (1983) even seems to suggest that it is the analysand, not the analyst, who imposes the terms of aggression and libido onto the analytic dialogue: "And if anyone emerges as a crude reductionist it is the analysand, viewed now as having unconsciously reduced too many events simply to infantile sexual and aggressive narratives" (p. 236). At this level of argument, Schafer is vulnerable. While some analysands may readily speak about psychosexual fantasies and themes, there are others who do not naturally take their associations in this direction. Therapists from other analytic schools regularly conduct analyses without utilizing these narrative lines. To claim that drive narratives are imposed by the analysand is to fall back on objectivist thought. But this move to assign narrative responsibility to the analysand, while tempting and never completely abandoned by Schafer, does not represent the main current of his thought. He is clear that the unconscious is never just discovered, and that the interpretative conventions of psychoanalysis remain narrative constructions. He (1993) writes:

> But just who is it that decides on the when and where of a phallus? Traditionally, analysts have maintained a simple positivist stance in claiming that they observe their analysands making these phallic reductions or being controlled by these unconscious phallic fantasies. In this view, the analyst's inferences are determined or compelled by the data; it is said that the conclusions are inescapable. The data emanate from the analysand's unconscious, and the analysand's unconscious is, of course, in the analysand. Today, however, this positivist stance in relation to data seems obsolete. I think it is now necessary to accept some form of the following interrelated propositions: one cannot distinguish sharply what the analyst finds and what the analyst introduces as a narrative organization [p. 184].

While convention provides a starting point for shaping analytic narratives, it does not provide an asubjective point of adjudication between narratives. At bottom, the constructive component in analytic narratives cannot be disguised or avoided.

When objectivism is abandoned, we have argued, adjudication between perspectival constructions must rest on pragmatic considerations. Schafer (1983) concurs with this standard of verification:

> That no history is the single and final one does not mean that each history is a mythic creation which is exempt from the rules of verification, coherence, consistency, and (for the time being) completeness. In this sense, the psychoanalytic life histories are versions of the truth, and the analyst at any rate regards them as more efficacious in bringing about beneficial change than those established by other clinical methods [p. 206].

For Schafer, questions of therapeutic efficacy must play a deciding role in mediating between competing versions of psychoanalytic truth. If we follow this reasoning, it becomes clear that he endorses the Freudian narrative out of a belief that it is the most useful mode of retelling a life to bring about therapeutic change, change that can be endorsed by both the analyst and the analysand. We must ask, then, what is the pragmatic efficacy of drive theory? Schafer's reply takes shape at several levels and the first of these concerns the possibility of retrieving disclaimed action.

Starting with the publication of *A New Language for Psychoanalysis* (1976), Schafer has directed a sustained critique at the reifications of metapsychology. The proliferation of internal agencies, the language of force, structure, and mechanism, have served to obscure the role of personal agency. This kind of reification is not peculiar to psychoanalytic habits of thought. Instead, it is a mode of disclaiming personal action that lies at the root of psychological defense and neurotic suffering. In the face of troubling affects and desires, the enduring tendency is to ascribe responsibility for their origin to forces beyond the self. According to Schafer (1983): "By attributing agency to impulses and thoughts rather than to oneself, the analysand disavows responsibility. Thereby the analysand attempts to preclude the experiencing of his or her actions in an anxious, guilty, ashamed, or otherwise disturbing manner" (p. 242). The problem with this defensive move, however, is that in disavowing agentive responsibility, the possibility of choice becomes obscured. Schafer argues that when analysands say "the impulse overwhelmed me" and "the thought of you slipped away" they become the victims of their experience: "Through such disclaiming, one simply appears as the victim or witness of happenings whose origins and explanations lie entirely outside one's own sphere of influence–outside the 'self,' as some would say" (p. 242). What is outside our sphere of influence cannot be changed, and to the extent that we are not the agent of our experience, we are helpless to overcome our suffering.

Drive theory, in drawing our attention to endogenous motivation and conflict, asks us to regrasp the experience of agency. When we describe our lives in the terms of drive, it forces us to confront the way we have helped construct our experience through motivated action. I suggest that Schafer's effort to recast the narrative of drive theory within the terms of an "action language" stems from his conviction that it provides the most effective means for recovering disclaimed action. By drawing out how our neurotic suffering, rather than something that has happened to us, is actively maintained as a compromise solution, drive theory relocates the possibility of choice. This is the second facet of Schafer's (1992) emphasis on the affirmative attitude. To remain affirmative is not only to make the analysand fully welcome, it is also to retain a consistent focus on the active quality of the analysand's suffering:

> In order to work analytically, however, the analyst must also anticipate, and go on to establish, that much more is involved in the analysand's suffering than having been victimized by her or his family's unmistakably cruel or otherwise disturbing exercises of power. What is that "more"? It is likely to include the analysand's having become, over the course of development, either a seducer of sadism or, through

> identification, a ruthless wielder of power and a cruel victimizer of others, often in the most subtle way; or, as is true in many cases, both at once [p. 128].

Here Schafer—in stressing the need to go beyond accounts of victimization—anticipates the critique we will offer of natural virtue. The analyst remains affirmative by attending to how the analysand, in reasonably trying to solve overwhelming difficulties, has authored a life that creates its own suffering. Yet the importance of reclaiming action cannot stand alone as justification for Schafer's endorsement of Freudian theory. The revelation of agency, while dependent on a theory of motivation, does not require the utilization of libidinal and aggressive narratives.

Schafer speaks of the analysand as a "seducer of sadism" or a "ruthless wielder of power." On the surface these are far from affirmative remarks, nor is this kind of description an isolated occurrence in Schafer's writing. He repeatedly speaks of the analysand "seducing" the analyst into negative enactments, of the "aggressive gratification" involved in defeating the analyst, of "phallic longing" and "anal soiling." These descriptions, to my mind, are reminiscent of Nunberg's account of the passive analysand who wished to be beaten; they have the same reprobative tone. Yet Schafer's decision to frame the analysand's action in these ways is not accidental or careless. For Schafer, this mode of speech, rather than undermining the affirmative attitude, represents its strongest embodiment. To understand this apparent paradox we must turn to his account of tragic and ironic understanding.

In his rejection of the scientific as a foundation for psychoanalysis, Schafer turns toward the humanities. He suggests that there are four guiding visions—the comic, the romantic, the tragic, and the ironic—that characterize the imaginative modes of understanding the human situation and its vicissitudes. The comic vision focuses on the possibility of overcoming difficulty and reaching a conflict-free realm of experience. According to Schafer (1976): "It sees conflict as being centered in situations and as being eliminated by effective manipulative action" (p. 27). Within the comic view, new beginnings are always available and utopian outcomes remain possible. The romantic view takes a similarly hopeful approach: "In the romantic vision, as conceptualized here, life is a quest or a series of quests. . . . The seeker is an innocent, adventurous hero, and the quest ends, after crucial struggles, with exaltation" (p. 31). These two visions, however, while profoundly optimistic, cannot provide a durable base for meaning. They overlook the linear quality of time: "Psychic structure is not abolished during analysis. The analysand can never be a child again and, so to speak, grow up right the second time around" (p. 30). Furthermore, by idealizing nature and individuality, they fail to acknowledge the internal conflicts that mark human existence. For Schafer (1983)—and here one cannot help but concur with his view—the weight of historical experience suggests that life, regardless of our approach, is intrinsically difficult, and the troublesome side of human nature cannot be avoided. The optimism of the comic and romantic approaches, then, holds out a false and unreachable goal, which when exposed can only lead to disillusionment. To endorse a narrative structure grounded in these visions is to undercut the range of our affirmative capacity. The focus on progress and pure virtue can lead to "sentimentally limiting the contents of empathizing only to those emotional experiences that are, in one or another sense, usually considered 'good' things to undergo in analysis, such as hopelessness and hope, conflict and mastery, and shame and joy, while forgetting about empathizing with avariciousness, overweening pride, sociopathy, sadism, and the like" (p. 36). Schafer remains allied with the narratives of Freudian theory, not despite their sparse and dark tones, but rather because of them. They provide, he seems to feel, a more embracing view of the human condition.

When we seek to resolutely face the difficult we come upon the tragic vision. For Schafer (1976) it is the tragic vision that lies at the core of psychoanalytic thought and represents the most profound and durable structure for virtue and meaning. By refusing to resort to palliative hopes, the tragic vision reveals a more solid form of value:

> The tragic vision is expressed in a keen responsiveness to the great dilemmas, paradoxes, ambiguities, and uncertainties pervading human action and subjective experience. . . . The person with a tragic sense of life knows the renunciations that are intermingled with the conditions of gratification; the necessity to act in ignorance and bear the fear and guilt of action; the burden of unanswerable questions and incomprehensible afflictions. . . . Of all the perspectives on human affairs, the tragic is by far the most remorselessly searching, deeply involved, and along with the ironic, impartial [p. 35].

To recognize the tragic is to see that ideals can only be imperfectly embodied, that ambivalence in human relationships is unavoidable, and that we are all divided within ourselves between competing desires and fears. For Schafer (1976), the capacity to accept the tragic view of life is a key accomplishment of maturity and a defining value of the therapeutic project (p. 55). Coupled with the ironic–the capacity to seek out paradox without losing perspective, the willingness to question our attachment to personal drama–the tragic vision lies at the core of mental health. Schafer (1992) embraces the Freudian narrative of sex and aggression because he feels it reflects the tragic and ironic view:

> Freud taught us to see the action in apparent inaction and accident, but he taught us, too, how much of our sense of power and control is illusory, is compensatory fantasy that denies and reverses the powerful and sometimes dire necessities of the body. He showed us that we share with others in our world a great amount of helplessness over our life cycles. In this, as in all of his psychology–a psychology of unconscious conflict and necessary ambiguities and paradoxes that pervade human experience and action–he introduced a modern tone into our conceptions of tragedy and irony; after Freud, our understandings and narrative of human existence could never be the same [p. 159].

To speak within the Freudian narrative, while seemingly reprobative, is, at a deeper level, a recognition that even our darkest aspects reflect a common humanity that, even if not indulged, are to be accepted. For Schafer, the progressed analysand knows love deeply enough to no longer need to keep from herself her aggressive and sexual feelings.

To read Schafer closely is to recognize the force of his argument. Yet to recognize the strength of the tragic view, does not require a commitment to Freudian theory. The ubiquity of suffering, of ambivalence, and of internal conflict can be accounted for within other narrative frames. Nor does this recognition require that we grant governing authority to the tragic view. Moreover, the demands of the affirmative attitude contraindicate the retention of the drive narrative. Schafer is clear that fear and shame are the driving force behind the disclaiming of action. The analysand, caught in the grip of a perceived danger situation, generates an amnesia of action to avoid recrimination. To be effective, then, analytic retellings must reframe the significance of the disclaimed action in both its intent and consequence. Before the analysand can reclaim authorship of action or can consider how she is implicated in creating her own suffering, the criminal penalties must be removed. The process of reclamation relies on the establishment of safety. To my mind the Freudian drive narrative is poorly suited for this task. Casting elemental desire as libidinal and aggressive creates a negative portrayal of our authorial intent. It paints a portrait of us as intrinsically aggressive and unmotivated to grow; it leads us to see ourselves as turgid and without grace. This mode of retelling is ill-suited for creating an atmosphere of safety. The translation from the language of need, vulnerability, and anger—the language that we naturally speak as analysands—to the terms of libidinal and aggressive drive marks a retreat to a view of the body caught in the problematics of transcendent virtue that cannot provide a consistently affirmative understanding of the self. While drive theorists may argue that the refusal to accept this language betrays denial, an unwillingness to accept the hard truths of analytic practice, I would counter that telling a life in this form leaves us without a foundation for valuing. It leaves us suspended between primitive motive and material reality, relying on sublimation to generate virtue. To create a workable aesthetic of virtue requires a language that can speak the intent of seminal motivation in affirmative terms, that recognizes the legitimacy and necessity of our desire. Even the tragic story line requires a protagonist who has some nobility.

Schafer argues that interpretation functions therapeutically through its capacity to destabilize the analysand's consciously presented narrative. It makes the familiar strange, and thereby reawakens the possibility of new action. To my mind, however, the capacity of Freudian narratives to unsettle our self-narration has been diminished. The rendering of experience in the language of drive theory, while once a provocative and daring act, has degenerated into a stale and unpoetic form of speech. At the time Freud practiced, the culture was dominated by the repressed world of the bourgeois. In that climate it was a startling and significant act to suggest that sexuality lay at the root of human behavior. Sexuality was excluded from immediate dialogue. As a result, it could draw on the energy of the forbidden and exert an invisible effect on behavior. In elaborate disguise, it sneaked into polite parties and overturned the tables. To pull away this disguise, then, was a moment of great excitement, and, as accustomed frames of understanding were uprooted, change became available. The unmasking of sexuality revealed that things were more than what they seemed, and in this expansion of meaning the foreclosure of intentional possibility was lifted. Part of drive theory's therapeutic power, its capacity to prompt the analysand to assume agentive responsibility, came from its fearless speech. But the Freudian revolution has been successful and sexuality, while still powerful and somewhat secret, has lost its taboo. To insist on telling our lives in its terms is no longer so startling or significant. It is an insistence that—having lost its freshness—has become conservative rather than radical. The narratively expansive potential of drive theory, its capacity to expand our sense of meaning, has subsided.

We can find evidence for this view even in the progression of Schafer's own work. In his book *Retelling a Life* (1992), Schafer moves toward increasingly literary modes of expression. While he continues to overtly endorse the primacy of Freudian theory, in most of his descriptions the narratives of sex and aggression have receded into the background. In their place, Schafer turns to more poetic forms of common speech. He speaks easily on "the idealization of unhappiness," "men who struggle against sentimentality," and "women lost in the maze of power and rage." In his case descriptions, Schafer's formulations increasingly center on the role of affect and relationship. He speaks of patients "dulling" themselves in order to avoid interpersonal abandonment or retaliation, of patients avoiding love relationships out of a fear that they would constitute an abandonment of their mother, as well as of the paralyzing fear of danger situations. Even when Schafer (1992) is dealing with overtly sexual content, he frames this material within the terms of affect and relationship. We can see this in his description of a female analysand who has brought in a disturbing sexual dream:

> For her, the danger was that the favorable changes would either chill the analytic relationship or overheat it, and they would bring about one or the other result because of the way the analyst would be affected both as a mother-figure and as a man. Thus, she had to disown parts of her self: her enthusiasm, her excitement, her gratitude, her wish to show herself and move closer freely, both emotionally and intellectually [p. 240].

While sexuality, in this case, remains an important part of the transference, its significance is determined within the context of affect and attachment.

The transcendent moral structure that permeates drive theory, I have argued, creates a problematic narrative structure. The negative construal of elemental desire undercuts the affirmative attitude and leads to an implicit subtext of criticism. The derogation of desire, however, creates difficulties that extend beyond the realm of interpretation. It leads to an account of psychoanalytic technique that is predicated on abstinence and neutrality. The emphasis on transcendence becomes a demand that the analyst work beyond the realm of affect or desire. In its extreme form, this view of the analyst demands an aseptic stance in the analyst. It is a portrait of the therapeutic process, as we have outlined, that has been well contradicted by the historical pressure of the analytic encounter. Yet even more subtle versions of the classical approach cannot stand up to epistemological critique. As analysts we remain embedded in affect and, to the extent we are concerned with the analysand's suffering, we function as moral agents. We cannot avoid bringing our values to the table and to obscure this act is to invite iatrogenic difficulty.

In the current analytic dialogue, the defenders of drive theory have increasingly acknowledged the limitations of the traditional portrait of the analyst. The analyst, they recognize, is not immune to the pressures of affect, and the countertransference is an inevitable part of the analytic encounter. Yet even while conceding this necessity, they continue, on the whole, to bracket the affective experience of the analyst as a kind of aberration, a necessary but less than fully useful reaction. The awkwardness of revisionist drive-theory accounts of the countertransference can be seen in the writing of Chused (1992a). On one hand Chused is familiar with the critique of objectivism. She acknowledges that the analyst cannot function as a purely objective augur of truth: "Analysts today no longer have the same confidence in the correctness of their interpretations or their theoretical assumptions as did their predecessors. . . . The analyst's view of the analysand and the analytic process is far from objective; it is filtered through distortions created by his own compromise formations" (p. 91). She realizes that the analyst cannot merely contain the countertransference within the boundaries of the self. It becomes part of the interactive space: "Much as he tries to maintain a position of abstinence and neutrality, if the analyst is open to the demands of the patient's transference (often both intense *and* disguised), it may become impossible for him not to participate in an enactment" (p. 105). In this passage Chused, while still speaking the language of abstinence and neutrality, acknowledges that even the most competent analyst will be drawn into participatory enactment. We are wired to respond to interactional pressure. Yet, although Chused acknowledges the inevitability of enactment, she continues to segregate it from adequate technique: "In general, countertransference enactments delay analysis of the patient's transference distortions and may even make them unanalyzable. Although they may be *the only means by which an appreciation of some aspect of the patient's psychic reality is reached*, they are mistakes nonetheless" (italics added; p. 112). If enactments are not only inevitable, but the singular route to certain forms of analytic understanding, what does it mean that they are mistakes? In calling these moments of analytic process mistakes, Chused reverts to the reprobative tendency within transcendent virtue. She continues to equate the analyst's virtue with the capacity to transcend the pressures of human affectivity. The historical gravity of drive theory, even in modern practice, draws technique back toward transcendent moralizing in its forms of understanding. It cannot escape its censorious portrait of the motivational ground.

In the realm of technique, however, as in the realm of metapsychology, it is Schafer (1992) who provides the most subtle defense of classical technique. While Schafer continues to advocate therapeutic neutrality, he adopts a more inclusive view of the analyst's affectivity. Schafer not only concedes the inevitability of countertransferential reaction, he acknowledges its value. He suggests that the analysis of countertransference has supplanted the analysis of resistance as a primary component of psychoanalytic technique. The countertransference offers the capacity to "illuminate the analysand's current emotional status and aims" (p. 229). Schafer, then, accepts the portrayal of countertransference as a mode of interpersonal knowing. By taking this relatively modern stance, Schafer avoids the kind of difficulties that plague other proponents of Freudian technique. Neutrality, in Schafer's account, does not require the repudiation of countertransference.

Schafer's (1983) defense of classical technique gains further force from his willingness to distance himself from the Freudian view of the psychic economy. In Schafer's account, the necessity of abstinence and neutrality stems not from the indolence of the will but from the importance of avoiding the imposition of virtue on the analysand: "The analyst must always be careful not to impose his or her value judgments on the analysand by unilaterally prescribing change" (p. 168). Not only does the analyst have no right to demand change, the attempt to impose change preempts itself. When the analyst departs from the analytic attitude—from a position of neutrality and interpretation—and begins to actively exert personal force, either positive or negative, the analyst has abandoned the affirmative attitude. Not only does the move away from neutrality signal a failure to fully welcome the analysand in the analytic relationship, it betrays a misunderstanding of the analysand's agentive nature. To champion change is to forget that the analysand actively maintains a neurotic character as an adaptive solution. When the analyst fails to see this, becomes seduced by the image of the analysand as a victimized or damaged individual, the temptation is to resort to supportive measures grounded in the positive countertransference. Yet these interventions of kindness fail to access the underlying conflict and so only serve "to consolidate implicitly paranoid and depressive positions" (p. 258). The analyst, rather than changing the terms of the analysand's internal object world, merely enters it as a benevolent figure juxtaposed against the persecutory. Schafer (1992) makes this point explicit in his discussion of sexism and the analytic treatment of women:

> Yet another countertransference may induce declarations of support for the patient's angry view of men and our sexist society. But this move will only make it harder to analyze the distortions and provocations that the patient has come to rely on defensively and through identification with the aggressor; specifically, it will obscure the play of these factors in the transference [p. 140].

To depart from neutrality and manifestly join in an alliance with the analysand is to leave in place the actively maintained conflicts that prevent more productive adaptations.

The danger of transgressing neutrality is equally strong in the opposite direction. In the face of analytic impasse the analyst may lose sight of the affirmative attitude and fall into an adversarial countertransference. To quote Schafer (1983):

> It is all too easy for the analyst to lose sight of . . . the importance of resisting to the analysand. The analyst's narcissistically needing to get "results" plays a big part in developing this blind spot. As the analyst loses sight of this broad conception, he or she begins to feel impatient with analysands who, despite analysis, further analysis, further clarification of origins, and obvious disadvantages and benefits of character traits, nevertheless continue to maintain certain forms of mistrust, affectlessness, intellectualizing, fear of rejection, scatteredness, or whatever other forms of resisting they insistently enact. Then the analyst's attitude tends to shift toward "attacking the resistance," and thus proceeding in a way that, at least implicitly, is alienated, irritable, and hopeless, and in any case unempathic [p. 73].

While the analysand may willingly submit to this coercive countertransference—may relinquish overt forms of resistance, enact behavioral changes—this submission should not be mistaken for genuine characterological change. For Schafer, neutrality represents the repudiation of all adversarial conceptions of the analytic relationship. When virtue is imposed, it becomes a standard of right and wrong that must create further internal conflict and greater paradoxical action. By turning away from demand or judgment, from supportive or antagonistic action, the analyst creates an environment of true safety and exploration.

At this level, Schafer's defense of classical technique remains pertinent. His vision of neutrality corrects the grosser flaws of traditional accounts and serves as a reminder that pedagogic correction cannot offer more than palliative help. Yet despite the validity of this insight, Schafer's prescription of analytic neutrality remains inconsistent with his account of narrative truth. At its core, constructivism maintains that understanding must always remain embedded in perspective. In the face of alternate perspectives, our choice of narrative frames must stem from pragmatic considerations. The way we understand the world and our interpretive system already reflect our personal values. To interpret, then, regardless of the particular narrative frame from which we operate, is to engage in a retelling of the analysand's life that must reflect the analyst's values. While Schafer (1992) knows this well, it is a knowledge he seems to surrender when he speaks about analytic technique: "The analyst will not participate in this empathic way in order to implement or enforce any particular value other than the health-value of knowing reality inside out, as it were, for it is this kind of knowledge that helps the analysand work out less costly and painful solutions or compromises than those with which he came into analysis" (p. 126). Which reality is the analysand guided toward knowing? In Schafer's case it is a reality, both tragic and hopeful, where the analysand is the agent of her experience. But this version of reality, as Schafer elsewhere acknowledges, is adopted as a result of pivotal values.

Even if we step beyond the problem of narrative frame, we cannot escape the pervasive presence of value in the analytic process. To take constructivism seriously requires that we apply its insight to itself. The epistemological understanding of constructivism cannot transcend the process of construction; it is not *objectively* true. It too is a mode of understanding that gains its veracity from pragmatic considerations. To see this is to acknowledge the impossibility of asubjective inquiry. The analytic process of inquiry cannot be divided from the theory of virtue. To suggest that thinking about oneself is useful, to begin an analytic dialogue, is to already assert a set of values. The analytic attitude, then, cannot be seen as merely "even-handed" as Schafer maintains. It reflects a particular theory of virtue. The metastructure of analytic inquiry and the focus on agentive awareness is not merely a theater in which narratives may be told; it too is a narrative that flows from a theory of virtue. Schafer's loyalty to the Freudian language of neutrality leads him to adopt an unbalanced and inconsistent view of the analytic cure. As we have shown, Schafer repeatedly stresses the importance of maintaining an affirmative view of neurotic suffering. The analyst must keep sight of the intrapsychic roots and the adaptive value of psychopathology. By empathizing the constructed and motivated quality of the neurotic character, Schafer remains consistent with constructivist understanding. When he moves from the problem of pathology to the question of health, however, he seems to abandon this constructivist understanding. Schafer (1983) seems to suggest that once the unconsciously maintained roots of suffering are brought to light and resolved, the way to health will become immediately apparent to the analysand:

> By sorting out the past from the present and the imagined from the actual, the "patient's" sense of danger is diminished and he or she can open as well as reopen the possibilities of action. Increasingly during this process, the "patient" will present apparent demonic forces and unyielding structures as personal actions and begin to live his or her life less painfully, apprehensively, self-deceptively, and unintelligibly. The "patient" will construct other and better situations to live in and will do so with an enhanced and more rational sense of personal responsibility [p. 112].

And again:

> Structural change is shown by obvious differences in the way analysands conduct themselves in the analytic relationship as well as in other relationships. In particular, it is shown by the way they generate *independently* new kinds of life situations and new ways of understanding these situations, and their doing so in ways that are better for them (in whatever adaptive sense the word "better" may be applied in each instance [p. 66].

Schafer (1992) believes that the analyst, through interpretation and neutrality, works to reveal the danger-situations that have governed the analysand's construction of reality, and so acts to "free up" the analysand's growth potential (p. 306). Yet if we accept that life is framed by tragic parameters, why would we imagine that the path toward growth should be immediately apparent? Within the tragic vision, life is necessarily difficult and the course of skillful action requires consideration. Health is dependent on the deliberate reworking of our affective and relational forms of behavior. The schemata of those affective-relational skills are not preformed in the body; they can not be read immediately in the text of reality. To recognize this is to see the untenability of characterizing analytic behavior solely in terms of neutrality. The analyst must offer some vision of virtue as a beacon. Again, we can turn toward Schafer's own work for support. In a section on empathy, Schafer (1983) writes: "Does art imitate life, or is it the case, as Oscar Wilde (1889) suggested in earnest, that to a great extent life imitates art? In the latter case, art is viewed as the creation of new ways of constructing experience and thus as the maker of new modes of living generally and new retrospective considerations specifically" (p. 55). It is my contention that psychoanalysis, in both metapsychological and technical practice, is a form of art that creates new modes of living. The analytic context, its mode of dialogue, is as much a new creation as whatever is spoken about in that context. As a participant in an artistic project, the analyst is always more than neutral, is always making apparent his vision of virtue.

The distrust of desire that lies at the core of drive theory leads to a theory of technique that is too insistent on analytic neutrality. If desire, at root, is egocentric and ruthless, to grant it a place in the analytic context is insensible. Schafer's writing on analytic technique makes it clear that he takes a more affirmative view of the analysand's motives and transferential struggles. Yet even while he seeks to separate the drive-model theory of technique from analytic moralism, he subtly endorses a transcendent account of the analyst's virtue. By arguing that there is no "appropriate" moment for the analyst's desire (1983, p. 12), and so there is no cause for frustration, Schafer implies that the analyst is required to rise above agenda driven affect. The analyst's virtue requires the transcendence of aspiration. In the attempt to spare the analysand, the analyst becomes the object of moral critique. At various points in his writing, Schafer speaks of the lapse from neutrality as "narcissistic," as "defensive grandiosity," and as a striving for "omnipotent mastery." While I agree with Schafer's warning that we must avoid imposing virtue on the analysand, I believe this caution is compatible with a more affirmative view of the analyst's desire and affect.

The transcendent impulse is a resilient and singularly human tendency. It arises quickly in the face of anxiety and to suggest that it belongs only to drive theory would be a naive generalization. In the face of impulse's chaotic uncertainty, the appeal of the transcendent route to virtue is not easily extinguished. Even those who have moved toward a more relational account of human motivation and development continue to speak about abstinence and neutrality as if these concepts could readily survive the transplantation to relational soil. Kernberg (1988), an openly relational theorist, acknowledges that the countertransference is a useful aspect of analytic technique. "If the analyst tolerates his countertransference, he can use it to clarify the dominant object relation in the transference, provided, of course, that professional boundaries are maintained" (p. 461). Here the "of course" is a kind of homage to a standard of decorum whose justification is no longer clear. What is the "professional boundary" and why can we assume that its structure is known and accepted? We can see this same deference to the strictures of transcendent virtue and to drive theory's vision of technique in Modell's (1976) account of the analytic holding environment. He argues that the provision of an analytic holding environment is congruent with the proscriptions of classical technique:

> We wish to reiterate, therefore, that the caretaking elements we have described are implicit in the classic analytic technique itself (in Eissler's terms, without parameters). If active measures are introduced into the analytic situation, there is the paradoxical effect of weakening the analytic holding environment. . . .
>
> The gratifications that result from the analyst's functioning as a "holding environment," we must again emphasize, are not the consequence of the analyst's special activity, that is actively giving reassurance, love, or support, but are an intrinsic part of "classical" technique [p. 432].

In arguing that the caretaking elements of psychoanalysis are not active, Modell aligns himself with the classical call for abstinence. But to speak of holding in the terms of drive theory seems problematic. Even if the analyst's caretaking occurs only through refraining from retaliation, by responding to the patient's affects, by remaining constant, the analyst has actively done something. "Abstinence" is not nothing. It too is an action, and its use and significance must be accounted for, not assumed.

The transcendent route to virtue, I argue, cannot provide a serviceable platform for psychoanalysis. Yet the transcendent impulse gains its strength from the durable realization that our innate tendencies are frequently fallible, and the reworking of our moral theory must attend to that knowledge. Drive theory—in its strong awareness that the biologically innate, in its raw form, inherently leads to suffering—knows something about the necessary boundaries of therapeutic technique. We cannot heal through naive kindness or unlimited support. The willingness to remain silent, the avoidance of hollow reassurance, the refusal to impose solutions—analytic procedures that we have inherited from the drive model—are necessary components of technique. In turning to constructed virtue, then, we must ask, if it rejects the language of gratification and abstinence, how it understands these facets of psychoanalytic technique? Constructed virtue, I will argue, takes an inherently more affirmative and paradoxical view of human motivation; it understands the route to virtue as a process of transformation rather than transcendence. Before we can provide a full accounting of this understanding, however, we must first return to the preparatory stages of virtue. We must detail the critique of natural virtue.

Natural Virtue and the Faith in Innocence

The presence of natural virtue as a moral position within psychoanalysis is less readily visible than transcendent virtue. While the split between Freudian and relational analysts is readily recognized, the division between naturalist accounts of virtue and constructed virtue, between developmental-arrest theorists and the relational-conflict theorists (Mitchell, 1993) has only recently entered the analytic conversation. Within psychoanalysis, natural virtue has been embraced as an antidote to the excesses of drive theory and its transcendent moralizing. Writers like Winnicott (1965), Fairbairn (1952), and Kohut (1984) have rejected the relentless agentive focus of the drive narrative and its tendency to blame analysands for their difficulties. By pointing to the earliest periods of development and the relational context in which the self comes into being, these writers have drawn attention to the role of dependence in the formation of character. The psychoanalytic account of natural virtue—by stressing the necessary rather than the indulgent quality of the infant's needs—takes an inherently more affirmative view of human motivation. The infant is not driven by the voracious demands for gratification but by the need for safety and interpersonal connection. These are righteous needs and they must be met for the infant's organismically grounded vitality and compassion to emerge. Our aggression is not primary; rather, it is a reaction to unbearable failures in the developmental environment. By viewing the self through this affirmative perspective, the analytic theory of natural virtue offers a generative source for value. What we begin with—our elemental self, our seminal motivation—is worthy of reverence.

While we begin in virtue, these writers suggest, we cannot consolidate that value without support. For the virtuous core to unfold, we require critical environmental provisions. These relational events provide the nourishment from which structure and skill are built: formations that serve as the scaffolding for the realization of the authentic self. In Winnicott's (1960) terms, for the true self to flourish, the holding environment must protect the infant from impingements. By creating a context of stillness, the caretaker allows the infant to experience an ongoing being. That continuity permits the integration of the self, where potential virtue can become actual. Kohut (1984), in his account of the selfobject, stresses a similar view of developmental dependency. In order to develop narcissistic stability we need caretakers who act as reliable selfobjects. Our parents and siblings must provide twinship, mirroring, and merger experiences before these functions can be internalized into a structured self.

Regardless of how we frame the necessary alimentary actions, it is clear that they do not lie in the realm of the infant's agency. As infants we are the object of our experience; what happens to us depends on our parents and their societal context. Our suffering is less the product of our elemental nature, than of how that nature is shaped by the pressure of family and society. We suffer because failures in the developmental environment have kept us from developing necessary skills. Those failures have left our development fixated and our selves inchoate. Winnicott (1960), describing the consequence of failures in the holding environment, writes: "In the extreme case the infant exists only on the basis of a continuity of reactions to impingement and of recoveries from such reactions" (p. 52). In reactivity, our love becomes desperate and manipulative rather than reparative and concerned. We become alienated from our virtuous core.

In the paradigm of natural morality, the route to virtue requires that the traumatically spawned layers of disauthenticity be cast off. In order to undo the pathological fixation and restart the true self's developmental process, the analyst must provide a therapeutic environment that is safe enough to allow the analysand to relinquish her distorted modes of self-preservation. Winnicott (1956) writes: "The behavior of the analyst, represented by what I have called the setting, by being good enough in the matter of adaptation to need, is gradually perceived by the patient as something that raises a hope that the true self may at last be able to take the risks involved in starting to experience living" (p. 417). Through providing adequate adaptation, the analyst allows a return to the conditions of infancy where the traumatic failures can be reversed. We can see this same emphasis on the recovery of the infant in Bollas' (1987) work: "The psychoanalyst's establishment of mental neutrality is akin, in my view, to the creation of an internal potential space . . . that functions as a frame . . . through which the patient can live an infantile life anew without the troublesome impingements of the clinician's judgments" (p. 201). Having created an environment where the analysand can risk the reanimation of the infantile, the analyst acts to provide critical adaptive experiences that will allow the analysand to resume the authentic development of the self.

Before turning to the problems of the psychoanalytic paradigm of natural virtue, I must acknowledge my reluctance to critique this model. By constructing an affirmative portrait of the motivational ground, this theory of development and the psychoanalytic process has played a critical role in righting the reprobative aspects of the transcendent impulse in psychoanalysis. It is an inherently more compassionate approach. Kohut (1984a), in a critique of analytic realism, writes:

> It is only when we recognize that the patient has no healthier attitude at his disposal than the one he is in fact taking that we can evaluate the significance of "defenses" and "resistances" appropriately. . . . Such recognition serves the patient better than anything else the analyst can offer, however deeply ingrained his traditional "realism" may be at such moments.
>
> But why do we continue to have difficulty acting in accordance with this principle? . . . The more important reason is that we are steeped in a morality-tinged theory about the therapeutic centrality of truth-facing that is interwoven with a comparably morality-tinged scientific model about the need to make the unconscious conscious. In

> terms of this model, anything that opposes "making conscious" or "becoming conscious" is a resistance [pp. 140–141].

By focusing on the legitimate needs of the analysand, psychoanalytic accounts of natural virtue have strengthened the analyst's empathic capacity. They have worked to overcome the moralism of drive theory and so have increased the sense of safety in the analytic environment.

If we move past the obvious strengths of natural virtue, however, we encounter other, more subtle difficulties with this psychoanalytic approach. The first of these concerns its epistemological status. At the center of the developmental-arrest model is the image of the baby. It suggests that under the layers of traumatically distorted adulthood we continue to hold an internal baby. Mitchell (1988) writes: "Thus, patients suffering from severe psychopathology (or sometimes all of us) are depicted as containing an inner baby, fixed in time" (p. 146). What begins as a metaphor becomes reified and treated as actuality. We have to ask, where does this baby live? Clearly not in our body in physical form, like a larva in a cocoon. The inner baby is part of our imaginative constructions, and that constructive aspect should not be lost. To mistake the constructed for the scientifically mandated, Mitchell (1993) argues, leads to "a tendency to see patients in regressive, infantile terms, to an inattention to the analyst's role in cueing for the seemingly regressed material he finds, and also to a tendency to take theories of early development much too seriously, as fact rather than as fruitful metaphors and mythologies" (p. 69). The moments of regression in an analysis are not a literal resurrection of a baby. They are moments of altered consciousness, of relational vulnerability, that parallel what we imagine occurs in an infant, but they are still events that occur in the present, to an adult. The acts of holding, of empathic attunement, of mirroring response, while arguably profoundly healing, cannot duplicate the efforts of the parent; they do not take us back in time to a moment that became frozen outside the wash of becoming. While both participants in the analytic dyad may find it useful to occupy the perspectival construction of the frozen baby for significant periods of time, we fall prey to epistemologically naive objectivism if we treat the metaphor as actual or true.

This epistemological critique is more than mere ideological severity. While the metaphor of the virtuous baby offers deliverance from the shaming tendencies of transcendent virtue, it becomes problematic when reified. The benevolent optimism of the metaphor, its belief in reparation and wholeness (a romantic vision in Schafer's terms), can turn on itself and become a narrative of damage and unattainable care. By focusing on how the analysand was the object of the developmental environment, psychoanalytic theories of natural virtue stress the way we are victimized by experience. "What is difficult about the metaphor of damage," Mitchell (1988) writes, "is that the analysand does not experience the sense of damage as something desired by him, cultivated and protected because it plays a central role in holding together his sense of connectedness to others. He sees himself as passive in relation to his past, as victimized by it. He sees the damage not as metaphorical but as real" (p. 268). If damage is real, to be cured we must have an adequate reparative experience where those aspects of our self that were damaged may now be recovered through adequate provision for their needs. The danger of this framing, Mitchell suggests, is that it can lead to the analysand's belief that what was "missed is still missing and needs to be provided essentially in the form in which it was missed the first time around" (p. 170). The analysand comes to feel that she must find a limitlessly expansive caretaker. But any actual caretaker, any real analyst, will be fundamentally human and limited in what he has to give. The analysand, in the face of these failures, may retreat into a pessimistic sense that while curative reparation might be possible, it is unattainable, and the analysis cannot go deep enough, early enough, to uproot the damaged aspects of the self. The romantic vision, when confronted with tragic limitations, collapses into desperation. "Such needy patients," Shabad (1993) writes, "may become immersed in endless spirals of 'malignant regression' . . . or passive repetition . . . as they search for an ever-elusive gratification that will justify and magically heal old wounds" (p. 492). The recognition of trauma, a critical aspect of natural virtue, becomes co-opted by the analysand's anxiety, and is transformed from a compassionate act into a statement of hopelessness.

The problem with natural virtue as a psychoanalytic paradigm is that it fails to recognize the paradoxical way in which we are both the object and the agent of our experience. While it protects the analysand from the blaming interpretations of agency present within transcendent virtue, it can leave the analysand pessimistically mired in the role of object. Greenberg (1992), in his attempt to reconstruct the theory of drive, argues that when we fail to see the motivated quality of our experience we become pawns of our experience. In the paradigm of natural virtue "negative or aversive reactions do not have a life of their own; they do not reflect (or serve) any kind of internal process. Instead, they are always reactive; their occurrence is evidence of some failure of the analyst's" (pp. 84-85). While this framing frees the analysand from blame, it also leaves her with no means to change her situation and her suffering beyond exhorting the analyst to behave better. By recognizing the analysand's role in preserving her sense of damage, in creating empathic breaches, Greenberg argues, we actually extend a more significant form of compassion, a compassion that lifts the sense of helpless despair.

By arguing for the utility of interpretations of agency, it may seem we have come full circle. In drawing attention to the analysand's responsibility, have we not simply returned to the transcendent underpinnings of drive theory? I argue that this is not the case. The emergent theory of constructed virtue seeks to preserve a deliberately more affirmative view of human motivation while recognizing our biologic vulnerability to adaptive error. To make sense of this duality calls for an inherently more paradoxical approach to our experience. The theory of constructed virtue asks us to recognize that we are simultaneously both the object and the agent of our experience. Within that paradox lies the possibility of a compassionate move toward responsibility and choice. To see that the inevitable exists alongside the accidental in tragedy, is to step beyond the imputation of guilt. To understand this we must turn back to the question of metapsychology and trace the development of constructed virtue's understanding of human nature and health.

VIRTUE = goodness, well-being
VIRTUOUS LIFE = ethical joyful simple true to one's self

virtue = reduce suffering & enrich meaning.

affect chosen b/c not derivative

- successful analysis → ability to dev. <u>dependent</u> relationships (Kernberg)
  1. when depend on others to perform tasks we had to master
  2. when we master what we had others do for us.

1. Reading this book, not for Carnochan but for myself
2. ~~When~~ Discussing this book w/ Carnochan

foundational skill in virtue: accepting & holding our different feelings toward an object

CHAPTER TEN

CONSTRUCTED VIRTUE: THE ARCHITECTURE OF PSYCHOANALYTIC MORALITY

To engage in a therapeutic process requires a theory of virtue. Without an account of virtue, we cannot distinguish between problematic and auspicious modes of living, we cannot plot a course of curative action. The recognition of virtue lies at the core of any attempt to restructure our life through deliberate action–it locates the therapeutic objective. When we argue for the value of psychoanalysis, when we maintain that engaging in analysis can reduce suffering and amplify our sense of meaning, we implicitly evoke virtue's name. To merely critique past accounts of virtue, then, is inadequate. If we stress the flaws in the transcendent and natural accounts of virtue, without constructing an alternative, we leave analysis without justification. This chapter, then, seeks to provide an account of what is meant by "constructed virtue."

The theory of constructed virtue owes its introduction to its epistemological cousin, constructivism. The constructivist critique of knowing, through its attack on the possibility of detached objectivity and the reification of the narrative metaphor, lies at the heart of the current psychoanalytic revolution. It has demanded the rethinking of metapsychology. Constructivism would argue that the inadequacy of drive theory and developmental-arrest models stems from the pragmatic consequences of adopting those narrative frames. Metapsychology does not represent a mirroring of the actual, the thing-in-it-itself of human existence; it acts as a narrative construction of our experience. The stories of drive and developmental arrest, while vulnerable to iatrogenic impasse, remain viable and often useful ways of understanding our experience. Those frames continue to illuminate aspects of our experience. To embrace constructed virtue as an analytic platform, then, cannot require the surrender of all reference to libido or holding environments. That kind of demand can only spring from a reassertion of objectivist understanding. Instead, the metapsychological understanding of constructed virtue must rest on a narrative view of truth or reality. The task in specifying the metapsychology of constructed virtue is to retain this remembering without abandoning argument.

The metapsychology of constructed virtue argues that the narratives of affect and relationship offer a more durable and serviceable structure for the therapeutic discourse. These narrative constructions are stronger therapeutic forms because they retain a sense of paradox that allows them to maintain an affirmative account of our motivational ground without falling into blame or passivity. The theory of constructed virtue recognizes the righteousness of our aims while keeping in sight the active quality of our suffering. The narratives of affect and relationship are more durable because they retain an awareness of their constructed quality and stay in closer proximity to felt experience. The emergence of this new narrative understanding, while still contested, has been supported by the process of agreement and irreversibility in the analytic community. It marks the forward edge of our understanding.

When we take the gauge of the current analytic dialogue, it is apparent that the language of affect has moved to the center. Accounts of anxiety and rage, self-esteem and soothing, mourning and vitality have become the vernacular of analytic literature. The capacity to inhabit and modulate affect is intimately tied to our health and our suffering. The growing emphasis on affect is clearest in Spezzano's work. Affect, he argues, is the seat of our subjective sense of identity; it is what defines our sense of being real. Yet the full recognition of this fact has been slow in coming. Psychoanalysis, while repeatedly concerned with the presence and reshaping of affective experience, has turned away from making this understanding explicit. Spezzano (1993) writes:

> Upon reaching this point, which constitutes the ontological terrain of psychoanalysis, all major theorists have implicitly treated affect as the ontological ground of human psychology while explicitly postulating something else–drive, undifferentiated matrix, object representation, self–as that ground. What I have been trying to show . . . is that affects are, according to every psychoanalytic theory...the preexperiential,

> "wired-in" capacities that constitute our fundamental categories of meaning. We would have no human experience as we know it without the specific array of affects we are universally capable of generating [p. 113].

Affect is fundamental. Yet to present affect as the explanatory heir, as the actual ontological ground, seems to risk falling prey to objectivist understanding. "Affect" is as much a construction, a mode of interpreting experience, as "drive" or "object." When we attend to affects—to our anger, our anxiety, our grief—they too change shape and significance with the angle of consideration. The language of affect is chosen not because it constitutes an imaginary pre-perspectival ground of experience, but because it does not require reference to a second-order source of phenomena. It does not ask us to refer to a generative ground of being—an invisible world of libidinal drives that can only be inferred, not directly encountered—that lies below the phenomena of our experience. When we turn to our experience, what comes first in awareness is the sensation of feeling. The recognition of affect as the ontological ground, then, stems from its immediacy, from its sensible tangibility, from the way it enters our speech before we have learned more elaborate constructions.

Affect matters because it is the medium of meaning. As we outlined in the previous chapters, affect, understood as a strategy for adaptive action, serves as the experiential link to our innate concerns. Our motivation is determined by the attempt to reach critical forms of affective experience. Greenberg suggests that there are two primary feeling states, safety and effectance, that constitute the teleological aim of our drives. While the terms may vary, the focus on safety and effectance (vitality, authenticity, creativity) reflects an understanding of affect and motivation that is shared by a growing number of analytic thinkers (Mitchell, 1993; Spezzano, 1993). On one hand we seek a sense of well-being, to remain free from pressing need or affective discomfort and anxiety. This sense of relaxation and surrender is the affective ground of the experience of safety. At the same time, however, we are also driven by the desire for excitement and vitality. This sense of vigor and competence marks the experience of effectance. These affective goals form the agentive ground, and it is through tracing the conflict between these needs that the theory of constructed virtue works to recover disclaimed action. Virtue depends on our capacity to meet both of these affective drive demands.

Well-being, this account of virtue holds, requires a deep sense of safety. The experience of safety must come first in human experience. Without a sense of safety, according to Winnicott (1962), the infant cannot come into being:

> At the stage which is being discussed it is necessary not to think of the baby as a person who gets hungry, and whose instinctual drives may be met or frustrated, but to think of the baby as an immature being who is all the time *on the brink of unthinkable anxiety.* Unthinkable anxiety is kept away by this vitally important function of the mother at this stage, her capacity to put herself in the baby's place and to know what the baby needs in the general management of the body, and therefore of the person [p. 57–58].

The security of being held is what allows the infant to develop an internal sense of continuity that forms the foundation of identity and creates the possibility of integrating feeling states into a cohesive center of subjective agency.

The necessity of safety does not end with the completion of infancy. As children and adults, the dictates of safety continue to shape our behavior. When our sense of security is undermined, our attention and behavior is determined by the need to reestablish safety. In a moment of anxiety we become urgent and our wider concerns are pushed out of awareness. In the practice of analysis, safety has demanded our attention through the operation of the resistance. In early psychoanalytic thought, resistance was understood as the byproduct of the adhesiveness of libido. That model of therapeutic action, however, failed to relieve the analytic impasse. Kohut's (1984) critical insight is that resistance does not spring from lust or aggression. Instead, it is the product of fear. The analysand resists the analytic process out of a feeling of being threatened, and until the analyst and analysand can reestablish a sense of safety the analysis cannot proceed. In this account of morality, the route to virtue requires the establishment of an atmosphere of safety. It also suggests that virtue itself is comprised in part by the capacity to create and maintain a sense of security. From the standpoint of technique, we must find ways to avoid chronic danger and anxiety, and develop our ability to skillfully confront and work through the unavoidable moments of threat.

When safety is established, the importance of effectance comes into play. As the infant begins to consolidate a sense of self, the initiative urge slowly takes shape. The infant moves his hand, directs his eyes, and in this triumph of deliberate will comes a wave of excitement. It is here, in this emergent intentionality, in this creative act, that the other root of our authenticity lies. To be well, this account of virtue holds, our intentionality must remain grounded in the agentive core of our affective self. While still speaking the language of drive theory, Loewald (1960) touches on this idea in his account of "replenishing regression." He suggests that optimal health requires that our conscious experience must remain in communication with the intensity of the instinctual ground. Without this communication "human life becomes sterile and an empty shell" (p. 30). In the current analytic dialogue the understanding of vitality has expanded beyond the genital, to embrace a wider sense of potent creativity. In constructed virtue, the manifold forms of human action—art, sport, work, relationships—each hold their own deed of meaning. To access that meaning we must remain in contact with our affectivity. It is the fabric of our caring and the source of our creative aliveness.

Mitchell (1993) argues that "what is inspiring about psychoanalysis today is not renunciation of illusion in the hope of joining a common, progressively realistic knowledge and control, but rather the hope of fashioning a personal reality that feels authentic and enriching" (p. 21). In this portrait of virtue, health and the capacity to form sustaining relationships depends not on "a rationality superseding fantasy and the imagination, but out of feelings experienced as real, authentic, generated from the inside, rather than imposed externally, in close relationship with fantasy and the imagination" (ibid, p. 21). Constructed virtue rejects the claim that moral progress requires the suppression or overcoming of emotion. The coolness of a surgeon, while necessary at times, cannot provide generative meaning or energy. When the channels of affect are closed, we are severed from the ground of our intention. Without emotion we have no internal basis for excitement and meaning becomes a veneer. We can see this view of affect in Schafer's (1992) account of destructive mother-daughter relationships:

> The second additional factor in the mother-daughter context is the deadening effect on emotional experience that could be traced largely to the mother's critical and possessive invasiveness. These mothers and mother-presences were experienced as constantly pulling the rug out from under the spontaneous enthusiasms of their developing daughters. The enthusiasms ranged from girlfriends, boyfriends, teachers, clothes, and makeup to intellectual interests and creative endeavors. These mothers had a devastating way of being unresponsive when they were not directly inflicting shame, guilt, or anxiety on their

> daughters, thus making them doubt even more their spontaneous feelings. As they grew older, these daughters came to inflict this affect-destruction on themselves [p. 138].

To be well—to experience meaning as intrinsic to experience—we must preserve the fluidity of desire. In this revised account of virtue, it is the spectrum of affect that provides the vitalizing ground for the experience of effectance and agency.

If the narrative of affect forms the first pillar of modern analytic understanding, the concern with relational experience must be recognized as the second. Increasingly, psychoanalytic theorists have stressed the primary importance of interpersonal experience (Fairbairn, 1952; Winnicott, 1960; Bowlby, 1969; Mitchell, 1988; among others). In the paradigm of constructed virtue, the necessity of attachment is recognized as a basic motive;[1] as infants and adults, we are compelled by the need for connection and intimacy. Our motives are both wider and more complex than acknowledged by drive theory, and the pull toward relationship is misunderstood if we see it as only libidinal. Mitchell (1988) writes: "Attachment is not, as in the drive model, derived from more basic biological needs; attachment is itself a basic biological need, wired into the species as fundamentally as is nest-building behavior in a bird" (p. 22). The infant depends on others for more than oral pleasure. Soothing, holding, affective regulation, mirroring, and play are all necessary parts of the attachment relationship. These relational behaviors play a critical role in shaping the infant's sense of cohesion; they make up the foundation for the infant's feeling of security and narcissistic equilibrium. While these aspects of interpersonal connection can all be rendered in the language of drive—just as the movements of the planets can be plotted geocentrically—it is a translation that becomes increasingly awkward and cumbersome. In the metapsychology of constructed virtue, there is a greater willingness to admit a polygenetic understanding of human connection.

We have identified affect and relationship as the foundational com-

[1] In speaking of a "basic" motive, we may seem to lapse into an objectivist frame. To identify a motive as "basic," however, is not to suggest that it has an epistemological status that is transcendent to perspective and interpretation. Rather, we speak of this motive as "basic" in the sense that the group of discussants, the analytic community, observing the data, can reach an agreement that this level of description is the most useful (at least for the moment).

ponents of modern metapsychology. Affect and relationship are both granted primary explanatory responsibility because they act in an interdetermining manner. On the one hand, our affects are determined and shaped by the interpersonal environment. While affects are endogenous, their structure is radically shaped by relational pressure. Mitchell (1988) writes: "In this vision the basic unit of study is not the individual as a separate entity whose desires clash with an external reality, but an interactional field within which the individual arises and struggles to make contact and to articulate himself. *Desire* is experienced always *in the context of relatedness,* and it is that context which defines its meaning" (p. 3). Affect occurs in a relational community, and the responses of that community will mold its structure through the developmental process. We learn to contain our anger, to modulate our anxiety, through the ministrations and exhortations of our caretakers and peers. It is in the interpersonal world that the need for safety and effectance are shaped, and it is in that context that we develop our characterological approach to meeting these needs.

Yet we can reverse the vector of explanation, and view relationship as determined by affect. The safety and effectance drives impel us toward relationships. It is only there that these needs can be adequately met. We seek out relationships because they are a primary source of security, and what occurs in relationships is shaped by the need to regulate the experience of safety. Even as adults, our capacity to form secure relationships lies at the heart of emotional health. This is a point where Kernberg and Kohut—writers who have disagreed sharply on questions of analytic technique—nevertheless agree on a definition of health. Kernberg (1988) argues that the therapeutic outcome of a successful analysis is marked by the emerging "capacity to establish authentically dependent relationships with others" (p. 459). In stressing the adaptive role of dependence rather than autonomy, Kernberg implies that even in adulthood, safety needs can only be adequately met in the context of interpersonal connection and support. Kohut (1984a) stresses a similar vision of the therapeutic outcome: "According to self psychology, then, the essence of the psychoanalytic cure resides in a patient's newly acquired ability to identify and seek out appropriate selfobjects—both mirroring and idealizable—as they present themselves in his realistic surroundings and to be sustained by them" (p. 77). Health, in the view of constructed virtue, depends in part on the capacity to form relationships that help us meet our needs for safety. Relationships, though, provide more than a background of safety.

They also act as the critical context for the expression of effectance needs. We need others to act as mirrors for our achievements. When we reach forward in our skills, part of our sense of pride comes from the gauge provided by the reflection of the interpersonal environment. We feel effective when we are able to master tasks that we once had to rely on others to perform. Furthermore, it is in the way we play with others—whether in games of imagination, sexual encounters, gatherings of art and sport, or business transactions—that we get our strongest moments of excitement. When we seek out others, we strive to form relationships that meet our needs for safety and excitement.

THE ACTIVITY OF HEALTH, THE STRUCTURE OF SUFFERING

The concerns of affect and relationship define the primary ground for motivation. Our virtue depends on the capacity to establish durable relationships where we can meet our needs for safety and effectance. This capacity, however, is not automatic. We cannot discover it merely through the recovery of the unconscious or the renunciation of infantile fantasy. Nor does it exist preformed in our natural self. To imagine that there lies within us the schematic for a competent adult that merely requires adequate nourishment to unfold is to mistakenly ascribe destiny to the desired. To reach virtue we cannot just remove distortion—whether understood as perceptive error or traumatic imposition—to find an immediate and sustaining reality. Experience is constructed and to create a life of meaning requires activity. At the core of this account of virtue lies a belief that health depends on a union between the inherent and the deliberate. While we begin with righteous motives, our biological capacity to realize those aims is inchoate. Although emotion provides an innate architecture for adaptive strategies—it is the basis for our capacity to fight, to flee, to grieve, to rejoice—its means are indiscriminate and lack complexity. The intrinsic components of our emotional behavior—hitting, yelling, fleeing, hiding, sobbing, laughing—are inadequate to overcome the difficulties of adult life. For us to be well, the biologically determined templates of emotion must be restructured. While the attachment system creates a fabric for the infant-parent relationship, it provides less sure guidance in childhood and beyond. At birth our understanding of the intersubjective world is rudimentary. The capacity for mutuality, while an innate potential, is not preprogrammed, merely requiring time and freedom from disturbance to unfold; instead, it is a particular outcome, one of many ways of structuring the innate, that is the result of specific developmental experiences. To reach virtue, then, we must discover modes of adaptation that extend beyond the innate.

In the theory of constructed virtue, moral progress depends on the purposeful reshaping of our innate strategies for action. It requires the construction of critical affective-relational skills. Our well-being depends on the ability to create modes of affective expression and action that serve our innate goals. It depends on the ability to develop relational understanding that allow us to negotiate the intersubjective needs for safety and effectance. The shape of this teleological end point, while dependent on the parameters of the innate, is not preprogrammed. We cannot, then, equate virtue with wholeness or the unfolding of a true self. It is a construction, adjudicated by the affective scale of value, that we progressively invent and discover through the course of cultural history. Our task is to locate its optimal architecture.

To claim that virtue depends on the acquisition of skill is controversial. If the acquisition of skill is the benchmark of health, does this imply that analytic technique should move toward the didactic? Are we suggesting that there is a single preferred structure for character? If this is the implication of our position, we are contradicted by the weight of psychoanalytic history. To speak of skill, however, does not necessarily imply a standard of conventional behavior or a backdrop of guilt. In this account of virtue, the acquisition of skill is not motivated by a chastising demand to behave well, but by the compassionate understanding that there are modes of action that are more effective in realizing our goals. While adaptive affective expression can take many forms, the presence of diversity is compatible with the claim that these diverse adaptations share elements of a common deep structure. When I speak of skill, I refer to that deep structure.

The concept of skillful action, I argue, is intrinsic to any analytic theory of health. To make sense of this claim I will return to Schafer's work. When he describes the process of analytic action and its therapeutic effect, he implicitly refers to skillful action. We can see this in his case history of a young man who experienced himself as "unworthy and unable to love." In Schafer's (1983) reconstruction, this man's parents had been unable to provide him with critical holding experience. They failed to tolerate and contain his rage. These developmental failures left the analysand compromised in his capacity to love:

> In relation to these parental imagos the son had established a mistrustful, despairing, and hateful outlook on himself and others.
>
> This analytically established picture of a boyhood illustrates how a familiar condition for loving was not met: the condition of the convincing, sustained readiness of those who are loved to contain one's more or less projective assaults on them, to tolerate the role of bad breast or phallus, arbitrary authority, or villain of some other kind, and to endure being abandoned.
>
> Ideally, the analyst provides this containing, tolerating, and enduring within the transference relation. The analyst even fosters these crises through interpretation of the defensive measures by which the analysand forestalls making this crucial test of the relationship. And the analyst passes this test, not through ordinary loving-kindness, but by standing fast as the interpreting analyst, recognizing the assault frankly, allowing it to be developed and sustained in the light of its developmental importance, and helping the analysand to endure it through understanding it more fully in all its crucial contemporary as well as infantile significance. Having met this condition for loving, the analyst is loved gratefully as a good mother, father, breast, womb, phallus, friend, and analyst. . . .
>
> In achieving this experience within the transference relationship, the analysand engages in less "splitting of ambivalence" and idealizing, and so begins to view the analyst, and each parent, more objectively, openly, and sturdily as a whole figure [p. 120].

I have quoted this passage at length because it provides an account of critical affective-relational skills at three levels: the parent, the analyst, and the analysand. Schafer—blending the theories of Freud, Winnicott, and Klein—suggests that the root of the analysand's suffering can be traced to failures in the holding environment. These failures in holding left the analysand mired in a paranoid-schizoid position. During the course of the analysis, the analyst's task is to provide this missing experience of containment. By "standing fast" the analyst allows the analysand to work through the experience of rage, and reach an experience of objective loving. That kind of loving requires the ability to sustain ambivalence, to reside in the depressive position. At each of these levels—parent, analyst, analysand—adequate function requires the presence of skill. In order to provide a durable holding environment, the parents and analyst must have constructed an affective capacity for forbearance. Rather than responding to assault with counterassault or withdrawal, they must be willing to maintain a firm but compassionate attitude. The ability to stand firm, though, is not innate. When a child is attacked his first impulse is to retaliate; that is the ordinary course of emotional behavior. To act as a parent or an analyst, then, we must rework this innate emotion plan. The first step is to rework the emotion appraisal process. Rather than viewing the child or analysand simply as a threat to be eliminated, the parents and analyst must also see him as an object needing care. By reworking the governing perception of the other, an emotion loop is generated that acts on the initial aggressive impulse of anger. The analyst's ability to retain this insight and to allow it to reshape emotional response—to generate an attitude of forbearance—is a skill. To provide an experience of holding requires more than the suspension of aggression. The parent or analyst must actively listen, must reflect understanding, and finally, perhaps, set limits when the rage threatens to become destructive. The necessity of skill continues when we turn to the analysand. Schafer (1983) writes that the locus of analytic progress lies in the analysand's growing capacity to tolerate ambivalence without resorting to splitting and idealization. The analysand gains the capacity to see that the loved other is also disappointing and imperfect, but that these blemishes are not catastrophic. To sustain the depressive position requires the ability to link conflicting affective states over time. Schafer continues: "Now, at last, he had integrated hitherto unintegrated bodily, emotional, and verbal constituents of experience" (p. 121). The ability to integrate the constituents of experience, in contrast to Freud's claim that synthesis is an automatic function, requires activity, and it is an activity that can only be learned through experience.

When we take a wider view of metapsychological accounts of human development and behavior, it becomes apparent that in the background of each theory is an implicit understanding of skill. Cohesion, narcissistic stability, the depressive position—each of these is an account of an affective-relational skill and the developmental experience that makes its construction possible. In Winnicott's work, the first and critical skill is the ability to integrate the divergent sense motilities and affective reactions into a unified experience of self. The cohesiveness of the true self requires the scaffolding of an adequate holding environment. For Kohut, the critical skill concerns the ability to regulate one's self-esteem and seek out appropriate selfobjects in the interpersonal environment. Before we can learn how to provide mirroring and idealizing experiences for ourselves, we must first find these experiences in our caretaking environment. For Klein, health requires the ability to tolerate ambivalence. We must accept the difficult truth of the depressive position and develop a capacity to offer reparation. This requires that we find objects that can endure our greedy and envious assaults. In each of these theories, health depends on active adaptation and environmental provision. When we accept the perspectival quality of understanding, we can no longer expect to find static sources of value.

In the language of constructed virtue, these critical skills are respoken in the terms of affect and relationship. That language remains closer to the vernacular of ordinary experience. The foundational skill in the development of virtue is the capacity to gather our varied affective states into a cohesive sense of self. Before the infant can develop a center of agency, he must draw within himself the sensations of affect. They must be felt as internal, as part of the self's reaction to the world, rather than as external pressures that impinge on consciousness. The schizophrenic who feels controlled by voices that impel him toward violence lacks the capacity to experience his rage as part of himself. Yet even in those less markedly impaired, the capacity to integrate affect is elusive. Affects are walled off, repressed, disowned. The integration of affect requires more than the ability to identify the interiority of emotion. To be well we must develop the ability to actively attend to our emotions, to draw the diverse and sometimes troubling stirrings of affect into our consciousness. Spezzano (1993) writes:

> In every good analysis a wide variety of events increases the analysand's capacity to hold (keep alive in himself) certain affective states long enough to be able to think usefully about them (that is, long enough to be able to use them as information about the nature of his unconscious processing of his position—the position of the self—in his object world at that moment and as information about his options for action within that world). . . .
>
> Within the analytic holding environment, the analysand gets a second chance to achieve competence in using affects as information about his unconscious psychic activity, especially his processing of contacts with others [p. 216].

The capacity to hold affects within our awareness is critical, in part because they are a fundamental way we know the world and ourselves. As we outlined in the section on epistemology, emotions act as communications about our primary concerns. To know ourselves—to understand how our needs have been impacted by the world, to make sense of how we are prepared to respond—requires the ability to tolerate and expand our intimacy with emotion. But emotions are also a way we know others. At the preconscious level, we process information about others' facial expressions, tone of voice, muscular tension; we read their affective states and our conclusions register in our own affective state. To know others—to understand how we have affected them, how they are disposed to behave—we must attend to the reverberations of our emotions; this is the root of intuition.

The necessity of attending to affect, however, should not be read as license for affective tyranny. To be aware of our affective totality is not to grant authoritative control to any part of that response. Emotions, in their elemental form, are imperfect strategies for adaptive action. Rage may lead us to destroy relationships and the interpersonal contexts we depend on; fear can lead us to phobically avoid new situations; grief can mire us in past loss. Emotions are also prone to misread the interpersonal context. We may sense another's discomfort, yet misattribute its source. The potential unreliability of affect creates a second reason for the necessity of keeping it in awareness; the capacity to constrain affect is what makes possible the move from the impulsive to the deliberate. When multiple affective states are held, we can realize that to act on impulse—to strike at a frustrating parent, to flee from the anxiety of work—while assuaging one aspect of our affective distress, may elicit ramifications unwelcome to other aspects of our affective reality. Holding the multiplicity of affect is a necessary precursor to evaluating options.

The capacity to sustain affective ambivalence is the first step in constructing a portrait of virtue. It marks the realization of impulse's unreliability and the necessity of restructuring affective templates. Yet just as the call for awareness should not be construed as license for affective tyranny, the emergence of ambivalence should not be seen as a demand for affective abstinence. While the innate templates for emotion are myopic, they hold orienting intentions that are essential. Without fear we could not sense the urgency of danger; we would have no motive for restraining ourselves or circumventing hazard. Without anger we would have no means of resisting unwarranted impositions; we would be left to passively endure insult, to sacrifice our integrity. To be well, we must find ways of restructuring our affective templates, of creating emotion skills, that provide more effective means of meeting our multiple and sometimes conflicting goals.

The process of affective restructuring occurs on multiple levels. We have described emotions as structured action tendencies that emerge out of the appraisal of the interaction between events, concerns, and coping potential (Frijda, 1986). Emotion skills are constructed through the reworking of each of these components (Fischer, Shaver, & Carnochan, 1989). As we grow older and our cognitive skills mature, we develop the capacity to make more complex appraisals of the intrapsychic and interpersonal environments (Fischer, 1980). In part the change in appraisal complexity is reflected in the strengthened ability to anticipate the consequences of emotional action. The child comes to expect that certain forms of emotional behavior, rather than solving situational difficulties, will evoke deleterious consequences. This expectation forms the root of the emotion loop that acts to reshape the emotion template. As the infant emerges from the state of dependence, the capacity to recognize the subjectivity of the caretaker slowly develops. According to Piaget, the child moves out of egocentric modes of understanding through the process of decentering, and develops a capacity to adopt the other's perspective. This ability to understand the subjectivity of the other is a critical part of health. Aron (1991), referring to Benjamin's work, writes: "The child must come to recognize the mother as a separate other who has her own inner world and her own experiences and who is her own center of initiative and an agent of her own desire" (p. 30). This emergent awareness is the basis of concern. The awareness of the subjectivity of others, their independent agenda of desire, provides the foundation for the depressive position. It is an awareness that directly impacts the emotion-appraisal process and leads to the development of new affective constructions.

As we mature, our capacity to restructure the action tendencies of emotion also becomes more subtle. We move from the realm of physical acts, from pure vocalizations of distress, to the use of the communicative-symbolic acts of language. As emotion increasingly finds voice through language, the ability to have our behavior serve multiple affective needs expands. At the most complex symbolic levels, the restructuring of emotion-action becomes quite subtle. The affective-relational skills that create the fabric of virtue are complex. My aim here is not to provide a detailed account of their structure; instead, by pointing to the component of skill, I want to refocus our understanding of health, suffering, and the route to virtue. When we recognize the skillful component in health, I will argue, our approach to psychoanalytic technique and the countertransference changes. The question is no longer merely how to undo the neurotic overlay but how to actively foster the development of these affective-relational skills.

Paradox and Compassionate Vision

The answer to this question is not straightforward. Constructivism, in its willingness to span manifold and divergent perspectives, leads toward paradox. It suggests that within the tension of opposites, there is more than confusion and contradiction. The tension that emerges from perspectival thought is a source of both creative understanding and analytic wisdom. As we turn to the problem of analytic technique the importance of paradox becomes central. The parameters of technique, I have argued, are determined by our understanding of motivation, need, and necessity. What is the nature of the analysand's desire? What are the conditions that make change possible? And what are the limits of human adaptation? The conclusions we reach will shape both what we do and how we feel toward the analysand. In the following sections we will take up the problem of narrative structure, aggression, personal agency, wishes and needs, and progressive versus repetitive forces in the transference, to trace how paradox informs constructed virtue. In each case, this paradoxical view impacts how we understand the problem of gratification and abstinence, and the role of the countertransference; furthermore, this paradoxical envisioning of the analysand, a kind of affective appraisal, serves to reshape the analyst's emotional response to the analysand. It creates a particular climate of countertransference. Within the framework of constructed virtue, the effort is not to overcome the tension between gestalts, but to accept the congruent validity of the competing perspectives.

The move toward paradox begins with the structure of the narrative frame. In placing affect and relationship at the metapsychological center, what kind of dramatic vision is shaped by the theory of constructed virtue? To speak of "safety" and "effectance," of "affective-relational skills," may evoke a sense of too easy warmth. This mode of speech may seem too quickly optimistic, too superficial to contain the tragic elements. We might ask, then, whether in seeking to right the reprobative excess of drive theory have we simply cast a patina of romantic and comic sensibility over the psychoanalytic narrative? Have we resurrected a prescriptive and formulaic account of correct behavior? If this were true the theory of constructed virtue could not offer a durable platform for the therapeutic project. In the section on Schafer, we concurred with his argument that life is inescapably marked by tragic elements. The conditions of our existence bring suffering—we are bound by mortality, must tolerate interpersonal strife and ambivalence, and must negotiate conflicted desire. Nor are these difficulties merely external; in thought and action, we are implicated in the creation of our own torment. Yet while the capacity to recognize the tragic is a necessary component of virtue, it does not form the endpoint for consideration. The essential depth of the tragic vision, as Schafer acknowledges, does not displace the validity of ironic, comic, and romantic narratives. We are simultaneously bound by our mortality, our insignificance, our relentless stupidity, and the great poetry of human existence. With a slight turn of our head, the aspect in view changes, like one of those 3-D cards that shifts as it moves across the line of sight. When we remember this flickering quality of meaning—exercise a spanning awareness, a capacity to inhabit multiple perspectives—what emerges is compassion. In compassion there is no concession to either false hope or grim resignation. The compassionate vision recognizes both the benevolent aspirations of the romantic and comic impulses, and the darker shadings of the tragic flaw; it knows the value of ironic levity and nonattachment. Within the larger frame of compassion there is a willingness to remember our value even in the midst of self-created suffering. When we extend compassion to the world, we show a willingness to forgive even in the moment of our persecution. This is not a posture of submission. We may forgive even while vigorously (and perhaps even violently) opposing oppression. We have argued that the theory of constructed virtue assumes a deliberately affirmative attitude toward human intention. Yet here we should also say that this affirmative approach emerges from compassion; it is the spontaneous reaction, the reliable affect, that follows paradoxical perception. This willingness to emerge from the tumultuous waters of greed and generosity, hatred and love, to gather these seeming opposites within redeeming care, forms the basis of compassion, and it lies at the heart of constructed virtue. To my mind it is compassion, rather than neutrality, that forms the ground of the analytic attitude.

We can begin to make more concrete sense of the paradoxical and compassionate view that underlies constructed virtue by turning to the problem of aggression. What sense does constructed virtue make of our aggressive and destructive capacity? This is a critical question because so much of our suffering, so much of the tragic, is conditioned by the operation of hate. Within drive theory, the aggressive impulse is seen as a primary drive. We are motivated to procure outlets for our aggressive energy. In Schafer's view, the willingness to accept the primary force of aggression is a critical part of the tragic vision. To reclaim our agency we must have the courage to call a spade a spade, to face our aggressive desire and recognize its role in creating our suffering. Although the willingness to make aggression primary serves our capacity to embrace the tragic, it creates a non-affirmative ground where we must always remain distanced from our actual motive. In this climate of transcendent virtue the analytic relationship can easily become a theater of guilt. Within the developmental-arrest paradigm the Gestalt is reversed and aggression is seen as reactive rather than primary. We begin in a state of altruism and our anger emerges only as a reaction to traumatic imposition. While this account of aggression offers an affirmative view of motive, it too easily becomes a story of victimization and incorrectly suggests that anger is not a necessary component of relationships. To avoid the opposed dangers of shame and victimization, the problem of aggression must be reframed.

The theory of constructed virtue takes a more paradoxical and integrative approach to the problem of aggression. It suggests that it is both reactive *and* inevitable. When we return to the theory of affect, aggression is drawn back into the fold of emotion. Rather than existing as a free-standing concern, it is seen as part of the behavioral component of anger. Violent action stands as an action strategy for overcoming obstacles. We can see this view of aggression in Mitchell's (1993) account of its adaptive function: "The biology of aggression is understood to operate not as a drive but as an individually constituted, prewired potential that is evoked by circumstances perceived subjectively as threatening or endangering" (p. 161). While aggression is biologically mediated, it does not function as a primary motivation, an end desired for itself. It is reactive and pragmatic rather than propulsive. Aggression serves as a means to reach the primary goals of safety and effectance. This view of aggression is seconded by Spezzano (1993) in his account of Kleinian theory: "In this type of relational world, our innate rage is . . . highly functional. It is a state of readiness to cope with the inevitable relational conflicts and disturbances that must occur among a group of creatures who are all ambivalent about each other and who, however much they may have the capacity to care for each other, have personal agendas that will diverge" (p. 95). To conceive of aggression as working reactively in the service of other, more affirmative motives, however, does not entail a naively romantic view of the human condition. While we begin with righteous motives—a desire for safety and effectance—they are urgent and not easily compromised. The infant, while expressing reasonable needs, is demanding, and the vicissitudes of self and other lead even the most responsive parent to provide repeated situations of frustration. Altruism is dependent on an experience of plenty. While we each have reasonable motives, our desires cannot remain perfectly coordinated over time, and in these moments of relational disjunction, conflict must emerge. As Mitchell (1988) writes: *"Conflict is inherent in relatedness"* (p. 160). The inevitability of relational conflict makes anger and aggression universal qualities in human experience. We cannot always get what we want and we are bound to be upset by the disappointment. Mitchell (1993) writes: "Because of the universality of the subjective experience of endangerment, rage and destructiveness are powerful experiences for all of us, playing a crucial role in the shaping and vitalization of the self" (p. 163). The centrality of aggression in human development can make it resemble a drive. In the face of enduring wounds suffered in a context in which responding aggressively would incur a second round of endangerment, the impulse toward aggression may become constant. The thwarted aggressive response makes ready use of the transferential capacity to find alternate outlets. We tease those who seem weak or we search out opportunities for aggressive triumph because these acts provide a kind of transitive restoration of our integrity. Or, through an identification with the aggressor (A. Freud, 1936), we come to make use of aggressive response as a stable pattern of adaptation. Yet regardless of the apparent intractability of aggression, and its sadistic coloration, the compassionate view looks beyond the inclination toward violence to examine the underlying sense of fear and endangerment. Although it remains unspoken, this compassionate view of rage is implicit in Schafer's account of the affirmative attitude. The theory of constructed virtue does not seek to obscure the prevalence of rage, or to deny destructiveness, yet it retains an affirmative understanding of our intent.

The necessity of paradox remains when we turn to the problem of responsibility and inculpability. To complete this account of virtue, we must say something about the acquisition of the affective-relational skills that are the cornerstone of health. What kinds of experience are required for their construction? This question matters because our understanding of the process of acquisition will influence our approach to technique.

When we create a course of therapeutic interaction, it is implicitly based on how we understand the structure of suffering and the possibilities for reworking that structure. To take up these questions is to collide with the problem of agency.

Our response to this problem, I have suggested, must navigate the narrow straits between blame and victimization. The theory of constructed virtue suggests that we are, simultaneously, both the agent and the object of our experience. On the one hand, we are clearly the object of our experience. We come into the world deeded a genetic inheritance and we encounter a caretaking environment that we did not choose. These givens are outside of our control. We are born in a state of absolute dependence and our survival is determined by the response of our parents. To develop the critical affective-relational skills that are the foundation of our being, much less our virtue, we must encounter an adequate response from the world. When we attend to this backdrop of necessity our objectness is apparent. At this level of analysis, however, we have dropped below the presence of a self. Within the determinism of the object perspective, the body is not the self; its reactions are not the self, and there is no volitional center of experience. If we are anywhere, if we locate an "I" in the swarm of causal relations, some part of the determined must be reclaimed. In this account of virtue, the self is equated with the affective core of consciousness. Once we retrieve the "I," the agentive aspect of experience reemerges. When the holding environment fails us, we react with anger and fear. In the attempt to adjust to the family, we actively form relational schemata and expectations. We deliberately create modes of affective expression. At this level of analysis, we *are* the agent of our experience, and actively participate in the construction of our health or suffering. The imbrication of the agentive and the objective gestalts pushes the theory of constructed virtue beyond victimization and blame.

When we extend our sight along the causal linkages of becoming, the hegemony of determinism becomes clear. The self is created out of some uncertain mix of heredity and experience, and neither of these forces is chosen. With Heidegger, we can say that we are thrown into the world, and where we are thrown and what we arrive with come from beyond ourselves. To understand the hegemony of determinism is to see how we are, completely, the object of experience. While this fact may seem enslaving, it also offers a profound liberation from blame. The errors in our life are not our fault. This recognition lies at the heart of the relational perspective. By attending to the significance of dependence in human development, relational theorists draw the narrative structure of psychoanalysis away from transcendent virtue's account of will and blame. The necessity of the clinical encounter, Spezzano (1993) writes, has led the field to relieve "analysts and patients of the burden of grounding the responsibility for each patient's psychopathology, and the affective distress and pain to which it makes the patient vulnerable, largely, if not solely, in the history of the patient's intrapsychic life" (p. 128). Infants are born in a state of pervasive vulnerability. Their well-being, the shape of their adult self, depends on the adequacy of the holding environment.

Sampson (1992) writes: "Certain kinds of actual events or interpersonal experiences tend to produce characteristic beliefs in those who experience them. This regularity demonstrates that actual experiences may decisively shape our construction of beliefs about reality. The beliefs are lawful–that is, regular and predictable–consequences of an actual experience" (p. 540). These beliefs, enduring affective appraisals, play a determining role in the construction of affect skills. While the different relational narratives describe the critical provisions in their own terms, each is clear about the pivotal role of relational experience. When these provisions are not forthcoming the individual will develop a view of the relational world that prohibits well-being. To overcome this trauma, the analyst must provide a curative or restorative relationship. In this view, abstinence cannot provide a ground for the restorative action of psychoanalysis; it cannot provide the material from which new skills could be built.

To see the world in terms of determinism is to put into question the tenets of classical analytic technique. At the core of the classical approach lies a committed focus on the intrapsychic determinants of experience. We can see this in Giovacchini's (1989) description of a resistant analysand: "He was trying to draw my attention to external situations and thereby move away from an intrapsychic perspective. In fact, he was trying to cling to the view that the sources of his reactions, feelings, and behavior resided in the external milieu" (p. 95). From the vantage point of the object, the insistence on maintaining an intrapsychic focus appears unbalanced. In important ways we *are* the product of what has happened to us. To obscure this basis of determinism is to truncate inquiry. In Giovacchini's unwavering focus on the intrapsychic, he implies that the analysand is wrongly, disobediently, denying responsibility. Yet not only is the inquiry into the experience of objectness intellectually coherent, it can serve the therapeutic process. When we make sense of how we have been affected by what lay beyond us, the impending presence of shame is reduced. Once we are liberated from shame, the need to keep parts of experience unthought recedes. Inquiry along determinist lines, then, may speed the process of insight, and paradoxically make possible a return to a consideration of agency.

To make sense of this we must see that the absolving recognition of determinism does not eliminate the possibility of agentive responsibility. While the configuration of our biological being is not our doing, it is a doing that is us. If we accept that the suffering we feel through traumatic experience is part of ourselves rather than part of the world beyond self, if we see affect as significant, as an object of our care rather than as an event to be watched dispassionately on a screen, we begin to claim a center of subjectivity—what was world becomes self. In the biological basis of affect lies the root of caring, of distinguishing between the desired and averred. At this level of analysis, where the volitional emerges out of the determined, we can locate an agentive self. We have flipped the problem of agent and object on its head, and when we inhabit this perspectival vantage point our narrative of development and suffering is rewoven.

From the moment of birth we are active in the construction and shaping of experience. The infant actively scans the visual field, cries when distressed. We are not a version of modeling putty, merely receiving the imprint of experience. The infant, no less than the adult, lives in a constructivist world and must actively construct the meaning of experience. Instead, we are motivated agents striving for desired ends. In the face of obstacles we intentionally seek to affect the world; we actively employ and reshape solution strategies. This process of affective reshaping, while a reasonable response to a traumatic environment, is nonetheless done by the child. Poor self-esteem, when viewed through the agentive perspective, is not a deficit or an absence, but an actively shaped strategy of adaptive action. It is founded on the child's cognitively immature tendency to generalize from the specific context of the family environment to the relational world at large, to egocentrically assume responsibility for events that are not his doing. The child who lives in an atmosphere of violence and develops a pattern of chronic rage is not merely shaped by his world: it is not that this child has no awareness of the possibility of restraining anger, but that this possibility is seen as problematic. The child actively resists the pressure for containment out of the belief that to relinquish violence is to risk subordination. He looks around and watches how the significant figures in his world cope with difficulty. He sees the benefits of rage (partial, self-defeating, although the child cannot make sense of all of this), and tries it on for size.

When we make the move from determinism to agency, when we locate the affective core of the subjective, the etiology of suffering is seen in a more active light. As the child becomes an adult, the dysfunctional solutions generated in childhood, the misadaptive affective-relational skills, are not merely endured for lack of anything better, they are actively maintained. Our sense of being damaged is not merely something we suffer from–it is also a well-protected mode of attachment and a claim of entitlement. In order to gather new experience that might lead to the reconstruction of affective-relational skills, old modes of adaptation must be set aside. But these problematic adaptations are seen as necessary forms of protection, as the only templates for gratification or intimacy, and the thought of deactivating them, even for moments, is terrifying. Out of fear, we actively avoid traversing the route to virtue.

When we accept the simultaneous and overlapping coherence of determinism and free will, the question of agentive responsibility changes. Within the constructivist sensibility it no longer makes sense to claim that we actually are always the agent of our experience. The movement toward agentive responsibility is not dictated by the demands of truth. Instead, the more encompassing perspective requires that we understand how we are, simultaneously, both the object and the agent of our experience. To know how we and those around us are determined by experience is to lay the groundwork for compassion. When we do not abandon this half of the paradoxical gestalt, fault becomes an empty concept and we are thrown back to a sense of forgiveness. Yet at the same time the capacity to claim our subjective identity, to assert our agency, lies at the basis of transformation and the possibility of virtue. At this level, responsibility emerges. Within the theory of constructed virtue, the analyst will retain a more fluid relationship to both of these perspectives. As Spezzano (1993) writes: "While the analyst's assigning of personal agency to all the patient's subjective experiences . . . may well be vital to the process of opening up new options, it is often not until the analyst can empathize with the patient's sense that his parents are to blame for at least certain aspects of his current affective distress and pain that the patient can assume responsibility for making important changes" (p. 123). The act of assuming agentive responsibility for one's life, an act that is critical to the process of transformation and the movement toward virtue, is not an acquiescence to truth and does not come at the expense of determinism; it is an act of courage, an artistic extension of the sense of self. We might say that the basis of constructed virtue is the willingness to take on complete responsibility not only for oneself but also for others as we shape them affectively through our actions, while not forgetting our own objectness and the compassion that we might require. As analysts, part of what we bring to the therapeutic relationship is a willingness to recognize both parts of this paradox.

The use of paradoxical understanding remains central when we move to the problem of psychic inertia and growth. In shaping analytic technique, we must ask whether the analysand's desire is sedentary, expressive of the resistance to change, or progressive, and a statement of legitimate need. Within drive theory, the emphasis on abstinence stems from the quantitative postulates of the pleasure principle. As Shabad (1991) writes: "This technical posture of abstinence is predicated on the assumption that the patient's curiosity for self-knowledge is not as powerful as the resistance against it, therefore necessitating its coercion by means of the analyst's abstinence" (p. 338). The individual, motivated by the desire to reduce internal tension, seeks to preserve accustomed modes of gratification. The adhesiveness of libido drives the individual to actively repeat the prototypical object relations experienced in childhood. From this perspective the analysand is more concerned with avoiding change, with resisting relinquishing infantile pleasures, than with seeking new opportunities or growth. The advent of psychoanalytic theories of natural virtue, however, reverses this gestalt. Within this paradigm, the resiliency of transferential function stems from fear and deprivation rather than from desire. The individual's core motivation is to reclaim the authenticity of the true self. The corollary of this view, Shabad suggests, is that the provision of key developmental experience will act to reawaken hope and allow the analysand to move spontaneously towards higher levels of maturity and psychic functioning: "In this view, there is an assumption that, by and large, the gratification of needs facilitates a spontaneous, natural process of organismic growth, and that the stagnation of experience will continue indefinitely until the need is fulfilled" (1991, p. 339). The theory of natural virtue suggests that it is gratification (perhaps rightly renamed "provision," "empathic attunement," or some other term that reflects the relational emphasis on nurturance over sexuality), not abstinence, that stokes the motivation to change. In some sense, then, the distinction between the transcendent and the natural accounts of virtue can be reduced to their understanding of desire. As Shabad (1993) writes: "One must empathize with the needs of patients with narcissistic and borderline disorders, whereas one cannot gratify the wishes of the Freudian neurotic" (p. 486). The controversy becomes whether the desires of the transference are expressive of libidinal wishes or unmet developmental needs.

Both of these views on inertia and change, however, are flawed. To see only the recalcitrant nature of the analysand is to create an antagonistic foundation for the analytic alliance. To see only the hopeful, progressive urges is to overlook the active quality of suffering and underestimate the allure of the familiar. To maintain this dichotomy is to suggest that the actions of technique are determined beyond the realm of subjectivity. On one side of the dichotomy, the analyst argues that abstinence is a necessary corollary of the alliance with reality; it provides the means to overcome hallucination. On the other side, the analyst suggests that the therapeutic provisions are determined by the invariant sequence of developmental needs. In regard to the latter stance, in a critique of Trop and Stolorow's (1992) work, Mitchell (1992) writes:

> Cloaking this preference, this choice, in the term "developmental" seems to be to claim for it an arbitrary authority and to shelter it from open consideration on its own merits. . . .
>
> One of my concerns about the developmental approach suggested here is that it implies too great a certainty about what is and what is not possible at any particular time [pp. 450–451].

Both sides, then, by appealing to "fact," obscure the necessity of aesthetic judgment about the shape of morality and virtue. To correct the imbalance of each of these approaches, we must acknowledge both the repetitive and progressive trends in human motivation (Stern, 1994). The theory of constructed virtue suggests—as it does with the problem of agency and object—that we simultaneously seek to reenact and preserve familiar modes of relationship while also striving to repair the traumatic past and establish more pervasively loving relationships.

Transference Reconsidered

We have stressed the importance of an affirmative portrait of motivation. This moral prescription, however, should not lead us to abandon the foundational insights of psychoanalysis. As Freud realized in his early practice, analysands seek to re-create early patterns of experience in the transference relationship. He saw that analysands, responsive to hypnotic suggestions concerning pedestrian acts, would selectively reject ostensibly desired hypnotic suggestions that countermanded core symptoms. From this angle of consideration, the transference is shaped by the analysand's attempt to protect symptomatic modes of functioning and re-create familiar forms of relationship. The drive toward the familiar is a resilient force in the psychoanalytic relationship. Stern (1994) calls this aspect of the transference "the repeated relationship." To see the repetitive element in the transference, however, does not wed us to reprobative or economic views of the motivational force behind this drive. In the affective-relational language of constructed virtue, the drive toward the familiar does not stem from the indulgent lassitude of the pleasure principle but from the constricting force of fear. The analysand enters into repetitive relationships because these are seen as the best outcome available. The analysand may repetitively create relationships centered around affective upheaval out of a belief that the alternative is isolation. In this unconscious equation a bad relationship seems better than none. Furthermore, in this kind of familiar hell, the analysand knows the rules of the game: he has gained expertise in this form of relationship. The drive toward the familiar, then, arises out of the need for security and effectance. We repeat because it gives us some sense of security and competence.

To view the transference as expressive only of repetitive impulses that must be thwarted, however, would be to take a myopic perspective. When we open both eyes it becomes apparent that we can coherently view the desires of the transference as a progressive force for change. The analysand, emerging from a problematic history of interpersonal relationships, is in pain and is actively looking for a relationship that can alter this pattern. At this level of analysis, we have reached what Stern (1994) calls the "needed relationship": "The needed relationship is not simply a stereotyped model of mother-infant interaction derived a priori from developmental theory, but rather an evolving, mutually constructed model of the kinds of responses the analysand wants and needs from the analyst in order to get better" (pp. 324-325). The argument for the coherence of the needed relationship, Stern suggests, need not rest on the reification of the internal infant. It is a concept that suggests more broadly that the analysand, despite his fear, hopes for change. In this sense, as Sampson and Weiss have argued, the analysand is actively looking to disprove the painful beliefs of the transference. Sampson (1994) writes:

"Therapy is a process in which patients (unconsciously as well as consciously) work to obtain, with the help of the therapist, experiences and knowledge that will enable them to change pathogenic beliefs and overcome their problems. Weiss's patient actively seeks those experiences and the knowledge needed to change his pathogenic beliefs" (p. 358). While the transference may stem in part from the constricting force of fear, it also expresses an equal measure of hope. Even when the analysand brings to bear interactive pressure of the most destructive kind, we can view this act as a furtive hope that this iteration of the same will somehow lead to a different, more constructive outcome. From this perspective, when the analysand's needs are met, needs for security and effectance, the progressive force of the analysis is strengthened rather than diminished. As the Ornsteins (1994) write: "It is only then, as the analyst's expanding capacity to respond in accordance with the patient's needs and his requirements for sustaining the analytic dialogue, that the working through (can) lead to structure-building and initiate the visible process of change" (p. 992). The analysis creates an environment where new experience becomes possible and alternative affective-relational skills can be generated and internalized.

When we bring together these two views of the transference, understood as both defensive repetition and progressive hope, the dichotomy between transcendent and natural virtue is overcome. Rather than asking what is the actual status of the analysand's intent–is it repetitive and resistant or progressive and collaborative–the theory of constructed virtue looks instead toward the question of what is the effect of each framing? Stern suggests that both are important and useful in analytic work. By concentrating on the progressive aspect of the transference we create an affirmative basis for the analytic intervention. But this must be supplemented by an acknowledgment of the repetitive impulse. Provided we avoid the danger of blame, to speak of the defensive and repetitive aspect of the transference, the motivated quality of resistance, creates an opening to focus on the analysand's agentive role in shaping experience. To accept this paradoxical description is to move beyond the objectivist focus on wishes versus needs. The question is not whether something *is* a wish or a need, but what is the utility of each position for the development of virtue. Within constructed virtue the question becomes: what actions do we, as analysts, believe are helpful to the analysand, what actions do we believe are not helpful or are harmful, and, finally, what are the limits of what we are willing to give? This problem must always be considered in conjunction with the issue of what actions the analysand thinks are necessary for his well-being. The alliance is built when the analyst and the analysand agree that there is something the analyst can provide that will be helpful to the analysand. Moments of disjunction occur when the analysand and the analyst disagree over the therapeutic effect of a specific action. The analysand may feel that a particular provision is necessary for his growth, while the analyst believes that such an action would ultimately serve as an impediment, and so resists the analysand's entreaties. At these moments, the analyst, working within this paradox, while holding firm in her decision, remembers the inherent uncertainty of the analytic project, the analysand's plausible conviction concerning need, and so preserves a more affirmative stance toward the analysand's desire even while remaining momentarily frustrating.

We have described virtue as dependent on the development of critical affective-relational skills. When this idea is combined with the understanding of the repetitive and progressive desires, it becomes clear that change occurs, roughly speaking, in a two-step process.[2] To reshape ourselves we must both recognize and suspend our misadaptive modes of affective-relational modulation, *and* piece together new and alternate modes of affect regulation and interpersonal connection. To attempt to directly install new skills without first locating and disassembling our problematic adaptations is to become distanced from our affective core. It would be like trying to build a new building without first clearing the ground. The resulting structure cannot help but be precarious and unstable. This kind of jury-rigged system, still conditioned by unaddressed fear, is prohibitive of vitality. As Greenberg (1992) writes:

> Oddly enough, it is my impression that many analyses, including some superficially beneficial ones, conclude on this note. My hunch is that such analyses become a kind of behavior modification: patients are made aware of and are pushed to renounce their dangerous impulses, but their sense that they are dangerous is never adequately addressed. Renunciation has been facilitated by a reinforcement of the patients' capacity for self-control brought about through a reintrojection of the analyst's countertransferential identification with the harshest aspects of the patients' superego. Patients are left with the feeling of being

[2] In speaking of a "two-step" process I do not mean to suggest that this is a sequential or clearly delineated process. The undoing of misadaptive skills overlaps the process of building alternate patterns of relationship.

> "sadder but wiser," able to make themselves behave better without ever having the chance to experience fully why they became so convinced in the first place that they were bad [p. 68].

To go beyond this kind of behavior modification, this strengthening of inhibition, the analyst must allow the repeated relationship to make itself felt, so that its driving fears can be addressed. Without this return to the motive for the neurotic adaptation, change can only be experienced as a deadening resignation. Yet if health is dependent on particular skills, skills that are the province of a culturally held portrait of virtue, analysis must go beyond recovering the past, beyond undoing. To rely only on the therapeutic powers of disassembly is to naively expect that the analysand will automatically perceive the structure of virtue once free of the old modes of constricted experience. But if we understand virtue as an aesthetic construction, there is no reason to expect that this will occur. To be of real use, the analysis must also serve as a context for discovery. The events of the analytic relationship must act as a kind of demonstration of what else might be possible. As Schafer (1992) writes (and I deliberately choose him here as a representative of the more conservative tradition):

> We would be inclined to follow the storyline that when analysis is effective, it frees the analysand to develop toward levels of integration higher than those reached so far. This development occurs in the field of the analytic relationship. The primary and forever influential precursor of the analytic field is the field of the mother-infant relationship, the field in which development necessarily and fatefully originates. In both fields, first the mother and later the analyst represent a higher level of being, relating, and mutual definition of selves; they hold out their higher level and create a tension relative to more primitive levels, thereby giving direction and focus to the developmental strivings of the child, and, later, the patient [pp. 305–306].

The analyst, Schafer suggests, gives direction to the creation of new affective-relational skills. This is not a didactic or coercive process. Instead, it is more like a studio for art. It provides materials, offers demonstration in technique, but ultimately these component elements must be selected and woven together anew by the analysand. Only when the analysand has appropriated the skills of virtue, made them personal, can virtue reveal its radiant aspect.

These paradoxes of virtue are more than epistemological cleverness. They matter because they shape a climate of understanding. By holding to the paradoxical view, the analyst moves beyond blame and innocence toward the more affirmative view of compassion. When the analyst can tolerate the contradictions of agent and object, aggression and defense, repetition and need, she creates a view of virtue. It is a view that begins with a focus on the role of affect and relationship, but ultimately goes underneath itself to reshape that starting place. When these paradoxes are held they become forms of affective appraisal, ways of constructing the world that work to determine the analyst's affective responses to the analysand. They saturate the countertransference, create emotion loops that form the basis of the analytic attitude and determine the analyst's dominant impulse to action.

The Actions of Psychoanalytic Technique

Having established the broad outline of constructed virtue–its view of health and suffering, its approach to motivation and development, its understanding of the transference–we can now turn to the question of psychoanalytic technique. To make sense of the countertransference in this revised terrain, we must revisit the problem of gratification and abstinence. It is here that the proscription of the countertransference gained its strength. To reclaim the countertransference as a source of therapeutic action, the lingering fear of gratification, both reasonable and unreasonable, must be addressed. We have already argued that the tenets of classical analytic technique are grounded, at least in part, in genuine insight. Perhaps the most important of these is the realization that to impose virtue, to demand or seduce change, may bring about behavioral changes and symptomatic relief, but cannot lead to a durable and extensive change in the conditions of suffering. The generation of meaning must proceed from radiant rather than veneered virtue. This insight remains both valid and foundational in analytic practice, and we should be clear that the rehabilitation of the countertransference is not to be read as a call for wild analysis or capricious affective displays. What we have called "neutrality" and "abstinence" are modes of analytic behavior that retain importance in the therapeutic repertoire of constructed virtue. But if we accept the necessity of subjectivity, the premises of constructivism, the framing of motive in terms of affect and relationship, the characterization of health as a set of skills—it is no longer tenable to speak of these technical behaviors as an absence or a negation of the analyst's subjective and affective participation in the analytic relationship. As Hoffman (1992) argues, the analyst's silence, the use of reflection and interpretation, the avoidance of affective reactivity, are all actions, actions that are "invariably personally expressive and cannot be understood merely as the application of a principle of technique in any simple sense" (p. 3). There is no place where the analyst may stand that transcends subjective perspective. Even when we are merely sitting in the same room with the analysand and listening, we reveal ourselves. Again, as Ornstein and Ornstein (1975) point out, our words are only one mode of communication: "It should be remembered in this connection that what is communicated by the analyst in his non-verbal behavior, his attitude, and the analytic atmosphere he creates may speak louder than his verbal interventions" (p. 262). The analytic acts of neutrality and abstinence cannot arise from the elimination of affective subjectivity—there is no action that lies outside that realm. They can arise only from the deliberate reshaping of the analyst's affective stance in relationship to the analysand. If we follow Schafer's argument concerning action language, it would seem that the classical portrait of the analyst as a blank screen must rest on a profound disclaiming of personal agency. To suggest that we are not acting, not feeling, when we sit in the analyst's chair represents a failure to take agentive responsibility for ourselves. It seems strange that a therapeutic approach that takes such pains to emphasize the intrapsychic, the personal participation of the analysand in structuring his world, would then imagine that something so subtly pervasive could be quarantined when a trainee makes the short walk from couch to chair.

To provide a coherent account of analytic technique, then, we must move toward a language of action. We must find a way of speaking of what we are doing as analysts, rather than of what we are not. What is occurring in the analyst's silence? What choices and interpersonal appraisals lie behind the analyst's emotional balance? To take this step is to breach the traditional divide between abstinence and gratification. At all times the analyst is actively shaping a therapeutic environment, and must be concerned with the provision of a particular kind of relational experience. When we move beyond the division between truth and value, the idea that the curative force of analysis lies solely in insight loses appeal. In its place rises a sense that it is the analytic relationship, the encounter with a "new object," that is the locus of therapeutic action. In the meeting between analyst and analysand, as safety is gradually established, lies an opportunity to draw back into conscious experience the activity of problematic emotion loops, to lessen their dictatorial grip on the present, and encounter new modes of affective-relational experience and skills. Mitchell (1993) writes:

> New forms of experience of self cannot be taught to the analysand in didactic fashion. Rather, they are learned only by being lived in, through participation in the psychoanalytic process, in a variety of different ways: through the analyst's interpretations, curiosity, and other features of a distinctly analytic situation; through the profound form of intimacy created and protected by the structure of the analytic relationship; and, finally and perhaps most important, through the model of the analyst's sense of herself, in the countertransference, as a container of multiple versions of self, providing a vehicle for understanding the manifold intricacies of relatedness [p. 121].

In Mitchell's account of therapeutic action, the analyst's understanding and personal manifestation of virtue comes to the forefront. To suggest that intimacy and the analyst's relationship to her own countertransference are critical parts of the analytic cure is to go far beyond traditional conceptions. In this section we will provide an account both of the activity involved in the maintenance of the therapeutic frame, and of the necessity of analytic gratification.

This is obviously controversial ground. To suggest that analytic technique depends on the provision of specific relational experience is to evoke the specter of the corrective emotional experience. When Alexander and French (1946) argued that therapeutic action depended on the provision of a corrective emotional experience, they elicited an avalanche of criticism. The momentum behind this negative reaction stemmed from their recommendation that the analyst should deliberately act in ways that were opposite to the parent's problematic actions. They were read as suggesting that the analyst behave as a kind of actor, deliberately manifesting a particular emotional presence irrespective of her actual countertransference. To the analytic world, this kind of deliberate provision seemed obviously manipulative; it lacked authenticity and was guaranteed to offer no more than palliative help. The corrective emotional experience, seen in this light, is antithetical to the analytic ideal of honesty and the unwavering pursuit of truth. At this level of understanding, we must agree with this critique of Alexander and French's work. To attempt to provide a curative relationship through an act of dissembling is an ill-fated project. This kind of false front is vulnerable to the analysand's empathic perception. The analysand is likely to see through ungenuine affect and feel betrayed. But the difficulty goes further. If the analyst provides an emotional response that is not grounded in an authentic subjectivity, that response acts as a distorting force. Though the appeal is made to the force of real experience, in actuality the analyst's response bears no relationship to the world beyond analysis, and the changes it might evoke are unlikely to be serviceable in the wider interpersonal realm. The positive reflection provided by the analyst, while momentarily bolstering the analysand's self-esteem, is unlikely to be repeated outside the consulting room, and this creates a paranoid split between the two worlds. This is a point that Strachey (1934) makes clear:

> But it may be equally unwise for the analyst to act really in such a way as to encourage the patient to project his 'good' introjected object on to him. For the patient will then tend to regard him as a good object in an archaic sense and will incorporate him with his archaic 'good' imagos and will use him as a protection against his 'bad' ones. In that way, his infantile positive impulses as well as his negative ones may escape analysis, for there may no longer be a possibility for his ego to make a comparison between the phantasy external object and the real one [p. 349].

To provide a corrective experience, a nurturing presence, without investigating the roots of the neurotic character structure, is to leave in place the misadaptive affective-relational skills that drove the analysand into analysis. What is gained through this kind of supportive therapy can only augment an additional story to an already awkward structure.

The outrage over Alexander's work, however, also gathers strength from another, more subtle factor. Implicit in this controversy is an idea about affect. Affect, we have argued, provides the adjudicative scale of value for questions of truth; it acts as the motivational core. In keeping with this view of affect as the core of our agentive identity, we seem to feel that affect should be found, not created. As the found element within ourselves, affect seems to offer something more stable, more indicative of necessary truth than cognition with its mercurial capacity to dart between perspectives. This faith in affect (an ironic inversion of the traditional hierarchy of cognition and affect), leads us to be wary of the attempt to manipulate it. We can see this caution in Aron's (1992) account of analytic enactments:

> The analyst's goal, however, is to understand these patterns with the patient, and while recognizing the inevitability of participating and enacting and even welcoming this development as the necessary next step in the progress of the analysis, the analyst should not be participating, that is, taking on any particular role, purposefully or deliberately. Participating should be done inadvertently, as much as possible as a response to the patient, rather than as a deliberate provocation or suggestive interpersonal influence. Viewing the analyst's participation as inevitable is a description, rather than a prescription of analytic activity [p. 493].

While we are not inclined to think about the choice to speak or remain silent as a question of authenticity (at least not necessarily), we feel differently about emotion. Emotion, to be authentic, should be something that happens to us, or perhaps we should say "is us," rather than something we do. We grant ourselves freedom to choose how we respond to affect, but we insist that something truthful lies behind these states.

Yet to equate affective authenticity with inadvertency is too restrictive. While the caution against play acting seems valid, and the warning to avoid manipulative enactments is important, these should not be read as contradicting the idea of relational provision. The analyst is always involved in the attempt to manage the countertransference in order to shape a therapeutic presence. When we speak about the importance of empathy, of the affirmative attitude, of non-judgmental listening, we are referring to the analyst's deliberate management of her affectivity. Schafer (1983) speaks to this deliberate reworking of affect in his account of the affirmative attitude. With clients who have markedly negative self-presentations–sick, miserable, destructive, or grandiose–the analyst's empathic capacity is challenged:

> The analyst cannot clarify and experience these affirmations empathically all at once. Understandably, it takes considerable analytic work, which means considerable development and interpretation of the forming of transferences and resistant strategies, before this work can be done genuinely and in a manner that is specific to each analysand. Before, then, the analyst's affirmative appreciation must

> be mainly theoretical and anticipatory; however, even in that limited form, it will still be important and useful [p. 60].

Schafer argues that the analyst, in order to maintain an affirmative attitude, in order to create an environment of safety, cannot avoid participating deliberately. Our theories of development and defense, from this point of view, function to support us in the process of deliberately reaching for empathy. If we return to the theory of affect, psychoanalytic theory serves to modify the appraisal process that lies behind the evocation of emotion. The couplets of paradoxical understanding that we traced in the previous section work to create a climate of compassion. They are modes of understanding that evoke a particular affective response in the analyst. By consciously bringing to mind the desperation that lies behind the analysand's action we change our emotional response. This kind of empathy does not rest on dissembling but on the deliberate reshaping of our affective terrain. To suggest that therapeutic action stems from the provision of specific relational experience, then, does not entail a prescription of a manipulative or ungenuine corrective emotional experience. Rather it suggests that the theory of psychoanalytic technique is concerned with the process through which we try to reach specific emotional experiences with the analysand. It asks us to view even our silence, our interpretations, our "neutrality" as part of this effort. In the following sections I will reframe the behaviors that have traditionally been described as part of the analyst's abstinence or neutrality as deliberate affective acts. Through this redescription, a movement away from the obsolete notion of abstinence toward an idea of stillness, we reaffirm the necessity of the therapeutic frame and make more explicit its utility in the analytic process. But stillness alone, while a foundation for analysis, cannot support the whole process of transformation. Gratification, I will argue, forms an essential part of analytic technique. To be of use we must find ways of engaging the analysand more fully, of bringing our affectivity to bear in the service of new development.

The Activity of Abstinence: Securing the Therapeutic Frame

As we turn to the problem of psychoanalytic technique, I want to begin with a defense of the behaviors that have been equated with neutrality and abstinence. Within the approach of constructed virtue, silence, reflection, non-judgmental presence, and caution around the issue of self-disclosure, remain valued. All of these acts play a critical role in establishing the therapeutic frame for analytic engagement.

Within this new school of psychoanalysis there is a growing cadre of analysts who stress the benefits of affective engagement—engagement that would have been seen as destructively gratificatory within the old paradigm. It should be clear that on the whole I am sympathetic to this effort. Yet at times, it seems, this call for analytic participation is inadequately grounded in a comprehensive theory of the psychoanalytic process. Having recognized the tenuous epistemological and metapsychological justification for abstinence, there is a tendency to reject the whole concept. Greenacre (1954), in a defense of abstinence, writes:

> So much time has been spent on these very elementary conditions for analysis because recently there has been a tendency to disregard them somewhat, and sometimes to ignore—on the basis that they are unnecessary, cumbersome or just so much rigid ritual anyway—the restrictions and to resent the deprivations which, admittedly artificial, are designed to promote the development of the full display of neurotic manifestations in the transference [p. 19].

While, in its rigid form, abstinence is a problematic and unjustified therapeutic stance, this does not mean that some part of this behavioral approach should not be salvaged.

Before we can sort out how the analytic attitude might be constituted in this revised theoretical terrain, we must be clear about what is and is not mandated by the insights of constructivism. In the wake of constructivism, there has been a tendency to make direct claims about what this epistemology demands of psychoanalytic technique. We can see this in the more recent writing of Hoffman (1992). He suggests that if knowing depends on perspectival constructions and the intersubjective process of dialogue and agreement, then the demand for anonymity and personal constraint is diminished:

> Do these features of the social-constructivist paradigm imply that the analyst can never speak with any sense of conviction to a patient? Do they require that the analyst always be riddled with self-doubt or that the analyst always adopt the patient's point of view? What is left of the analyst's authority in such a model?
>
> Paradoxically, the analyst is freer in this model to speak his or

> her mind. With the elimination of the standard of doing just the "right" thing according to some external criterion, there is more leeway for a spontaneous kind of expressiveness than there was before, and that spontaneity might well include expressing conviction about one's point of view. . . . What is not possible in this point of view is a total transcendence by analytic therapists of their own subjectivity. The resulting special kind of "uncertainty" frees analysts to "be themselves," that is, to be the people they are within their analytic role [p. 293].

In Hoffman's mind, the conclusions of constructivism mandate a greater permissiveness in analytic expressiveness. This conclusion, I will argue, is not an immediate corollary of constructivism. To see that objectivism is untenable, that the personal cannot be transcended, does not entail any particular kind of behavior in the analytic setting. While constructivism shatters the claim to a priori truth about classical technique, it cannot by itself install an alternate standard of behavior in its place. Constructivism only states that truth is inevitably tied to ideas of value, and to suggest that the analyst's behavior should look like a constructivist's account of inquiry is to mistake analogy for corollary.

In the wake of the constructivist critique there is a tendency to level the distinction between different modes of behavior. If silence and speech are both forms of behavior whose significance must be determined through contextual analysis, the advocates of participation question why silence should be given precedence. Wachtel (1993) argues that if silence is a form of influential doing, than active interventions should not undermine the possibility of analyzing the transference:

> From this perspective, the patient's reactions to so-called active interventions are no less analyzable than are any of the events or experiences that occur in a more traditionally conducted analysis. In each instance, what one attempts to understand is what the therapist's behavior meant to the patient [p. 595].

While in principal Wachtel's argument is concordant with the conclusions of constructivism, it errs in equating the possible with the practical. The point in analysis is not whether the analysand is actively engaged in a constructional perception of the analyst's behavior, but whether this constructivist participation can be meaningfully brought to the analysand's attention. The analysand comes to analysis burdened by an experience of necessity: The analysand, understood in this view as an unnamed objectivist, feels that his perceptions of the interpersonal world are mandated by external reality. The task of analysis, then, is to reveal the constructional nature of perception to the analysand so that new modes of experience can develop. At this pragmatic level silence and activity are not equal in their ambiguity. The analyst who gives advice is much more likely to be perceived as acting like a parent figure than is the analyst who remains silent. The power of conventional perception and significance, a form of corroborative agreement, will make the seemingly fixed meaning of the analyst's behavior more salient and thereby obscure the active quality of the analysand's perceptive participation. To suggest, then, that activity and silence are equally analyzable is to ignore the difficulty of helping the analysand reach a constructivist understanding.

The movement toward democratizing the analytic situation may lead at times to a failure to place the analysand's needs foremost. When Tansey (1992) writes that "for the relational-conflict analyst, the injunction to try to see things exclusively from the patient's point of view would be tantamount to a substitution of one form of perspectival tyranny for another" (p. 312), he seems to suggest that "tyranny" must automatically be excluded from the analytic arena. But this is not clear to me. While it may be a kind of tyranny to demand that the analyst always see things from the analysand's point of view, it remains conceivable that it might be a useful and therapeutic form of tyranny. Although it may be difficult to sustain, if it is helpful to the analysand in making critical therapeutic changes, then it seems that the analyst should accept this form of subjugation as part of his role. While I am ultimately sympathetic to the various arguments for analytic participation, we should be clear that these arguments cannot rest on epistemological claims. To make that argument is to once again obscure the role of value in the determination of truth. "Truth" independent of pragmatic considerations is mercurial and cannot support one mode of analytic behavior over another.

Having undercut the epistemological and metapsychological foundation for abstinence and neutrality, we have left this area of technique unmoored. While we may sense that some part of our inherited ideas around psychoanalytic technique remain useful, we no longer have a clear justification as to why. To overcome this confusion we must find a way to articulate these actions in a language that is congruent with the constructed theory of virtue, that recognizes these as acts of commission rather than omission. Abstinence is much more than the withholding of action. For the analyst to remain silent, to avoid expressing personal opinions or offering advice, to modulate her affective response, to do any of these acts of "abstinence" or "neutrality," requires skill. To do them well, the affective-relational patterns of response must be reworked both in terms of the appraisal process and in terms of expression or response. At this level, the analytic idea of abstinence is closer to Buddhist practice than to transcendent standards of value. In describing the practice of meditation, the Tibetan lama Chögyam Trungpa (1988) writes:

> Meditation is not a matter of trying to achieve ecstasy, spiritual bliss or tranquillity, nor is it attempting to become a better person. It is simply the creation of a space in which we are able to expose and undo our neurotic games, our self-deceptions, our hidden fears and hopes. We provide space through the simple discipline of doing nothing. Actually, doing nothing is very difficult. At first, we must begin by approximating doing nothing, and gradually our practice will develop [p. 2].

The difficulty of doing nothing is an unexpected idea. To be difficult means to require effort and this seems the opposite of doing nothing. In this sense, then, doing nothing becomes an expression of the desire to create a particular kind of space where the actuality of the subject can become manifest. That space, in analytic language, is the therapeutic frame. In keeping with this notion, it seems to me that these behaviors, rather than a kind of abstinence, are a manifestation of stillness.

For the analysis to be joined, a sense of security is a necessary precondition. To begin the process of unraveling unserviceable affective-relational skills the analysand must have a sense that the analytic relationship offers new possibilities. The process of unraveling, though, cannot occur without revisiting the affective ground that was operative in the initial formation of character. This ground, marked by primitive cognition and virulent emotion, can be threatening, and the analysand needs a sense that these experiences can be contained. Before we explore murderous impulse, incestuous desire, shattering terror, we must have a sense that this exploration will not devolve into an enactment where thought becomes actual.

The therapeutic frame, then, must serve to delineate a paradoxical realm, a transitional space where the symbolic and the actual coexist. As Szasz (1963) writes: "Just as the pre-Freudian physician was ineffective partly because he remained a fully 'real' person, so the psycho-analyst may be ineffective if he remains a fully 'symbolic' object. The analytic situation requires the therapist to function as both, and the patient to perceive him as both" (p. 35). The behaviors that have been known as abstinence, I suggest, are better understood as the actions that are taken to maintain a therapeutic frame. Our stillness creates a transitional space. Within this frame real events happen, but they are events that are contained within protective boundaries.

The first function of the therapeutic frame is to create a space where the patterns of character may make themselves felt. It is here that the analyst's silence first gains importance. To not speak, to shut up and listen, is a remarkable act. It is an invitation and an opening for the other to come forward. In this sense, analytic silence is different from many other forms of silence. It is the antithesis of the angry, punishing refusal to speak to another: a refusal that says, "I will have nothing more to do with you until you say what I want, until you apologize." In its alert quality of listening, this silence is the antithesis of the silence that emerges when there seems nothing more to be said and both conversants retreat into private thoughts. The silence of the analyst does not reflect the absence of emotion but rather a particular quality of emotion. The analyst listens out of an affective sense of interest and care. To be in the presence of this kind of listening is to enter into an altered state. Bollas (1987) writes:

> The psychoanalyst's establishment of mental neutrality is akin, in my view, to the creation of an internal potential space (Winnicott, 1974), that functions as a frame (Milner, 1952) through which the patient can live an infantile life anew without the troublesome impingement of the clinician's judgments. The psychoanalyst's neutrality functions as a dream screen (Lewin, 1946) [p. 201].

By remaining still, the analyst creates a dream space where the nuances of the analysand's experience may be revealed.

Analytic stillness serves a magnetic function for the transference. If we understand transference as a set of convictions or expectations about relational interactions, then to remain still is to evoke a sense of surprise or uncertainty in the analysand. In the absence of more overt signs of behavioral reciprocity, the analysand must wonder about the significance of the silence. In a climate of ambiguity, as the analysand tries to establish what is the interpersonal reality, the expectations of the transference become louder rather than quieter. Greenacre (1954), describing this magnetizing quality of stillness, writes: "The nonparticipation of the analyst in a personal way in the relationship creates a 'tilted' emotional relationship, a kind of psychic suction in which many of the past attitudes, specific experiences and fantasies of the patient are reenacted in fragments or sometimes in surprisingly well-organized dramas with the analyst as the main figure of significance to the patient" (p. 18). While the description of the analyst's behavior as "nonparticipation" is no longer tenable under constructivist understanding, the analyst's contained mode of behavior does create a kind of suction. Although we have argued that silence is a significant act that manifests emotional presence, this is not to say that silence is equivalent to more ordinary forms of behavior. Given the relative ambiguity of silence (at least before the silence has been coopted by the transference-countertransference matrix), it can offer more openings for the analyst to point out the analysand's transferential constructions. It is to this point that Glover (1924) speaks in his critique of active interventions:

> Do not active interferences on the part of the analyst disturb the transference picture as a spontaneous repetition, since the recognition by the patient of transference material *as such* is greatly facilitated by the passive role of the analyst and his impersonality? In other words, when the father-imago is revived by a figure that does not advise, persuade, convert, or command, it is more easily recognized *as such* than when it is anchored to the present by a *real* situation in which a physician actually does advise, persuade, convert or command a patient [p. 136].

While we are now more inclined to recognize the repetitions of abandonment, silent condemnation, and censure that may be enacted through silence, this should not lead to a complete abandonment of silence as a starting point for analysis. By remaining still, the analyst will often have a better chance of bringing the constructional quality of transference into relief.

The activity of abstinence, however, serves functions beyond ambiguity, beyond fostering the regressive phenomena of the transference. While in the perspective of transcendent virtue, abstinence is geared toward frustration and the renunciation of false desire, the stance of doing nothing may also serve the aims of compassion. As the transference begins to take shape it creates an interactional pressure on the analyst. The analyst, as a subjective other, is bound to have emotional reactions to complement the analysand's. Racker (1972) speaks to this point:

> Every transference situation provokes a countertransference situation. . . . These countertransference reactions are governed by the laws of the general and individual unconscious. Among these the law of talion is especially important. Thus, for example, every positive transference situation is answered by a positive countertransference; to every negative transference there responds, in one part of the analyst, a negative countertransference [p. 183].

To remain still in the face of the negative countertransference represents the first effort to break the vicious circle of transference expectation and realization. From this perspective the behaviors of abstinence mark an attempt to move beyond impulsive reactivity. While in the moment we may not immediately perceive the analysand through an affirmative attitude, the moment of repose creates time for us to look more deeply, to move from the complementary to the concordant perception that lies behind empathy (Tansey and Burke, 1989). The analyst's stillness, then, reflects an attempt to move beyond the immediate identification with the countertransference. From this perspective, "abstinence" is reframed as the attempt to sustain emotion within the analytic relationship and create a breach in the vicious circle of the transference repetition. Finally, the analyst's stillness serves as the best protection against the urge to impose a model of virtue upon the analysand. By remaining still, the analyst allows the analysand to weigh the evidence, to make personal moral choices, and regain a sense of radiant vitality.

When we understand the activity of abstinence as directed at creating and preserving a therapeutic frame, the traditional warnings to avoid countertransference disclosure regain some of their importance. We have argued that the analyst's stillness functions to bring the transference into relief. The immodest use of countertransference disclosure, then, can cloud the projective space and lead to pervasive uncertainty about the origin of the transference. While the absolute distinction between neutrality and participation has been rendered insensible by the constructivist critique, the relative distinction remains useful. When understood in this relative sense, the argument of more conservative theorists is pertinent. Blum (1986) writes:

> However clamorous the countertransference may be, its interpretation to the patient is generally silent. I do not advocate, and question conveying reports of the analyst's inner life to the patient. . . .
>
> To my mind, countertransference explanation too readily becomes exhibition and confession which only further "contaminates" the transference [pp. 102–103].

While I think the use of the word "contaminates" is unfortunate, suggesting a false distinction between pure and sullied objectivity, Blum's basic argument seems correct. If we move too quickly to speak about our own emotional reaction to the analysand, the analysand will tend to be caught more in reaction than in discovery. Because analysis must primarily be in the service of the analysand, the focus must remain more on the transference than on the countertransference. This realization unites Schafer and Greenberg, analysts from quite different schools of thought, in a common prescription. Schafer (1992) writes:

> Analysts should not split off countertransference from acceptably accurate reality testing. . . . "Reality" is known to be a good defense. . . . Thus, in the clinical situation, even when it is recognized that the patient has correctly perceived a trait of the analyst's, even a countertransference manifestation, as a rule it is still best to keep the focus on the transference significance of this piece of good reality testing [p. 232].

For Schafer, the task of analysis is to reveal the analysand's agency. When the analysand becomes aware of some part of the countertransference, what is pertinent is not so much the analyst's affective participation (although it should not be denied), but the intrapsychic use the analysand makes of this. Greenberg (1992) stresses a similar point:

> A vision of transference based on appreciation of the patient's convictions about the analyst returns us to the wisdom of Freud's early advice. I am not, in this connection, suggesting that it is helpful either to confirm or to dispute any convictions the patient might express. At this phase of the work, the analyst must follow the often more difficult path of maintaining an openness to the patient's impressions and an awareness of their plausibility, even when doing so gets uncomfortable [p. 248].

While Greenberg is more ready to acknowledge the plausibility of the analysand's perceptions, he too is concerned with the importance of maintaining a space where the analysand's associations, rather than the analyst's disclosures, are the central focus of the treatment. In taking this more reserved approach, however, it is critical to distinguish between compulsion and invitation. The analyst's silence, in contrast to the militaristic accounts of resistance, is not motivated by an attempt to force the analysand to take responsibility for the transferential projection. Analytic stillness should arise from a feeling of compassion and be presented as a gift.

The value of stillness goes further than protecting a projective space. When the analyst resorts to a too facile use of countertransference disclosure, it can become a palliative measure that forecloses emotional depth. In an argument against the use of countertransference disclosure as a tool in restoring the therapeutic alliance, Kanzer (1975) suggests that the apparent positive effects of disclosure may not represent true analytic progress: "The subsequent calming of the patient may represent not so much a restoration of the therapeutic alliance as a seduction and a stifling of the inherent trends of his thoughts and feelings" (p. 315). Kanzer believe that the analyst's willingness to speak candidly may not represent a true generosity. By resorting to countertransference disclosure, the analyst actually staves off material that, while potentially threatening, is vital to the analytic work. Greenberg (1992) makes this same point in terms unburdened by the reprobative overtones of drive theory:

> Frequently, when personal information is given to the patient, unless it comes from a countertransferential outburst, it is given in the interest of promoting either trust or some kind of identification. These goals are generally incompatible with the establishment of a neutral atmosphere because they embody the analyst's decision that he should support or bolster one aspect of the patient's tendencies at the expense of another. Unsurprisingly, the effect of many personal revelations is to stifle feelings [p. 221].

While the ostensible goal behind these revelations is the benevolent attempt to foster trust, Greenberg argues, the actual motivating force may stem from the analyst's need to avoid the analysand's rage. By installing herself as a benevolent figure the analyst may create a superficially warmer relationship, but avoid an exploration of the analysand's anger and its use in interpersonal relationships. In this sense, countertransference disclosure, although it may serve the analyst's comfort, loses track of the analysand's interest, and so becomes a selfish rather than a generous act.

To engage in countertransference disclosure can also limit the process of exploration by prematurely demarcating the boundary between reality and projective fantasy. If the analyst confirms or disconfirms the analysand's perception of the countertransference, the analyst appears to be the final arbiter of reality. It also suggests that the analyst, unlike the analysand, is free of an unconscious, that the analyst knows herself exactly. Yet clearly this is not the case. Aron (1992), although supportive of cautious self-disclosure, points out this danger of self-revelation:

> What I believe to be particularly problematic are self-revelations in which the analyst states what she or he feels about a patient in a way that closes off further discussion, for example, saying to a patient, "Yes, you are right, I was annoyed when I said that!" or "No, I'm not aware of feeling impatient with you." These types of self-revelation are troublesome, not because they reveal too much of the analyst, but rather because they imply too much certainty on the analyst's part and minimize the extent to which the analyst too has an unconscious, and hence they discourage further exploration by the patient [p. 481].

Ironically, the argument here for caution around countertransference disclosure comes not from an advocate of objectivism but from a supporter of constructivism. If we accept that the meaning of an action is perspectivally determined, it becomes clear that we as analysts cannot serve as the final arbiter of our own affectivity. To disclose the countertransference without reference to its ambiguity, then, serves to obscure the constructional nature of introspection. Analytic reserve, rather than denying the significance of the countertransference, becomes a way of allowing its multiple and open-ended meanings to become manifest.

Finally, the caution against countertransference disclosure gains strength from the necessity of protecting the analysand from the retaliatory urges of the analyst. As we argued above, the analyst's stillness plays a critical role in allowing the analyst to rise above the full weight of the transferential gravity. By remaining quiet, by concentrating more on the process of understanding than on transformational action, the analyst protects her affirmative attitude toward the patient. To abandon this position is to risk entering into a regressive series of enactments. Hoffman

(1983) cautions that "regular self-disclosure is likely to pull the therapist's total personality into the exchange in the same manner that it would be involved in other intimate social relationships" (p. 417). The analyst remains human, subject to confusion and aggression, and to become involved at that level of intimacy must necessarily lead to damaging consequences. The altruism of the analyst depends in part on the protection afforded by analytic stillness.

Let me end this discussion with a caution. While analytic stillness plays a central role in establishing the therapeutic frame and securing an environment of safety, its value is heuristic. But, when the heuristic value of analytic stillness is treated as canonical, rigidity begins to pervade the field of psychoanalytic technique. At its worst, the canon of abstinence and anonymity becomes a prescription for robotic behavior. Modell (1991), in describing the extreme versions of abstinence, writes: "When I began my psychoanalytic training in the 1950s, I heard of stories, possibly apocryphal, of analysts who remained silent even when the analysand said, 'Good morning'" [p. 27].

When analytic stillness becomes rigid, what was intended to bring clarity serves only to obscure the conditions of inquiry. Chused (1992b), an advocate of neutrality, writes:

> Analysts frequently do not answer questions, and occasionally a patient will mention that he or she has stopped asking questions because the nonresponse seemed to mean that the analyst did not like to be questioned. But ever since one child patient said to me, "You must have a lot of secrets if you can't tell me anything," I have wondered how many other children (and adults) assume I have "secrets" [p. 178].

While Chused goes on to stress the importance of exploring the issue of secrets with the analysand (an approach that seems predominately correct), she fails to address the reality of the child's perception. For Chused, the child only "assumes" that she has secrets; it is part of the child's fantasy life. To my mind, however, the child has correctly perceived Chused. In her belief in anonymity, in refraining from a mutual exploration of the countertransference, Chused does harbor a kind of secret, and the child is right to wonder what kind of material this secrecy conceals.

The rigid maintenance of analytic reserve reflects an uneven approach to the problem of agency. We have argued that agency is best seen through the lens of paradox: we are simultaneously the agent and the object of our experience. In holding only to analytic anonymity, however, the role of the analysand as an object of experience is ignored. We can see this in Kantrowitz's discussion of a patient who had raged at her repeatedly. Kantrowitz had tried to remain empathic with this patient, had refrained from setting limits, and as a result of the disavowed negative countertransference, had ended a session with this patient ten minutes early. As Kantrowitz (1992) tries to sort through the events that precipitated her analytic retaliation, she comes to the conclusion that she went too far in self-abnegation:

> Was I sharing the patient's problem in not appreciating the importance of limits? Did I believe, as he claimed his mother had, that with sufficient patience, tolerance, and care from me over time, he would move on of his own accord, that it was not necessary to set limits? After careful reflection and self-analysis, I concluded this was true. I saw that, like the patient's mother, I had implicitly given him permission to avoid responsibility for his behavior. I had made something my task that should have been his [p. 181].

When she speaks of giving permission to avoid responsibility for a task that should have been the patient's, Kantrowitz has resorted to transcendent moralizing. If we are to ask the analysand to refrain from continued rage, to explore his agentive role in creating the disappointing situation, this must be justified, ultimately, by reference to the analysand's well-being and suffering. We will do better to say, then, that the analysand would profit from taking responsibility, rather than raising the specter of guilt by stating that he should. To only interpret, to remain doggedly anonymous, to reside in a position of abstinence, subverts the potential of stillness and strains the working alliance. Unless we can integrate the necessity of gratification into the practice of analytic technique, I will argue in the following section, analysis must remain an imperfect response to our suffering.

The Necessity of Gratification

We have come a long way to dismantle the bias against affective engagement in analytic treatment. The preceding pages have served as a sustained argument concerning the historical, epistemological, and moral forces that initially maintained and now contradict the prescription of pervasive analytic abstinence. Taken as a whole, this work, if coherent, will have strengthened our capacity to recognize and tolerate the necessity of both the analyst's affectivity and the advent of gratification in the analytic process. These two questions are intertwined. The affective-relational approach suggests that analysands have needs that must be met by the compassionate action of the analyst, for the prospect of change to unfold. To meet these needs for engagement we must rely on the countertransference. It is from the countertransference, from the core of our affectivity, that our capacity for authentic provision stems. We have already argued this point in regard to analytic stillness. In this final section, however, I will argue that the boundaries of analytic technique must be expanded to encompass more than stillness. The analysand's potential for change requires that we foster modes of engagement that are both more personal and more active than classical tradition would permit. To create a context of inquiry and experimentation, the analyst must offer the analysand help in managing distressing affect, and in loosening the reactive grip of fear. To make the possibility of virtue tangible, the analyst must bring forward alternate models of relationship and affective action. This kind of affective participation, I will argue, does not entail the abandonment of analytic boundaries or disciplined technique, but it does require that we find ways to act from the countertransference without acting it out.

The fear of succumbing to the temptation of gratification is obstinate. Even when we recognize the possibility of non-sexual gratification and the need for human contact, the anxiety around affective influence can remain. In part this reflects a useful caution, a respect for the value of stillness. But the fear is deeper than that. It gains strength from the reverberating echo that suggests that the urge to make our affect present in the analytic context stems not from clear thought, but from unresolved neurosis. This is a critique Schafer (1992) directs toward the overactive analyst:

> The danger of successful analytic pretense becomes particularly great when the analyst departs from the reserved Freudian model and becomes overactive and personally obtrusive. . . . There are many reasons why an analyst may hold this belief in the ultimate triumph of interpretation, among them narcissistic strivings for omnipotent mastery, guilty emphases on reparation, and intolerance of feelings of boredom or helplessness [p. 275].

Schafer's critique of the intrusive analyst is valid. We have already discussed the danger of coercive technique and the value of stillness, and clearly there are analysts who lack the personal resources to subordinate their immediate needs to the treatment process. Yet the familiarity of this critique acts as an indiscriminate professional superego, evoking guilt too quickly in the face of any movement away from analytic reserve. To counter this trend we should see that the gestalt of this critique can be reversed, leading us to question the neurosis that lies behind the refusal to acknowledge the value of affective engagement. From the affective-relational perspective of constructed virtue, we can argue that the rigid maintenance of analytic reserve can itself stem from the analyst's need to deny vulnerability, and from fears of intimate engagement, discomfort with affective vitality or spontaneity, or a sadistic need to punish the patient. The critique of abstinence as a neurotic outcome is of questionable validity and cannot settle this debate; yet by balancing the accusations leveled at the inclination toward engagement, it may serve to prevent the larger argument from being too quickly derailed by a lingering sense of guilt.

In trying to rehabilitate the pariah of gratification we can take further comfort from the necessity of the task. As we have argued, analysts from a wide array of theoretical backgrounds have reached a consensus that the analyst's subjectivity is inevitably revealed in the analytic encounter. Writers like Schafer, Hoffman, and Gill, among others, have rejected the Freudian image of the purely reflecting analyst. They have recognized that the process of inquiry and interpretation is always personally expressive. The impossibility of pervasive abstinence, however, goes beyond affective engagement. In even the most traditionally conducted analysis, the analytic relationship itself is a source of significant gratification. Modell (1991) writes: "What Freud did not elaborate, and what we must consider, is that the therapist, acting appropriately as a therapist, can be a source of very meaningful gratification" (p. 25). The act of being listened to non-judgmentally, of having dependable interpersonal contact, and of being understood are all satisfying experiences. In even this most limited sense, then, psychoanalysis operates through the provision of corrective experience. Kohut (1984a) is one of the earliest writers to make this realization explicit:

> The more accurately our theories correspond to the psychic realities that underlie our patients' disturbances, the closer our interpretations

> will come to providing for the patient, in an adult setting and in an adult form, the optimal frustrations that were not forthcoming from the imperfect selfobject responses of early life. Should an ill-disposed critic again claim gleefully that he has caught me red-handed, that once more I have openly admitted that–*horrible dictu*–we are indeed providing "corrective emotional experience" for our patients, I could only reply once more with "So be it!" I would add, however, that the only way by which we could avoid gratifying the patient's need to be understood would be by consistently confronting him with erroneous, inaccurate, or untimely interpretations [p. 153].

When we recognize the inevitability of gratification in the analytic situation, this recognition directs us more firmly toward the task of clarifying what kinds of gratification are genuinely therapeutic and what kinds are palliative or, worse, destructive.

When the analyst tries to hold tight to anonymity, the analysand cannot help but question this posture. The countertransference is not invisible and the analysand can see through the mirror. To deny the presence of affective reaction, to cordon off this area of inquiry, is a distorting and inauthentic act. At this level, abstinence becomes manipulative. Gill (1979) writes: "If the analyst remains under the illusion that the current cues he provides to the patient can be reduced to the vanishing point, he may be led into a silent withdrawal. . . . What happens then is that silence has become a technique rather than merely an indication that the analyst is listening" (p. 75). To deny the necessity of affective engagement and revelation, to attempt to remain merely abstinent, is to create an inhuman context for analysis. When the analyst tries to eliminate all vestiges of affective engagement, tries to corral any action that could offer gratification, the analysand cannot avoid feeling brutalized by the analyst. Ferenczi saw this truth when he broke away from the tacit sadism contained in his active technique. The scale of affect calls for empathic response in the face of traumatic memory. Spezzano (1993) phrases this realization in affective-relational terms:

> If a person in pain attempts to use another person to contain, regulate, and ultimately replace the bad feeling with a good one, and if that person does not understand what the hurt person is trying to do or will not allow him to do it, then a second moment of pain occurs. It is this second type of breach that often precipitates a therapeutic impasse. . . .

> If the patient views the analyst as refusing to allow herself to be used by him in his effort to contain and regulate affective pain, which the patient attributes to the analytic relationship—and the analyst has not consciously or unconsciously intended to turn away from the patient—a *transferential breach* will ensue. If, however, the analyst were *actually* to withdraw from the patient's pain, perceived, for example, as an unreasonable or threatening demand for comfort, a painful breach would be created *in vivo* during the analysis [pp. 135–136].

When the analyst tries to deny the interpersonal ground of analysis, deny that it too is governed by the rules of reciprocity and care, the therapeutic alliance is breached and the analysis must be caught in an impasse. While some patients may tolerate this kind of aseptic environment, the history of analytic practice suggests that there are many who will not.

The process of affective engagement is both inevitable and necessary in the analytic relationship. If we understand the origin of suffering to lie in the realm of relationship and reciprocal affectivity, for the analysis to be engaged two people must be in the room. The analyst who remains as unwavering as a stone can only be experienced as inanimate. The inanimate offers a poor medium for the transference. Analytic stillness, then, should not be understood as an immovable affectivity. In the section on epistemology, we discussed how the countertransference served as the receptive medium for analytic understanding. Here we should say that the countertransference, the analyst's affective engagement, also serves as an invitation to the analysand to bring both his desire and his fear into the consulting room. Bollas (1987) speaks of this willingness to be affectively impacted as critical to the creation of the transferential context:

> By establishing a countertransference readiness I am creating an internal space which allows for a more complete and articulate expression of the patient's transference speech than if I were to close down this internal space and replace it with some idea or notion of absolute mental neutrality or scientific detachment. . . . Indeed, by maintaining an internal space for the reception of the patient's transference, the analyst is more likely to fulfill the intention of Freud's concept of the analyst's mirror function. . . .
>
> More often than not we are made use of through our affects, through the patient generating the required feeling within us [pp. 204, 205–206].

The analyst's countertransference readiness signals a willingness to enter the affective terrain of the analysand's life. It is this willingness that separates analysis from non-transferential therapeutic approaches, and allows the analysand to move beyond merely reporting difficulty to making the actions of suffering manifest and available to dialogic observation. Mitchell (1988) argues: "Unless the analyst affectively enters the patient's relational matrix or, rather, discovers himself within it—unless the analyst is in some sense charmed by the patient's entreaties, shaped by the patient's projections, antagonized and frustrated by the patient's defenses—the treatment is never fully engaged, and a certain depth within the analytic experience is lost" (p. 293).

The necessity of affective engagement, however, goes beyond merely evoking the full depth of the transference. Without this openness to transference-countertransference enactment, the events of analysis can never offer a reality substantial enough to counterbalance the felt certainty that maintains neurosis. Some degree of repetition, Greenberg (1992) suggests, must precede meaningful reparation or new experience: "On a purely cognitive level, I suspect that the analyst whose actions are designed to disconfirm pathogenic beliefs would simply be miraculous, from the patient's point of view. And that has strong implications, because if the analyst's behavior is too discrepant from what the patient has experienced throughout the rest of his life, I doubt that the patient could experience it for what it is" (p. 535). The analyst who does not allow some degree of natural emotional response, either by remaining too sterile or too supernaturally affectively benevolent, fails to represent humanity at large, and the events of the analysis will feel inapplicable to the larger domain of the analysand's life.

In addition to the role of insight, then, we must acknowledge the place of empirical conviction in therapeutic action. Analysis cures, in part, by evoking the transference expectations, creating the context of dread, and resisting the pulls of reenactment to offer an alternate mode of experience. Weiss and Sampson (1986) have spoken clearly to this form of therapeutic action. They suggest that the critical moment in analytic progress comes when the analyst is able both to acknowledge the analysand's expectant though habitually unspoken fear, and, through specific action, disprove the expectation. Sampson (1994) argues that "therapy is a process in which patients (unconsciously as well as consciously) work to obtain, with the help of the therapist, experience and knowledge that will enable them to change pathogenic beliefs and overcome their problem" (p. 358). This capacity to disprove expectation, we should be clear, does not emerge from non-participation by the analyst, but from the capacity to participate in a way that is less traumatic and more sustaining than what the analysand has previously experienced. In this sense the analyst functions as a new object, where, even if we move beyond the metaphor of the baby, the analysand has the opportunity to suspend old forms of defense and adaptation, and begin to remake the affective-relational skills that comprise virtue.

The importance of affective engagement, however, extends beyond the process of discovery. When we understand virtue as a constructed presence, when we reject the idea that it is preformed, we must move beyond the idea that the therapeutic action of psychoanalysis can rest solely on the undoing of pathology. If virtue depends on the presence of affective-relational skills, then it is inadequate merely to bring to light and recognize the unmandated quality of the transference convictions. To acknowledge only that aspect of therapeutic effect is akin to suggesting that an expert golfer could be shaped solely by pointing out the technical faults of his swing: "Your grip is wrong; you swing too hard." These interpretations may undo bad habits, but they offer little help in creating better ones. What is needed is assistance in understanding the mechanics of a powerful and accurate swing. The necessity of demonstration is equally true in the domain of the analytic relationship. Within the affective-relational perspective, the skills that form the foundation of virtue must be built, and their architecture can only be apprehended within the context of particular relational events. Ehrenberg (1992), describing her effort to move beyond the sense of immobilization with a particular patient, writes:

> From this vantage point it appeared that my refusal to remain in a paralyzed deadened state or to be locked into the painful kind of interaction that had been evolving, as well as my ability to find my way out of it independently, turned out to be not simply a way of indulging my own need but also an extremely important analytic step. Once again, I was impressed with the degree to which new experience within the analytic relationship can become a locus of therapeutic action [p. 174].

In this way the analyst's personal action, the way the analyst works with her own emotion, serves to illuminate a wider range of interpersonal possibility. Insight is not possible when we cannot imagine that alternate modes exist. The impossible is not an object for reflection. When we recover the sense of possibility, insight can begin. The analyst brings more to the analytic relationship than an understanding of neurosis and suffering. She brings a sense of the structure of virtue and, through the quality of the analytic attitude, demonstrates aspects of this new mode of living.

From the perspective of constructed virtue, then, therapeutic action stems from the intertwining force of insight, countervailing experience, and the internalization of alternate affective-relational skills. When taken together these perspectives on therapeutic action suggest that the work of analysis concerns the attempt to reach particular affective-relational states with the analysand. The analyst's ability to foster these states, moments where safety and vitality can coexist, is what creates the therapeutic potential of psychoanalysis. Hoffman (1991) suggests that it is the analyst's personal presence "that creates the opportunity for a special kind of affective contact with the analyst that is thought to have therapeutic potential" (p. 75). The presence of safety and vitality both define the necessary preconditions for inquiry and the environment for skill development. The capacity to reach these affective states, initially aimed at developing a therapeutic alliance, becomes a medium of learning. The analyst grounded in the compassionate attitude provides an affective presence that is both more complex, more capable of handling ambiguity and ambivalence, and simultaneously more benevolent. This kind of engagement, which initially serves as a supporting scaffold, is slowly internalized, personally and idiosyncratically, by the analysand in the process of restructuring affective-relational skills.

The establishment of safety is not only an essential component of virtue, it is also the necessary foundation for analytic work. From this perspective the willingness to pursue analytic work does not stem from frustration or from the deliberate amplification of the analysand's suffering, but from the alleviation of fear. Greenberg (1992) argues that for the analysand to tolerate a full range of self-representations, the analyst must foster an environment of safety: "The work involves facilitating the patient's sense of safety in the face of emerging transference experiences that evoke dangerous archaic experiences and intolerable re-representations. When this aspect of the work has gone well, the patient is able to maintain his self-assurance while confronting an increasing variety of self representations" (p. 203). The capacity to free associate, to inquire without boundary, then, cannot be seen as a precondition for analysis; instead, it is the result of an effective therapeutic alliance. To establish a sense of safety, however, it is not enough for the analyst to merely avoid threatening action. Safety depends on more than the analyst standing her ground against libidinal temptation or aggressive response. The analysand rightly fears not only these acts of commission, but also acts of omission. When we recognize the centrality of attachment needs, it becomes clear that the danger of abandonment, of unspoken reprobation and withdrawal, are equally threatening eventualities. The analysand expects this kind of relational trauma, trauma that undermines self-esteem. As Kaiser (1934) argues, in a commentary that somewhat anticipates Kohut's work, resistance is not the product of wanton stubbornness, but is the reaction to endangered self-esteem: "The kind of *character-armor* in which many single but interrelated features are shaped into a system not only has a history in which the genetic development of each element may be pursued, but it also forms something like a thought system (comparable with a paranoid delusional system), the core of which expresses the particular style by which self-esteem is regulated" (p. 398). The analysand's narcissistic vulnerability marks both the pathological aspect of character and a potential obstacle to therapeutic inquiry and progress. Before analysis can proceed, the conditions of narcissistic safety must be met. Whether we understand these in the language of self psychology, and speak of them as selfobject functions, or in the language of affect and relationship, the underlying point remains—the analyst must provide help in managing the devastating effect of painful feelings. Spezzano (1993) writes:

> Every therapy, in other words, must provide a means of containing and regulating the patient's affects; that is, the treatment must take over the psychic work being done by the patient's character. Only on this basis will the patient feel safe enough in the therapeutic encounter to begin to enter into a relationship with the analyst that has a chance to change the patient's character. . . .
>
> Unless the therapist and the patient can construct a relationship that takes over the functions of containing and regulating the patient's bad feelings, the patient's character will continue to do that work and will remain essentially unchangeable [p. 184].

The analyst and the analytic relationship serve as an auxiliary system of affective management. This external support diminishes the urgency of defensive action and allows the analysand latitude to examine and reform affective-relational skills.

The actions behind the therapeutic provision of safety, on the whole, are familiar components of analytic technique. The first part of this provision depends on the analyst's willingness to pay attention to the analysand. The analyst listens, and makes this listening manifest through non-verbal cues. The analyst's willingness to listen has a significance that goes beyond inquiry. It indicates, implicitly, that the analysand is worth listening to. Listening, then, becomes an indication of the analysand's value. The communication of value is reinforced by the analyst's empathy. When the analyst provides an empathic reflection, this becomes a suggestion that the analysand's subjective view of the world matters. Again it is self psychology that has been most vocal in speaking to this function of empathy. Ornstein (1993) writes: "Self psychology directs our attention to the recognition of empathic failures that inadvertently repeat infantile or childhood traumata, and thereby provoke the ensuing withdrawal, depression, anger or fury. . . . Such a disruption necessitates an active search for how the patient experienced our interventions and it demands that we view it from the vantage point of the patient's perspective and not our own" (p. 33). The analyst's affirmative and empathic response to the analysand, then, can be understood as therapeutic provisions that are in the service of helping the analysand manage his self-esteem. This kind of help is not an empty reassurance or a false reflection. It is grounded in the analyst's genuine affectivity.

The demands of safety, however, cannot always be met within the bounds of conventional technique. To move beyond the iatrogenic difficulties that can stem from anonymity, the analyst must be willing to bring the countertransference more fully into the analytic dialogue. To make sense of this claim we must acknowledge the potential humiliation involved in analysis. For the analysand to enter into a regressive transference to speak candidly about his strongest desires and fears, is to take a tremendous risk. In the face of an entirely self-possessed analyst, this kind of self-exposure can readily sour. The analysand may come to feel that the tumult of the transference marks him as weak or sullied in the eye of the unperturbable analyst. This kind of inference, while it may be inaccurate, is not unreasonable given the ordinary rules of interpersonal interaction. In the face of disturbing material most people will respond with condemnation; why should the analysand, without positive evidence to the contrary, expect the analyst to be any different? If the analyst is without apparent countertransference, is not an affective participant in the relationship, then the analysand must infer that the transference is without basis and all suffering that arises within the analytic relationship is the analysand's unnecessary creation. Now the analysand not only suffers but feels humiliated for suffering. To go past this kind of iatrogenic effect the analyst must acknowledge her subjective participation in the analytic relationship. Little (1951) writes: "In my view a time comes in the course of every analysis when it is essential for the patient to recognize the existence not only of the analyst's objective or justified feelings, but also of the analyst's subjective feelings" (p. 149). In part this recognition comes from the analysand's emerging capacity to recognize the analyst's affective terrain. Yet it is not enough for the analysand to speak about this in a one-sided conversation. At some point the analyst must be willing to disclose something of herself. In this sense, the analyst's use of self-disclosure serves the demand of analytic safety in two ways. On the one hand, the analyst's acknowledged affective participation confirms the universality of human subjectivity and vulnerability. For the analyst to bring the countertransference visibly into the room becomes a statement that the difficulty of human relationship is the responsibility of both the analyst and the analysand. Ehrenberg (1992) points this out in her discussion of her anger: "For example, one time I became so angry at a patient that I assumed it would no longer be possible for me to work with her. I was amazed when the patient reported how much it meant to her to know that I, too, could 'lose it.' For once she felt that she was not the only bad one in the room" (p. 19).

This is a complex therapeutic moment. On one hand, I am hesitant to salute a therapeutic interaction that culminates in the relieving "recognition" that the analyst shares in the analysand's "badness." The term "bad" suggests that the paranoid appraisal system of self and other remains intact, and that the felt relief comes primarily from reapportioning blame. However, I do believe that this piece of Ehrenberg's work, while incomplete, points to how the use of affective expression may begin to dislodge fixed appraisals of self and other. If the analyst is unwilling to acknowledge her affective and idiosyncratic participation in the analytic relationship, it places all the neurosis in the analysand's corner. This kind of partitioning of agentive responsibility not only undermines the analysand's self-esteem and sense of safety, it can also act to create unrealistic expectations about the structure of virtue. If the analyst is emotionally implacable, it tacitly implies that health is determined by the capacity to rise above vulnerability. But virtue does not rest on the elimination of painful affect; rather, it rests on the capacity to inhabit a broad range of affect without devolving into destructive enactment.

The establishment of analytic safety is closely related to a second component of affective provision. For the analysand to relinquish misadaptive affective-relational behavior, the analytic relationship must offer hope for something better. Loewald (1960) writes: "The patient can dare to take the plunge into the regressive crisis of the transference neurosis which brings him face to face again with his childhood anxieties and conflicts, *if* he can hold on to the potentiality of a new object-relationship, represented by the analyst" (pp. 17–18). In the same vein, Winnicott (1956) argues: "The behaviour of the analyst, represented by what I have called the setting, by being good enough in the matter of adaptation to need, is gradually perceived by the patient as something that raises a hope that the true self may at last be able to take the risks involved in starting to experience living" (p. 417). To take an affirmative attitude toward the analysand's character, with all its difficulties, is to acknowledge that it represents the analysand's attempt to protect hope and is his best effort to reach some degree of safety and effectance. To relinquish this mode of living, no matter how tortured, the analysand must first have a believable experience of a workable alternative. For change to become possible, the analysand must encounter in the analytic relationship a more workable way of being with another person.

What is required is that the analysand experience the analytic relationship as both authentic and more satisfying than what has come before. In this sense the analyst's empathy marks a beginning point for the analysand's hope. Kohut (1984a) argues that the analytic relationship serves as the catalyst for the patient's "increasing realization that, contrary to his experiences in childhood, the sustaining echo of empathic resonance is indeed available in this world" (p. 78). The analytic relationship offers proof that relationships can be grounded in compassion. But it is not enough for the analyst to merely be kind or understanding. If the relationship remains fully asymmetrical the analysand will fail to experience these provisions as specific to himself, will be unable to feel that it is a giving that is related to the analysand's presence. At this level, countertransference disclosure plays an important role in infusing the strictly professional relationship with human actuality. Ehrenberg (1992) writes: "For many patients, finding that they can have an emotional impact on the analyst, positive or negative, or that the analyst is interested in knowing them may be what matters most" (p. 20). The analyst's willingness to become present serves the analysand's self-esteem, but not through false reassurance or a collaboration with the analysand's sense of narcissistic grandeur. Instead it meets the analysand's need to be recognized in an authentic and particular fashion.

For hope to be made tangible, for the analytic relationship to offer a reparative connection, not only does the analysand need to be recognized, he also needs to be allowed to touch the analyst's subjectivity. Without this reciprocity, the new experience of the analysis must always remain fictional. As Aron (1991) writes:

> Patients probe, more or less subtly, in an attempt to penetrate the analyst's professional calm and reserve. They do this probing not only because they want to turn the tables on their analyst defensively or angrily but also, like all people, because they want to and need to connect with others, and they want to connect with others where they live emotionally, where they are authentic and fully present, and so they search for information about the other's inner world [p. 37].

The analysand's need to know the analyst, to know the countertransference, has roots that go deeper than defensive retaliation. If we accept the primacy of attachment, we have recognized that the analysand is motivated by the need to form a connection to a subjective other. For this new relationship to offer believable hope, the analysand must have some sense that the analyst's actions are genuine, not dissembled. To reach that conviction, the analysand must be able to see that the analyst is also capable of feeling the full range of human emotion and lives within the same predicament of affectivity as does the analysand, and yet still finds a route to compassion.

Part of what the analysand needs from the analyst's countertransference, then, is an experience of durability. Before the analysand can reach a point of trusting the analytic relationship, before he can risk bringing the full range of his own affective experience into view, he must gain a sense of the analyst's capacity to stay affirmatively engaged in the relationship. In a discussion of Fairbairn's view of security, Spezzano (1993) writes: "What supplies this feeling of certain security? Fairbairn's answer is that we get the feeling when our expressions of affection and hate are accepted by others. We love other people and they love us back; we hate them and they at least stay put" (p. 98). Without this kind of affective durability, the analysand cannot risk acknowledging the full range of his affective reality. He must continue to embrace paranoid strategies of splitting and idealization. Part of what the analysand must find an answer to, then, is what the analyst does with her hate. If the analysand is attacking the analyst, is voicing strident demands, the analysand will reasonably expect this kind of transference enactment to evoke a negative response from the analyst. It is at these moments where the analysand may most need to have access to the analyst's countertransference. In a provocative article on hate in the countertransference, Frederickson (1990) describes a patient who repeatedly yelled at him:

> In the sixteenth month of our work he raged at me because he could not have his old hour back after we had made a change at his request. He finally stood up and towered over me screaming. He had become increasingly provocative but this was the worst. I quickly stood up with my face only three inches from his. In as loud a voice as I could muster I yelled, "Shut up!" I sat down. Jolted, he sat down too as I continued: "I can't take it. I can't take your screaming. I can't take your kicking the furniture. I don't know if people did this to you in your past or what. I just know I can't take it." "Good," he replied, "The first human response I've gotten from you" [p. 483].

Frederickson's response is an extreme reaction to an extreme patient. We might argue that setting a limit earlier in the process of enactment, with less rage, would be more effective. Nonetheless, we should see that in this moment of acting from the countertransference, Frederickson shows that he can contain the analysand's rage, can set a limit, without having to abandon him. It is an affective action that makes manifest the analyst's capacity to tolerate ambivalence. The analysand's pleasure at evoking Frederickson's anger, then, may be more than masochism. It reflects the analysand's relief at discovering the analyst's affective reality and capacity to tolerate hate.

The affective activity of the analyst, however, serves functions beyond providing affective management to the analysand. The analyst's willingness to acknowledge and reveal his affectivity can also serve as a kind of demonstration for the analysand. The analyst, through his manifest relationship to the countertransference, provides a model of constructed virtue. The analysand, in turn, may then internalize these skills and make them personal. The role of demonstration makes itself felt first in the use of affect as information about oneself and the other. We have already argued that the analyst's countertransference is a critical source of interpretive understanding. Yet, Spezzano (1993) argues, "We have not considered in any rigorous way the alternative of analysts saying to themselves, to each other, and to patients that our main clue to what our patients feel is what we feel" (p. 46). Why have we not yet taken up this question in a serious fashion? In the constructivist approach, the capacity to integrate and make use of affect as a guide to understanding and action is a primary component of virtue. The analyst's ability to make this manner of understanding manifest, I would argue, fosters the analysand's emerging capacity to attend to his own affectivity. Bollas (1987) speaks to this in his discussion of the analyst's self-relating:

> The analyst demonstrates his own form of self-relating in the way he perceives and relates to his own interpretations in the presence of the patient. For example, when in the midst of an interpretation to a patient I may suddenly realize that I am slightly off base, and I will stop myself and say something like 'Nope, that's not it, I can't quite find what I want to say' . . . I am well aware that I live out a form of self-relating in the presence of the patient, with one part of me functioning as the source of material—like the patient in the analysis—and another part of me functioning as the analyst [p. 207].

When the analyst allows this internal process of appraisal and uncertainty to be spoken, she makes tangible the capacity to engage in provisional thought, the confidence to risk being wrong. At times, Bollas takes this kind of visible self-relating further, and speaks directly about his affective states. Bollas, having challenged an analysand by saying "nonsense" in response to the analysand's claim to be without feeling, writes: "I was intent upon speaking up for and valuing subjective states as potentially valid" (p. 216). The analyst's willingness to ground understanding in the countertransference, while potentially challenging, also serves to support the analysand in coming to more fully trust his own subjectivity. As analysts, part of our expertise is the capacity to hold affect in order to make better sense of its meaning and its potentials for action. As Modell (1991) argues: "This split between the analyst's experiencing ego and observing ego can be thought of as a form of consciousness that we hope that our patients will acquire from us" (p. 20). Part of what the analyst models is a relationship to the countertransference as a route to understanding.

The analyst's participation in the analytic relationship, however, cannot be understood as merely interpretive, and the function of modeling touches on skills beyond understanding. The analyst's neutrality does not entail an immunity from participation. In the give and take of the transference-countertransference field, we have argued, representation is gradually overtaken by enactment. As Levenson (1972) argues, analysis is concerned with "extricating oneself from the equifinality of systems, not of avoiding it" (p. 158). In this model the analyst will be drawn into complementary countertransference roles that reflect the intersubjective positions that have ensnared the analysand. For the analysand, these quandaries have no adequate solution, no solution better than the neurotic adaptation. The analysand has come to feel that the only option is the untenable choice between sacrificing authenticity and vitality or losing the interpersonal connection. To reverse this sense of pessimistic foreclosure, the analyst must do more than merely interpret the predicament; the analyst must find a mode of affective action that makes plausible a third option. Levenson (1972) writes:

> Resolution may require that the therapist be able to put his/her money where his/her mouth is; that is, be able to enact with the patient a resolution to a problem which the patient believes is unresolvable.
>
> If the patient were to leave therapy with the traditional insight that he is distorting, carrying over a childhood experience into the present; he may reform, learn to be nice to his presumably deserving wife, and inattend his anger [p. 389].

The idea that working through enactments is a critical part of therapeutic action can also be seen in the work of Sampson (1994). He suggests that analytic progress stems from the analyst's capacity to disprove pathogenic beliefs:

> There are two broad types of tests: transference tests and passive-into-active tests. In a transference test, the patient repeats by carrying out a trial action involving the expression of an attitude, affective state, or behavior that (the patient believes) led in childhood to a traumatic experience. In carrying out a transference test, the patient risks retraumatization. In a passive-into-active test, the patient repeats a pathological childhood relationship with the roles reversed. The patient behaves like the traumatizing parent and actively inflicts the trauma on the therapist, who is in the role of the child. The patient

> unconsciously hopes that the therapist will not be as traumatized as he himself was as a child and the therapist can model a capacity that the patient needs [p. 358].

Within the model of constructed virtue, this capacity is an affective-relational skill that allows the interpersonal dilemma to be approached in a way that addresses the need for both safety and effectance without sacrificing the attachment relationship. In this sense, the analyst must be willing to not only speak of the countertransference, but act from it.

In the midst of what Sampson calls transference tests, the analyst's ability to remain affirmative, to provide needed experience, serves as a model of the kind of caretaking that is available in the world and that the analysand may partially come to provide for himself. In the passive-into-active tests, however, the challenge is how to deal constructively with interpersonal assaults, assaults that occur within the context of a valued relationship. In this kind of situation, we must find a way to protect our integrity without damaging the person who has made us angry, but whom we value. To speak this in the language of affect, we would say is there a way of behaving with anger without resorting to destructive rage. In traditional analytic discourse this mode of action has been spoken of as "confrontation." The analyst, in the face of obstructing resistance, must be willing to use confrontation to open the field for inquiry. In a discussion of a patient who, on initial presentation, utilized extensive idealizing defenses, Schafer (1992) writes: "This phase of the work required some forceful confrontations on the analyst's part. Only subsequently could the more fundamental aspects of transference and defense be taken up analytically and a similar account of his relationship to the analyst be developed" (p. 106). In the classical model of analytic action, the element of force behind the confrontation is not explicitly linked to the analyst's affective energy. The analyst confronts impersonally, without countertransferential arousal. To my mind, however, that version of action fails to account for the universality of affective involvement. To confront, to resolutely press one's point in the face of opposition, requires, at some level, the utilization of anger. It may be a highly sublimated form of anger, an anger that has been carefully modulated and infused with a remembrance of the analysand's well-being, but it still has roots in that affective subsystem.

Within the more relational analytic schools, the utilization of anger is more explicit. Perhaps the earliest advocate of this approach was

Winnicott. To provide an adequate holding environment, to be convincing, Winnicott (1947) argued, the analyst has to go beyond sentimentality:

> It seems to me doubtful whether a human child as he develops is capable of tolerating the full extent of his own hate in a sentimental environment. He needs hate to hate.
>
> If this is true, a psychotic patient in analysis cannot be expected to tolerate his hate of the analyst unless the analyst can hate him [p. 202].

The analyst's hate, though, is necessary not only to make the analysand's hate tolerable, but because it provides a sense of reality to the analytic relationship. Unless the analysand can access the analyst's realistic hate, the analyst's realistic love must remain in doubt. The analyst's capacity to hate or to be angry, without reverting to destructive action, lies at the root of the analysand's emerging capacity to tolerate his own ambivalence. When Frederickson yells at his patient and tells him to sit down he protects the analytic frame, models a form of productive limit setting, and works his way out of an analytic enactment. It is a kind of standing-up for oneself that is simultaneously a standing-up for the analysand and for the legitimacy and potential of affective reaction. Ehrenberg (1992) describes a similar result from her use of countertransferential anger: after she tells a patient that she has been irritated with her, the patient replies by saying that "she was finally beginning to understand that it was possible for people to be angry at each other without necessarily becoming sadistic toward each other or ending the relationship" (p. 72). What seems important in this more unfettered use of countertransference disclosure is a capacity to speak about the countertransference reaction while simultaneously trying to make sense of its transferential significance in regard to the analysand. To maintain an affirmative attitude, to protect the analysand's sense that the analysis is for him, rather than for the analyst, the affective communication must carry a sense that the negative affect is spoken not merely to unburden the analyst, but to preserve the relationship and move beyond the obstructing elements. In speaking about the countertransferential anger, then, the analyst must convey, at some level, simultaneous caring for the analysand's well-being.

In this section we have argued that there are occasions when the analyst must be willing to bring the countertransference more directly into the analytic encounter. This use of affectivity is essential both in providing an environment of safety and hope, and in the process of modeling alternate solutions to transferential quandaries. These kinds of modifications in technique, Ehrenberg (1992) argues, "do not constitute a violation of analytic integrity nor an abandonment of an analytic process; rather, they may be *essential* to establish or preserve an analytic possibility" (p. 50). The paradigm of constructed virtue suggests that at times it is the analyst's skillful use of the countertransference, in utilizing both positive and negative affects, that forms the basis of therapeutic action. In calling for a more extensive form of analytic engagement, we should not forget the danger of coercive technique, of expressing that our compassion is contingent on the analysand's compliance with our agenda for change. Therapeutic zeal, as we have argued, cannot provide a foundation for durable change. Yet at the same time we should acknowledge that although we cannot cure through love alone, it is equally clear that we cannot cure without love. This kind of use of countertransferential affect should not be seen as pedagogical or moralistic. It occurs within a relationship and so remains personal. To my mind the task that lies ahead for analytic thought is to take up more specifically the contours of affective action, and to specify the parameters of engagement. For analysis to remain vibrant and coherent we must be willing to risk speaking and acting from the countertransference.

A Final Perspective on Countertransference

The countertransference, over the last three decades, has moved onto the center stage of analytic thought and technique. This book has been a sustained attempt to create a coherent foundation for that discussion. Through a consideration of history, epistemology, and virtue, I have tried to make clear both the inevitability and necessity of the countertransference. The historical record, I have argued, strongly suggests that the countertransference cannot be sequestered. To avoid or deny the countertransference is not only an ill-fated project, but one that undermines the therapeutic alliance and precipitates iatrogenic impasse. Analysands will not tolerate the aseptic authority of an unresponsive, emotionally remote analyst. From an epistemological perspective, the proscription of the countertransference is no longer sensible. The phenomena of the analytic encounter have demanded that we relinquish objectivist epistemologies in favor of constructivism. Knowing is inherently a perspectival and subjective event. Within this framework, emotion is recognized as more than an obstacle to rationality. It serves as a necessary promontory for interpersonal understanding. To see this is to recognize that the countertransference serves as an essential means for knowing the analysand; it is what allows our understanding to become dimensional, to gain a pulse. Finally, I have described the interdependence between theories of metapsychology and theories of virtue. Psychoanalysis, I have argued, is inevitably concerned with aesthetic portraits of virtue and the acquisition of affective-relational skills. This understanding suggests that the analyst must do more than merely remain abstinent. The transformation of character is dependent on a context of provision. The analyst must provide long moments of stillness as well as periods of active affective engagement.

The intent of this work has not been to provide radical new approaches to the countertransference. It is not a polemic that would demand sweeping gestures or vivid affective displays. In this sense, the specific prescriptions concerning the countertransference will seem familiar. I suggest a middle road between the poles of pervasive stillness and radical engagement. What is new in this work, however, is the attempt to systematically ground our understanding of the countertransference in a wider theoretical context. This is a necessary step in bringing coherence to the debate. The foray into history, epistemology, and moral theory has been an attempt to make these sometimes scattered areas of thought congruent. My hope is that this discussion will bring order to what has often been a confusing debate. Perhaps I have cleared away some of the lingering fears of the countertransference, some atavistic prejudice, and opened our thinking to the full potential of the countertransference. For psychoanalysis to remain pertinent, we must go further in exploring the parameters of provision and affective participation, without sacrificing the foundational insight of psychoanalysis that virtue imposed must remain a fragile and shallow form of living.

References

Abend, S. M. (1989), Countertransference and psychoanalytic technique. *Psychoanalytic Quarterly,* 58:375–395.

Abraham, K. (1919), A particular form of neurotic resistance against the psycho-analytic method. In: *The Evolution of Psychoanalytic Technique,* ed. M. Bergmann & F. Hartman. New York: Basic Books, 1976, pp. 82–88.

Alexander, F. (1925), A metapsychological description of the process of cure. In: *The Evolution of Psychoanalytic Technique,* ed. M. Bergmann & F. Hartman. New York: Basic Books, 1976, pp. 99–108.

Alexander, F. & French, T. M. (1946), *Psychoanalytic Therapy.* New York: The Ronald Press.

Aron, L. (1991), The patient's experience of the analyst's subjectivity. *Psychoanalytic Dialogues,* 1:29–51.

—— (1992), Interpretation as expression of the analyst's subjectivity. *Psychoanalytic Dialogues,* 2:475–507.

Balint, M. (1953), *Primary Love and Psycho-Analytic Technique.* New York: Liveright.

Bernstein, R. (1983), *Beyond Objectivism and Relativism.* Philadelphia: University of Pennsylvania Press.

Bettelheim, B. (1990), *Freud's Vienna and Other Essays.* New York: Knopf.

Bird, B. (1972), Notes on transference: Universal phenomenon and hardest part of analysis. In: *Classics in Psychoanalytic Technique,* ed. R. Langs. New York: Aronson, 1990, pp. 51–67.

Blum, H. (1986), Countertransference: concepts and controversies. In: *Countertransference,* ed. E. Slakter. Northvale, NJ: Jason Aronson, 1987, pp. 87–104.

Bollas, C. (1987), *The Shadow of the Object.* New York: Columbia University Press.

Bowlby, J. (1969), *Attachment.* New York: Basic Books.

Brenner, C. (1976), *Psychoanalytic Technique and Psychic Conflict.* Madison, WI: International Universities Press.

—— (1985), Countertransference as compromise formation. In: *Classics in Psychoanalytic Technique,* ed. R. Langs. Northvale, NJ: Aronson, 1990, pp. 449–452.

Bretherton, I., Fritz, J., Zahn-Waxler, C., & Ridgeway, D. (1986), Learning to talk about emotions: A functionalist perspective. *Child Development,* 57:529–548.

Chused, J. (1992a), The patient's perception of the analyst: The hidden transference. *Psychoanalytic Quarterly.* 41:161–184.

—— & Raphling, D. (1992b), The analyst's mistakes. *Journal of the American Psychoanalytic Association,* 40:89-116.

Cohen, M. B. (1952), Countertransference and anxiety. In: *Essential Papers on Countertransference,* ed. B. Wolstein. New York: New York University Press, 1988, pp. 64–83.

Crowley, R. M. (1952), Human reactions of analysts to patients. In: *Essential Papers on Countertransference,* ed. B. Wolstein. New York: New York University Press, 1988, pp. 84–90.

Davies, J. & Frawley, M. (1992), Dissociative processes and transference-countertransference paradigms in the psychoanalytically oriented treatment of adult survivors of childhood sexual abuse. *Psychoanalytic Dialogues,* 2:5–36.

Delgado, J. M. (1967), Social rank and radio-stimulated aggressiveness in monkeys. *J. Nerv. Ment. Dis.* 144:383–90.

Dewey, J. (1929), *The Quest for Certainty.* New York: Minton, Balch.

Doi, T. (1973), *The Anatomy of Dependence.* Tokyo: Kodansha International.

Duke-Elder, S. & Scott, G. (1971), *System of Ophthalmology.* London: Henry Klimpton.

Eissler, K. R. (1953), The effect of the structure of the ego on psychoanalytic technique. In: *Classics in Psychoanalytic Technique,* ed. R. Langs. New York: Aronson, 1990, pp. 397–418.

Ehrenberg, D. B. (1992), *The Intimate Edge.* New York: Norton.

Ekman, P. (1984), Expression and the nature of emotion. In: *Approaches to Emotion,* ed. R. Scherer & P. Ekman. Hillsdale, NJ: Lawrence Erlbaum Associates, 1984, pp. 319–344.

—— & Friesen, W. (1975), *Unmasking the Face.* Englewood Cliffs, N.J.: Prentice-Hall.

Fairbairn, W. R. D. (1944), Endopsychic structure considered in terms of object-relationships. In: *An Object-Relations Theory of the Personality.* New York: Basic Books.

—— (1952), *Psychoanalytic Studies of the Personality,* London: Routledge & Kegan Paul.

Fenichel, Otto. (1938), Problems of psychoanalytic technique. In: *The Evolution of Psychoanalytic Technique,* ed. M. Bergmann & F. Hartman. New York: Basic Books, 1976, pp. 271–272.

Ferenczi, S. (1919a), On the technique of psycho-analysis. In: *The Evolution of Psychoanalytic Technique,* ed. M. Bergmann & F. Hartman. New York: Basic Books, 1976, pp. 89–98.

—— (1919b), Technical difficulties in the analysis of a case of hysteria. In: *The Evolution of Psychoanalytic Technique,* ed. M. Bergmann & F. Hartman. New York: Basic Books, 1976, pp. 110–117.

—— (1930), The principle of relaxation and neocatharsis. In: *The Evolution of Psychoanalytic Technique,* ed. M. Bergmann & F. Hartman. New York: Basic Books, 1976, pp. 288–303.

—— (1988), *The Clinical Diary of Sándor Ferenczi.* ed. Judith Dupont. Cambridge, MA: Harvard University Press.

—— & Rank, O. (1923), The development of psychoanalysis: A historical critical retrospect. In: *Essential Papers on Countertransference,* ed. B. Wolstein. New York: New York University Press, 1988, pp. 25–35.

Feyerabend, P. (1975), *Against Method: Outline of an Anarchistic Theory of Knowledge.* London: NLB.

Fischer, K. W. (1980), A theory of cognitive development: The control and construction of hierarchies of skills. *Psychological Rev.*, 87:477–531.

——, Shaver, P., & Carnochan, P. (1989), From basic to subordinate category emotions: A skill approach to emotional development. In: *Child Development Today and Tomorrow,* ed. W. Damon. San Francisco: Jossey Bass, 1989, pp. 107–136.

Fliess, R. (1942), The metapsychology of the analyst. In: *Classics in Psychoanalytic Technique,* ed. R. Langs. Northvale, NJ: Aronson, 1990, pp. 219–226.

Frederickson, J. (1990), Hate in the countertransference as an empathic position. *Contemporary Psychoanalysis,* 26:479–496.

Freud, A. (1936), The ego and the mechanisms of defense. In: *The writ-*

ings of Anna Freud (Vol. 2). Madison, CT: International Universities Press, 1966.

Freud, S. (1887-1904), *The Complete Letters of Sigmund Freud to Wilhelm Fliess,* ed. J. M. Masson. Cambridge, MA: Harvard University Press. 1985.

—— (1886a), Report on my studies in Paris and Berlin. *Standard Edition*, 1:5–15. London: Hogarth Press, 1966.

—— (1886b), Observation of a severe case of hemi-anaesthesia in a hysterical male. *Standard Edition*, 1:23–31. London: Hogarth Press, 1966.

—— (1887), Review of Weir Mitchell's "The Treatment of Certain Types of Neurasthenia and Hysteria." *Standard Edition*, 1:36. London: Hogarth Press, 1966.

—— (1889a), Preface to translation of Bernheim's "Suggestion" (1888–1889). *Standard Edition*, 1:75–87. London: Hogarth Press, 1966.

—— (1889b), Review of August Forel's "Hypnotism." *Standard Edition*, 1:89–102. London: Hogarth Press, 1966.

—— (1891), Hypnosis. *Standard Edition*, 1:103–114. London: Hogarth Press, 1966.

—— (1892), Sketches for the "Preliminary Communication" of 1893. *Standard Edition*, 1:147–172. London: Hogarth Press, 1966.

—— (1894a), A case of successful treatment by hypnotism. *Standard Edition*, 1:115–128. London: Hogarth Press, 1966.

—— (1894b), Preface and footnotes to the translation of Charcot's "Tuesday Lectures." *Standard Edition*, 1:133–143. London: Hogarth Press, 1966.

—— (1893–95), *Studies on Hysteria. Standard Edition*, 2:1–309. London, Hogarth Press, 1955.

—— (1895), *Project for a Scientific Psychology. Standard Edition*, 1:295–397. London, Hogarth Press, 1966.

—— (1896a), Heredity and aetiology of the neuroses. *Standard Edition*, 3: 141–156. London: Hogarth Press, 1962.

—— (1896b), Further remarks on the neuro-psychoses of defence. *Standard Edition*, 3:162–185. London: Hogarth Press, 1962.

—— (1896c), The aetiology of hysteria. *Standard Edition*, 3:191–221. London: Hogarth Press, 1962.

—— (1898), Sexuality in the aetiology of the neuroses. *Standard Edition*, 3:263-285. London: Hogarth Press, 1962.

—— (1900), *The Interpretation of Dreams. Standard Edition*, 4 & 5: 1–625. London: Hogarth Press, 1962.

—— (1901), On dreams. *Standard Edition*, 5:633–714. London: Hogarth Press, 1953.
—— (1904), Freud's psycho-analytic procedure. *Standard Edition*, 7:249–254. London: Hogarth Press, 1953.
—— (1905a), Fragment of an analysis of a case of hysteria. *Standard Edition*, 7:7–122. London: Hogarth Press, 1953.
—— (1905b), *Three Essays on the Theory of Sexuality*. *Standard Edition*, 7:130–243. London: Hogarth Press, 1953.
—— (1905c), On psychotherapy. *Standard Edition*, 7:257–268. London: Hogarth Press, 1953.
—— (1906), Psychical (or mental) treatment. *Standard Edition*, 7:283–302. London, Hogarth Press, 1953.
—— (1907), The sexual enlightenment of children. *Standard Edition*, 9: 129–139. London: Hogarth Press, 1959.
—— (1908a), Creative writers and day-dreaming. *Standard Edition*, 9:141–153. London: Hogarth Press, 1959.
—— (1908b), 'Civilized' sexual morality and modern nervous illness. *Standard Edition*, 9:181–204. London: Hogarth Press, 1959.
—— (1908c), On the sexual theories of children. *Standard Edition*, 9: 209–225. London: Hogarth Press, 1959.
—— (1909a), Analysis of a phobia in a five-year-old boy. *Standard Edition*, 10:5–149. London: Hogarth Press, 1955.
—— (1909b), Notes upon a case of obsessional neurosis. *Standard Edition*, 10:155–318. London: Hogarth Press, 1955.
—— (1910a), Five lectures on psycho-analysis. *Standard Edition*, 11:9–55. London: Hogarth Press, 1957.
—— (1910b), The future prospects of psycho-analysis. *Standard Edition*, 11:139–151. London Hogarth Press, 1957.
—— (1910c), A special type of choice of object made by men (Contributions to the psychology of love: I). *Standard Edition*, 11:163–177. London: Hogarth Press, 1957.
—— (1910d), Wild psycho-analysis. *Standard Edition*, 11:219–227. London: Hogarth Press, 1957.
—— (1911a), Formulations on the two principles of mental functioning. *Standard Edition*, 12:218–226. London: Hogarth Press, 1958.
—— (1911b), The handling of dream-interpretation in psychoanalysis. *Standard Edition*, 12:89–96. London: Hogarth Press, 1958.
—— (1912a), The dynamics of transference. *Standard Edition*, 12:97–108. London: Hogarth Press, 1958.

—— (1912b), Types of onset of neurosis. *Standard Edition*, 12:231–238. London: Hogarth Press, 1958,

—— (1912c), On the universal tendency to debasement in the sphere of love (Contributions to the psychology of love: II). *Standard Edition*, 11:177–190. London: Hogarth Press, 1957.

—— (1912d), Recommendations to physicians practicing psycho-analysis. *Standard Edition*, 12:109–120. London: Hogarth Press, 1958.

—— (1912e), Contributions to a discussion on masturbation. *Standard Edition*, 12:243–254. London: Hogarth Press, 1958.

—— (1913a), On beginning the treatment (Further recommendations on the technique of psycho-analysis: I). *Standard Edition*, 12:121–144. London: Hogarth Press, 1958.

—— (1913b), Two lies told by children. *Standard Edition*, 12:303–309. London: Hogarth Press, 1958.

—— (1913c), The disposition to obsessional neurosis. *Standard Edition*, 12:317–326. London: Hoagrth Press, 1958.

—— (1914a), Remembering, repeating and working-through (Further recommendations on the technique of psycho-analysis: II). *Standard Edition*, 12:145–156. London: Hogarth Press, 1958.

—— (1914b), On the history of the psycho-analytic movement. *Standard Edition*, 14:7–66. London: Hogarth Press, 1957.

—— (1915a), Observations on transference-love (Further recommendations on the technique of psycho-analysis: III). *Standard Edition,* 12:157–171. London: Hogarth Press, 1958.

—— (1915b), Instincts and their vicissitudes. *Standard Edition*, 14:117–140. London: Hogarth Press, 1957.

—— (1916a), Some character-types met with in psycho-analytic work: III. Criminals from a sense of guilt. *Standard Edition*, 14:332–333. London: Hogarth Press, 1957.

—— (1916b), *Introductory Lectures on Psycho-analysis. Standard Edition*, Part III. London: Hogarth Press, (1963).

—— (1917), Mourning and melancholia. *Standard Edition*, 14:243–258. London: Hogarth Press, 1957

—— (1918), From the history of an infantile neurosis. *Standard Edition*, 17:7–122. London: Hogarth Press, 1955.

—— (1919), Lines of advance in psycho-analytic therapy. *Standard Edition*, 17:157–168. London: Hogarth Press, 1955.

—— (1921), *Group Psychology and the Analysis of the Ego. Standard Edition*, 18:69–143. London: Hogarth Press, 1955.

—— (1924), The economic problem of masochism. *Standard Edition*, 19:159–170. London: Hogarth Press, 1961.
—— (1925), An autobiographical study. *Standard Edition*, 20:7–74. London: Hogarth Press, 1959.
—— (1926), *Inhibitions, Symptoms and Anxiety. Standard Edition*, 20:87–175. London: Hogarth Press, 1959.
—— (1933), *New Introductory Lectures on Psychoanalysis. Standard Edition*, 22:3–182. London: Hogarth Press, 1964.
—— (1937), Analysis terminable and interminable. *Standard Edition*, 23:216–253. London: Hogarth Press, 1964.
—— (1940), *An Outline of Psycho-analysis. Standard Edition*, 23:144–207. London: Hogarth Press, 1964.
Frijda, N. H. (1986), *The Emotions.* Cambridge: Cambridge University Press.
Gadamer, H. G. (1960), *Truth and Method*. New York: Crossroad.
Gay, P. (1988), *Freud: A Life for Our Time.* New York: Anchor Books, Doubleday.
Gill, M. (1979), The analysis of the transference. In: *Classics in Psychoanalytic Technique,* ed. R. Langs. Northvale, NJ: Aronson, 1990, pp. 69–82.
Giovacchini, P. L. (1989), *Countertransference Triumphs and Catastrophes.* Northvale, NJ: Aronson.
Glover, E. (1924), Active therapy and psycho-analysis: A critical review. In: *The Evolution of Psychoanalytic Technique,* ed. M. Bergmann & F. Hartman. New York: Basic Books, 1976, pp. 126–143.
Greenacre, P. (1954), The role of transference. In: *Classics in Psychoanalytic Technique,* ed. R. Langs. Northvale, NJ: Aronson, 1990, pp. 17–23.
Greenberg, J. R. & Mitchell, S. A. (1983), *Object Relations in Psychoanalytic Theory.* Cambridge, MA: Harvard University Press.
Greenberg, J. R. (1992), *Oedipus and Beyond.* Cambridge, MA: Harvard University Press.
Greenson, R. R. (1971), The "real" relationship between the patient and the psychoanalyst. In: *Classics in Psychoanalytic Technique,* ed. R. Langs. Northvale, NJ: Aronson, 1990, pp. 87–96.
Harre, R. (1986a), Emotion talk across times. In: *The Social Construction of Emotions,* Ed. R. Harre. Oxford, England: Blackwell.
Harre, R., ed. (1986b), *The Social Construction of Emotions*. Oxford, England: Blackwell.

Heimann, P. (1949), On countertransference. In: *Classics in Psychoanalytic Technique,* ed. R. Langs. Northvale, NJ: Aronson, 1990, pp. 137-142.
Hoffman, I. (1983), The patient as interpreter of the analyst's experience. *Contemporary Psychoanalysis,* 19:389-422.
—— (1991), Discussion: Toward a social-constructivist view of the psychoanalytic situation. *Psychoanalytic Dialogues,* 1:74–105.
—— (1992), Expressive participation and psychoanalytic discipline. In: *Contemporary Psychoanalysis,* 28:1–15.
Izard, C. E. (1977), *Human Emotions.* New York: Plenum.
James, W. (1884), What is an emotion? *Mind*, 9:188–205.
—— (1907), *Pragmatism.* Cambridge, MA: Harvard University Press, 1975.
Kaiser, H. (1934), Problems of technique. In: *The Evolution of Psychoanalytic Technique,* ed. M. Bergmann & F. Hartman. New York: Basic Books, 1976, pp. 383–413.
Kantrowitz, J. (1992), The analyst's style and its impact on the analytic process: Overcoming a patient-analyst stalemate. *Journal of the American Psychoanalytic Association,* 40:169–194.
Kanzer, M. (1975), The therapeutic and working alliances. In: *Classics in Psychoanalytic Technique*, ed. R. Langs. Northvale, NJ: Aronson, 1990, pp. 305–318.
Kernberg, O. (1988), Object relations theory in clinical practice. In: *Classics in Psychoanalytic Technique,* ed. R. Langs. Northvale, NJ: Aronson, 1990, pp. 451–462.
Klein, M. (1932), *The Psycho-analysis of Children.* London: Hogarth Press.
—— (1946), Notes on some schizoid mechanisms. In: *Envy and Gratitude*. New York: Delacorte Press, 1975, pp. 1–24.
—— (1964) *Love, Hate, and Reparation.* New York: Norton.
Kohut, H. (1978), The search for the analyst's self. In: *The Search for the Self, Vol.2,* ed. P. Ornstein. New York: International Universities Press, 1991, pp. 395–446.
—— (1984a), *How Does Analysis Cure?* Chicago: University of Chicago Press.
—— (1984b), The role of empathy in psychoanalytic cure. In: *Classics in Psychoanalytic Technique,* ed. R. Langs. Northvale, NJ: Aronson, 1990, pp. 463–473.
Lacan, J. (1953-54), *The Seminar of Jacques Lacan: Freud's Papers on Technique.* New York: Norton.
Landauer. K. (1924), Passive technique: On the analysis of narcissistic illnesses. In: *The Evolution of Psychoanalytic Technique,* ed. M.

Bergmann & F. Hartman. New York: Basic Books, 1976, pp. 174–181.

Lange, C. G. (1885), *Om Sindsbevoegelser: Et psyko-fysiologiske Studie* (*The Emotions*). Baltimore: Williams & Wilkins, 1922.

Langs, R. (1981), *Classics in Psycho-analytic Technique.* Northvale, NJ: Aronson.

—— (1993), Psychoanalysis: Narrative myth or narrative science. *Contemporary Psychoanalysis,* 29:555–594.

Lazarus, R. S. (1984), On the primacy of cognition. Am. Psychol., 39:124–129.

Levenson, E. A. (1972), *The Fallacy of Understanding.* New York: Basic Books.

—— (1993), Shoot the messenger. *Contemporary Psychoanalysis,* 29:383–396.

Little, M. (1951), Counter-transference and the patient's response to it. In: *Classics in Psychoanalytic Technique,* ed. R. Langs. Northvale, NJ: Aronson, 1990, pp. 143–151.

Loewald, H. W. (1960), On the therapeutic action of psycho-analysis. *International Journal of Psycho-Analysis,* 41:16-33.

—— (1971), On motivation and instinct theory. In: *Papers on Psychoanalysis.* New Haven, CT: Yale University Press, 1980.

Mendelsohn, R., Bucci, W., & Chouhy, R. (1992), Transference and countertransference: A survey of attitudes. *Contemporary Psychoanalysis,* 28:364–390.

Milner, M. (1952), The role of illusion in symbol formation. In: *New Directions in Psychoanalysis*, ed. M. Klein, P. Heimann & R. Money-Kyre. London: Maresfield Reprints.

Mitchell, S. A. (1988), *Relational Concepts in Psychoanalysis: An Integration.* Cambridge: Harvard University Press.

—— (1993), *Hope and Dread in Psychoanalysis.* New York: Basic Books.

Modell, A. H. (1976), The therapeutic setting and hold. In: *Classics in Psychoanalytic Technique,* ed. R. Langs. Northvale, NJ: Aronson, 1990, pp. 429–438.

—— (1991), The therapeutic relationship as a paradoxical experience. *Psychoanal. Dial.*, 1:13–28.

Nunberg, H. (1926), The will to recovery. In: *The Evolution of Psychoanalytic Technique,* ed. M. Bergmann & F. Hartman. New York: Basic Books, 1976, pp. 182–191.

—— (1928), Problems of Therapy. In: *The Evolution of Psychoanalytic Tech-*

nique, ed. M. Bergmann & F. Hartman. New York: Basic Books, 1976, pp. 192–206.

Ornstein, P. & Ornstein, A. (1975), On the interpretive process in psychoanalysis. *International Journal of Psychoanalytic Psychotherapy,* 4:219–271.

—— (1994), On the conceptualization of clinical facts in psychoanalysis. *Internaional Journal of Psycho-Analysis,* 75:977–994.

Ornstein, P. (1993), On the function of theory in the interpretive process. Unpublished manuscript.

Racker, H. (1968), *Transference and Countertransference.* Madison, WI: International Universities Press.

—— (1972), The meanings and uses of countertransference. In: *Classics in Psychoanalytic Technique,* ed. R. Langs. New York: Aronson, 1990, pp. 177–200.

Reich, A. (1951), On counter-transference. In: *Classics in Psychoanalytic Technique,* ed. R. Langs. New York: Aronson, 1990, pp. 153–159.

Reich, W. (1933), The technique of character analysis. In: *The Evolution of Psychoanalytic Technique,* ed. M. Bergmann & F. Hartman. New York: Basic Books, 1976, pp. 230–270.

Reik, T. (1933), New ways in psycho-analytic technique. In: *The Evolution of Psychoanalytic Technique,* ed. M. Bergmann & F. Hartman. New York: Basic Books, 1976, pp. 370–382.

—— (1948), The surprised psychoanalyst. In: *Essential Papers on Countertransference,* ed. B. Wolstein. New York: New York University Press, 1988, pp. 51–63.

Rorty, R. (1982), *Consequences of Pragmatism.* Minneapolis, MN: University of Minneapolis Press.

Rousseau, J. J. (1750), *The First and Second Discourses.* New York: St. Martin's Press (1964).

Sampson, H. (1992), The role of "real" experience in psychopathology and treatment. *Psychoanal. Dial.,* 4:509–528.

—— (1994), Repeating pathological relationships to disconfirm pathogenic beliefs: Commentary on Steven Stern's "Needed relationships." *Psychoanalytic Dialogues,* 4:357–361.

Schafer, R. (1976), *A New Language for Psychoanalysis.* New Haven, CT: Yale University Press.

—— (1983), *The Analytic Attitude.* New York: Basic Books.

—— (1992), *Retelling a Life.* New York: Basic Books.

Searles, H. F. (1975), The patient as therapist to his analyst. In: *Classics in*

Psychoanalytic Technique, ed. R. Langs. Northvale, NJ: Aronson, 1990, pp. 103–135.

Segal, H. (1967), Melanie Klein's technique. In: *Classics in Psychoanalytic Technique,* ed. R. Langs. Northvale, NJ: Aronson, 1990, pp. 357–368.

Shabad, P. (1991), The unconscious wish and psychoanalytic stoicism. *Contemporary Psychoanalysis,* 27:332–350.

—— (1993), Resentment, indignation, entitlement: The transformation of unconscious wish into need. *Psychoanalytic Dialogues,* 3:481–494.

Shaver, P., Schwartz, J., Kirson, D., & O'Connor, C. (1987), Emotion knowledge: Further exploration of a prototype approach. *Journal of Personality and Social Psychology,* 52:1061–1086.

Slakter, E. (1987), *Countertransference: A Comprehensive View.* Northvale, NJ: Aronson.

Spezzano, C. (1993), *Affect in Psychoanalysis: A Clinical Synthesis.* Hillsdale, NJ: The Analytic Press.

Stein, S. (1991), The influence of theory on the psychoanalyst's countertransference. *International Journal of Psychoanalysis,* 72:325–334.

Sterba, R. F. (1934), The fate of the ego in analytic therapy. In: *Classics in Psychoanalytic Technique,* ed. R. Langs. New York: Aronson, 1990, pp. 263–270.

—— (1953), Clinical and therapeutic aspects of character resistance. In: *The Evolution of Psychoanalytic Technique,* ed. M. Bergmann & F. Hartman. New York: Basic Books, 1976, pp. 273–286.

Stern, D. B. (1991), A philosophy for the embedded analyst. *Contemporary Psychoanalysis,* 27:51–80.

Stern, S. (1994), Needed relationships and repeated relationships: An integrated relational perspective. *Psychoanalytic Dialogues,* 4:317–345.

Strachey, J. (1934), The nature of the therapeutic action of psycho-analysis. In: *The Evolution of Psychoanalytic Technique,* ed. M. Bergmann & F. Hartman. New York: Basic Books, 1976, pp. 331–360.

Sullivan, H. S. (1953), *The Interpersonal Theory of Psychiatry.* New York: Norton.

Sulloway, F. J. (1979), *Freud, Biologist of the Mind.* New York: Basic Books.

Szasz, T. (1963), The concept of transference. In: *Classics in Psychoanalytic Technique,* ed. R. Langs. New York: Aronson, 1990, pp. 25–36.

Tansey, M. J. & Burke, W. F. (1989), *Understanding Countertransference.* Hillsdale, NJ: The Analytic Press.

Tansey, M. (1992), Psychoanalytic expertise. *Psychoanalytic Dialogues.* 2: 305–316.

Titchener, E. B. (1908), *Lectures on the Elementary Psychology of Feeling and Attention.* New York: Macmillan.

Tower, L. E. (1956), Countertransference. In: *Essential Papers on Countertransference,* ed. B. Wolstein. New York: New York University Press, 1988, pp. 131–157.

Trop, J. & Stolorow, R. (1992), Defense analysis in self psychology: A developmental view. *Psychoanalytic Dialogues,* 2:427–442.

Trungpa, C. (1988), *The Myth of Freedom.* Boston, MA: Shambala.

Wachtel, P. (1993), Active intervention, psychic structure, and the analysis of transference: Commentary on Frank's "Action, insight, and working through." *Psychoanalytic Dialogues,* 3:589–603.

Weiss, J. & Sampson, H. (1986), *The Psychoanalytic Process: Theory, Clinical Observation & Research.* New York: The Guilford Press.

Winnicott, D. W. (1947), Hate in the countertransference. In: *Collected Papers: Through Paediatrics to Psychoanalysis.* London: Hogarth Press, 1958.

—— (1956), On transference. In: *Classics in Psychoanalytic Technique,* ed. R. Langs. Northvale, NJ: Aronson, 1990, pp. 413–418.

—— (1960), Parent-infant relationship. In: *The Maturational Processes and the Facilitating Environment.* New York: International Universities Press, 1965, pp. 37–55.

—— (1962), Ego integration in child development. In: *The Maturational Processes and the Facilitating Environment.* New York: International Universities Press, 1965, pp. 56–63.

—— (1963), From dependence towards independence in the development of the individual. *The Maturational Processes and the Facilitating Environment.* New York: International Universities Press, 1965, pp. 83–92.

—— (1965b), *The Family and Individual Development.* London: Tavistock, 1965.

—— (1971), *Playing and Reality.* New York: Basic Books.

Wittgenstein, L. (1958), *Philosophical Investigations.* New York: MacMillan.

Wundt, W. (1903), *Grundriss der Psychologie.* Stuttgart: Engelmann.

Zucker, H. (1993), Reality: Can it be only yours or mine? *Contemporary Psychoanalysis,* 29:479–486.

INDEX